1940

This b

FOUR FRENCH NOVELISTS

Four French Novelists

MARCEL PROUST

ANDRÉ GIDE

JEAN GIRAUDOUX

PAUL MORAND

BY GEORGES LEMAITRE

Agrégé de l'Université
Docteur ès-Lettres
Associate Professor at McGill University

OXFORD UNIVERSITY PRESS

London New York Toronto

1938

Printed in the United States of America

TO MY WIFE

PREFACE

I TAKE *this occasion to offer gratefully my thanks to Dr. C.E. Fryer,* F.R.HIST.S., *Kingsford Professor and Head of the Department of History, McGill University. With unfailing and untiring kindness Dr. Fryer gave me his scholarly advice and editorial assistance in preparing the final draft of these sketches for publication.*

I am indebted to my colleagues, Dr. C.W.Hendel and Dr. W.D.Woodhead, for invaluable criticism while the work was in progress; also, and in particular, to Miss Janet Oswald for secretarial services necessarily of an arduous and exacting kind. To these I would add the names of M.H. Bougearel, Miss Margaret McKay, Miss Naomi Jackson, Miss Ada Klett, Miss Josephine Hemphill, and Mlle Marthe Sturm for several useful suggestions.

I wish to express my sincere thanks to the Librairie Gallimard—Editions de la Nouvelle Revue Française—(Paris) for permission to quote passages from the collected works of M.Proust and A.Gide and from P.Morand's OUVERT LA NUIT, FERMÉ LA NUIT, *and* FLÈCHE D'ORIENT; *to M.Bernard Grasset (Paris) for passages from the works of J.Giraudoux and from P.Morand's* LEWIS ET IRÈNE, RIEN QUE LA TERRE, BOUDDHA VIVANT, MAGIE NOIRE, CHAMPIONS DU MONDE, PAPIERS D'IDENTITÉ, *and* AIR INDIEN; *to the Librairie Plon (Paris) for passages from P.Morand's* LONDRES *and* BUCAREST; *to the Librairie Ernest Flammarion (Paris) for passages from P.Morand's* NEW-YORK *and* HIVER CARAÏBE.

I have to acknowledge the courtesy of Messrs. Chatto and Windus (London) and of Random House, Inc. (New York) for permission to reproduce extracts from the translation of

M.Proust's A LA RECHERCHE DU TEMPS PERDU *by C.K.Scott Moncrieff and F.A.Blossom. The edition of* REMEMBRANCE OF THINGS PAST *used for references and quotations is the edition in four volumes published by Random House, Inc. (New York),* 1934.

For authorization to translate into English passages from French texts for which they have the exclusive copyright, my thanks are also due to the publishers listed below: Random House, Inc. (New York) in the case of SI LE GRAIN NE MEURT *by A.Gide; G.P.Putnam's Sons (New York) in the case of* SUZANNE ET LE PACIFIQUE *by J.Giraudoux; William Heinemann, Ltd. (London) in the case of* NEW YORK *by P.Morand; Robert M.McBride and Company (New York) in the case of* RIEN QUE LA TERRE *by P.Morand; Alfred A.Knopf, Inc. (New York) in the case of* L'IMMORALISTE, LA SYMPHONIE PASTORALE, L'ECOLE DES FEMMES, LES CAVES DU VATICAN *by A.Gide and of* BELLA *by J.Giraudoux.*

Every effort has been made to discover the owners of all the copyrighted quotations. If any passage from any author mentioned in this book has been cited without express permission and proper acknowledgement, it is not through lack of effort on my part to find to whom acknowledgement is due. I hope and trust that any copyrightholder who may have been overlooked will kindly consider this as an adequate expression of my regret and my thanks.

Except in the case of Proust, all quotations have been translated directly into English from the French original.

The dates given in the footnotes refer to the edition used, which is not necessarily the original edition. The date of each original edition is indicated in the Bibliography.

GEORGES E. LEMAITRE

McGill University, Montreal
October 1937

CONTENTS

II. ANDRÉ GIDE

III. JEAN GIRAUDOUX

INTRODUCTION

In the course of the last quarter of a century, and especially since the Great War, French manners and ideas have undergone such rapid and extensive changes that the authors of the immediately preceding period appear to us hardly less remote than the writers of, say, the classical or the romantic school. However, even though we are fully aware of the sharp general contrast between ourselves and the generation that went before us, it is by no means easy to trace with accuracy the various stages and the multifarious aspects of that profound and complex transformation. Amidst the confusing medley of 'modern' tendencies, the works of Marcel Proust, André Gide, Jean Giraudoux, and Paul Morand offer perhaps the most provocative and enlightening *exposé* of certain essential trends in contemporary French civilization and literature. Of course each of these four writers has approached his problems in his own particular way and has found his own personal solution for his difficulties. Nevertheless in every case, the problems involved have such a broad human bearing that Proust, Gide, Giraudoux, and Morand may be considered as well qualified exponents of some of the most typical aspirations, anxieties, and perplexities of this rather restless and unbalanced, yet highly interesting and perhaps supremely important new generation.

At the threshold of our 'modern' era, Proust appears as an outstanding figure in the realm of French, and, it may even be said, of world literature. His works, it is true, were mainly elaborated before the war and the material on which he drew belonged to a period that is past: indeed, the 'society' which he set himself so faithfully to portray, has now almost completely disappeared. In the field of psychology, however, Proust set an example and inaugurated a method which, when conjoined with discoveries coming from other quarters about the same time, profoundly altered, nay revolutionized, the generally accepted views on the working of our conscious and subconscious minds. On his work undoubtedly hinges to a large extent the conception that many contemporary French writers still hold of human psychology. In that respect, though Proust himself is sometimes already regarded as of an earlier generation, his influence, direct or indirect, on the France of today can hardly be overestimated.

André Gide likewise garnered the most important elements of his life experience during the pre-war period. As in the case of Proust, however, real fame only came to him in very recent years. The moral problems which had perplexed him for a long time happened to correspond almost exactly to the difficulties that beset a great many young men in the days following the Great War. He seemed to embody the spirit of free, sincere, and independent search for a new truth, while his zest for life—untrammelled by old-fashioned, conventional ideas—his deep longing for a genuine personal morality on a higher plane, appealed strongly to a young generation which had lost its way and was eager to find its bearings again, to start afresh and to reconstruct, amid the ruins of the past, a richer and a better world.

This task of reconstruction was not an easy one. The past had deposited its substratum of facts which could neither be abolished nor ignored, and the new edifice could not be reared on a purely theoretical and abstract foundation. This problem was indeed not altogether a

new one: for some time it had been becoming more and
more apparent that the most precious heritage of the
past—the old classical culture, with its undeviating intellectual and moral standards—was not at all in accord
with the modern world as it tended spontaneously to take
shape before our eyes. Of that opposition between modern
reality and the old classical ideal, only scholars were keenly
aware in the years before the war. One of their number,
Jean Giraudoux, profoundly appreciated both the value of
the classics and the attractions of th modern world, and
he had explored, though in an imaginative and desultory
fashion, the possibilities of reconciling the one with the
other. The circumstances that arose in all countries after
the great upheaval of the war, turned this underlying
antagonism into an open clash. Many felt that they must
choose between classical culture and modern life. Not a
few definitely turned their backs on culture. For most
French people, this conflict had an aspect almost of tragedy, as traditionally the French have always set the
greatest store by their cultural past. It was then that
Giraudoux came to the fore. Previously his reputation had
hardly reached beyond a narrow circle of cultivated con-
noisseurs. Gradually it became more and more evident
that behind the veil of poetic fancy with which most of
his literary productions are delicately wrapped, he was
attacking with determination one of the most vital problems of our modern times. Even though Giraudoux's suggested solution for effecting a harmony between classical
ideals and modern reality may not be accepted by all as
decisive and final, his clever and penetrating investigation of the difficulties and the possibilities will undoubtedly hold for every cultured man a vivid and engrossing
interest.

Indeed, the solution propounded by Giraudoux is not

final—in fact, no satisfactory solution of that crucial problem seems to have been evolved so far by anybody. To many people, the world of today presents but a glittering, and somewhat meaningless, spectacle of moral disintegration and decay. The spectacle, though disheartening, is by no means lacking in beauty. The strange fascination of the modern world, as well as its fundamental disjointedness has been intensely felt and powerfully expressed by Morand. Few recent writers have more aptly rendered the atmosphere of tragic uncertainty, of headlong flight forward which seems to be among the most characteristic features of our modern world. The new manners—if not the ideas—of today have indeed in Morand an extremely shrewd observer and an extraordinarily brilliant painter.

The views presented by Proust, Gide, Giraudoux, and Morand on the man of today and the world he lives in do not by any means exhaust the content of contemporary French literature. But they may be considered as striking examples of some of the main trends of French civilization. Proust in the field of psychology, Gide in the field of personal morality, Giraudoux in a more purely intellectual demesne, Morand in the swiftly moving current of fast changing manners, have given us their several testimonies on the spirit of our age, and these will undoubtedly remain as outstanding landmarks in the general perspective of our present era.

MARCEL PROUST

I. MARCEL PROUST

1. *Proust's Life*

MARCEL PROUST was born in Auteuil, a suburb of Paris, July 10, 1871. In the preceding months the French capital had been besieged by the German armies, bombarded and starved into surrender. As a sequel to this disaster, a furious civil war, known as 'La Commune,' broke out within Paris itself. Barricades were erected, buildings were set on fire and, before order was restored, the government troops had slain thousands of the insurgents. Proust's father actually was wounded by a bullet whilst walking peacefully from one part of the city to another in pursuit of his profession.

Born shortly after these trying months, Marcel Proust was never to be quite normal. His younger brother, Robert, two years his junior, was a strong and sturdy youngster. Marcel, however, was destined to bear all his life the consequences of the nerve-racking experiences which his mother must have gone through before the time of his birth.

The father, Dr. Adrien Proust, was a well known physician and a university professor as well. He appeared as a strong, stout, bearded man, distant and cold in his manner, and yet active, energetic, and always preoccupied with his professional duties. His personal influence upon his son amounted practically to nothing; there was never any real understanding or deep sympathy between them. But the material assistance which Marcel derived from his father was by no means negligible. Dr. Proust enjoyed

3

a large income, and during his lifetime he provided his
son generously with money. At his death he left Marcel
enough to enable him to pursue the life of a gentleman of
leisure and the career of a man in society, which had
already been his only calling for a great number of years.

Yet by his family origins Marcel Proust did not belong
to 'society.' In France at that time a professor, even with
money, had ordinarily no access to the charmed circle and
Dr. Adrien Proust had never been able or had never cared
to break through the conventional barrier. Mme Proust
constituted a further handicap in that respect. She was a
Jewess—her maiden name was Jeanne Weil—and 'society'
in the nineteenth century had very decided ideas about
Jews.

Mme Proust was a remarkable woman, highly cultured,
endowed with an almost oriental charm, gifted with a
strong and captivating personality. As any mother would,
she lavished the stronger affection and love upon Marcel
because he was a weakly child. Marcel, responding to her
love, gave her worship for worship and haunted her very
shadow. At the age of thirteen, in answering a question-
naire, opposite the query 'Your idea of misery?' he put
down, 'Etre séparé de maman.' [1] All his life, he retained
this passionate and jealous devotion to his mother.

Brought up away from any strong masculine influence,
Marcel Proust was spoilt if ever a child was. In his case
there seems to have been no question of anyone's enforcing
discipline or inculcating self-control. He grew up in an
atmosphere of unrestrained caprice, tempered with affection. Although nominally Catholic, he never received any
real religious training. His Catholic father and his Jewish
mother had the tact, perhaps the wisdom, to exclude

1. Pierre Abraham, *Proust*, Rieder, Paris, 1930, pl.viii. The question is asked in
   English in the original.

Church controversies from the home. Religion and morals are frequently linked together in the mind of a very young man; but Proust was not to be troubled by either.

The general indulgence which he received at home may be accounted for—if not excused—by the very poor state of his health. At the age of nine, returning one day from a walk in the Bois de Boulogne, he had a violent attack of suffocation and nearly succumbed under the very eyes of his distraught father. He never fully recovered from this, and remained a semi-invalid for the rest of his life. The doctors were unable to agree upon a diagnosis; but whatever the cause, all the year round coughs, colds, insomnia, hay fever, asthma, singly or together, would attack and shake his sickly frame. He had periods of partial recovery or temporary improvement, though these never lasted for long, and even at his best he was weak and ailing.

Naturally he had to go to school. More important for him though was the time that he could spend away from his teachers on Thursdays and Sundays, the traditional French school holidays, and during the spring and summer vacations. On the Thursdays and Sundays, and even at times after school on other days, he would go to the 'Champs-Elysées' and play with children of his own age. Actually he took little part in play; he preferred to talk, and he seems to have known precociously how to keep his young friends under the spell of his words. He generally appeared muffled in a number of shawls and comforters, and went about displaying the most perfect manners, showering delicate attentions on elderly ladies sitting on benches near by, no doubt to their amused delight. But his interests were not only in the elderly ladies there. He found amongst his youthful friends round the gingerbread stand his first childhood sweethearts. Proust himself said that he experienced then 'le grand amour de ma vie, sans qu'elle l'ait jamais su.' [2] Who the object of that 'grand amour' was, is still unknown.[3] But the point is immaterial. Combined perhaps with a few others of the same group, undoubtedly she now lives in the person of Gilberte, the red-haired daughter of Swann.

If it be true that the impressions of early childhood tend to form our deepest aspirations, such as may afterwards manifest themselves as irrepressible cravings, then this first sentimental adventure of Proust will account perhaps for certain features of his later mental evolution. This precocious experience of love probably left in him the deep-rooted conviction that this passion is the thing that counts most in life.

In his spring and summer holidays he went sometimes to the home of a great-uncle on his mother's side, Louis Weil, who lived in Auteuil. Auteuil, now a part of Paris, was then a rural suburb full of the gardens and the flowers which Proust loved. There he came into intimate and familiar contact with the Jewish members of his family and their friends in the typical atmosphere of Jewish family life. Among the friends and visitors of Louis Weil, there was a man—Charles Haas—who used to fill young Marcel with admiration and awe. Charles Haas must have possessed a strange power of fascination, for—though he was a Jew and not particularly wealthy—he was received and even sought after by the most exclusive aristocratic families of the time. He made such a strong impression on the young boy that, later on, Proust chose him as the proto-type for one of the main characters of his books: Swann.

Sometimes the family went to visit another uncle of

2. *Hommage à Marcel Proust*, Nouvelle Revue Française, Paris, 1927—Proust's letter to J.de Lacretelle, p.202.
3. R.Dreyfus in his *Souvenirs sur M.Proust*, Grasset, Paris, 1926 mentions two sisters of foreign birth, the elder of whom seems to have inspired Proust with more than ordinary admiration (p.12).

Marcel, on his father's side, Jules Amiot, who had a house at Illiers, not very far from Chartres. Here reigned Aunt Amiot, perpetually ill—or believing herself to be so—punctiliously attended by her devoted maid, Ernestine Gallou. At Illiers young Proust learned to know the characteristic types of a small provincial town. But above all, he here received his initiation into the love of Nature and all things beautiful. The countryside round Illiers had no very striking features, but a subtle and delicate charm seemed to hover about the place. In one direction were gardens and woods, brooks and ponds, all in an atmosphere of repose and quiet mystery; on the other side lay a broad expanse of open country, where the only landmarks were the white road cutting across the plain and the sharp outline of some far-away steeple, etched against the sky. These two directions became respectively *Guermantes' Way* and *Swann's Way*, the *Côté de Guermantes* and the *Côté de chez Swann*, in *A la Recherche du Temps Perdu*, for Illiers, with a few added touches, provided all the main features of the imaginary *Combray* of the book. The fanciful name of *Combray* itself is but the harmonious transformation of *Combres*, the actual name of a neighbouring village. Proust enjoyed here some of the happiest and most intense moments of his life. The simplest spectacle, such as the play of light on some distant steeple, would throw him, young as he was, into a lyric ecstasy. The hawthorn in bloom in the hedges roused in him a mystic passion. It also brought him almost unremitting physical torment, for, as a sufferer from asthma, he could not endure the perfume of flowers. On this account he was obliged subsequently to renounce Illiers-Combray for ever.

His parents gradually came to repair in preference to Cabourg or Trouville, both rather fashionable resorts on

the coast of Normandy. There the family used to take
quarters in one of the large and showy seaside hotels.
Marcel did not find much to do except watch the sea or
observe the groups of boys and pretty 'jeunes filles' enjoying the comparative freedom permitted on the beach in
strictly conventional pre-war France. Proust seems to have
liked the life there and Cabourg became for him a permanent centre of attraction.

Between holidays Proust attended classes at the 'Lycée
Condorcet.' On account of poor health he was obliged to
make up by his instinctive cleverness what he missed
from irregular attendance. In history he was markedly
proficient. One of his teachers, Jallifier, aroused in him a
keen interest in the seventeenth century. The *Memoirs* of
Saint-Simon with their picture of the court of Louis XIV
became his favourite reading. All the secret and complex
background which lay behind the heroic deeds, the great
disasters, or the actual daily routine of the reign were
unfolded before his eager curiosity. He became thoroughly
familiar with the great aristocratic names of the time. In
his imagination he lived at the court of Versailles. For him
that world was suffused with the glamour attached, in
the eyes of a sensitive adolescent, to something which
has been magnificently great and which has receded into
the mists of a supremely romantic past.

From Saint-Simon, whose Memoirs he kept on reading
throughout his life, Proust learned to discover the reasons
concealed beneath a man's every action, word, or glance.
Furthermore he learned to find in hidden motives the only
realities of life or of history, motives more or less covered
by a screen of pretence. Perhaps even at that time, but
undoubtedly later, he dreamed of being the 'Saint-Simon'
of his own era and of recording the thousand imperceptible
trifles which go to make our modern world.

The past, however, had an irresistible attraction for him. He wanted to see, perhaps even to meet, the descendants of Louis XIV's illustrious retainers and courtiers. By its very inaccessibility the mysterious world of the upper aristocracy became for this young, half Jewish *bourgeois* an object of fascination and irrepressible longing. It acquired the halo of charm and grandeur which his young imagination had already created round the majestic memory of the 'Grand Roi.'

Among his school friends, there were a few of aristocratic birth, such as Louis de la Salle and Jean de Tinan; but most of them were wealthy young *bourgeois*, such as Henri Rabaud, Marcel Boulenger, Jacques and Paul Baignières—a few being Jews or half Jews, like Marcel Proust himself: Léon Brunschwicg, Robert Dreyfus, Fernand Gregh, Jacques Bizet, Daniel Halévy. Many of them belonged to the group of his playfellows in the Champs-Elysées. They formed the first solid group of friends he made, and these friendships lasted throughout the years of his youth.

All these boys were keen and clever; with the advent of adolescence and early manhood they were bubbling over with longings, aspirations, illusions, ambitions of all sorts. Proust for his own part felt that he himself had something to say—perhaps too much to say—though he did not know exactly what. 'J'ai tant à dire. Çà se presse comme des flots,' he wrote at eighteen to Robert Dreyfus.[4] At a still earlier age it had happened that, in the face of the beauty of things he had felt an intense emotion, which had to express itself in words, however inarticulate; 'The tiled roof cast upon the pond, whose reflections were now clear again in the sunlight, a square of pink marble, the like of which I had never observed before. And seeing upon the

4. R.Dreyfus, *Souvenirs sur M.Proust*, p.33.

water, where it reflected the wall, a pallid smile responding
to the smiling sky, I cried aloud my enthusiasm, brandish-
ing my furled umbrella, "Damn, damn, damn, damn." But
at the same time I felt I was in duty bound not to content
myself with these unilluminating words, but to endeavour
to see more clearly into the source of my enjoyment.' [5] He
had the distinct conviction that he had a message to impart, though he did not know exactly its nature; and he
trusted that the future eventually would reveal the secret.

At eighteen—an interlude. Proust was called up for his
military training. He was a most indifferent soldier for the
single year (1889) during which he was attached to the
76th Infantry stationed at Orléans. His family knew personally Colonel Arvers, in command; so for Marcel duties
were rather light, and furloughs plentiful. Nevertheless he
was supposed to be interested in strategy and later on he
liked to talk and even to write on the subject. In Orléans
he acquired a new and interesting friend, Gaston de Caillavet, who was to be of great assistance in helping him to
further his social ambitions.

When Marcel returned home to Paris, Dr. Adrien Proust
insisted upon his taking up a career. He suggested the
French diplomatic service. Marcel wanted to be a 'society
man,' and perhaps a writer. Ultimately there was a compromise and Proust registered simultaneously at the 'Sorbonne,' at the Law School, and at the 'Ecole libre des Sciences Politiques.' From the 'Ecole des Sciences Politiques'
he drew very little, except a friendship with Léon Blum,
who was his co-disciple. In Law he failed to pass his exam-
inations at the end of the second year. At the 'Sorbonne'
literature, psychology, philosophy most attracted him.

5. M.Proust, *Du Côté de chez Swann*, Nouvelle Revue Française, Paris, 1919,
Part I, Chap.II, p.224—*Swann's Way*, Random House, New York, 1934, I,
p.199.

In the field of philosophy Bergson's famous book, *Essai sur les données immédiates de la conscience*, published in 1889, had created a great sensation. It is difficult to say whether Bergson's influence on Proust was altogether direct, or whether Proust merely absorbed part of Bergson's ideas, as practically every young man did who lived in the intellectual atmosphere of Paris in the early 1890's. At any rate, Proust became joined by family ties to the philosopher when Bergson married one of Marcel's relatives, Mlle Neuburger. He was even best man at their wedding, so it is probable that this relationship helped to make the young Proust an admiring, though independent, disciple.

One of the main points in Bergson's philosophy was his conception of Time. Bergson pointed out that there are two different ways of considering time. One is the way scientists and watchmakers look at it—as an impersonal, empty, and perfectly homogeneous entity, which is identically the same for all observers, which can be cut into sections of precisely the same length: seconds, minutes, hours, etc. and the course of which can be measured by the motion of some material object in space, the sun in the sky, for example, or the hands on the dial of a clock. Each and every moment of this time, once gone, vanishes altogether into nothingness. But psychological time, according to Bergson, is of a very different nature. It is a matter of common experience that time flies very quickly in certain circumstances and in others crawls haltingly along. On certain occasions it is crammed with feelings or thoughts, on other occasions it seems perfectly empty and flat. It is not annihilated when it slips away. What would a melody mean to us if the sounds, just past, did not remain, hidden as it were but actually present? Past and present are inextricably mixed. Time considered in this way cannot be cut into separate, independent sections. It

is a continuity, identical with the irregular and living flow
of our consciousness. It cannot be marked or measured by
lines or dots. It can be grasped by intuition alone. It is indeed so different from scientific, astronomical time, that it
deserves, so Bergson said, an entirely different name: duration. It is duration alone that counts in our psychological
life. In fact it is one with our psychological life itself. It is
an aspect, perhaps the most important aspect, of our ever-
changing personality. We are swept along in its tide. If we
could know Time, we would know ourselves. Time-duration
is ourselves.

These ideas made the deepest impression on Proust. In
his hours of illness he had heard the clock ticking away
Time; empty seconds, minutes, and hours passed which
had no meaning for him. What had this to do with real
Time, with the vital flow of his soul? To him, Time was a
wonderful and terrible enigma, concealing the secret of life.
Then Bergson's theories presented themselves as a key to
this enigma, imperfect perhaps but well worth trying.

Bergson put forth other theories to which Proust re-
sponded with equally keen interest. For instance Bergson
asserted that our clear ideas do not represent our true
selves at all. Our real selves lie in subconscious tendencies,
sometimes outwardly manifesting themselves by accident,
but most of the time completely hidden, even from ourselves. It is the task of the psychologist to detect from
these occasional fleeting appearances the development of
the all-important, underlying mental trends. Bergson also
stated that there is, interposed between the apparent reality of things and the depth of our consciousness, a kind of
wall, constituted by a practical, almost mechanical set of
customary reflexes, conventional feelings, and ready-made
ideas. We resort to them in order to deal conveniently with
the very complex world that confronts us at every mo-

ment. One of the privileges of the artist is to penetrate this artificial wall and to discover the true course of nature, by a sort of intimate communion revealing its reality to himself and to all others at the same time.

By the time Marcel Proust left the Sorbonne, after taking the degree of 'licencié' (1892), he had formulated for himself a definite set of ideas, almost a programme. Life was before him and he approached it cherishing two great dreams. He hoped to feel the pangs of a great love, which, perhaps on account of his childhood adventure, appeared to him as the most magnificent and glorious experience to be had in life. He expected everything—at least everything beautiful—from love. At the same time he wanted to be received by the proud aristocrats, whose illustrious names dated back to the reign of Louis XIV, and who, in his imagination, were the essence of all that is elegant and truly great on earth.

Behind these two main aspirations loomed two ideas which were less conspicuous, but nevertheless deeply rooted and bound to grow; first, the vague belief—not yet a certainty—that he had something to say. But what? Was he going to sing of the beauty of Nature, which he had felt so intensely at Illiers? Or like Saint-Simon was he going to write the memoirs of his time? Or again, was he going as a psychologist, to try to extract the innermost secrets of everyman's soul? Time would tell. But was not Time, as Bergson had shown, Marcel Proust himself? If Time ran on too fast, would it not mean that Marcel Proust also would go at the same pace?—for he was not so robust. . . . The conception that Time was something infinitely precious and terribly dangerous lurked at the back of his mind.

. . . .

'Un prince napolitain pour roman de Bourget.' This is how Proust appeared in his twenties to a friendly though somewhat malicious observer.[6] He was slender and pale, with long black hair and large, soft, rather expressionless dark eyes. His nose, which was long and somewhat curved, to his great despair, gave him an oriental look. He dressed with great care, yet without ever attaining a neat appearance. His shirt fronts would be of a special creamy-pink shade of his own invention—of which he was very proud—but his suit would be too big for him and would hang about his person as if it had been bought—God forbid!—at any ready-to-wear clothes shop. He tried hard to be a dandy, but failed, and this gave him an uncertain and artificial air.

The impression of artificiality was further accentuated by his manners. He affected the most embarrassing humility towards everyone he met, no matter whether it were an old friend or a new acquaintance, a lady of fashion or a cab-driver in the street. He was always sensitively apprehensive he might incommode someone, even a servant, and apologized profusely on all occasions for things of the most trifling import. His over-politeness expressed itself in extravagant fussiness, also in exaggerated though always very delicate flatteries. The Duchesse de Clermont-Tonnerre, who knew him well, said that his attentions were like the 'soft little jammy paws of very small children, patting your face and clothes—tender and sweet but sticky. You feel flattered and at the same time a little annoyed.' [7] Proust's friends had invented a special word, 'Proustifier' for these peculiar mannerisms and behaviour.

Humble as he was, or pretended to be, Proust loved to talk, and he would talk for hours if he could find a patient listener. When invited to a dinner-party, he used to have his own meal at home first in order to be able to talk dur-

---

6. *Hommage à Marcel Proust*, Fernand Gregh, p.35.
7. E.de Clermont-Tonnerre, *Robert de Montesquiou et Marcel Proust*, Flammarion, Paris, 1925, p.11.

ing the dinner hour as well as the entire evening afterwards. Once started, his flow of conversation, not exactly brilliant, would be subtle and captivating. A thousand small trifles, which nobody else would ever notice, through his insight and his often tortuous implications, took on an importance which left the other guests puzzled but always, in the end, admiring. At other times he would make the cleverest imitations of some absent friend. Throughout his intricate sentences there was often an undercurrent of irony and sarcasm; at times the sudden flash of an illuminating idea. This might have revealed, behind his too polite and smooth bearing, something more than the languid and equivocal charm which seems to have struck most of the people who met Proust at that time and who, as Barrès did, generally saw in him nothing but a 'gentil compagnon.' [8]

Young Proust had made it one of his ideals and at the same time one of the definite purposes of his life to be accepted in 'society.' High society in France round 1890 was very different from what it is in our own day. It was a self-contained and very exclusive world. The descendants of the great aristocratic families gathered in certain *salons*, adopting an attitude of affected superiority towards the rest of mortals. They had not given up all their illusions and hopes concerning the possibility of a monarchic restoration, and they believed that they were to be the lords of tomorrow. Probably several of them had already begun to entertain doubts about the future—which was one more reason for being on the defensive and remaining protected behind the barrier of a silent and distant pride. Nevertheless they admitted to their midst some outstanding personalities,—artists, writers, and even a few *bourgeois* men of leisure, as it were, on sufferance. The 'Affaire Dreyfus,'

8. *Hommage à Marcel Proust*, Barrès, p.13.

which started in 1894, made them for a while at least still
more exclusive. Besides these aristocratic *salons,* and to
some extent aping them, were other gatherings, more miscellaneous, such as the *salons* of a few rich and enterprising
bourgeoises, anxious to have a little circle of their own and
striving to attract all those who were *distingués.* A nobleman of course was a good 'catch,' but a well known artist,
or even a politician was not to be despised. On the same
level were certain aristocratic *salons,* which for one reason
or another had not been able to maintain their aloofness,
and therefore their standing. The *salons* of this kind were,
of course, comparatively easy of access, but in the eyes of
a connoisseur they were only second choice.

It was in these less considered *salons* that Marcel first
succeeded in gaining a foothold. His school friendships
gave him several openings. Jacques Bizet introduced him
to his mother, Mme Straus, a daughter of the Jewish composer Fromental Halévy. She had been married first to
Georges Bizet, the composer of *Carmen,* and then to the
lawyer, Emile Straus. Hers was essentially an intellectual
and musical circle. Proust repaired to her *salon* assiduously. Jacques Baignières invited him to Mme Arthur Baignières' receptions and also to those of Mme Henri Baignières. Thanks to Gaston de Caillavet, he was asked to the
famous gatherings of Mme Arman de Caillavet and here
he could see and admire Anatole France. Anatole France
was kind to the young man, even to the extent of writing
a preface for his first literary effort. Further he was invited
to Mme Aubernon's house. He was even admitted to
the company of the famous Princesse Mathilde, a niece of
Napoléon I.[9] Gossips maliciously, and probably without
cause, linked the name of the aging dowager with that of
Marcel, who used to crouch at her feet like a page in the

9. The daughter of Jérôme Bonaparte, a younger brother of Napoléon.

romances of old. There was a great deal of etiquette and ceremonial surrounding the Princesse Mathilde. Nevertheless, her noble lineage was not a century old—a mere trifle when it comes to genealogical trees. . . . Madeleine Lemaire had a studio, something quite new at that time, and there gave very smart parties, where the artistic and aristocratic world used to meet. Proust became an assiduous caller upon Madeleine Lemaire as well as her friend; but then Madeleine Lemaire had so many callers and friends! Admission to the most exclusive circles, which he himself so ardently coveted, was still beyond his reach.

It was in Madeleine Lemaire's studio that he discovered Robert de Montesquiou, the man who was to give him the key to the magic world and change his whole outlook on life. Montesquiou was one of the strangest characters of the time. He was a member of the most exclusive 'blue-blooded' aristocracy and belonged by right of birth to the highest society. Of all this M.le Comte Robert de Montesquiou was inordinately proud. His insolence towards his inferiors, that is to say, towards practically all the rest of the world, was slightly tempered by a friendliness akin to the protective feeling which many people have for dumb animals. At the same time he was uncannily clever and penetrating when it came to discovering the hidden motives and secret lives of the people around him. He knew everybody, and everything about everybody. He was indiscreet, and loved to talk about what he knew, especially if his vanity was touched—as it easily was. With all this he was a poet, with extraordinary refinement of feeling and expression and not without a certain bizarre charm. Striking in appearance, he combined a nonchalant air with the dash of the three legendary musketeers. But Montesquiou, to put it mildly, lacked normal affections. His passion for

the musician Delafosse and for the Argentinian Gabriel de
Yturri was the open secret of Paris.

Proust knew all that; but Montesquiou could give him
two things he wanted—access to the most exclusive *salons*,
and information about the people who frequented them.
Young Proust was alive with curiosity, and he was ready
to pay the price. So he attached himself deliberately to
M.le Comte and accepted everything from him 'avec une
patience qui allait plus loin que la patience.' [10] Montesquiou certainly was not an easy person to get on with; he
had uncontrollable outbursts of temper; he would insult
Proust, taunting him with his Jewish parentage; he even
went so far as to call him in public 'petit être usagé.' [11] So
Proust, as one may well understand, came to hate him in
his heart with a ferocious hatred; but apparently was more
humble and polite to him than ever, and plied him regularly with the most fulsome flatteries, which the *gentilhomme* swallowed whole. But at the same time Proust,
remembering what he wanted, asked for gossip and begged
for introductions, and got both.

Montesquiou introduced him to his beautiful cousin, the
Comtesse Greffülhe, née Chimay, to the Princesse Edmond
de Polignac, and to the Princesse de Wagram. Soon the
exclusive houses of the Comtesse de Beaulaincourt, of the
Comte d'Haussonville, and of many others, were open to
him, and for a while Proust swam in the blissful atmosphere of unbelievably high connexions. Now he was welcome everywhere, everywhere treated with politeness and
respect, even sometimes sought after in the most flattering
way—and this by the most particular and haughtiest
aristocrats in France. One of his dreams had indeed come
true.

10. E.de Clermont-Tonnerre, *Robert de Montesquiou et Marcel Proust*, p.26.
11. *Ibidem*, p.33.

But by and by he came to discover that the people his young imagination had placed on a pedestal, high above all other beings, were after all only men and women. In fact they were frequently much worse than other men and women, being full of silly prejudices, empty-headed on account of their lack of contact with the realities of life, and absorbed in petty intrigues and rivalries; they were all pretence, conceit, and idle vanity—in a word, they were snobs. Proust himself has been accused of snobbery, and in a way undoubtedly he was a snob; but that was only one side of his personality. Society people, he found, had nothing in them, except perhaps a few vices; and these proved all the more devastating to people who had the means and the time to indulge in them. Here kindness, and courtesy even, were superficial—just a veneer concealing selfishness and cruelty. The realization of all this came to Proust by degrees. He was possessed by the demon of investigation. Was it the influence of Saint-Simon?—of Montesquiou?—or perhaps just the nature of Proust's mind? He had to find out what really was behind appearances, actions, and words. And the more he discovered, the more he wanted to go further still. Bit by bit the wonderful castle of his youthful dreams was crumbling and falling at his feet; after ten years of this life practically nothing was left of the dream. Of course he had grown to know better then—he was wiser—but one of his great ideals was completely ruined.

His other great dream, love, had not fared much better. In this case again he had started life in search of the absolute, and had been disappointed. It is not always easy to distinguish between his friendship and his love; and to make matters still more complicated, a number of his adventures seem to have been purely imaginary. His first group of friends, those he knew as a boy, were mainly his school-fellows from the Lycée Condorcet: Robert Dreyfus, Jacques Bizet, Daniel Halévy, Fernand Gregh, etc.; these friends he did not keep much beyond his twenty-fifth year. He knew them and they knew him only too well. They used to tease him, as young fellows will, and over-sensitive Marcel could not endure teasing. He did not actually break with them; but when the aristocratic world was opened to him, he dropped them.

In these aristocratic circles he met Charles Haas again. Haas had succeeded in what appeared to Proust, at that time, to be the most wonderful and enviable achievement; he was received by the highest 'society.' He was actually a friend of the Prince of Wales (the future Edward VII) and also the friend of many other distinguished personages —in fact, he was 'one of them'! For Proust, Haas was the ideal model of what he himself wanted to be. Yet Haas seems not to have shown anything beyond a rather condescending politeness to his youthful admirer.

It was among the young aristocrats themselves that Proust found his real 'affinities.' He began a very close and intimate friendship with the young and attractive Comte Bertrand de Fénelon and two young Roumanian princes, Antoine and Emmanuel Bibesco. The four of them formed a kind of mystic fraternity, having special names for each other and secret signs. Fénelon became 'Nonelef,' and the two Bibescos, 'Ocsebib,' and Marcel, 'Lecram.' [12] Secret confidences and literary effusions were their bond of union. Quarrels would sometimes disturb their friendly relations which, however, were invariably restored with impulsive and effusive displays of affection. Proust wrote to Antoine Bibesco: 'Si le peu que je sais peut t'intéresser, il est à ta disposition, mon petit Antoine, dans la même

12. M.L.Bibesco, *Au bal avec Marcel Proust*, Nouvelle Revue Française, Paris, 1928, p.11.

mesure que mon cœur, mes forces, ma vie et le peu d'uti-
lité que je pourrais occasionnellement avoir dans la vie, c'est
à dire tout entier. J'ai naturellement en t'écrivant la
légère émotion qui accompagne inévitablement des assertions si véhémentes. . . .'[13] However flowery and emphatic the normal epistolary style of Proust may have
been, one cannot help feeling here the throb of a deep and
sincere emotion. Several others—d'Albuféra, Léon Radzi-
will, Guiche—all belonging to the most distinguished families, played a more or less episodic part in Proust's in-
satiable craving for affection. That craving was never to
be satisfied; he wanted too much, too many contradictory
things—and when he was disappointed, he had violent
outbursts of despair. He was jealous of Antoine Bibesco's
friendship with Bertrand de Fénelon,[14] and yet did everything he could to promote that friendship; sometimes he
would keep them together, sometimes he tried to separate
them and set them one against the other. His letters are
full of recriminations and complaints: nobody ever loves him
enough; he continually detects, or believes he can detect,
indifference and deception; he is the ever-disappointed.

With women his associations were no happier. Long
after his boyhood love in the Champs-Elysées, there was
a youthful affair with a courtesan, a Mlle Clomesnil,
which does not seem to have gone beyond the stage of ex-
changing photographs.[15] A more serious affair, though still
a very innocent one, linked him with another beauty of
the day, Laure Hayman, famous under the nickname of
Gladys Harvey.[16] Later on he indulged himself in a great

13. M.Proust—Letter xxii to Antoine Bibesco, quoted by M.L.Bibesco in
op. cit., pp.13–14.
14. M.L.Bibesco, op. cit., pp.127–128.
15. *Hommage à Marcel Proust*, Proust's letter to J.de Lacretelle, p.202.
16. The name of an imaginary courtesan in a book, *Pastel de Femmes*, by Paul
Bourget, then the recognized painter of high—and fast—life.

but platonic love for a lady of fashion—probably Mme de C.[17]—whom he used to watch walking, or driving in state, along the smart Avenue Marigny. His heart does does not seem to have been touched seriously, but all his imaginative faculties were brought into play in this aristocratic affair. It was distinctly an 'amour de tête.' He had numerous adventures besides, generally with persons of a not very elevated social rank—as, for instance, a short liaison with an Austrian girl [18] and a long flirtation with an actress, Louisa de Mornand. In each of these cases his boundless expectations of happiness were doomed to disappointment. With uncanny and destructive penetration he questioned the value and doubted the sincerity of any love offered to him, and by and by he came to question and to doubt love itself. To his over-exacting and oversensitive nature, the little ripples in the stream of his affections became waves of suffering and bitterness; battered by them his beautiful dreams slowly crumbled away.

While his two great enthusiasms—social ambition and love—were bringing disappointment and even disgust, other aspirations were progressively growing and developing within him. Even when very young he had felt in a dim and confused way the yearning to express his feelings and experiences in literary form. In his early twenties that yearning took a more definite shape and he decided that he would be a writer. But what was he to write about?

When Proust was twenty-one, certain young men, most of them belonging to the Lycée Condorcet group and regular frequenters of Mme Straus's *salon*—Fernand Gregh, Jacques Bizet, Daniel Halévy, Léon Blum, Proust himself, and a few others—founded a literary magazine called *Le*

17. Léon Pierre-Quint, *Marcel Proust*, Kra, Paris, 1928, I, 4, pp.74–75.
18. R.Dreyfus, *Souvenirs sur Marcel Proust*, Chap.II, pp.50–51. Letter of M.P. to R.D., 25 September, 1885, and note p.50.

Banquet. The attempt was shortlived and *Le Banquet*, which first saw the light of day in 1892, perished in 1893 after the publication of eight numbers. Proust had contributed a few little sketches and notes, clever and dainty as a rule, but showing no spark of genius. About the same time he wrote pretty trifles for the symbolist *Revue Blanche*. Finally in 1896 he published a rather insignificant pamphlet, *Portraits de Peintres*, and also *Les Plaisirs et les Jours*.

Les Plaisirs et les Jours was nothing but a collection in book form of the articles which he had published previously in *Le Banquet*, in the *Revue Blanche*, and in *Portraits de Peintres*, with the addition of a few new pieces of the same kind. His friend Madeleine Lemaire consented to do the illustrations for the book; a second friend, Reynaldo Hahn, contributed a few musical compositions; and Anatole France, another friend, wrote the preface. The whole thing was printed very luxuriously, and Proust's friends had perforce to purchase copies. There were practically no other purchasers. Proust won the appreciation of the small circle which alone counted with him. To the general reading public, however, he was still unknown, or, considered at best, a 'mondain amateur.' [19] Articles which he subsequently contributed to *Le Figaro* only confirmed that impression.

In fact, though in these early publications many of the most typical characteristics that he later displayed can be detected, Proust had not yet found himself. He probably realized this, as in the following years he gave up entirely the attempt to produce anything new and original and he put himself to the school of another man's thought. For six years he immersed himself in Ruskin. At first he knew scarcely any English; but he had a dictionary and plenty of tenacity.

19. An expression of André Gide.

Proust found in Ruskin the same dominant idea concerning the place of art and beauty in life, which was his own problem and interest at the time. To Ruskin beauty is not a mere ornament nor an object of superficial entertainment and pleasure, but a deep reality, giving life its very meaning. In beauty itself, conceived as the great reality in life, there is a profound mystery. Proust was sensible of this, and he felt that a personal solution must be discovered, or rather experienced, before he could create anything worth while himself. Ruskin was not to provide him with a ready-made æsthetic philosophy; the moralizing Englishman was too unlike Proust to exert on him a very direct influence. But Ruskin actually did inspire him and guide him through a maze of delicate and complicated problems. He helped Proust to find himself; in the face of certain striking similarities in the two writers it is difficult at times to tell whether there was identity of æsthetic experience or whether Proust, perhaps unconsciously, was fecundated by the master mind with which he had lived in spiritual communion for upwards of six years. As an example, the idea that an artist must grasp the essence of reality with his senses only and refrain as much as possible from allowing intelligence to be its interpreter, thus spoiling its freshness, is common to both writers.[20] The theory also, which is perhaps the keystone of Proust's general conception of art, namely, that the sentimental colour associated with a past experience may be involuntarily and yet forcibly revived by a new physical sensation analogous to the earlier one—this theory is definitely to be found in a very similar form in Ruskin.[21]

Proust translated two of Ruskin's books, *The Bible of*

20. Ruskin, *The Eagle's Nest*, Lecture VII, §§ 125–126, cf. Proust, *Pastiches et Mélanges*, Nouvelle Revue Française, Paris, 1919. En Mémoire des Eglises Assassinées, III, p.169.
21. Ruskin, *Modern Painters*, Part III, Section I, Chap.4, Paragraph 9.

Amiens (1904) and *Sesame and Lilies* (1906). The translations, as might be expected, are rather free, but Proust's own long prefaces show that Ruskin had provided him with abundant food for thought.

Meanwhile Proust had started making notes about people and things around him. He does not seem to have known at first exactly how he would use them. Friends who were privileged to read some of the lines he scribbled on any scrap of paper at hand could never discover anything of interest in his long and minute descriptions of the most insignificant facts, nor in the detailed accounts of perfectly banal everyday happenings. He was accumulating these notes carefully, however, as precious material for a large work which was now secretly taking shape in his mind. He was not without misgivings concerning his vocation as a writer, and often, after trying to express reality as he himself so deeply felt it, he would realize how inadequate were all his attempts. His despair however was only momentary, for the conviction that he had a message to deliver was in spite of everything becoming stronger in him every day.

Would he have time to grasp this message fully himself —time to give it complete expression, and ultimately to achieve fame? The daily life he led really needed more hours than he had at his disposal. He continued to live with his parents, in a flat on the Boulevard Malesherbes, until 1901, and afterwards at 45 Rue de Courcelles. Dr. Proust, at first disgruntled at the 'idle' life of his son, had been dazzled finally by his amazing social success and had accepted the situation, content to provide the necessary funds. His mother, as dear to him as ever, kept in the background. So Marcel was entirely free. He was in fact extremely busy. He had been caught in a whirl of invitations, engagements, visits, dinner parties, and dances, and for a while enjoyed them all thoroughly. With Jean Lorrain he even fought the Frenchman's inevitable bloodless duel, the occasion being a disparaging article which Lorrain had published in *Le Journal* in 1897. Proust himself gave the smartest receptions, sometimes in his own home, but more frequently at the Ritz. He was exceedingly fastidious in the choice of his guests, and the preparations for his entertainments were of an inordinate elaborateness and expense. Nothing he ever did was natural and simple, and he turned the slightest occasion into the most complicated matter.

At one time he had planned extensive travel abroad. He did manage to take a few short journeys, one in particular to Venice, in 1900, which like all his other plans proved a disappointment to him. For the most part he practically never left the region of Paris—and Normandy. Regularly every summer he went either to the 'Hôtel des Roches Noires' at Trouville, or more frequently to the 'Grand Hôtel' at Cabourg. Here he felt quite at home, and gradually the two places combined in his imagination to form the fanciful picture of Balbec.

Strangely enough in Paris as well as in Cabourg, Proust, the snob, seems to have been on familiar terms with servants, waiters, elevator-boys, bell-boys wherever he went. He may have been attracted at first by the possibility of obtaining through them secret information about people; but very soon the habit seems to have revealed itself as a matter of personal predilection. He liked their company, felt happy with them. In one of his letters he even compared a duke to a taxi cab driver to the latter's advantage, indeed 'le chauffeur a plus de distinction.' [22] He was always welcome amongst this class of people because of the generosity of his tips, which frequently verged on the extravagant.

But this life of uninterrupted social activity put a great

22. M.L.Bibesco, op. cit., p.182—Letter of M.P. to Mme Sert.

strain on Proust's vitality. Frayed nerves and asthma were still tormenting him; partly to avoid the rush and the 'heavy air' of the day-time, partly to keep his whole strength for the brilliant evening functions he liked so well, he acquired the habit of sleeping during the day and really living at night. If sleep refused to come, Proust would have recourse to drugs. If threatened with an attack of asthma when an important engagement was impending and his frail body failed to respond to his demands, he would turn to alcohol or take a dozen cups of coffee, one after another, and then swallow a narcotic. As a result of this way of living his nerves grew rapidly worse; his irritability became extreme, his sensitiveness morbidly acute and miraculously perceptive. Sounds or smells which were scarcely noticeable to any normal person caused him distress to the very depths of his being. Every minute of that almost painfully intense existence was progressively killing him, and he realized it. For Proust, Time had always been a factor to reckon with; now it was devouring him. It had furnished, and was still furnishing him with splendid and extraordinary adventures; now it threatened to take them all away and to annihilate them for ever. Proust did not want them to be annihilated; he wished them to be recorded in his *magnum opus*, as any great writer would. But was he a great writer? Of course his faith in himself had grown more and more in the last few years, but he was not absolutely sure of himself yet. Perhaps after all he had hoped in vain.

It was at this time that a very unusual personal experience, almost mystical in its nature, came to him unexpectedly like a revelation. Then only did he feel sure that he had found the secret—that secret which was to grasp Time and hold it and compel it to give back everything that had existed before, but had seemed irretrievably lost. That was his message. At once all his doubts about his

vocation as a writer vanished. Now he was certain he had
something to tell the world. Society and love had betrayed
him, but he had discovered that Time and his vocation
as a creative artist were in truth the great existing realities.
But it was going to require many volumes on Proust's
part to explain how through his various disillusionments he
had come to this final conclusion.

The way was made easy. His father had died in 1903,
leaving him an independent income. His mother died in
1905 and her death severed the only deep sentimental
ties which linked him with the outside world. As for his
innumerable friends and acquaintances who would try
to rob him of his precious time, his ill-health was a ready
excuse which satisfied the demands of his everlasting
politeness. Now at thirty-five, he was aware that he was
to create a work of outstanding import. He would retire
and pursue his ideas in peace. His mind was made up; by
1906 his life had taken a new turn.

. . . .

He moved to a new flat, on the Boulevard Haussman.
He was to live, or rather to camp, there almost until his
death. Most of the furniture was left in the large reception
hall. Unpacked trunks, crates full of odd things were deposited helter skelter. On the chairs were books, old photographs, letters full of memories of the past. Later on he had
the walls of his bedroom lined with cork to deaden the
noises from outside, walls which he never cared to have
covered with wall-paper or paint. By now his work had
become everything to him. Besides, his sensitiveness had
grown so painfully intense of late that contact with the outside world could only hurt him. Once (August–September,
1907) he could not resist the longing to see the hawthorn
in bloom again and went all the way to the country in a
cab with the windows tightly shut lest the springtime fra-

grance should overcome him altogether. At times he would repair to his dear Cabourg. On these occasions he had to rent several rooms adjoining his own, one on the right, one on the left, one above, and one below. He left these rooms empty; and then, after a large dose of narcotics, in the midst of a dead silence, he was at last able to sleep.

Servants came to play a more and more important part in his life. His cook and general servant, Céleste Albaret, who knew him of old, accepted and respected his incredible manias, serving him faithfully—though not without grumbling—and also quarreling with him in the most picturesque language. When he returned to any great hotel which only recently had witnessed his brilliant triumphs, after making a short social appearance, he would repair to the porter's office and stay there talking and making notes far into the night. The head-porter's booth at the door of the Ritz became a second headquarters to him. Here he would check his notes or gather fresh intelligence. Waiters and valets were his most available source of information and he received plenty of it from them, as his tips grew more lavish than ever.

Occasionally, like a ghost, he would return to his old life for one night, perhaps to revive old impressions, though more often with a definite purpose, such as to obtain from some lady of fashion a detailed description of the hat or dress she had worn for such and such an event, ten or fifteen years before. Generally the lady remembered what Proust wanted and he could give a correct account of it in his book. By now he was writing with enthusiasm—the healthy enthusiasm of genuine creation. Looking back on his past life, he could not but feel melancholy, as his two great dreams, social success and love, had brought him nothing but disappointment. At the time he felt more ironical than bitter towards his past illusions. All the agitation

of his twenties, his youthful longing for the *salons*, for the
affection of some woman or friend, appeared to him idle
and ridiculous, but certainly not tragic. He bore people no
grudge for being what they were; his memory of them,
though critically clear-sighted, was after all comparatively
lenient and kind. What struck him most in 'society' was
the vanity of all that brilliant display; and when he came
to think of the part he himself had played in it, he discovered that his case was just one particular instance of the
general trend of society. Society had changed; if he,
Marcel Proust, a young half Jewish *bourgeois*, could break
through into the most exclusive circles, it was because
there was in progress at the time a distinct movement of
fusion between the aristocratic world and certain elements of the *bourgeoisie*. This fusion had been effected,
and Proust wanted to be the historian of the great social
transformation.

Love he recalled without rancour; his adventures appeared to him as a chain of rather pleasant memories. His
boyhood sweethearts, his first bashful acquaintances with
celebrated courtesans, his devoted admiration for a titled
lady, his affair with the young Viennese girl, his many
other attachments of various kinds, all made a light gar-
land, fragrant though not enduring. His experiences had
not come up to his own expectations—far from it! But he
would show at least the delicate charm of his young loves,
together with their emptiness and their fragility.

He was still young, he was still a poet. Time had taken
the best part of his life and all the people, young or old,
all the places near or far, which had made up the very
texture of his being. Now thanks to memory, Time was
giving back its victims, and they were transfigured and
rendered more radiant and beautiful than ever. Proust re-
lived the past in a kind of mystical day-dream, which

brought out all the inherent beauty in persons and things he had known.

At the same time, his mind remained clear enough to enable him to draw a perfectly coherent, well balanced picture of what he had planned to portray; and in 1912, having completed his work—1500 pages of text—he started out in search of a publisher. But his reputation as a society man, perhaps also the thickness of the manuscript, created apprehension. The great publishing firms of *La Nouvelle Revue Française*, *Le Mercure de France*, of Fasquelle, and of Ollendorf, turned it down, one after another. In the end he had the book printed at his own expense by a then little known publisher, Grasset.[23] The first volume, *Du Côté de chez Swann*, appeared in 1913. It attracted scarcely any notice at all. Before the two other volumes which had been planned could be published the Great War broke out. Grasset was called to the colours and the attention of the public was completely withdrawn for a long period from the type of literature represented by Proust's books. So Proust, deprived of his expected glory, was left alone, nursing another disappointment.

He remained in Paris throughout the war. Though he was physically unfit and unable to take any active part in the conflict, he shared in an intense and almost mystic way the collective emotions roused by the great upheaval. He wrote at that time, 'Comme on vivait en Dieu, je vis dans la guerre.' [24]

He lost a number of his friends. Bertrand de Fénelon was killed in 1914; others followed. Emmanuel Bibesco committed suicide in London in 1917. Proust felt for them

23. The proofs have been completely printed. They have been kept intact. Cf. A.Feuillerat, *Comment Marcel Proust a composé son roman*, Yale University Press, New Haven, 1934, Avant—Propos, p.5.
24. Letter to Paul Morand, quoted by Léon Pierre-Quint—*Marcel Proust*, I, 4, p.104.

more than an ordinary sorrow. His health was giving way more and more under the strain of the general tension, the mental shock of the air raids, and physical privations. Fever scarcely ever left him. He was not only in poor health, but actually ill most of the time. The war played havoc with morality, private and public. This did not escape Proust's still keen and clear-sighted observation, and it filled him still further with disgust and despair. Soured and disappointed, he had lost faith in everybody and everything except his work.

One volume, *Du Côté de chez Swann*, had been published before 1914, but because of war the manuscript had to be returned to him. Having nothing else to do, he began reading it again and then revising it. Since the first writing he had undergone a complete change himself. Then he had been young and comparatively optimistic. In the course of a few years he had aged greatly, and his outlook on life was becoming blacker every day. He thought of his past dreams of great affection no longer with an amused scepticism, but with almost a blind rage. He wanted to say exactly what he thought, and he said it, somehow, in marginal notations. Writing to Lucien Daudet about this change he remarked: 'Alors je croyais à l'amitié. Aujourd'hui, tu verras ce que j'en dis dans Swann et qu'elle n'existe plus pour moi! Et je ne dis pas que personne en soit la cause. Ce serait trop long à expliquer.' [25] The explanation was within Proust himself. What about his past social ambitions? Society he now felt was stupid and rotten to the core. Rotten! Well, was Proust himself so unexceptionable after all? But then it is only human to expect in those we admire—or have admired—something better than we find in ourselves. As for the stupidity of society,

25. Quoted by E.Seillière—*Marcel Proust*, Nouvelle Revue Critique, Paris, 1931, VI, 4, p.233.

it was obvious, and, to Proust, unforgivable. He knew he was a thousand times superior to any of those outmoded noblemen, who once had put on such airs when he, an unknown young man, had offered them his naïve and poetic worship. They had disdainfully slighted him; that would have to be paid for. Amidst the paragraphs of his work he inserted scathing, satirical remarks upon aristocracy and upon society. M.de Montesquiou came in for more than his share of this denunciation. Proust still resented the humiliation he had had to go through in order to gain and to retain the protection of this haughty *gentilhomme*. Now he would betray all that he knew of his former friend's secret and degrading vices—not exactly in revenge, but to get rid of all that lay heavy on his own heart. Thus was developed his wonderful but horrible portrait of M.de Charlus and the whole background of his work *Sodome et Gomorrhe*.

Meanwhile the war had drawn to a close. With the coming of peace came also time for literature. *Du Côté de chez Swann* had already won recognition from a number of critics. *La Nouvelle Revue Française*, influenced by this success agreed, after lengthy negotiations, to take over from Grasset the future publication of Proust's work. His writings had no longer the clear and well-balanced form which they first possessed, but had been enriched by a quantity of corrections and additions which increased them in size to approximately double what they had been originally.

In 1919 a second volume, *A l'Ombre des Jeunes Filles en Fleurs*, was published. It brought the author almost instantaneous success,—nay even fame and glory. For it Proust received the 'Prix Goncourt.' First the attention and then the admiration of the whole literary world was bestowed upon him, and this regard he retained to the

end of his life. Proust enjoyed his triumph almost like a
child. He relished the praise immensely and also chafed
under the criticism. Once more he went out into the world;
once more he gave brilliant and costly receptions. Now he
found time to write a small volume, *Pastiches et Mélanges*,
in which he displayed his virtuosity and at the same time
paid clever compliments to many of his old friends who
had been a part of his once beloved 'society.'

Alas! 'Society' was no more. The war had destroyed it
beyond hope of recovery. The *salons*, which formerly shel-
tered and protected a closed world of birth and breeding,
were thrown open to the *nouveaux riches*—in fact to all and
sundry. A hopeless mixture and confusion prevailed. Good
manners—or any manners at all—were all gone. All the
barriers were down. This transformation changed the
meaning of all Proust's work; it was not only the fusion
of the aristocracy and the *bourgeoisie* which he had to
show, but also the breakdown, the agony and death of a
distinctive form of social life. He was sensible of the change
during the war itself; but it must have been only in the
post-war dissolution that he became aware of the magni-
tude of the collapse. He would record it—if he had time.

He was by now a complete invalid, practically never
leaving his chamber and keeping the air thick with vapours of fumigation which he resorted to in order to calm
his spells of asthma. His window was always closed and no
cleaning of the room was allowed lest it should raise a dust.
He received practically no visitors and scarcely ever left
his bed. He had to rely upon an almost excessive use of
drugs, alternating veronal in order to sleep, with adrenalin
and caffein in order to be able to write. For at this stage
he was working frantically. He felt a morbid longing to say
everything, everything he had seen and experienced during
his whole life. Being ill he recalled these experiences under

anything but a rosy hue. In his imagination, his disappointments turned into disasters, things ridiculous became tragic, old friends and companions became hated enemies. Homosexuality acquired the force of obsession with him. He had touched upon the subject before but now it was growing upon him, and developing like a cancer, changing almost the entire meaning of his work. While the manuscript was increasing in bulk, from pages of additions and corrections penned in feverish haste, Proust sought to give a consistency to the whole, by improvising alterations to characters and details, in order to make the changes look like part of the original and thus prepare the reader for a conclusion not foreseen at the start.

Volume after volume was published, rousing worldwide curiosity and interest. Proust continued to write feverishly. Was he going to have time to say all he had to say? He had come to realize it really meant a race with death. Time was for him the all-devouring monster, which might at any moment crush and destroy his dying hopes— it was indeed the great adversary. No longer is Proust a poet now; the philosopher in him takes the upper hand, prompts him to pour out all his sad and bitter reflections upon life and people.

Fortunately for the rounding off of his work—for at this stage Proust could not desist from his hectic writing—the actual conclusion had been penned years before in the original text. At the end of 1922, becoming ill with pneumonia, he remembered that one of his characters, Bergotte, had been portrayed in the agony of death. The description which Proust had given of him to show how a dying man feels, he saw every reason to change. Proust now knew correctly the sensation—he was dying himself. So he asked for his manuscript and dictated the necessary alterations.

. . . .

2. *A la Recherche du Temps Perdu*

THE works of Proust were published partly during his lifetime and partly after his death, under the general title: *A la Recherche du Temps Perdu*. They do not form by any means a homogeneous whole; it is easy to detect the most disconcerting differences between one volume and another. These discrepancies are, to a large extent, to be accounted for by the untoward conditions under which the composition was carried on. Proust began writing about 1905, with a more or less definite outlook on life, and completed his work originally in 1912. He took it up again during the war and went on enlarging it, in an entirely different frame of mind which prevailed with him until his death in 1922. The first version fell naturally into three parts; the second version extended to seven volumes. The fusion between the two aspects of his mental evolution was never perfect and, to add to the complexity, the transition from one mood to the other was only gradual and the growing difference between the two phases of his moral attitude became strongly marked towards the end only.

When Proust began writing he had, as we have seen, a clear plan and very definite views. He wanted to give an account of the great experiences of his life up to the age of thirty-five. On the one hand he had to show how it had fared with the two great dreams of his youth. Social ambition had driven him away from his own natural environment, the middle class half Jewish circle of *Du Côté de chez Swann*, into the aristocratic surroundings of *Le Côté de Guermantes*. But a more sophisticated insight into the object of his aspirations had brought disappointment and his exalted fancies concerning society had finally dwindled into ironical contempt. Love had carried him through a series of light, entertaining affairs, as seen in *A l'Ombre des*

Jeunes Filles en Fleurs, but he had failed to fulfil his youthful expectations; and by and by its vanity and emptiness had become more and more apparent to his mind. On the other hand while 'society' and love were betraying him, there was growing within him, first, the feeling that he had something to say, then, the belief that he was an artist, and finally, the knowledge that his real vocation was to be a creative writer. Together with this conviction, and as if parallel to it, there was developing within him the realization of the all-importance of Time. Time had shown the hollowness of 'society' and love. Time had shown the enduring power of beauty and art. Time was all that had been, that was, and that would be. When he felt sure that the past could be recaptured, he was convinced that he had attained the absolute. The general plan of the three volumes: *Du Côté de chez Swann, A l'Ombre des Jeunes Filles en Fleurs*, and *Le Côté de Guermantes*, which constituted the first version of Proust's work, can be easily understood and pictured in the following fanciful manner, which is offered only for its diagrammatic value: Imagine on the framework of a loom two twin threads running diagonally and downwards; let them represent 'Society' and Love, the two ideals which stood so high with Proust at the beginning of his career, but which subsequently declined, following a continuous descent throughout the course of his life experience. Crossing them obliquely, imagine two other twin threads, representing his Vocation and the idea of Time, moving also diagonally, but in this case upwards, starting at the lowest level, unobtrusively as it were, when Society and Love were at their topmost position—and ascending regularly so as to reach *their* highest level when the two others are at their lowest. On that schematic background Proust wove clever and colourful patterns by his remarks and annotations upon society, upon psychology, and upon art. For society he showed the progressive fusion between the aristocratic and the *bourgeois* worlds; in psychology he threw unexpected lights into the most secret recesses of the human soul; in art he evoked things of beauty with an ardent and mystic enthusiasm.

When Proust began revising his manuscript, he kept, generally speaking, to the same ideas and the same plan; but by introducing ruthlessly in the very middle of his original work a mass of new material, all elaborated at an entirely different period of his mental evolution, he disarranged his first harmonious conception. He had mentioned casually the subject of homosexuality before; this subject now had become an obsession with him. The vice of M.de Charlus and the abnormality of Albertine, in *Sodome et Gomorrhe, La Prisonnière, Albertine disparue* are almost entirely the outcome of Proust's new preoccupation. His picture of society is no longer limited to the fusion of the aristocracy and the *bourgeoisie*; it becomes rather the complete history of a given social group in its development, evolution, and decay. In this sense *Le Côté de Guermantes* was thoroughly overhauled and thus part of *Le Temps Retrouvé* came into being. Love had been considered before as a harmless though rather vain pleasure; it is now an omnipotent passion relentlessly torturing its victims. The friends of long ago, once painted with kindliness, sometimes even with humour, have turned into grotesque puppets or disgusting monsters, living a nightmare life. All this is explained and made real by a wealth of psychological comment, satanically clever and penetrating. These psychological comments give to the work of Marcel Proust a lasting interest and an enduring value; but by their very bulk they are likely in no small way to interrupt, and even to conceal the continuity of his thought. When the long deferred conclusion of the original book—the key to the seven volume enigma—is reached at the end of *Le Temps Retrouvé*, the reader is left in a state of bewilderment—rather at a loss to co-ordinate the many divergent impressions he has received, dazzled by the delicate beauties, at the same time horrified by the disgusting monsters he has seen, and left giddy after the depths he has been made to explore.

The conditions under which the work was written must be borne in mind when one is trying to understand the obvious irregularities of composition in the book as it stands, and when one attempts to explain the numerous discrepancies in the development of the characters. However, the seven volumes of *A la Recherche du Temps Perdu* have been presented to the reader by Proust as one whole and therefore must be examined as such.

The first book, *Du Côté de chez Swann*, takes us to the imaginary town of Combray, lying somewhere within a radius of a hundred and fifty miles from Paris. There little Marcel is spending a part of his holidays with his parents at the house of a great aunt, Tante Léonie. He is a nervous boy, subject to fleeting and confused gusts of imagination and memory. Going to sleep is a little tragedy enacted every night, and relieved only by the kiss his 'maman' gives him after he is tucked in bed. He is a whimsical child, often moody and sad in spite of the warm affection of his grandmother and the care of the cook and general maid, Françoise. Combray is a little world by itself, which for Marcel is divided into hemispheres, determined by the two standard walks which the family takes. On one side is the road to the village of Méséglise, known in the family as 'Swann's way,' because to get there one has to pass along the boundary of M.Swann's park. In the opposite direction is 'Guermantes' way' because there lies the estate of the aristocratic family of the Guermantes. The modest household to which Marcel belongs is socially far removed from that of the proud Guermantes. At church on Sundays Marcel could see and admire from afar the most decorative of them all, the Duchesse Oriane. But Swann, a very intelligent and wealthy dilettante, of Jewish extraction, would sometimes drop in and chat with Marcel's parents. They were far from suspecting that he was a man in society, eagerly sought after by the most exclusive aristocrats. Marcel had a great admiration for him, and very soon also for his little daughter, Gilberte. There were other neighbours, such as Vinteuil, an insignificant looking music teacher, who in reality was a composer of genius. He died, however, without anybody suspecting his genius, and his graceless daughter did not reverence his memory overmuch. . . . Since Marcel was going to school now, he brought home one of his school friends, Albert Bloch; but Bloch failed to win the appreciation of the family. Marcel, with all the curiosity of a growing boy, wondered why Mme Swann never came to the house to call.

He did not learn the reason till much later. Swann had fallen in love, a long time ago, with a *demi-mondaine*, Odette de Crécy. Swann used to meet her in the *salon* of a certain Mme Verdurin—and a strange *salon* it was. With few exceptions only *bourgeois* were to be found there, men like Dr. Cottard, Brichot, or Saniette. Mme Verdurin pretended to despise people in high society. Hers was supposed to be an intellectual *salon*. It was certainly musical. There Swann heard for the first time Vinteuil's sonata . . . He succeeded in winning Odette—a much less difficult achievement than he imagined it to be. But it brought him neither peace nor happiness as he was the victim of retrospective jealousy, especially when he came to suspect a former liaison between Odette and a certain Comte de Forcheville. In time he grew calmer, but once at a reception in the house of the Marquise de Saint-Euverte, on hearing the strains of Vinteuil's sonata again, he experienced a recrudescence of all the tortures of doubt which had already caused him so much suffering.

Years rolled by and Swann married this woman of dubious character whom his friends would not receive. A daughter was born to them, Gilberte. Marcel had seen the little girl at Combray and met her again in Paris playing in the Champs-Elysées. The poor lad was very much taken with her, but got no response to his feelings of affection. This his first love affair brought him little else but pain. Fortunately he was able to forget.

It was in Balbec, a seaside resort on the Channel coast, rather than in the Champs-Elysées, that he really found himself, *Within a Budding Grove—A l'Ombre des Jeunes Filles en Fleurs*. One day on the beach he beheld a group of young and pretty girls, like a frieze outlined against the seascape; almost immediately he fell in love with all of them indiscriminately and collectively. He succeeded, not without trouble, in procuring introduction to the group, and his fancy delightedly flew from one to another, resting sometimes on Andrée, sometimes on Gisèle, sometimes on Albertine. In Balbec he also made less frivolous acquaintances—the great painter, Elstir, and the famous writer, Bergotte. There in fact he made his first appearances in society. He met the Marquise de Villeparisis, a childhood friend of his grandmother, and through her he came into contact with the Princesse de Luxembourg, with the charming Robert de Saint-Loup, and also with the disconcerting Baron Palamède de Charlus.

Meanwhile the collective attraction he felt towards the little band of girls had gradually narrowed down to a very special interest in one of them—Albertine. It was nothing really serious as yet. Once, when Albertine, who was obliged to stay in her room on account of a cold, let Marcel know that he might come to see her, he could but indulge himself in all sorts of vague hopes from the interview. Finding her in bed, he felt his head begin to swim and he bent over to kiss her. But immediately he was startled by the sudden, prolonged jangle of a bell—Albertine had rung with all her might.

Back in Paris, society claimed him once more. Mme de Villeparisis was again of assistance to him, and invited him to a reception, at which Albert Bloch was present, as well as Charlus, the Marquis de Norpois (a very intimate friend of the hostess), Saint-Loup, the Duchesse Oriane, and many others. Marcel could say that he had been completely accepted by the genuine, old aristocracy, constituting *le Côté de Guermantes*, when he received an invitation to a large dinner-party given by the Duc and Duchesse de Guermantes themselves. The fact was that Marcel, in spite of a brief interest in a Mlle de Stermaria, had fallen in love with the Duchesse de Guermantes; he even confessed his feelings, but they were so truly admirable and platonic that they caused neither alarm on the one side nor suffering on the other. Real suffering however did come to Marcel when he lost his grandmother. Real suffering also was in store for him when he found Albertine again. She had been completely transformed since their last meeting, which had terminated so abruptly. She expressed herself in a very different way now. The young man detected some encouraging symptoms in the change; and a new friendship was struck up between them. At the same time the friendship of Saint-Loup for Marcel had developed amazingly, though the former was kept rather busy by his duties as a non-commissioned officer in a

regiment of cavalry and by his deep and tormenting attachment to a Jewish courtesan, Rachel.

M.de Charlus at that time was also paying much attention to the young Marcel, preserving however an attitude
that was never anything but enigmatic—for M.de Charlus
felt at home only in the *Cities of the Plain*. To anyone who
cared to hear about such things he gave curious and abundant details concerning the manners of the inhabitants of
Sodome et Gomorrhe. Indeed, M.de Charlus, though he
had been a good husband and was secretely but passionately loved by no less a person than the Princesse de
Parme, often preferred the company of, let us say, a plain
waistcoat-maker, Jupien, or a young musician, Morel.
Albertine in her own way was probably no better. Her
friendship with Marcel had grown to be very close. Marcel
even thought of marrying her, but their relations were
poisoned by the equivocal attitudes and the patent lies
of the young girl. A trip which they took to Balbec did not
improve matters and Marcel was about to leave her, when
he heard that Albertine was a friend of Vinteuil's unprincipled daughter. This confirmed many suspicions which
he had entertained before and strangely enough induced
him to become more attached to her than ever.

In order to protect Albertine from herself, as it were
he took her to his own home, where she was to be *the
Captive, La Prisonnière* of his love and jealousy. Marcel's
parents, who of course were living there also, do not seem
to have objected to the arrangement. Françoise, the maid,
had little liking for the stranger but was compelled to
confine the manifestations of her hostility to indirect hints
or expressive silences. Meanwhile M.de Charlus had arranged with Mme Verdurin to give a concert at her house,
at which Morel was to play and to conduct the Vinteuil
septet. Charlus promised to bring his aristocratic friends

so that Morel might acquire the reputation he needed and Mme Verdurin the high social connexions she really craved. But at the reception the noble ladies and gentlemen paid no attention whatever to their *bourgeoise* hostess, and in a fury of spite Mme Verdurin provoked Morel into a bitter quarrel with the disreputable Baron, who was shaken to the depths at the insults he received and collapsed morally under the shock. Marcel himself fared not much better when Albertine, unable to stand any longer the jealous inquisition of her gaoler, decided to leave his house unexpectedly and never to see him again.

With *The Sweet Cheat Gone—Albertine Disparue*—there was nothing left for the young man but to nurse his pain, his regrets, his memories. But the memories fade, the regrets dwindle, and the pain recedes. The process is analysed by him with the most minute accuracy. One day he hears that Albertine is dead, killed in a riding accident. Then, through their common friend, Andrée, he learns all about Albertine's real past and finds a strange relief for his curiosity in seeing at last her character in its true light,—how different it is from what he thought, how much worse than his worst suspicions!

This is not the only way in which the past comes back to him. Gilberte Swann, his first love, has been adopted by the Comte de Forcheville, who after Swann's death had married Odette. Gilberte is now a titled young lady, well received by the Duchesse de Guermantes, and rather ashamed of her late father and her Jewish ancestry. She finally becomes the wife of Robert de Saint-Loup, failing nevertheless to find happiness, as her husband proves to be a thoroughly corrupt character. One more disappointment awaits Marcel! He makes the journey to Venice which he had so long wanted to take. Again the banal reality falls short of his high expectations.

Years pass; the Great War comes, and with it the end of the social world which Proust had known. Saint-Loup is killed; Charlus has fallen into indescribable depths of degradation. Jupien prospers as the owner of a house of ill fame. Morel is a deserter. After the war things grow still worse. Mme Verdurin by marriage has become the Princesse de Guermantes! She gives a reception. Marcel is invited, and as if in a nightmare he sees all the people he has known pass before him transformed by Time into ghastly skeletons or bloated monsters. Could he suffer more than to see Gilberte middle-aged and fat, or Morel honoured, decorated, and rich? On that very day, however, Marcel makes another discovery about Time, which gives meaning to all this fantastic display of living ghosts: *Le Temps Retrouvé—The Past Recaptured*—brings enduring happiness to Marcel himself.[26]

It is by no means easy to classify the work of Marcel Proust. At first reading it seems like a semi-autobiographical novel; but, as can be readily perceived from the short outline given above, the plot does not present any vivid and striking features. The reader is never held in suspense by an unexpected turn of action; he follows the fate of the various characters without any deep emotion. The writer himself seems more than once to forget the course of events for a while, and launches without warning into some interminable digression. In spite of this, there is a gripping fascination about the whole work. Open the book at random; begin to read almost any page, interest is aroused and attention held. Obviously the interest does not lie in the tale itself, but in something else. In fact the novel is of minor importance, and the real merit of Proust is to be found in his exhaustive and living picture of

26. This discovery will be dealt with in a later chapter, when its involved nature will be more fully explained.

French high society in the course of the past half century; in his unbelievably penetrating investigation of almost unknown corners of the human mind; in his original conception of beauty and art; and, last but not least, in his strange, new vision of Time. In all these fields, descriptive of society, psychology, æsthetics, philosophy,—though he may have been influenced by Saint-Simon, by Ruskin, by Bergson—Proust formed his own personal and thoroughly original views.

3. *Society*

THE study and minute description of the special characteristics of French high society from 1890 to about 1920 may not seem at first to be a matter of engrossing interest. It was a highly sophisticated and artificial community, which, apart from a certain temporary brilliance, did not produce anything of real value. It is dead and gone by now, and there is not the slightest chance of its revival even in a remotely similar form. Nevertheless, in studying the circumstances of the development of that particular group, Proust discovered and brought to light the general, almost universal laws governing the formation, growth, and decay of any social group in any place and at any time. 'From the changes which had occurred in society,' says Proust, 'I could all the more readily extract some important truths . . . because they were in no way peculiar to our time, as I might at first have been tempted to believe.' [27] So French society, in Proust's work, is only a representative case, a definite example, of a much broader and infinitely more important phenomenon: the life of practically any 'society' group.

27. M.Proust, *Le Temps Retrouvé*, Nouvelle Revue Française, Paris, 1927, Chap.III, p.150. *The Past Recaptured*, Random House, New York, 1934, Chap.III, p.309.

The original cell, as it were, of society is the 'coterie' or clan. A coterie is made up of a variable but usually limited number of people, who have, or who adopt, similar views on certain unimportant things. There is no question of creating this social unit on the basis of a real agreement about the essentials of life. Each individual has his own secret aspirations, his own deep rooted tendencies, at times apparent, and even his own personal ambitions openly confessed. Aspirations, tendencies, personal ambitions would inevitably conflict, thus rendering the formation of a unified group impossible. But by a sort of tacit convention, the members of the coterie refer as little as possible to things *fundamental*; and, when together, they confine themselves to certain activities, use a common stock of familiar expressions, adopt the same mannerisms, profess the same prejudices, sometimes even affect the same bearing, be it haughty or nonchalant. They acquire in time a certain superficial similarity, which links them all together. This similarity does not imply real affinity, nor even affection or friendship; it is the result of casual association, not entailing any real, deep community of interests. 'Swann and the Princess had the same way of looking at the little things of life—the effect, if not the cause of which, was a close analogy between their modes of expression and even of pronunciation. . . . On important matters, Swann and the Princess had not an idea in common.' [28]

Such social clans are exclusive—and, indeed, they must be, if they are to endure any length of time. They must exclude carefully all those elements which are not in agreement with the superficial but very definite tone of the group. Such inharmonious strains, if admitted, would at once bring about the dissolution of the coterie. But, on

28. *Du Côté de chez Swann*, Part II, p.179. *Swann's Way*, Part II, p.442.

the other hand, the coterie must recruit new and accept-able members in order to survive—if only to make good the inevitable losses caused by time. Hence the great problem in 'society': whom to receive, and by whom to be received. It is the real test of social success. A completely successful society man is one who is accepted everywhere, and who is sought after by all hostesses. The ambition of a climbing *mondain* is to break into the most exclusive sets. At the same time, the social status of a particular set may be accurately measured by its inaccessibility: the fewer the people that can gain admission to it, the higher will it rank and the more will it be appreciated. Were a certain group, a certain *salon*, to become too lenient and too easy of access, it would lose its character, its power of attraction, and eventually would disappear altogether. A lady of fashion is an object of consideration and envy in proportion to the number of people she ignores and can go on ignoring. Hence a subtle and sly little game where everyone is trying to be accepted into more exclusive circles and at the same time to keep free from too easy associations and to avoid misplaced or valueless intro-ductions. Intelligence, morality, or talent have practically nothing to do with the matter. Strong or striking person-ality is rather a handicap, since the prevailing tone of any group is inclined to mediocrity; to be of the group one must be in harmony with the prevailing tone. So from top to bottom, in spite of its rigorous hierarchy, society is per-petually agitated by internal currents and cross-currents; those at the bottom are always forging ahead and up-wards, those at the top pushing them back, at times stren-uously, at times half-heartedly, according to their individ-ual dispositions or to special circumstances in which they are placed. There are periods of quick change and periods of slow progress but the motion never ceases.

Society people have—or should have—a common ground: politeness. Politeness does not attest kindness of soul. It is born of pride. A social superior, thoroughly conscious of his own social value, in pity for a social inferior, tries to make the latter forget for a while the tremendous distance between them. Nothing that he can do will really bridge the abyss, of course, but he tries his best, and with the most flowery expressions, the most flattering gestures, may delude the poor fellow as to his standing. But it is part of the game that the unfortunate should realize his standing and return compliment for compliment, gratefully protesting against attentions of which he is so unworthy. If he fails to grasp the situation, a piece of insolence will be shot home, to remind him that he must not mistake convention for reality.

Pride, or rather vanity, is the real keystone of 'society' as a whole. No tangible profits, no moral or intellectual advantages are to be gained from the company of titled ladies and gentlemen. Only pride can make you enjoy being counted as one of them. And their pride is no less than yours and their contempt for you, and others, is almost unbounded. Among people with such a sense of superiority, and so much feeling for hierarchy and caste, any slight hurt which their vanity may receive becomes an almost incurable wound—hence the bitter hatreds, always carefully concealed, the petty but venomous slanders, the cruel and subtle revenges. There is no friendship, no sincerity, no true generosity among them. Everybody is on the alert, and, provided there is no danger of retaliation, ready to strike. Of course Proust had not always held such bitter opinions about society. He had loved it when he was young, and his first published volumes were more satirical than indignant; but in his last writings his radical pessimism insists vehemently on the fundamental hardness, even ferocity of society people in general.

On the subject of their stupidity he is inexhaustible. Very early he was impressed by the absence of real culture among them. He had found it amusing to note their sometimes astonishing lack of serious knowledge. Soon he discovered that the cause of this lay in the nature of society itself: to maintain the unity of the clan, ready-made opinions are the best guarantee of uniformity. Independent thinking is heresy. It is forbidden to speak earnestly about important things. One must either not mention them at all, or else speak lightly and superficially about them, lest conflicting views rend the apparent harmony of the mutual relationships. A cultured man like Swann in the Verdurin home or in the *salon* of the Duchesse de Guermantes, must either keep silent or express his ideas in an innocuous way, depriving them of all pungency and vigour. Not only are society people ignorant and stupid, but in contact with them a man of real worth, an artist, becomes insignificant and sterile. In the eyes of society people the world resolves itself into a collection of trifles and commonplaces. For they are, at the bottom of their souls, common; their so-called elegance is just a thin veneer barely concealing the fundamental vulgarity of their minds. How could it be otherwise, since a deep culture is incompatible with the manners of the tribe? So Proust, older and more virulent in mood as he nears the end of his book, finds an almost cruel joy in exposing this ugly, naked truth.

Society, like any organism, must start from a certain nucleus, pass through a number of transformations, sometimes opening to admit new elements of growth, sometimes closing tightly to fend off intruders, and finally, when the capacity for reaction is exhausted, end with a period of decay and dissolution. This seems to be a law which applies to the development of any community group. In the particular case of French high society, Proust clearly shows the following stages: Shortly after the war of 1870 there were a few aristocratic *salons* and a few *bourgeois* gatherings all self-contained and distinctive. Generally they had at their centre an ambitious woman, perhaps attractive, perhaps only scheming, such as the Duchesse de Guermantes or Madame Verdurin. Then the aristocratic circles, in need of fresh recruits, opened their ranks slightly to a few well-educated and talented *bourgeois*—Swann for example. That practice, in some cases, was not without unpleasant consequences. Then the aristocrats recoiled and Swann, for instance, who had married a demi-mondaine, did not succeed in introducing her to those by whom he had formerly been received. But with the feeling of safety, engendered by this power of veto in reserve, a certain relaxing of standards set in; more and more of the *bourgeois* took advantage of the weakening of resistance, and tried to gain admission into the upper strata. A few succeeded, Marcel among them. However, the inevitable reaction followed, all the more marked because of the *affaire Dreyfus*, which was just then beginning to make Parisian society more class conscious. Mme Verdurin, who had tried to take advantage of Charlus's vice in order to worm her way into aristocratic circles, failed dismally in her attempt. Yet the Dreyfus case, more than anything else, contributed to the breaking down of the old divisions and barriers. Some of the best of the aristocrats were convinced of Dreyfus's innocence; they found themselves in sympathy with many of the *bourgeois*, and associated freely with them; the rush into the once exclusive circles became general. Intermarriage was accepted as normal. Gilberte, Swann's daughter, became the wife of Saint-Loup, who was the nephew of the Duc de Guermantes. *Bourgeois* and aristocrats found themselves brought together socially as members of a mixed society though in every other respect the two classes remained separate and distinct. Proust's original book ended approximately here. Then the war came and the picture had to be completed. The war, as Proust shows, resulted in a complete dislocation of the whole ordering of society. It was the end of his 'society' as a self-contained and exclusive body. The capacity for expulsion of outside elements was exhausted. One could speak no longer of a fusion between *bourgeoisie* and nobility; the two had become a composite, a shapeless mass, a moral and social chaos. As a symbol of this, in the last volume, the Prince de Guermantes, a widower, marries Mme Verdurin herself.

In spite of the mixing of classes shown at the end of the book, Proust's original idea—the fusion between the aristocratic and the *bourgeois* worlds—remains apparent in the grouping of the characters. The noblemen are led by the *coterie de Guermantes*; the *bourgeois* by *le petit noyau* of the Verdurins. Jews and artists move freely back and forth between the two sets. Behind them all—reflecting the manners and habits of their masters—are the servants, always an important ingredient in a Proust picture.

The Duchesse Oriane is certainly the most brilliant of the Guermantes. By birth a member of an impoverished branch of that illustrious family, she marries her cousin the Prince de Laumes, who on his father's death inherits the older and therefore more distinguished title of Duc de Guermantes. The Duchesse first appears as a model of good breeding and charm, with her natural elegance, her blond beauty, her undoubted virtue, her reputation for intelligence and wit. She is one of those rare aristocrats who prefer the company of men of real worth, no matter what their birth, and with supreme tact she carefully

avoids speaking to them of their own technical speciality,
be it philosophy, science, or art. No wonder young Marcel
falls in love with her! He tries to get to the heart of her
celebrated *esprit*, which is the *esprit* of the Guermantes
clan. He does not detect much, for it is never easy to discover the essence of a character when that essence merely
resolves itself into the most subtle shades of emotion and
thinking. By and by he finds out that this elusive *esprit*
is nothing but a cultivated contempt for any hackneyed
idea or expression: at all costs one must be different. But
of real originality of thought he sees in her mind no trace
whatever. Her pride of caste and her prejudice against
Jews show that she is not as open-minded as she seemed
at first. Her acquaintance with intelligent men is probably
only a special form of snobbery, for she is not able to
appreciate them at their real value. And at the end of the
book comes the final judgment: 'Comme elle est bête!' [29]
Is this because Marcel knows her better? Is it because she
has grown old? Is it because Proust himself has aged and
now sees her through different eyes? In any case she now
appears as but a very ordinary woman.[30]

Her husband, the Duc de Guermantes, is not treated
with any greater kindness. He never loved his wife and
was never faithful to her. But he has a decided character—
a haughty and immensely wealthy landlord, of a hard and
violent nature, stingy yet ostentatious. He refuses to give
his wife money for charities but he wants her to spend
lavishly on her dresses and to keep up a magnificent carriage and pair. Incompatible as they are in temperament,
nevertheless he is inordinately proud of her, yet only as
one of his most enviable possessions. With all this he combines a certain superficial, almost comical benevolence.

29. *Le Temps Retrouvé*, Chap.iii, p.202.
30. *Ibidem*, Chap.iii, p.206.

He appeared in the drawing room of Mme de Villeparisis with 'a half-open hand floating like a shark's fin by his side, which he allowed to be vaguely clasped by his old friends and by strangers who were introduced to him.' [31] But the polish wears off—or Proust's own forbearance becomes exhausted—until finally M.le duc reveals himself as a person of fundamental vulgarity with a mentality no better than that of a *petit bourgeois*.

His brother, the Baron de Charlus is introduced to us at first as an enigma. Without doubt he displays sincere generosity and a genuine kindness of heart. He shows himself completely devoted to those he loves, and to all who find favour in his eyes he exhibits the most charming manners. As a member of the highest aristocracy, he is welcome everywhere. His recognised good taste has made him the arbiter elegantiarum of 'society.' In fact, perhaps more than any other member of his circle, he feels and expresses the quaint, rather artificial charm of 'society' life. But the man sometimes looks at one in a strange way; he makes jerky movements, and shows unexpected turns of expression and attitude. Suddenly, for no apparent reason at all, he will flare up in a rage, and pour out a torrent of scathing, often vile insults. He never doubts his own towering superiority, and yet is abnormally sensitive about trifles. At heart he is essentially a good man, and yet he sometimes betrays a ferocity bordering almost on insanity. There is a solution to this puzzle: M.de Charlus constantly wears a mask. He is a homosexual; and it is his inhibitions that have produced in this proud aristocrat his amazing complexity of character. The older he grows the more suspicious he becomes of all his entourage. Mor-

---

31. M.Proust, *Le Côté de Guermantes*, Nouvelle Revue Française, Paris, 1920, Part I, p.201. *The Guermantes' Way*, Random House, New York, 1934, Part I, p.305.

bidly he breaks with his friends and acquaintances one by
one; soon he is alone—alone with his passion, his mania,
his disease. In the last stages of his life he descends into
an inferno of low vice and debauchery. The tale of his
degeneration and his end has in it something horrible and
sinister, like the sulphurous flames which consumed the
cities of Sodom and Gomorrah.

The Marquis Robert de Saint-Loup, nephew of the
Baron Charlus, has the same secret vices as his uncle; but
who would suspect it? He is young, wealthy, handsome,
a dashing horseman, ready to enter the brilliant cavalry
school at Saumur. He has a liaison with the notorious
Rachel and seems to be very much in love with this mistress. Thus M.de Saint-Loup appears at first. Marcel's
original impression of him is indeed not very favourable;
but Saint-Loup takes a fancy to him and showers him
with delicate and affectionate attentions. Marcel for his
part discovers that the young nobleman is keenly intelligent, that he despises his own caste, reads Nietzsche, medi-
tates on Proudhon. But he comes to tire of Saint-Loup's
admiring attentions, of which he feels he is undeserving.
Yet Saint-Loup remains almost to the end an impulsive
and enthusiastic young fellow, portrayed on the whole
sympathetically. But after he has married Swann's daughter, Gilberte, for her money, we learn to our dismay that
he is following in the footsteps of his unworthy uncle,
Charlus.

We catch glimpses of many other types of aristocracy
of high and low degree. The Princesse de Parme and the
Princesse de Luxembourg are most exalted figures of the
great world. The latter is so ineffably above all other living
things that she does not distinguish between various kinds
of creatures inhabiting the lower sphere. On one occasion
she met Marcel with his grandmother, and, eager to show

her friendliness, she offered them almost unconsciously a
little morsel of rye bread, as though she fancied she were
feeding animals at the zoo.[32] Madame de Villeparisis belongs to the highest aristocracy, but she has lost caste
somewhat because of her superior intelligence and her too
numerous love affairs. She is now indulging in a rather
obvious friendship with a solemn diplomat, le Marquis de
Norpois, who goes through life repeating high-sounding
but hollow formulas. The Prince de Guermantes is an old
fossil who, at a dinner, makes a scene if he is not placed in
accordance with the rank to which his family was entitled
under Louis XIV. The Courvoisiers, reserved and aloof,
hold to the narrow, traditional conventions of the Boulevard Saint-Germain. The Cambremers are of good, old
stock, but scarcely ever leave their provincial manor in
Normandy; in Paris they count for very little. When they
go there they have a chance to display themselves only
among the lesser nobility in second-rate *salons* like that of
Madame de Saint-Euverte.

Among the *bourgeois* Mme Verdurin plays an outstanding part. She is the centre of a small nucleus, *le petit
noyau* of 'faithful' friends. She is capable of doing anything to help her '*fidèles*' and to keep them attached to
her. Occasionally she is generous and kind, as when she
discreetly persuades her husband to give a pension to old
Saniette, who has been suddenly ruined. At the same time
she has no scruples about acting as a go-between in the
most immoral circumstance, or again she does not hesitate
to strike with a cold-blooded ferocity at any opponent,
especially if her vanity is wounded. In such cases she
descends to open insults, secret plotting, slander, lies—
all with equal malice and effectiveness. As she herself has

32. M.Proust, *A l'Ombre des Jeunes Filles en Fleurs*, Nouvelle Revue Française,
      Paris, 1919, Vol.ɪɪ, p.138.

been the victim of many disappointments in her society career, she has taken deliberately to embroiling people round her. It has grown to be a habit with her, and there is nothing she enjoys more than spreading distrust and enmity, ruining friendships, wrecking affections, destroying happiness. She is dangerous and cunning, but not strikingly intelligent. Nevertheless she is possessed of a genuine musical feeling and whenever a piece is about to be played, she goes through the same ritual, complaining and protesting that she is certainly going to be ill because of the intensity of emotion which the music will rouse in her! For a long time she pretends to despise all other *salons*: they were composed of nothing but 'bores and scoundrels'; but when she saw the possibility of herself entering the once-forbidden, enchanted circles, she set to work with invincible obstinacy to gain admission. After M. Verdurin's death she married the Duc de Duras; and, on becoming a widow again, she wedded the Prince de Guermantes.

His wife's stronger personality completely crushed M. Verdurin, and told with equal effect upon all her guests. Cottard represents the medical profession. He is supposed to be an outstanding doctor, but in private life he is a boor. Awkward and clumsy and incredibly vulgar, he tells questionable jokes and repeats age-old puns. At first he appears bashful and ill at ease in company; later on he is supercilious and domineering. Is this a new aspect of his personality which develops with time and success, or just an inconsistency between the first and second version of Proust's writings? The character of Brichot, a professor at the Sorbonne, bears traces of a similar divergence. At first he is a brilliant speaker, with a clear voice, who even in conversation seems to be delivering a lecture. This was the type of professor that was *à la mode* when Proust was at the University. Later on, Brichot is dull, interested in details, fond of philology and etymology—a new type, corresponding to a more recent professorial species, which does not naturally evolve from the former. Saniette is the society man more than half in his dotage. Everybody makes fun of him—his hostess taking the lead in this respect; and yet he remains in the circle, heaven knows why. . . .

Proust's interest in Jews is obvious. He himself had certain traits of character which may be the outcome of his own Jewish origin, thus: his nervous hypersensitiveness; his apparent humility before people more powerful than himself; his determination to elevate himself, and his amazing pertinacity in doing so; his plasticity and adaptability; his capacity for entering, as it were, into another's personality, and yet remaining thoroughly himself; his almost Talmudic predisposition for drawing distinctions and splitting hairs *ad infinitum*. It has been said that when he created the character of Swann he was portraying the Jewish half of his own personality. Within himself he was trying to reconcile the Jewish and the gentile strain; the problems involved in the assimilation took on an overwhelming importance both in his own life and in his books. In that respect, if we omit his minor Jewish characters, he drew two antithetic Jewish pictures: the good Jew and his opposite.

Swann is the good Jew. In fact he is hardly a Jew at all. His family has been converted for two generations. His nose has not quite lost the Semitic contour; but in his manner there is very little of the Jew left. On the contrary his characteristics are quite out of keeping with those generally considered typically Jewish. Thus the Jews are supposed to be tactless and pushing, and Swann avoids such blunders, carrying his reserve to a point which shows

clearly that he is still secretly obsessed with the idea that
people would take him for a Jew. Wealthy, cultured, and
refined, he has been admitted into the most exclusive
circles of the aristocracy at a time when such a privilege
was exceptional. Unfortunately he falls in love with a
demi-mondaine, Odette, and follows her into the circle
surrounding the Verdurins. Though he is infatuated with
her, it is not considered proper on his part for them to be
married. Yet eventually, when all his passion is spent, he
does marry her and then finds himself cut off almost entirely from his former friends. Then the Dreyfus case
shakes the very foundations of the French social order,
and Swann feels in himself the stir and the call of his
ancient Hebraic blood. He is a man; and now that the
Jews are out of favour, he will assert himself openly as a
Jew. He becomes more Jewish in appearance from
day to day, more like a Hebrew prophet, and the end
of his life is a lesson in moral heroism—or is it perhaps
just one of the strange and inescapable throw-backs of
heredity?

Bloch, on the contrary, is a caricature of the Jew—
pushing, blundering, snobbish, and nervously unbalanced.
He is brilliant, but too conscious of the fact, and anxious
to show off his brilliance. Smart and precocious in everything, he is always up to the minute with the fashions, if
not in advance of them. He is an *agrégé de l'Université*,
really intelligent and learned, nevertheless perfectly unbearable in spite of his intelligence. He cannot deny that
he is a Jew, so he keeps mentioning it all the time. He
thinks he is too clever to remain a professor all his life.
He therefore becomes an author, and writes plays. Meanwhile in his eager haste to become assimilated to his circle
he has turned anti-Semite. 'One day when we were sitting
on the sands, Saint-Loup and I, we heard issuing from a

canvas tent against which we were leaning a torrent of imprecation against the swarm of Israelites that infested Balbec. "You can't go a yard without meeting them," said the voice. "I am not in principle irremediably hostile to the Jewish nation, but here there is a plethora of them. . . ." The man who thus inveighed against Israel emerged at last from the tent. . . . It was my old friend Bloch.' [33]

Artists of all sorts are represented by Proust as personally rather insignificant: all their value lies in what they create. Society ignores them—or if they are accepted, they are either spoiled or held in contempt. Vinteuil fugitively appears as a music teacher, poor and unknown in spite of his great genius. Elstir, the painter, is spontaneously friendly and kind, as well as wise and good, but is generally misunderstood. He is received by the Verdurins; but displays in their company only the mean, vulgar side of his nature; and finally shrinks back into solitude. Bergotte, the clever and successful writer, at first trusted and admired, becomes later a target for Proust's irony and sarcasm.

' Tel maître, tel valet'—the proverb takes on a new and perhaps truer meaning in the light of Proust's observations. The world below stairs is an exact duplicate of the world of society. Between the kitchen and the drawing room there is an alarming but ludicrous parallelism. The servants have exactly the same feelings, the same prejudices, the same absence of ideas as the great lords and ladies whom they serve. They share in the pride of title and ancestry, although in their case it is one degree removed. Their sense of etiquette and caste, where their masters are concerned or even among themselves, is no

33. *A l'Ombre des Jeunes Filles en Fleurs*, Vol.II, p.190. *Within a Budding Grove*, Random House, New York, 1934, II, p.48.

less pronounced than that of their betters. Like their
masters they can crawl before a superior, or they can
crush the fellow beneath them with their assumed haughti-
ness. Again like their masters they can nurse in silence a
life-long, virulent hatred, or give vent to it in poisonous
lies and slanders.

The most typical of the servants is Marcel's own maid,
Françoise. Faithful as a watch-dog, she is especially devoted to Marcel, and proud of his wealth and of his high
connexions. Françoise dislikes strangers and treats them
with scant courtesy. Albertine she hates with a furious
jealousy. Aware of her own importance in the house, she
grows increasingly independent, nags continually, and becomes at the end thoroughly crabbed in her manners and
speech. Here again it is the effect of age no doubt, but
whether the alteration is in her or in Proust it is impossible
to decide.

The question has often been raised as to how much in
these portraits is taken directly from actual, living people.
Proust always protested against any attempt at identification. He insisted that every artist must borrow from reality in making his creations, but the creations themselves
are the result of so much imaginative combination and
transposition of details that there is no actual portrait of
any living person in his books. And this is true to a great
extent. But Proust could not prevent contrary rumours
from spreading, and people he had known could not be
restrained from publishing the names of the supposed
originals.

Thus practically all the critics agree that Marcel's
grandmother in the book has many of the features of
Proust's own mother. Françoise is the literary combination of Proust's housekeeper, Céleste Albaret, and of
Ernestine Gallou, Aunt Amiot's faithful maid. Charles

Haas served as a model for Swann. Odette de Crécy was modelled after Clomesnil, or Laure Hayman, or both. M.de Charlus is obviously Robert de Montesquiou, though some of the physical details of this character may have been taken from a certain baron Doisan.[34] Charlus's friend, Morel, the violonist, was in reality the pianist, Delafosse. Brichot seems in some respects to resemble Brochard, a professor at the Sorbonne.[35] Brunschwicg, another professor at the Sorbonne, and former school fellow of Proust, always maintained that he was the original of Bloch.[36] In fact Bloch seems to be a synthetic character representing Proust's little group of Jewish friends at the Lycée Condorcet.[37] Saint-Loup in many ways is very much like Bertrand de Fénelon,[38] but he seems also to stand as a symbol of the company of aristocratic young friends cultivated by Proust after his twenty-fifth year.[39] Madame Verdurin embodies the traits of Proust's first hostesses at the time of his *début* in society—Mme Arman de Caillavet, the two Mmes Baignières, Mme Aubernon, and in particular Mme Straus.[40] Oriane de Guermantes resembles slightly the object of his youthful worship—the Countess of C.[41]—but also the noble ladies who later on received him into their *salons*. The Princesse de Parme holds receptions in the style of the Princesse Mathilde.[42] Mme de Villeparisis is patterned after Mme de Beaulaincourt.[43] Bergotte reminds one of Anatole France also, to some extent, of Bergson; and Elstir seems to be a combination

34. Léon Pierre-Quint, *Marcel Proust*, i, 3, p.312.
35. E.Seillière, *Marcel Proust*, iv, 2, p.122.
36. Léon Pierre-Quint, op. cit., i, 3, p.312.
37. E.Seillière, op. cit., iv, 6, p.248.
38. E.de Clermont-Tonnerre, *Robert de Montesquiou et Marcel Proust*, p.288.
39. E.Seillière, op. cit., iv, 6, pp.148–149.
40. *Ibidem*, iv, 2, p.120.
41. *Ibidem*, iv, 5, p.130.
42. *Ibidem*, iv, 5, p.190.
43. E.de Clermont-Tonnerre, op. cit., p.228.

of several painters—Whistler (whose name is made up of
almost the same letters), Manet, and more especially
Monet. The most composite of all, however, is Albertine.
Albertine is a mixture of several persons all differing in
appearance, character, and social standing. As the fusion
between the various features has not been perfectly
achieved, it is fairly easy [44] to take the ensemble to pieces
and isolate at least some of the component parts. She
appears sometimes as a good soul, innocent, playful,
empty-headed like a pink-nosed kitten; [45] sometimes as an
'extremely intelligent' woman, not at all frivolous, very
fond of reading,[46] cultured, pure, and almost sisterly; [47]
sometimes as an impulsive, giddy, changeable little girl,
crying and laughing alternately; [48] sometimes as a past
master of lying and deception.[49] She may be rather
plump,[50] lazy, round-faced, pink-cheeked; [51] or on the
contrary eager, thin, pale; [52] or again she is a gorgeous
creature with marvellous hair.[53] Her eyes shine like the
facets of an opal, with mauve and silken reflections; [54] or
they are decidedly black.[55] In fact Albertine stands for a
number of individuals whom Marcel Proust loved; and no
particular name can be linked definitely to her protean
personality.

44. A.Feuillerat, *Comment Marcel Proust a composé son roman*, II, 5, pp.212–217.
45. M.Proust, *La Prisonnière*, Nouvelle Revue Française, Paris, 1923, Chap.I,
    p.103.
46. *Ibidem*, Chap.I, pp.84–85.
47. M.Proust, *Albertine Disparue*, Nouvelle Revue Française, Paris, 1925,
    Chap.I, p.220.
48. *La Prisonnière*, Chap.III, p.280.
49. *Ibidem*, Chap.III, p.230.
50. *Ibidem*, Chap.I, p.240.
51. *A l'Ombre des Jeunes Filles en Fleurs*, Vol.III, p.90.
52. *Albertine Disparue*, Chap.I, p.42. *La Prisonnière*, Chap.I, p.138.
53. *La Prisonnière*, Chap.I, pp.236–237.
54. *Ibidem*, Chap.III, p.245.
55. M.Proust, *Sodome et Gomorrhe*, Nouvelle Revue Française, Paris, 1922,
    Part I, Chap.III, p.79.

4. *Psychology*

THE haste with which Proust wrote his last volumes .
may account for minor inconsistencies in the portrayal
of a few of his characters; but generally the variations and
unexpected transformations in the characters are the
consequence of changes brought by Time. Psychological
novels usually place before the reader a given character,
making that character revolve, as it were, before the
reader, so as to present one by one all the different aspects
of his personality; or again the reader is shown the continuous evolution, over a number of years, of a definite
set of qualities and defects. Proust shows that character
does not develop so simply in real life. We make the acquaintance of a person, lose sight of him for a while and
when we meet him again he reveals to us, on account of
altered circumstances, another side of himself, not quite
the same as the one we knew before, while his personality
also may have inwardly changed in the intervening period.
Another lapse of time may occur, bringing new revelations of the other's character to the observer. Time
transforms people in our eyes for two reasons: first because new and unsuspected sides of their character are
presented to us; and, secondly, because the character itself
is subjected to an uninterrupted process of inward transformation and flux. As an instance of the first case, when
Marcel discovers that the Verdurins, whom he believed to
be thoroughly hard-hearted, have given old Saniette a
pension, he is impelled to express himself thus: '. . . at
the moment of my discovery, M. Verdurin's nature offered
me a new and unimagined aspect; and so I am brought up
against the difficulty of presenting a permanent image of a
character as of societies and passions. For it changes no
less than they, and if we seek to portray what is relatively

unchanging in it, we see it present in succession different aspects (implying that it cannot remain still but keeps moving) to the disconcerted artist.' [56] As an illustration of the second case, we find Marcel about to draw a mental picture of two girls who are dear to him. He hesitates, realizing that the very fact of fixing a feature is treason to reality, since a feature is never really fixed in a living being but is constantly changing and melting into something new. 'And, in themselves, what were Albertine and Andrée? To learn the answer, I should have to immobilize you, to cease to live in that perpetual expectation, ending always in a different presentment of you. I should have to cease to love you, in order to fix you, to cease to know your interminable and ever disconcerting arrival, oh girls, oh recurrent ray in the swirl wherein we throb with emotion upon seeing you appear while barely recognizing you in the dizzy velocity of light. . . . On each occasion a girl so little resembles what she was the time before (shattering in fragments as soon as we catch sight of her the memory that we had retained of her . . .) that the stability of nature which we ascribe to her is purely fictitious and a convenience of speech.' [57]

So there is no stability of any kind in any of us. Every minute we die and are born anew, and every effort to fix the characteristics of life destroys the very essence of life itself. If the motion of life is to be registered at all, it must be by an art as mobile and fluid as life itself. In this respect, Proust has attempted the almost impossible—and succeeded. His characters are revolving before us and simultaneously evolving within themselves, but the double motion is not continuous. Its continuity is broken by long

---

56. *La Prisonnière*, Chap.II, pp.167–168. *The Captive*, Random House, New York, 1934, Chap.II, p.444.
57. *La Prisonnière*, Chap.I, p.85. *The Captive*, Chap.I, pp.77–78.

intervals in which a man or woman will disappear for a while—to spring up again, barely recognizable. Thus we grasp the effects of Time and acquire an entirely new and disconcerting outlook on human psychology.

Classical psychology for a long time concentrated on the obvious and clear phenomena of the conscious mind. Intelligence was analysed and for centuries reason was made to account for nearly all our thoughts. Today the subconscious is an object of almost popular interest, but it was not so when Proust began observing people and things. The success of his writings was even to a large extent responsible for drawing the public attention to some of the most obscure, yet powerful potentialities of our nature. Proust held that all that we feel deeply, is practically beyond our understanding and control. As depth of feeling takes us down into the subconscious, we find its laws and manifestations frequently interfere and clash with the decisions of our conscious will-power. To discover some of those all-important and little known laws was one of the great interests of Proust's life; the results of his enquiries are among the most engrossing attractions of his books.

In order to be able to reach as far as possible into the depths of our subconscious life, Proust, whenever he can, will linger on the threshold of our conscious mental activity, during the uncertain moments when we are falling asleep, in the weary hours of persistent insomnia, or in the vision-haunted days when we are abed with fever. He will even, though more rarely, try to explore the mysterious world of dreams. In every case, his careful observation of the slightest and most elusive impressions, felt by almost each of us, though few are really aware of them, reads like the record of an illuminating revelation.

It is in his observations of every-day life, however, that Proust displays his most amazing virtuosity. He is not much interested in the actual meaning of what people say, nor in their ostensible motives, nor the obvious consequences of what they do. But he is intensely eager to catch exactly the particular manner in which they speak or act. Indeed, very little information as to the deep realities of a person's nature is to be gathered when he takes a definite stand or gives a perfectly clear explanation of his actions. In fact, the more definite the stand and the clearer the explanation, the more open to suspicion they become. Each of us is invariably acting a part, trying to appear different from what we really are, and intelligence provides us with the best mask with which to conceal our true face. The diplomat and the doctor, in the practice of their professions, have to dissemble, and do so honourably and systematically; the society man is an enigma behind the superficial polish, common to all his kind; the general prejudice against his race forces upon the Jew a complex desire to be himself and yet to appear different; the homosexual must pretend throughout his life that he feels as other men do. These are the types that Proust met with during his life, and which he put in his books. They are all eternally busy trying to appear what they are not; in a word, they are all actors—but not all accomplished actors. An unexpected gesture will often betray the real man. The mask does not fit closely all the time; a sudden move or a smile will lift it for a second and allow Proust to get a glimpse of the face beneath. Then Proust will meditate long and earnestly on what he has been able momentarily to see. Such an occurrence may seem entirely unimportant, and in itself very often is; but this is the only way we have of getting at the truth. The so-called important things in life may mean nothing at all, but a world of revelation sometimes unsuspected lies in trifles.

Proust therefore deliberately keeps out of his books the

great turns of events, the catastrophes, in which most
novel writers revel. For instance, in *Du Côté de chez Swann*,
there is a most complete picture of Swann's love affair with
Odette de Crécy, whom he ought not to marry for a number of excellent reasons. Yet he does marry her, and we are
never told how he came to make such a momentous decision. We understand, however, that the outcome was
not by any means an easy matter. Says M.de Charlus,
' . . . And the joke of it is that it was she who fired a re-
volver at him and nearly hit me. Oh! I used to have a fine
time with that couple; and naturally it was I who was
obliged to act as his second against d'Osmond, who never
forgave me. D'Osmond had carried off Odette, and Swann,
to console himself, had taken as his mistress, or make-
believe mistress, Odette's sister.' [58] But these thrilling
episodes receive no other mention in the book. On the
other hand, we find carefully noted the intonation Swann
gives a certain word in the most insignificant conversation.
'You know that I don't believe very much in the "hierarchy" of the arts,' he remarks; and then follows the com-
mentary: 'Whenever he used an expression which seemed
to imply a definite opinion upon some important subject,
he would take care to isolate, to sterilize it by using a
special intonation, mechanical and ironic, as though he
had put the phrase or word between inverted commas,
and was anxious to disclaim any personal responsibility
for it.' [59] All this seems true enough, though rather unimportant; but what does it mean? Swann is a man of culture
to whom, when speaking on a serious subject of general
interest, there comes spontaneously the abstract word to
fit the occasion. But society has put its stamp on him and

58. *La Prisonnière*, Chap.II, p.131. *The Captive*, Chap.II, p.406.
59. *Du Côté de chez Swann*, Part I, Chap.II, pp.143–144. *Swann's Way*, Part I,
    Chap.II, pp.122–123.

society has no use for that type of expression, wanting everything to be smooth and flat. Swann's real nature, however, though suppressed, is still there and a learned word may sometimes escape him by chance; when this happens, he excuses himself, as it were, by putting an ironical emphasis on it. Thus we suddenly discover the otherwise unsuspected disharmony that underlies the whole of Swann's life. In the same way a furtive glance cast by M.de Charlus at another man reveals more about his secret tendencies than would a long moral investigation. . . . Everyone has in use a certain number of stock expressions. If a new idiom is adopted by anyone in speaking, it is often possible to trace its origin to some change of surroundings or to some particular new acquaintance. When Albertine happens to use a brand new set of words, Marcel guesses right away, to her great amazement and notwithstanding her denials, that they are the outcome of a meeting with new friends; and from the very turn of the new expressions, he sometimes succeeds in guessing the social standing of the intruders, and even the type of relationship between them and Albertine. Proust, in using that original method of his, does not look *at* people but actually looks *through* them. As he himself said, speaking of certain guests at a dinner-party, 'je les radiographiais.' [60]

A la Recherche du Temps Perdu presents a very strange and at first disconcerting aspect. There is scarcely any plot, and even such episodes as would generally be considered dramatic and calling for development are just casually mentioned. Although nothing happens, Proust accumulates a mass of uncannily clever and interest-compelling observations about the little mannerisms, turns of speech, winks or glances of his characters. The observations and comments which he makes are sufficient to con-

60. *Le Temps Retrouvé*, Chap.i, p.37.

vince us that he has really struck something fundamental
and hitherto practically unknown. There is such a fascination about them that some readers have been tempted to
find in them the major, if not the only permanent interest
of the book. To such *A la Recherche du Temps Perdu* is like
a collection of notes made by a master of microscopic research.

Proust himself has vehemently protested against this
view of his work; the detailed notes he took were just the
preliminary labour leading towards the discovery of very
general psychological laws, which, though governing all
our affective life, are as remote as the stars from the ordinary conception which we have of our own nature. 'Even
those who were favourable to my conception of the truths
. . . congratulated me on having discovered with a mi-
croscope when I had, on the contrary, used a telescope to
perceive things, which, it is true were very small, but situated afar off and each of them a world in itself. Whereas I
had sought great laws, they called me one who grubs for
petty details.' [61]

Most of these great laws are about love, the great concern of Proust in the first half of his life. His conceptions
are in opposition to most current ideas on the subject. If
you ask an enamoured swain how he came to be so much
in love, he may tell you about the deep affinity between
himself and his lady; or he may even be convinced that
they were chosen for each other in all eternity. If he is not
so far gone as that, he may explain how he chose his
Dulcinea. If he has more sense, he may even admit that it
was she who selected him. Nonsense, says Proust—neither
predestination nor choice has anything to do with the
matter. Love lies within ourselves; and the personality of

61. *Le Temps Retrouvé*, Chap.III, p.251. *The Past Recaptured*, Chap.III, pp.393–
    394.

our partner, in spite of all illusions, counts for very little indeed.

The first stage in the process of falling in love is a certain state of unrest, a mental attitude of expectation, readiness to be favourably disposed to affection. If that state of receptivity is not present, there is no chance of love ever gaining a foothold and eventually developing. The main feature of that preliminary disposition is an indefinite, though sometimes intense, attraction to the young and beautiful. This feeling of desire is generally delightfully stimulating, and all the impressions received within its aura are tinged with a delicate and poetical happiness.

This vague longing spontaneously tends to find an object, but at the very beginning it rarely selects one particular individual. More often its manifestations are as indefinite, as general, as the desire itself, and it perhaps embraces a whole group of young men or young women as the case may be. And then the fancy flits from one to another like a butterfly. Sometimes imagination alone comes into play; sometimes the attraction leads to approach and conversation. As a rule this stage is so enjoyable and free from pain that many linger over it as long as possible. In *A l'Ombre des Jeunes Filles en Fleurs*, Proust portrays in a subtle manner the charm attached to these rather superficial but often pleasantly thrilling emotions.

In most cases the interest is concentrated sooner or later on one particular person; and then real love begins, with all its torments. The reason why we concentrate on one rather than on another has little, if anything, to do with mutual affinity. It is true that we all have our particular conception of the ideal type. This is a product of our own fundamental tendencies, and of our very early experiences; it has arisen out of the books we have read, the pictures we have seen, the respected opinions we have heard; it is related to the fanciful figures of our youthful day-dreams. It has obviously nothing to do with the person we meet and fall in love with. The latter has attracted our attention perhaps on account of some quite external cause; a glance, a smile, or—as in the case of Oriane de Guermantes—a name may have given our imagination a start. Very often the reason of our interest is that we encounter an obstacle to our wishes, which at once we ardently desire to overcome; as for instance if a lady refuses an invitation, declaring that she is not free on that particular day. Should our desire and curiosity be too easily gratified, all interest will vanish almost immediately; but if the opposition be serious, the desire may become fixed more or less permanently.

As soon as the desire is fixed our imagination begins creating an imaginary, ideal being out of the person in question. We generously grant that person a wealth of qualities drawn from our own fancy. All this of course is done quite unconsciously and we are convinced that the object of our devotion actually possesses the characteristics with which we have endowed her. The illusion is often so strong that we may sincerely believe the person to correspond by some strange coincidence to the ideal we have conceived and cherished in our inmost soul. In reality the actual person has been moulded by a heredity and by circumstances very different from those which formed us and gave birth to the ideal creature of our imagination. Of course if there is a violent contradiction between the ideal and the reality, the imaginary creation will not go far; but the power of our imagination will make up for any ordinary deficiencies. Then we are in love—in love with a person, as we fondly believe, but really the person is only the occasion, the pretext, as it were, and love, the child of our aspirations, our admiration and our desires, is within ourselves and completely subjective.

Love, says Proust, cannot possibly last for ever. In the first place, daily companionship provides a permanent comparison of the real person with the imaginary being; and however blind we may be we gradually come to realize that they are not one and the same. This is a disappointment. In the second place, there is the fact that *we* change. Time causes in us radical transformations both physical and mental. That fact is beyond doubt. Then since love is almost entirely within ourselves and depends on the real characteristics of our partner only in the smallest degree, if our ego had previously found in a net of circumstances sufficient reason for being in love, how could the ego of today, which has altered, respond to past influences which were different? Even if we are not disappointed—and we are practically bound to be—our own evolution would make us now indifferent to feelings which were formerly ours, but are so no more.

Still there is a chance for love to last a long time: that happens when an obstacle permanently prevents its natural fulfilment; or better still, when an ever-recurring menace periodically threatens the completeness of possession. An object, even of trifling importance, which we are about to lose, for that very reason acquires in our eyes a tremendous value. It is the same in our love for a woman. We may have become almost indifferent to her, but the prospect of losing her to a rival immediately makes her seem more than ever desirable to us. Along with the fear of losing her goes the painful anxiety of jealousy, and love is temporarily revived. When the feeling of safety returns, jealousy and love dwindle away. 'Afraid of losing her, we forget all others. Sure of keeping her, we compare her with those others whom at once we prefer to her.' [62] Should jealousy reappear, love will follow. The more elusive the woman, the more ardent is the pursuing male—or *vice versa*. This is true especially of physical love, which is probably the kind that strikes the deepest roots into human nature and therefore can be the most cruel and torturing. 'Generally speaking, love has not as its object a human body except when an emotion, the fear of losing it, the uncertainty of finding it again, has been infused into it. This sort of anxiety has a great affinity for bodies. It adds to them a quality which surpasses beauty even; which is one of the reasons why we see men who are indifferent to the most beautiful women fall passionately in love with others who appear to us ugly.' [63] Proust in the second part of his book, and especially in *La Prisonnière* has drawn a haunting picture of love feeding on jealousy and suffering. 'I must choose, either to cease from suffering or to cease from loving. For just as in the beginning it is formed by desire, so afterwards love is kept in existence only by painful anxiety.' [64]

To make matters still more complicated, love, alternately moved by painful anxiety and peaceful indifference, is subjected to the rhythm—independent and distinct—of the 'Heart's Intermissions.' Our love for another person could not be represented, if put on a chart, by an unbroken continuous line; there are intervals, intermissions, during which, for no apparent reason, we simply feel nothing at all. This means that our capacity for loving is temporarily exhausted, and though our head may be convinced that nothing is changed and that we are still in love, our heart for a while keeps silent. This applies not

62. *La Prisonnière*, Chap.I, p.125. *The Captive*, Chap.I, p.118.
63. *La Prisonnière*, Chap.I, p.125. *The Captive*, Chap.I, pp.117–118.
64. *La Prisonnière*, Chap.I, p.145. *The Captive*, Chap.I, p.137.

only to the development of amorous feelings but to all kinds of natural affection. Marcel loves his grandmother dearly. After her death his sorrow is deep, sincere, and lasting—seemingly as permanent as anything can be. Yet he did not fully realize what her death meant to him until about a year after her burial when the following incident occurred. On the first night of a stay at Balbec, he had one of his frequent physical collapses. 'I bent down slowly and cautiously to take off my boots. But no sooner had I touched the topmost button than my bosom swelled, filled with an unknown, a divine presence, I shook with sobs, tears streamed from my eyes. The person who came to my rescue, who saved me from barrenness of spirit, was the same who, years before in a moment of identical distress and loneliness (in a moment when I was no longer in any way myself) had come in and had restored me to myself.' [65] . . . that is to say his grandmother. And he adds, ' . . . and so in my insane desire to fling myself into her arms, it was not until this moment, more than a year after her burial . . . that I became conscious that she was dead. I had often spoken about her in the interval and thought of her also, but behind my words and thoughts . . . I retained only in a potential state the memory of what she had been. . . . For with the troubles of memory are closely linked the heart's intermissions.' [66]

This account of the 'Intermittences du cœur' is generally considered as one of Proust's cleverest psychological observations. He clearly shows that, behind an apparently consistent screen of conventional emotions, our affective life follows in reality an independent rhythm of its own. At times we may sincerely believe that we are feeling a

65. *Sodome et Gomorrhe*, Part I, Chap.I, pp.176–177. *Cities of the Plain*, Random House, New York, 1934, Part I, Chap.I, p.217.
66. *Sodome et Gomorrhe*, Part I, Chap.I, pp.177–178. *Cities of the Plain*, Part I, Chap.I, pp.218–219.

certain emotion: anger, love, joy, or sorrow; whereas in fact, precisely at that time we feel absolutely nothing at all. Then suddenly a trifling incident perhaps will suffuse our consciousness with genuine and powerful feelings. That emotional tide however does not remain permanently and unchangingly in ourselves. After a while, it begins to recede very slowly at first, so slowly in fact that very often the recession may not be noticed and we may persuade ourselves that our feelings are still at their high level. Yet they are gone—perhaps gone for ever—perhaps just hidden somewhere and ready to return, not however at our beck and call but in their own way and in their own mysterious time.

But after a number of such oscillations, love must gradually fade away; we forget the person who was so dear to us; the progressive weakening of our feelings follows almost the same course as was taken by our affection in reaching its climax, though in reverse order, until finally we arrive at the same state of sentimental receptivity, with the same indefinite vague longings that we had at the beginning.

On the whole, love, according to Proust, is a rather pitiful thing. The prelude—the initial desire and its first feeble, flighty attempts—may be pleasurable and charming; but the actual feeling, born as it is of casual accident, and fed on illusions, thrives on jealousy and suffering; then, after numerous intermissions, necessarily dies in disappointment, or perishes just because time has made us different, or because our ideal has changed. Then we begin all over again. . . . In his first version Proust, being still young, insisted more on the preliminaries; even in the present state of the book, the first volumes, with the notable exception of the gripping Swann-Odette episode, offer a rather pleasant picture of a set of light, amorous adventures, for instance Marcel's intrigues with Gilberte and Albertine in *A l'Ombre des Jeunes Filles en Fleurs*, with Mlle de Stermaria, and further with the Duchesse de Guermantes in *Le Côté de Guermantes*. Later on, as Proust grew older, he insisted on the serious side of love. The second version of his book—and the last volumes generally —bear the stamp of that deeper and more pessimistic mood. The story of Marcel's love for Albertine acquires, especially in *La Prisonnière*, an extremely complex and almost tragic quality. Marcel is constantly writhing under the sting of suspicion and doubt. Suspicion and doubt, however, serve to keep his love alive. He has some solace only when the pangs of love are quiet for a time—during his 'heart's intermissions.' But soon the obsession comes back. Has Albertine been unfaithful, and with whom? He dreads to learn the truth and yet craves to know it. He sets traps for Albertine, torments her with relentless cross-examinations. She involves herself in complicated explanations and intricate lies. He wants to break with her and then when he is about to lose her finds her more precious than ever. Time also comes into play: Custom dulls impressions; memory revives the past, making it actual, and painfully cruel; the future is anticipated by the imagination, but seldom in rosy colours. Even true lovers are not always sincere. If only by intuition they know a little psychology, and they pretend things just to discover what the reaction of their partner will be. The result is that these little comedies get hopelessly mixed with genuine manifestations of feeling. In that almost inextricable maze Proust tries to find his way; he has indeed an uncanny flair for picking up a scent, but his search only results in more doubt, more pain, more suffering.

Normal and abnormal love, says Proust, are governed by exactly the same laws. His writings leave the impression

that homosexuals are exceedingly numerous. It is somewhat disconcerting to discover at the end of the book that
nearly all the characters belong to Sodom or to Gomorrah.
Proust goes into the greatest details to make clear the
strange and peculiar ways of that extraordinary breed.

According to Proust homosexuality is a sort of nervous
disease: 'What they have been calling their love . . .
springs not from an ideal of beauty which they have
chosen but from an incurable malady.' [67] They must be
considered not as immoral but as sick men and women.
Precisely on account of that disease, homosexuals are, says
Proust, much more interesting as a rule than normal people.

They are more refined, more cultured, more musical
than the others. Their intelligence is keener and more
subtle. They are deeply sensitive. According to Proust
such people did their duty with the greatest bravery during the war. They have extreme kindness of heart and
great delicacy of feeling—so much so that occasionally
they turn to sadism. Mlle Vinteuil, in a burst of intimacy,
gives the portrait of her dead father to Léa, her friend, and
makes her spit on it. Surely this is a proof of wickedness!
Not at all, says Proust. 'Sadists of Mlle Vinteuil's sort
are creatures so purely sentimental, so virtuous by nature,
that even sensual pleasure appears to them as something
bad, a privilege reserved for the wicked. And when they
allow themselves for a moment to enjoy it, they endeavour
to impersonate, to assume all the outward appearance of
wicked people . . . so as to gain the momentary illusion of
having escaped beyond the control of their own gentle and
scrupulous natures into the inhuman world of pleasure.' [68]

Yet even if the original cause of their sadism is a

67. *Sodome et Gomorrhe*, Part I, p.268. *Cities of the Plain*, Part I, p.22.
68. *Du Côté de chez Swann*, Part I, Chap.II, p.236. *Swann's Way*, Part I, Chap.II,
p.211.

strangely perverted sense of purity, sadism is there. By
degrees, it spreads into their personality, develops progressively, and eventually infects and corrupts them
altogether. In *Le Temps Retrouvé*, Proust gave a horrify-
ing picture of the monstrous and disgusting practices to
which a man like Charlus may descend. Charlus is an
extreme pathological case, of course; but anyway, as the
inverts are compelled by society to conceal their feelings,
they are, all of them, condemned to a life of permanent
hypocrisy which is generally conducive to additional mental distortions. Those are added to their primitive anomaly
and react on it within a vicious circle. Proust, especially in
Sodome et Gomorrhe, has hauntingly conjured up the atmosphere of suspicion, anxiety, deception, and fear in
which homosexuals have to spend almost every moment
of their lives and at the same time he has minutely analysed all the repercussions of such an ever-present obsession on their moral outlook and on their behaviour.

Proust's picture of homosexuality has aroused a great
deal of controversy. On the one hand, he presents the
homosexuals as a moral and intellectual 'élite'; at the
same time he shows them doomed to an abject degrading
existence. But if the interpretation of facts given by Proust
may seem open to challenge, the accuracy of the facts
themselves can hardly be doubted, and it is one of his
most daring and original achievements to have made a
technical and almost scientific study of a passion once
considered taboo in literature.

5. *Art*

PROUST seems to have received some of his most vivid
impressions of beauty in the contemplation of flowers.
Throughout his writings, and particularly in the first and

earlier part, he composes again and again, like musical
themes, entrancing evocations of floral harmonies. The
two dominant motifs are the hawthorn which in the full
bloom of its loveliness is the adornment of Illiers-Combray, and in the orchards of Normandy, the apple blossoms, whose beauty he could admire on his way to Ca-
bourg-Balbec. In a minor key, as it were, he sings the
praises of the lilacs, flowering in profusion all around
Paris, and of the pear blossoms, inspired perhaps to some
extent by the enthusiastic descriptions which his friends,
the Bibescos, gave of springtime amid the orchards of
their Roumanian estate at Corcova. But the hawthorn,
above all other blossoms, impressed him so intensely as to
have for him almost a mystic significance. 'The flowers
. . . held out each its little hand of glittering stamens
with an air of inattention, fine, radiating "nerves" in the
flamboyant style of architecture, like those which in
church framed the stairs to the rood-loft or closed the
perpendicular tracery of the windows, but here spread
out into pools of fleshy white, like strawberry-beds in
spring. . . . I . . . stood before them as one stands before those masterpieces of painting which, one imagines,
one will be better able to "take in" when one has looked
away, for a moment, at something else. . . . The sentiment which they aroused in me remained obscure and
vague, struggling and failing to free itself, to float across
and become one with the flowers. They themselves offered
me no enlightenment, and I could not call upon any other
flower to satisfy this mysterious longing.' [69]

But the real revelation of beauty was to come to him
from still simpler objects, and in stranger circumstances.
Once while driving with his parents, not very far from

69. *Du Côté de chez Swann*, Part I, Chap.II, pp.200–201. *Swann's Way*, Part I,
    Chap.II, pp.176–178.

Combray: 'I experienced suddenly,' he writes, 'that special pleasure which bore no resemblance to any other, when I caught sight of the twin steeples of Martinville, on which the setting sun was playing, while the movement of the carriage and the windings of the road seemed to keep them continually changing their position; and then of a third steeple, that of Vieuxvicq, which although sep arated from them by a hill and a valley and rising from rather higher ground in the distance, appeared none the less to be standing by their side.' He gazed at them as 'they veered in the light like three golden pivots.' Of course there was obvious beauty in the spectacle, and yet, as he says, 'I felt that I was not penetrating to the full depth of my impression, that something more lay behind that mobility, that luminosity, something which they seemed at once to contain and to conceal' . . . then, all at once, 'their outlines and their sunlit surface, as though they had been a sort of rind, were stripped apart, a little from what they had concealed from me became apparent . . . an idea came into my mind which had not existed for me a moment earlier, framed itself in words in my head; and the pleasure with which the first sight of them, just how, had filled me was so much enhanced that, over-powered by a sort of intoxication, I could no longer think of anything but them.' [70]

Another mysterious experience was later on to make him want to go still deeper in his search for what lies at the source of beauty. It was near Balbec. He was driving in a carriage with Mme de Villeparisis when suddenly he was 'overwhelmed with that profound happiness . . . happiness analogous to that which had been given me by . . . the steeples of Martinville.' And what was the cause this

70. *Du Côté de chez Swann*, Part I, Chap.II, pp.258–260. *Swann's Way*, Part I, Chap.II, pp.232–233.

time? 'I had just seen, standing a little way back from the steep ridge over which we were passing, three trees probably marking the entrance to a shady avenue. . . .'[71] —nothing more. That was enough to throw him into a state of ecstasy. But this time, he tried to get to the bottom of his emotions: 'I looked at the three trees; I could see them plainly but my mind felt that they were concealing something which it had not grasped.'[72] He placed his hand over his eyes and with his thoughts 'collected, compressed and straightened . . .' tried to pierce the secret that was beneath their surface. Had he seen them before— or something similar even—years ago? Or were they 'but an image freshly extracted from a dream?'—'Like ghosts they seemed to be appealing to me to take them with me, to bring them back to life. . . . I watched the trees gradually withdraw, waving their despairing arms, seeming to say to me, "What you fail to learn from us today, you will never know. If you allow us to drop back into the hollow of this road from which we sought to raise ourselves up to you, a whole part of yourself which we are bringing to you will fall for ever into the abyss". ' But then 'the road having forked . . ., I turned my back on them and ceased to see them, with Mme de Villeparisis asking me what I was dreaming about.'[73]

The challenge offered by the trees of Balbec was not to remain unanswered, and Proust did discover in the course of time the root of the pleasure and the nature of the disturbance he had felt that day.

The key to the enigma is this. Though we all are looking

71. *A l'Ombre des Jeunes Filles en Fleurs*, Vol.ii, p.161. *Within a Budding Grove*, Vol.ii, p.20.
72. *A l'Ombre des Jeunes Filles en Fleurs*, Vol.ii, p.162. *Within a Budding Grove*, Vol.ii, p.20.
73. *A l'Ombre des Jeunes Filles en Fleurs*, Vol.ii, pp.163–164. *Within a Budding Grove*, Vol.ii, pp.21–23.

almost constantly at the world, we hardly ever really see it at all. We do get glimpses of lines or perceive patches of colour, but as a rule we do not exhaust our sensation, for immediately there is a rush of memories of past experiences, memories of pictures we have seen, of descriptions we have heard. They come to help interpret the original sensation and to give it a useful and practical meaning. The process is of course unconscious and in most cases so rapid that for us sensation and interpretation are one and the same thing. For instance, that green mass dotted with white, instantaneously appears to us as a hawthorn bush, a rather prickly affair but sweet-smelling and lovely; these few sharp, erect outlines in the distance are seen as a steeple, a striking landmark and a proper setting for church bells; the dark shapes in front of us are trees, which may give us shade or again may be an awkward obstacle to run into. Every sensation is transformed at once into practical information.

This is indeed of vital necessity to us. We have to move about in a wonderfully rich and motley world. In order to accept what is pleasant, spontaneously and automatically, and to avoid what is dangerous, we have to recognize as quickly as possible the nature of the forms perpetually being presented to us. If we had to make a fresh investigation of things every time we meet them we would waste many precious hours, on trifles; and on the other hand the nervous strain would be continuous and exhausting. It is a safe economy of time and energy to interpret our sensations in as practical a way as possible, as signs of the real world in which we all have to live.

Nevertheless there is a great difference between a sensation and a sign. A sign is in itself neither painful nor pleasant; it has meaning—that is its main character and purpose. Its affective value is practically nil; but it is laden with intellectual, informative elements. These latter come partly from our own experience, but also from conversations, drawings, or books. Who among us is personally acquainted with the essential 'being' of a steeple? Even our past sensations have been so much modified and schematized by the simplifying process of our mental activity that they have become mere sketches from which almost all the richness of reality has been drained. So we have at our disposal a mass of records undoubtedly of great practical value but at the same time of an abstract, impersonal, and conventional nature; and as we see things almost entirely through their medium, reality is robbed of practically all its original colour.

An original and pure sensation, so seldom experienced, is entirely different. Its general informative value in regard to our surroundings is small, but it subjectively tells us much about what we ourselves feel in contact with the world. In fact it is a sort of affective spark appearing when our ego and a part of external reality suddenly meet. In a way it is a kind of communion of our inmost selves with Nature. It is a matter of experience that this union of our personality with the unknown forces surrounding us is generally accompanied by an intense pleasure, a feeling of happiness, almost akin to a mystic trance—especially in the most sensitive natures.

For Proust a sure way of attaining an indestructible happiness is to revert to original sensations as much as possible. The thing is not easy; lying in wait, as it were, in our minds are the cohorts of ready-made intellectual conceptions, all prepared to leap forward on the slightest intimation of a sensation to smother it instantaneously with their cold and practical interpretations. In some cases the superposition does not work. If we travel into strange lands, the ready-made ideas we have of people, houses,

trees, and so on, simply cannot fit in with the new perceptions that we obtain. So these perceptions remain more or
less original and unmixed—hence a great part of the charm
of travelling. But more often than not, even when we are
travelling, the superposition does take place. When Marcel
went to Venice he experienced bitter disappointment at
its banality. What is banality if it is not the exact coincidence of what we find with that which we already know?
Sometimes, however, in the most ordinary circumstances
of life, and for reasons not well accounted for, the original
sensation remains unadulterated. For instance, when Marcel saw the steeples of Martinville, behind the outer covering of conventional conceptions, he was able to grasp the
pure sensation, and he felt himself in complete communion
with reality and experienced an ecstatic bliss. But such an
occurrence seems to be just mere chance or a gift of God.
Concentrating one's powers of intelligence and deduction
on the objective sensation does not help—indeed, it is
rather a hindrance. Marcel on seeing the three trees, after
a gleam of insight, tries to think and remember, but has
to abandon all hope of getting to the bottom of the mystery. So, although the way is by no means clear, the aim
is perfectly obvious: one must penetrate beneath the crust
of superimposed intellectual interpretations which give our
sensations their practical meaning and rob them of their
original flavour, if one is to enjoy in its purity the refresh-
ing and almost illuminating contact of ourselves with the
reality of Nature.

Some people are more gifted than others, and are better
able to retain the original freshness of their sensation in
spite of the pressure of convention: these are the artists.
Art is nothing but the result of original contact between
the artist's personality and the world, and the fixing of the
derived impressions by means of shapes, colour, sounds, or

words, as the case may be—in painting, music, literature, and so on. As Proust himself noticed, the original sensation, when grasped by chance, tends to manifest and express itself spontaneously—in words in the case of a writer. On the occasion when the steeples of Martinville are revealed to him as they really are, he remarks 'An idea came into my mind which had not existed for me a moment earlier, framed itself in words in my head' . . . [74] Without admitting to myself that what lay buried within the steeples of Martinville must be something analogous to a charming phrase, since it was in the form of words which gave me pleasure that it had appeared to me, I borrowed a pencil and some paper . . . and composed . . . to appease my conscience . . . the following little fragment.' [75] And after finishing his page he writes, 'I found such a sense of happiness, felt that it had so entirely relieved my mind of the obsession of the steeples and of the mystery which they had concealed, that, as though I myself were a hen and had just laid an egg, I began to sing at the top of my voice.' [76]

So the conclusion is reached that there is at least one sure way to reach happiness; after obtaining an original and thoroughly personal perception of some fragment of the world, to express it through the medium of a definite work of art.

How did Proust come to form such a theory? Ruskin may have influenced him to some extent. Bergson held a very similar doctrine. But quite probably it was in contact with artists and works of art that he found himself and

74. *Du Côté de chez Swann*, Part I, Chap.II, p.259. *Swann's Way*, Part I, Chap.II, p.232.
75. *Du Côté de chez Swann*, Part I, Chap.II, p.260. *Swann's Way*, Part I, Chap.II, p.233.
76. *Du Côté de chez Swann*, Part I, Chap.II, pp.261–262. *Swann's Way*, Part I, Chap.II, p.234.

discovered his own creed. Bergotte, a character drawn from the model of Anatole France, shows how a contemporary writer could inspire him and fill him with enthusiasm. France's artistic conception, however, was perhaps too remote from Marcel's potentialities. There was no real fecundation of one mind by the other; Marcel became aware of the great man's limitations, and disappointment followed. The impressionistic school of painting, symbolized in Elstir, played a more important part in his development. It was one of the most important tenets of the impressionistic theory that the artist should avoid elaborating with his intelligence the data of his first perceptions of things, because such a process would almost inevitably lead to an academic and conventional view of Nature. The painter had to meet Nature face to face and transfer to the canvas his own, spontaneous, direct and personal vision of the landscape. Throughout *A la Recherche du Temps Perdu* but especially in the first part, Marcel holds long conversations with Elstir, comparing his own experiences with the achievements of the artist.

But it is above all in music that Proust found inspiration. Proust was a young and receptive adolescent when, about 1885, after a long, dull interlude, there began a real renaissance of musical taste in France. At that time Wagner, who at first had been practically ostracized by the Parisians for nationalistic reasons, was now definitely sponsored by enthusiastic French admirers; and in his train came the magic throng of all the great German masters. When Proust took his first steps into society, he entered groups where good music was held to be one of the essentials of life. The *salon* of Mme Straus-Bizet was a centre of deep and genuine musical culture. Proust soon became personally acquainted with two composers of note: Reynaldo Hahn and Gabriel Fauré. Last but not

least, Proust himself was endowed with an uncommon, inborn feeling for music. Even ordinary noises had for him a
musical value. Once, listening in the silence of the night at
Combray, he feels that 'the most distant sounds . . .
could be distinguished with such exact "finish" that the
impression they gave of coming from a distance seemed
due only to their "pianissimo" execution like those movements on muted strings so well performed by the orchestra
of the Conservatoire. . . .' [77] Or, again, in describing the
sound of the autumn wind blowing outside the house, he
says: 'When the wind howled in my chimney, I would lis-
ten to the blows which it struck on the iron trap with as
keen an emotion as if, like the famous bow-taps with which
the C minor symphony opens, they had been the irresistible appeal of a mysterious destiny.' [78]

Among Proust's favourite composers, Wagner for long
held the foremost place. Proust seems to have been thoroughly filled with his music and to have lived, especially
when he was young, in a sort of mystic, Wagnerian atmosphere. To César Franck, who may be said to have brought
a little of the Latin love of order and clarity into the
powerful Wagnerian turmoil, and to Fauré, Franck's pupil, Proust had probably the closest personal affinity.
Beethoven he admired greatly; but it was only in later
years, when his enthusiasm for Wagner had taken a somewhat less exalted tone, that his predilection for Beethoven
came to the fore. Of course he knew and loved the Symphonies of Beethoven; but it was the string quartets of
this composer which seem to have had a special attraction
for him. Nor were Chopin and Schumann without their influence. Proust's tastes naturally followed the trend of the

77. *Du Côté de chez Swann*, Part I, Chap.I, p.53. *Swann's Way*, Part I, Chap.I,
    p.39.
78. *Le Côté de Guermantes*, Part II, Chap.II, p.36. *The Guermantes' Way*, Part II,
    Chap.II, p.49.

cultural period to which he belonged; yet his appreciation
of music showed no trace of affectation. The adulation
of the virtuosi, a failing rather common among 'society'
music-lovers, was utterly foreign to his nature. He loved
music, not for any technical display, but for the meaning
which it may hold.

To him music meant so much that throughout his writings references to musical themes are employed in order
to explain, to illustrate, and even to reveal the deep life
of the characters. For instance the love of Swann for
Odette develops under the influence of Vinteuil's sonata,
and a little phrase from its andante movement becomes,
as it were, the 'theme' of their love. Later, at a time when
Swann knows that Odette no longer loves him, he happens
to hear the theme again, and at once suffers the cruel
pangs of lost love; but by and by the music soothes and
comforts him, and lifts him to noble heights of finer and
more spiritual feeling. A long time afterwards, he hears
Vinteuil's whole sonata again; but by then his love for
Odette is completely past and dead, and the appeal
arouses in him no response. That very day Marcel meets
Swann and for the first time hears the sonata. Thus there
is established between the two a sort of mystic link, and
henceforward Vinteuil's music faithfully follows its new
admirer through many experiences and adventures.

Proust created for his work a new and amazing 'orchestration' of his own. Not only does he mention the 'rouge-
oyant septuor' and the 'blanche sonate' [79] but by a miracle
of metaphoric artistry he actually conveys to us the clear
messages and stirring appeals of that marvellous imaginary
music, with its variety of inflexions and unity of spirit:
'No doubt the glowing septet differed singularly from the
candid sonata; the timid question to which the little

79. *La Prisonnière*, Chap. II, p. 71.

phrase replied, from the breathless supplication to find the
fulfilment of the strange promise that had resounded so
harsh, so supernatural, so brief, setting athrob the still
inert crimson of the morning sky, above the sea. . . .
Those two dissimilar questions . . . the former breaking
into short appeals a line continuous and pure, the latter
welding into an indivisible structure a medley of scattered fragments, were nevertheless, one so calm and timid,
almost detached and as though philosophic, the other so
anxious, pressing, imploring, were nevertheless the same
prayer poured forth before different risings of the inward
sun. . . .' [80] His evocation of the famous 'little phrase'
has in it something gracefully poetical and powerfully
suggestive: 'more marvellous than any maiden, the little
phrase, enveloped, harnessed in silver, glittering with
brilliant effects of sound, as light and soft as silken scarves,
came towards me, recognisable in this new guise.' [81] More
than once Proust has been asked exactly what was in his
mind when he was referring to the 'little phrase,' and more
generally to Vinteuil's sonata. His answers show very well
the process of composition which he followed. The 'little
phrase,' as played at Mme de Saint-Euverte's reception,
is sometimes a charming but mediocre phrase from a sonata for piano and violin by Saint-Saëns, and sometimes
'l'Enchantement du Vendredi Saint' from Wagner's *Parsi-
fal*. When the piano complains alone, like a bird deserted
by its mate, and the violin hears and answers it as from
a neighbouring tree,[82] Proust thinks of César Franck's sonata. When performed at the Verdurins' house, the *trem-
olos* accompanying the phrase have been suggested by
the prelude to *Lohengrin*, and the phrase itself is 'some-

80. *La Prisonnière*, Chap.II, pp.71-72. *The Captive*, Chap.II, pp.344-345.
81. *La Prisonnière*, Chap.II, p.54. *The Captive*, Chap.II, p.337.
82. *Du Côté de chez Swann*, Part II, p.193. *Swann's Way*, Part II, p.455.

thing by Schubert.' That same evening at the Verdurins'
the phrase is also a 'ravissant morceau de piano par
Fauré.' [83] But from the medley of sources from which he
derived inspiration, Proust created a musical masterpiece
which is actually his own.

To Proust music was above all the revelation of a reality
beyond the reach of intelligence. It is the best way we can
find to penetrate the husk of conventional and impersonal
conceptions about people and things and to discover our
genuine, original impressions. It brings into conscious being the deeply concealed realities of the soul. Music is an
artistic fixation of the deepest and most inexpressible of
our feelings. As such it is closely related to the experience
which Marcel had in connexion with the steeples of Martinville or the trees of Balbec; but with something more
added to it. A feeling of fulfilment comes from the discovery of the truth that lies at the very core of our being and
from its complete and adequate expression. This expression is an absolute realization of one's personality and
brings about a supreme and unsurpassable happiness. The
little phrase 'was what might have seemed most definitely
to characterize—from its sharp contrast with all the rest
of my life, with the visible world—those impressions which
at remote intervals I recaptured in my life as starting
points, foundation stones for the construction of a true
life: the impression that I had felt at the sight of the
steeples of Martinville or of a line of trees near Balbec.'
Marcel, on hearing it, is filled with 'an ineffable joy which
seems to come from Paradise,' and, as he says, 'this appeal
to a super-terrestrial joy, was a thing which I would
never forget.' [84]

83. *Hommage à Marcel Proust*—Proust's Letter to J.de Lacretelle, p.190; cf.
   M.L.Bibesco: *Au bal avec Marcel Proust*—Letter cxi to Antoine Bibesco,
   pp.189–190.
84. *La Prisonnière*, Chap.ii, p.79. *The Captive*, Chap.ii, p.352.

So Marcel Proust, in his quest for happiness, after having been disappointed in his social ambitions and his sentimental expectations, finds at last the rock on which to build his life: that is, art. Art is not merely a game of skill or an entertainment for the frivolous. It is the strenuous effort to put aside the conventional, colourless notions about the world we live in—notions supplied by our intelligence—and to experience a genuine, personal communion with deeply hidden reality. Our original reaction to this reality will be our truth, the message vouchsafed to us. Discovering it, and above all fixing it in the form of a work of art, will fill the soul with an inexpressible, paradisaic joy. The pure, indestructible bliss of artistic creation is the reward of a long, slow, and sometimes weary search. In this search, though the goal was now clear to him, Proust still had to find his own way, and the way was to be shown to him in the course of time by Time itself.

6. *Time*

PROUST has several conceptions of time—which are not contradictory but are merely different views of the same reality. These divergences may give the impression that his ideas are more complicated than they really are. Sometimes he considers Time as an enemy, eager to destroy everything that is dear and precious to us, perpetually changing each one of us into another being. It kills our affections, subtly undermines our health, slowly but surely ruins our minds, turns pretty maidens into decrepit old hags. A great part—perhaps the greatest part—of Proust's writings is intended to show the havoc wrought in and round us by Time; and he succeeded amazingly not only in suggesting to the reader, but in making him actually feel, the universal decay invincibly creeping over everything and everybody with a kind of epic and horrible power. This conception of Time is a reflection of Proust's own experience. His whole life was a fight against Time—an endless struggle to last out a few more moments in spite of tremendous physical odds. He felt, especially in the latter part of his existence, more than ever threatened by the danger of having his thread of life cut short before he could express all that he had to say. Then the idea of Time became like a haunting nightmare and all his writings of that period bear the stamp of the ever-present, hostile obsession.

At other times, however, especially in the early part of his life, and mostly in the first version of his writings, Proust considers Time from a completely different angle. This conception of Time is closely related to the Bergsonian idea of duration. Time is not an abstract and theoretical vacuum; it is a reality filled with our own emotions and feelings. Since our present state of being is always to a very large extent conditioned by what we have been in the past, since our thoughts and passions of today are nothing but the development of our thoughts and passions of yesterday, the past is not completely abolished and dead. It still lives in us. Time past is implied by the very fact of our present existence. Indeed Time, that rich complex of personal experiences, has made us what we are, and is remaking us every moment. As a rule we do not even suspect it. Superficially personality might be conceived as something present, immediate, instantaneous—and nothing more; but a little attention will easily show that the past is there also, buried within us, really and actually.

To Proust 'an hour is not merely an hour. It is a vase filled with perfumes, sounds, places and climates.' . . . [85] 'The slightest word we have spoken or the most insignifi-

85. *Le Temps Retrouvé*, Chap.III, 2, p.39. *The Past Recaptured*, Chap.III, p.217.

cant gesture we have made at a certain moment in our life was surrounded and illumined by things that logically had no relation to it . . . ; and yet in the midst of these irrelevant objects—here the rosy glow of eventide on the flower-covered wall of a rustic restaurant, the feeling of hunger, the yearning for women, the pleasant sensation of luxury; there, blue volutes of the morning sea, wrapped in spirals around strains of music which only partly emerge, like mermaids' shoulders—the most insignificant gesture, the simplest act remain enclosed, as it were, in a thousand sealed jars, each filled with things of an absolutely different colour, odour and temperature. Furthermore, these jars, ranged along the topmost levels of our bygone years— years during which we have been constantly changing if only in our dreams and thoughts—stand at very different altitudes.' [86]

So we hold within us a fabulous treasure of impressions, clustered in small knots, each with a flavour of its own— impressions formed from contemporaneous experiences, at a certain moment of our past. But this treasure lies buried in our subconscious mind. It is as if it were enclosed in sealed jars, and even with all our intelligence we cannot reach it. Time past is Time as good as lost to us.

If only we could somehow rediscover the treasure and recapture the time that is past—and lost to us! If we could have one of these jars, open it and breathe again that wonderful, intoxicating perfume! We have seen that, according to Proust, a supreme pleasure may be derived from contact with unalloyed reality and in perpetuating, through the medium of an art, the original impression obtained thereby. Impressions that are genuinely pure and unadulterated come but rarely, however; intelligence is ready to interpret every present sensation to suit its own practical

86. *Le Temps Retrouvé*, Chap.III, 2, p.12. *The Past Recaptured*, Chap.III, p.195.

purposes and to rob that sensation of its sentimental content. But what of the sensations experienced in the past?
Here is an inexhaustible mine for art, if we could only
reach it.

At first sight, it seems simple enough. It is the function
of memory to bring back the past when needed; and we
can exercise this function almost at will. Proust, however,
with great cleverness and penetration, noticed that when
we give our memory an order to bring back a fragment of
our past, memory very intelligently proceeds to choose
from out of the past those elements which will be of practical use for our present requirements and those, and those
only, are brought back. Memory will tell us the number of
people who were present at a certain time, say, in some
rustic restaurant—what they did, what they said, perhaps
what they wore—but the sentimental perfume which impregnated this 'jar' in memory's collection, the original
flavour of the scene, will be left behind because it is no
longer needed today. Now this perfume, this flavour, is
the very thing that Proust considers priceless to an artist
that makes an hour unique, different from all others, and
causes it to be a certain definite moment in Time. Intelligent, voluntary memory is powerless to recall a moment
in its original completeness; it can only suggest the structure of it, or the skeleton. Of course no delirious joy accompanies this practical information, and the fixation of
it would have little artistic value. So Proust, when he was
at last sure of his vocation in the realm of art, was at a loss
how to fulfil it. He knew well enough that the treasure
lay in Time, but the way to reach it he could not find.

Nevertheless some strange incidents occurred which
gave him an inkling as to the general direction to follow.
Once, when a young man, he came home cold and weary
on the evening of a dull winter's day and his mother offered

him tea, which he did not ordinarily take. There were a few of those 'short, plump little cakes called "petites madeleines," which look as though they had been moulded in the fluted scallop of a pilgrim's shell.' [87] He raised to his lips a spoonful of tea in which he had soaked a morsel of his cake. 'No sooner had the warm liquid, and the crumbs with it, touched my palate,' he says 'than a shudder ran through my whole body . . . an exquisite pleasure had invaded my senses . . . at once all the vicissitudes of life had become indifferent to me . . . this new sensation having had on me the effect which love has of filling me with a precious essence.' [88] Marcel of course paused, intent on finding out the cause of that transcendent joy. It was obviously connected with the taste of the tea and cake. So he took a second mouthful and found in it nothing more than in the first, then a third which gave him rather less than the second; the beverage was progressively losing its magic. So he put down his cup and immersed himself in deep meditation, groping in the dark depths of his own subconscious mind. Suddenly, like a flash, light came. 'The taste was that of the little crumb of madeleine which on Sunday mornings at Combray . . . when I went to say good-day to her in her bedroom, my Aunt Léonie used to give me, dipping it first in her own cup of . . . tea.' [89] All that took place years and years before, when Marcel was a little child; but the taste of the madeleine in the tea, never experienced again till now, had forcibly brought back to him the integral memory of a past which he had thought to be completely obliterated, but which in fact had just

87. *Du Côté de chez Swann*, Part I, Chap.I, p.69. *Swann's Way*, Part I, Chap.I, p.54.
88. *Du Côté de chez Swann*, Part I, Chap.I, pp.69–70. *Swann's Way*, Part I, Chap.I, pp.54–55.
89. *Du Côté de chez Swann*, Part I, Chap.I, p.72. *Swann's Way*, Part I, Chap.I, p.57.

lain dormant within him, ready to be called back to consciousness. Indeed as soon as he had perceived the taste of the crumb of madeleine soaked in tea, 'immediately the old grey house upon the street . . . rose up like the scenery of a theatre . . . and with the house the town . . . the square where I was sent before luncheon, the streets along which I used to run errands . . . And just as the Japanese amuse themselves by filling a porcelain bowl and steeping in it little crumbs of paper which the moment they become wet, stretch themselves . . . take on colour and distinctive shape . . . so in that moment all the flowers in our garden and in M.Swann's park . . . and the good folk of the village and their little dwellings and the parish church and the whole of Combray and of its surroundings, taking their proper shapes and growing solid, sprang into being, town and garden alike, from my cup of tea.' [90] The explanation of such a miracle of resurrection is that, 'when from a long-distant past nothing subsists, after the people are dead, after the things are broken and scattered, still, alone . . . the smell and taste of things remain poised a long time like souls, ready to remind us, waiting and hoping for their moment, amid the ruins of the rest; and bear unfaltering, in the tiny and almost impalpable drop of their essence, the vast structure of recollection.' [91]

So beside the voluntary memory, practical, dry, and colourless, there is another form of memory, entirely beyond the control of our conscious will-power. In this the recollection is suggested by some unexpected physical sensation, generally unimportant in itself, such as a faint scent, taste, or sound. But that sensation has in the past

90. *Du Côté de chez Swann*, Part I, Chap.I, p.73. *Swann's Way*, Part I, Chap.I, p.58.
91. *Du Côté de chez Swann*, Part I, Chap.I, p.73. *Swann's Way*, Part I, Chap.I, pp.57–58.

been associated with a number of definite impressions—
and when by chance the identical sensation recurs years
afterwards, all the impressions associated with it also rush
back 'en masse.' Intelligence has absolutely nothing to do
with the process and therefore does not enter in to discrim-
inate or to select certain elements, rejecting others. It is
a complete fragment of the past, with its original 'perfume' as if fresh from the sealed jar—that is for a moment
given back to us.

Thus Proust seems to have found the starting point for
a new way of rediscovering the elusive and marvellous
past. But there was still something unexplained in that experience of his—the feeling of inexpressible joy which had
overwhelmed him for a moment. As he writes: 'I had
ceased now to feel . . . mortal.' [92] Did he then for the
briefest moment gaze upon 'Immortality'? The ecstasy
which he had felt at the sight of the steeples of Martinville
could not attain such a state of transcendence. On the
other hand, whether or not he had other experiences of
the same kind later in life, this exaltation remained for a
long time isolated and exceptional, something on which no
permanent doctrine could really be based. So for many
years Marcel felt himself at a loss in his quest to recapture
Time. He was on the verge of despair and ready to for-
swear literature and art for ever.

Suddenly one day, however, the darkness broke. Marcel
was going to an afternoon reception at the home of the
Princesse de Guermantes. He entered the court of the
Guermantes's residence absorbed in unhappy meditation,
and was nearly run over by an incoming automobile.
Stepping back, he stumbled over unevenly set flagstones
and attempting to recover his balance, put his foot on a

92. *Du Côté de chez Swann*, Part I, Chap.I, p.70. *Swann's Way*, Part I, Chap.I,
    p.55.

stone which was a little lower than the one next to it. Immediately all his discouragement left him; all his anxiety about the future, all his doubts about his literary vocation were ended as if by magic. The feeling of happiness was of the same order as that which he had experienced while watching the steeples of Martinville, or listening to the music of Vinteuil, or tasting the madeleine. This time, he felt, he had to find the solution to the enigma. A deep blue azure intoxicated his vision. The dazzling vision seemed to say, 'Seize me in my flight, if you have the power, and try to solve the riddle of happiness I propound to you.' [93] And presently Venice appeared before his mind's eye, Venice where once he had stood on two uneven flagstones in the Baptistry of Saint Mark's. Deeply moved, he entered the Guermantes mansion and stepped into a small library adjoining the buffet. Then it happened, so he explains, that 'a servant trying in vain to make no noise struck a spoon against a plate. The same kind of felicity as I had received from the uneven paving stones now came over me; the sensations were again those of great heat, but entirely different, mingled with the odour of smoke, tempered by the cool fragrance of a forest setting.' [94] The sound of the spoon striking the plate had recalled a very similar sound made by a workman's hammer during repairs to the wheels of a train in which Marcel had been travelling and which had been brought to a stop close by a clump of trees. The whole scene had come back to him. Just then, at the reception, a servant brought him some cake and a glass of orangeade. Marcel drank; and, as he used a serviette afterwards, another joyous vision spread before his eyes—Balbec. The serviette had precisely the

93. *Le Temps Retrouvé*, Chap.III, p.8. *The Past Recaptured*, Chap.III, p.192.
94. *Le Temps Retrouvé*, Chap.III, p.9. *The Past Recaptured*, Chap.III, pp.192–193.

same sort of stiffness, he said, as the 'towel with which I had had so much trouble drying myself before the window the first day of my stay at Balbec.' [95]

The challenge of these three successive revelations—when during all his past life only partial or fragmentary initiation had been granted to him—was too strong to be disregarded and allowed to dwindle and disappear without a response or an attempt to solve the problem. And indeed meditation brought Marcel the answer to the enigma, together with a sense of the full meaning of his vocation in life.

Resurrection of the past in the wake of an accidental, involuntary physical sensation is the keystone of Proust's conception of life and art. It combines past and present in a miraculous unity. It brings back from the past a rainbow of rich and varied impressions. These past impressions have been, as it were, purified, decanted, by the influence of Time in our subconscious mind. All that was commonplace in them, all that was not of their finer essence, has been discarded and eliminated. And here they stand more absolutely themselves than ever. Yet we cannot revive them except through the imagination. The imagination—and not the intellect—is the one faculty that can and does perceive beauty in things. So our imagination, working without our clear knowledge, achieves a sort of internal transfiguration whereby things appear beautiful. In its glow our past experiences become more radiant, more vivid, more intense, than at the actual moment of perception.

At the same time, these impressions, alive but deeply concealed within us, are conjured up out of our subconscious mind by a physical sensation which is overwhelmingly present. The present sensation adds something of its

95. *Le Temps Retrouvé*, Chap.iii, p.10. *The Past Recaptured*, Chap.iii, p.193.

own reality to the old impressions thus brought to light. Without this association, the recollection of the past would be like a dream, a mere phantom, having no solidity nor strength. But its close connexion with a sensation that we positively feel imparts to it a compelling actuality.

So Proust discovered a reality more wonderful than reality itself. Everyday reality is forcibly present, but is often adulterated by an intellectual elaboration which does not give our imagination a full chance of coming into play. The recreated reality retains unspoilt all the glamour of the past and even magnifies it, while it holds all the strength and savour of the most obvious present. 'How many times in the course of my life,' complains Proust, 'had I been disappointed by reality because, at the time I was observing it, my imagination, the only organ with which I could enjoy beauty, was not able to function, by virtue of the inexorable law which decrees that only that which is absent can be imagined. And now suddenly the operation of this harsh law was neutralised, suspended, by a miraculous expedient of nature by which a sensation . . . was reflected both in the past (which made it possible for my imagination to take pleasure in it) and in the present, the physical stimulus of the sound or the contact . . . adding to the dreams of the imagination that which they usually lack, the idea of existence.' [96] This concentration of past and present, of imagination and actual reality, into one compelling flash of our mental life would explain sufficiently from a simple psychological standpoint the enthralling pleasure experienced in such circumstance by Proust.

Proust, however, goes one step farther and plunges into

96. *Le Temps Retrouvé*, Chap.III, p.15. *The Past Recaptured*, Chap.III, pp.197–198.

metaphysics. Past and present have in fact been grasped as a complete whole, indissolubly mixed together—as a single tremendous experience. But then, according to our normal conception of Time, past, present, and future are clearly separated and cannot possibly overlap one another. Yet we feel that in defiance of all the laws generally accepted as governing our world, past and present on rare occasions do actually meet and unite. And what is that state in which past and present are one, if not Eternity? So, with Proust, we transcend our common human experience and penetrate, as it were, into a super-terrestrial realm. Then we understand the more than earthly joy suffusing any being who is able to reach beyond the human order of Time, and to step—though still inhabiting this world—right into Eternity. The future holds no fear for him—not even the fear of death. All petty worries and cares recede into insignificance before this great truth. Everything acquires a new meaning on a higher plane. A feeling of complete self-realization and perfect happiness pervades the whole being. The ultimate goal has been reached. Still meditating on the long-past experience of the madeleine, Proust says: 'In truth the person within me who was at that moment enjoying this impression enjoyed in it the qualities it possessed which were common to both an earlier day and the present moment,—qualities which were independent of all consideration of time,—and this person came into play only when, by this process of identifying the past with the present, he could find himself in the only environment in which he could live and enjoy the essence of things, that is to say entirely outside of time. That explained why my apprehensiveness of death vanished at the moment I instinctively recognised the savour of the little madeleine because at that moment the person within me was a timeless person, consequently unconcerned with the vicissitudes of the future.' [97] Later on he insists again: 'Our true self . . . awakes, takes on fresh life as it receives the celestial nourishment brought to it. A single minute released from the chronological order of time has recreated in us the human being similarly released, in order that he may sense that minute. And one comprehends readily how such a one can be confident in his joy . . . It is easy to understand that the word "death" should have no meaning to him; situated outside the scope of time, what could he fear from the future?' [98]—And all that mystic exaltation of Proust's had its roots in the fact that, thanks to the miracle of the suggestion of a simple sensation, he had at last been able, as he said, to 'recapture bygone days, times past, which had always balked the efforts of my memory and my intelligence.' [99] But he had in fact done more than recapture the past—he had succeeded in apprehending 'a fragment of time in its pure state.' [100]

Henceforth Proust's task is perfectly clear to him. He will fulfil himself by perpetuating in a work of art the tremendous discovery he has made—he will incorporate it in a book. These flashes of eternity will become the precious substance of his creation. He soon realized, however, that on account of their dazzling brilliance and their comparatively rare occurrence, they were not sufficient in themselves to constitute the whole matter of a literary work. At best, they could be used like brilliant jewels studding a less conspicuous surface. Then Proust thought of the mass of information he had collected regarding the main preoccupations of his early life: love, and society,

97. *Le Temps Retrouvé*, Chap.III, p.14. *The Past Recaptured*, Chap.III, pp.196–197.
98. *Le Temps Retrouvé*, Chap.III,p.16. *The Past Recaptured*, Chap.III, p.198.
99. *Le Temps Retrouvé*, Chap.III, p.14. *The Past Recaptured*, Chap.III, p.197.
100. *Le Temps Retrouvé*, Chap.III, p.15. *The Past Recaptured*, Chap.III, p.198.

and the great laws of morality and psychology that he had discovered, when he was applying all the power of his intellect to the search for that unknown principle which eluded the intelligence but which was finally revealed to him through the medium of some accidental sensation. He goes on to say: 'I felt that these truths which the intelligence draws directly from reality are not entirely to be scorned, for it may be that they enchase, in a grosser substance, it is true, but nevertheless pierce with understanding, those impressions which are brought to us, outside of all considerations of time, by the essential qualities common to sensations of the past and the present, but which, being more precious, are too rare for the work of art to be composed wholly of them. I felt surging within me a multitude of truths concerning passions, characters and customs which might well serve in that manner.' [101]

Yet what was the source of these truths about passions, characters, and customs if not the experiences Proust had had throughout his life? So after all, the great work of art he had planned to produce ever since he was young was nothing but the tale of his own life. All the notes he had taken—all the adventures he had had, great or small, thrilling or dull—were the elements of a work which had gradually been taking shape in his mind all through his life. 'Then a new light dawned within me,' he writes, '. . . I understood that all these materials for literary work were nothing else than my past life and that they had come to me in the midst of frivolous pleasures, in idleness, through tender affection and through sorrow, and that I had stored them up without foreseeing their final purpose or even their survival . . . and so my entire life up to that day could . . . be summed up under the

101. *Le Temps Retrouvé*, Chap.III, p.53. *The Past Recaptured*, Chap.III, p.228.

title, *A vocation.*' [102] Hence the strange and singular character of the book: it is at once a collection of memories and
an account of how and why the book was written. And as
Proust's life experiences draw to a close, the book which
has been produced under our very eyes, so to speak, finds
its justification and its excuse—and is finished.

Thus behind the well-maintained and obvious unity of
Marcel Proust's life experience and of his work, there is a
latent dualism having its origin in the very nature of his
mental evolution. He started his career with great expectations concerning society and love, and life failed to
fulfil its promises in these two fields. By and by he became
aware of his artistic vocation and therein found unshakable
happiness, thanks to an almost mystic revelation as to the
essential nature of Time. All his writings mark his transition from one conception of existence to the other, and
both phases are necessary for the harmony of the whole.
The 'truths' connected with beauty, art, Time, glowing
with the light of Proust's blissful illumination, are set in
the mass of greyish, intellectual information about people
and their ways of speaking and acting in society, or when
in love. It may be noticed that the 'truths' about beauty,
time, and art were discovered fairly early by Proust and
are practically all contained in the first version of his
works, written before the war. The psychological and
social facts had also a place in the first version, but they
have been extensively developed in the additions of his
later period.

With all these variations of thought there are corresponding variations in expression. Notwithstanding the
well-maintained unity, arising from the strong personality
of the man himself, the style of Proust changes its form

102. *Le Temps Retrouvé*, Chap.III, pp.53–54. *The Past Recaptured*, Chap.III, p.229.

and hue according to the aspect of the subject to be described. The general, more outstanding characteristics of his style are obvious. Verbs play the most important part in it. They are numerous, expressive, laden with meaning, powerful and rich. They give the sentence a swing, a push, an unusual forward motion. They carry the attention along as in the current of a lively stream. Yet Proust's style is far from flowing directly and smoothly forward; a multiplicity of subordinate clauses often breaks the flow of the sentence and forces the thought into a variety of narrow and sometimes singularly twisted channels. The reader generally comes out of them safely to find that, at the end of a long-drawn out sentence there stands a direct object—a noun. The noun is frequently rather ordinary, almost banal. The very fact that it has been relegated to such an inconspicuous place shows that Proust took but little interest in it. Indeed these thoroughly personal forms of expression are in close relation to his own philosophy. All his life he has been obsessed by the idea of irresistible, universal change. In everything and everybody an evolution is constantly going on. Proust considered a static description to be a contradiction of reality. Everything is moving along with Time as it passes. His effort to register that perpetual transformation expresses itself spontaneously in the preponderant use of the verb, which of all the grammatical elements is the one that best renders action, movement, and change. Linked to the dominant idea of change, there is in the view of Proust another extremely interesting feature—that is, the manner in which the change is taking place. The modalities of the transformation, the ways by which people or events turn into something else, are realities worth considering and noting in all their details. The subordinate clause is employed to give a complete and adequate account of the

various modes of this change. But the actual fact, or the
final result of the transformation, holds no mystery and
therefore no lure for the intelligence of Proust. So it will be
mentioned as it is entitled to be, more or less casually, and
the poor noun—the direct object—will just state what is
what and no more.

With that plain pattern as the foundation Proust displays a fanciful variety of *coloratura*. He is an artist, however, and not a virtuoso, and his effects of style are never
presented for their own sake but are always the reflexion
of a definite variation of thought or simply of mood. The
two chief aspects of his works help to distinguish the
two main varieties of his style: the poetical and the
abstract.

Whenever Proust tries to give an account of the true
reality of things, whenever he tries to bring to light the
treasures of our subconscious mind, his sentences take on a
supple rhythm to suit the elusive quality of our mental life.
Whenever he tries by intuitive sympathy to enter into
communion with things of beauty around him, there is an
almost musical throb in his accents. His subtle rendering
of the fugitive impressions of the half-waking state—his
eloquent descriptions of flowers, young women, scenery—
his inspired evocation of music—his mystic transfiguration
of Time—are all of them permeated with an intensely
poetical atmosphere. His style then presents some striking characteristics. The adjectives, otherwise rather scant
and restrained, suddenly and enthusiastically burst forth
like a dazzling display of fireworks. They come pouring
out, all richly expressive and intensely colourful, in a kind
of lyrical outburst. These accumulations of adjectives—
invariably used with an unerring sense of the most delicate
shades of meaning and with great power of suggestion,
occur at rare intervals, and are generally rather brief, but

act all the more potently on the imagination. More frequently, especially when Proust wishes to evoke the more subtle charm of a beauty only faintly perceptible to the senses but penetrating slowly and deeply into our inner consciousness, the imagery—again suggested by adjectives—takes on a more insinuating quality. The same imagery follows unobtrusively several successive sentences, as a musical theme reiterated in various keys on the piano may furnish the modest accompaniment to a violin solo. So the adjectives, all recording a similar modality of impression, though varying in their special mood, come again and again, imparting a certain quality and resonance to the whole sentence. These poetical effects in which the adjectives play a leading role, are more frequent in the earlier part of Proust's work and especially in those passages which he considered as jewels 'enchased in a grosser substance.'

The 'grosser substance' turns out to be by far the most extensive of his material. It extends wherever Proust tried with his keen intelligence to pierce the crust of pretence covering the actions and gestures of men. In this operation there can be no lyrical feeling whatever—in the account given, no poetical expression of any sort. The language is reduced to the level of its logical, abstract content. But even then it may have a beauty arising out of the sheer display of the author's power of penetration and investigation. Very often he applies his logic to discover reality as a wrench is used to force open a closed door. Then his sentence stands firm on solid ground; it may twist and turn like a wrestler who feints and gives way for a moment but only in order to gain a stronger hold. Then the subordinate clauses, which are a special characteristic of Proust's style, lean on a robust framework of conjunctions and relative pronouns. The sentence is a structure of heavy and sturdy build—not unlike the sentence of the seventeenth century French prose writers. Its beauty lies in its strength and perfect adaptation to its function. Sometimes also, when Proust feels that it is scarcely possible to penetrate the mystery by sheer brutal power of logic, his sentence wanders on the surface of the problem, exploring the slightest crevices, trying these one by one; and though a definite conclusion can hardly ever be reached by this method, nevertheless some approximate idea can be obtained of what lies at the bottom of the matter. Then the sentence will take on a special shape, not infrequently met with in Proust's work: the subordinate clauses are separate, independent, and parallel, each acting and searching as it were on its own account; between them, there is only the connecting link of a *soit que* . . . , *soit que* . . . , *soit que* . . . , repeated as often as is necessary. At last Proust may find an actual opening in the crust of reality. His exploring sentence, long and sinuous like a snake, then gropes its way in the dark. Its progress is slow and cautious; it hesitates, recoils, makes a fresh start. The subordinate clauses, loosely articulated, represent the various phases of the motion. Finally at the end of the long laborious search is found a little fragment of truth.

. . . .

A laborious search for fragments of truth, sometimes enlivened by a brilliant discovery—so appears the work of Marcel Proust to the reader. Since Proust's style faithfully reflects his persistent efforts, his few triumphs, and his numerous disappointments, the reader sometimes feels discouraged on account of the bulk of these compact volumes wherein 'nothing happens' most of the time.

A perusal of the first pages of Proust presents real

difficulty—even to a French reader. It is almost like trying to read a new language, at least it means entering into communion with a new and very original personality. When that first obstacle is overcome, however, there is undoubtedly a strange fascination in all Proust's writings; if the reader is patient as Proust himself was, from an arduous task he will, like Proust, reap the reward of great artistic enjoyment.

Proust had grown up without any religious or moral ideal. His prospect in life was limited to the pleasure to be derived from the feelings and sensations of the moment; and it was a programme of no mean order since his extraordinarily developed sensitiveness enabled him to feel more acutely and completely than others. Yet mere pleasure, intellectual or physical, betrayed his expectations, revealed itself as unstable and unprofitable, and in the end proved both dull and exasperating. Ultimately it turned against him. In his childhood he had been sickly; after a short surge of vitality in youth and early manhood, disappointment settled on his shoulders, he became *blasé*, and his last years were spent in the anguish of tortured nerves. Nothing was before him but final, black despair. Indeed Proust seems to have been touched more than once by its enveloping wings. Life after all seemed to him a tremendous disaster. Yet in that extremity salvation came to him. The indispensable sublime was discovered, in the idealization of sensation itself. A mystic revelation enabled him not only to snatch from Time its victim, evanescent sensation, but also to bring it back, more pleasurable than ever, with an added flavour of eternity about it. This was a thoroughly personal experience— especially in its overwhelming intensity. What may be of universal value in all this is the idea underlying it and the conclusion to which Proust himself came: that the momentous experience should be crystallized in a work of art; and that in the act of artistic creation complete self-fulfilment and consequent happiness will be attained. Out of the shipwreck of his life he had made a masterpiece and so found the bliss that nothing else could give.

ANDRÉ GIDE

II. ANDRÉ GIDE

1. *André Gide's Life*

THE very name of André Gide is anathema to the god-fearing and a horror to the *bourgeois*. On his own confession is he not an invert; and further is he not a professed communist? Moreover he holds views on religion which add a touch of the sacrilegious to his dangerously disturbing theories. Yet probably no man was ever brought up in a more pious or more strictly orthodox atmosphere. Gide was born in Paris, 22 November 1869. He came from old French Huguenot stock. These Protestants of France, as the result of the long, hard struggle they sustained for their faith, have acquired a stern and serious outlook on life and a kind of solemn stiffness of manner, which stamps them, even now, as different from their less gloomy Catholic countrymen. This was more marked at the time of Gide's youth than it is today and still more so in the generation to which Gide's parents belonged. They were inclined to consider spontaneous enjoyment of life as something dangerous which would lead inevitably to sin. The best way to keep on the straight and narrow path was to turn from the light and frivolous side of life and to follow quite literally the strict commands of God's Law. Life to them was not a glorious adventure but a trial of moral strength. Great would be the reward of those who struggled and prevailed; but it would require all the powers of a strong character to overcome the weaknesses and the evils to which human nature is prone, and to raise up in the heart of each one an altar of pure

115

sacrifice to the Lord. Duty, and the striving after the right, observance of God's Law and self-immolation before its exacting demands were, according to their views, the basis of righteous living.

Gide's moral and religious inheritance, however, was not exclusively Protestant. His father's family was Protestant through and through; and it was with a mixture of admiration, amazement, and awe that young Gide, during his holidays, met these severe Huguenots who appeared so completely outmoded in their manners and speech, that they seemed to belong to an almost extinct, fossilized age.[1] But on his mother's side, there was a definite strain of Catholicism. Mme Gide's grandfather, Rondeaux de Montbray, once mayor of the city of Rouen, was himself a Catholic, though he had taken a Protestant wife; one of his sons, Edouard, married also a Protestant and their children were brought up as Protestants. Gide's mother was one of these. The tradition of piety among the Rondeaux, though no less fervent than that of the Gides, was decidedly milder in tone and somewhat different in spirit.

There was another important difference between the two sides of the family. The Gides came from the south— from the region of Uzès. It is a country of stern beauty where under a blazing sun the sharp outlines of barren rocks jut out from amongst scanty vegetation. Everything suggests austerity and uncompromising clarity of thought. This is a land of pure intellectuality, of logic, where even asceticism is not out of place. The Rondeaux, on the other hand, were cradled in Normandy, that rich and fruitful province, where life is easy and the people prosperous, and where opulence is everywhere apparent. Money-

1. A.Gide, *Si le Grain ne meurt*, Œuvres Complètes, Vol.x, Nouvelle Revue Française, Paris, 1936, Part i, Chap.ii, p.68.

making, good living, enjoyment of all the pleasures of life, are the normal pursuits of the solid Normans. A fundamental sensuousness permeates every form of their life, art, and thought. At the same time they have a strength and depth of feeling which is frequently lacking in the brilliant but more superficial southerners.

Gide was well aware of the conflicting influences within himself; and once, when answering Maurice Barrès, who argued that the first condition of culture was to have taken root somewhere, he said, ' Né a Paris, d'un père Uzétien et d'une mère normande, où voulez-vous, Monsieur Barrès, que je m'enracine? ' [2] Gide himself was persuaded that this conflict of antagonistic tendencies had to a large extent been his urge to an artistic vocation as a writer. 'Nothing could be more different than the influences of these two families, or than these two provinces of France, whose contradictory influences unite in me. Often I have persuaded myself that I had been compelled to produce a work of art simply because it was the only way to bring about an agreement between these too divergent elements which otherwise would have fought constantly with each other or at least have pursued a dialogue within me.' [3] Whatever there may be of truth in these theories of heredity, it is worth noting that behind the apparent unity of Gide's early puritanic environment lies a dualism of deep, perhaps inborn, influences, on the one hand inciting him to enjoy the good things of life— on the other, telling him that stern duty must always be his guide.

Gide's father had heard only one of these two voices. He was a professor in the Faculty of Law at the University

2. A.Gide, *A propos des Déracinés*, Œuvres Complètes, Vol.ii, Nouvelle Revue Française, Paris, 1933, p.437.
3. *Si le Grain ne meurt*, Part i, Chap.i, p.46.

of Paris, and carried the family tradition of absolute probity so far that he had been nicknamed by his colleagues *vir probus*—the honest man.[4] But Professor Paul Gide was unable to exert any marked influence on his son, since he died when André was only eleven years old. The cause of his death was an intestinal tuberculosis.

Mme Gide, who up to that time had kept in the background, now came to the fore. She was a thoroughly good woman, a woman 'of good will' in the Scriptural sense, as Gide himself says.[5] She had a definite, though limited number of lofty principles: a complete and implicit faith in God, a respectful admiration for everything intellectual, and a high and uncompromising sense of duty. She had also on a humbler plan a set of equally imperative class prejudices and self-imposed obligations. In every case she would do what she considered right with inflexible rigidity. Her appreciation of people and their actions was confined within the narrow limits of her beliefs. Her way of dealing with evil was simply to refuse to consider it. At home the book-cases containing her husband's books were kept for years under lock and key. Once her young son, with childish curiosity asking the meaning of the word 'atheist,' had to be content with the illuminating explanation: 'It means a wicked and stupid man.' [6] Another time André was forbidden by his mother to go to a concert where some music by Chopin was to be played, because in her opinion Chopin's music was 'unwholesome' (*malsaine*).[7] André was her only child, in fact her only real interest in life. Without being very rich she had enough to enable the two of them to live comfortably without financial cares. As she had no one but her son to

4. *Si le Grain ne meurt*, Part I, Chap.I, p.38.
5. *Ibidem*, Part I, Chap.VI, p.210.
6. *Ibidem*, Part I, Chap.IV, p.142.
7. *Ibidem*, Part I, Chap.VI, p.213.

be concerned about, she applied herself with all the more thoroughness to the warding off systematically of all the evil that threatened him. She concentrated on him the burden of her constant attention and overwhelming devotion. The little fellow was simply crushed beneath it all.

His mother was not the only one supervising André's moral welfare. There was another saintly woman who was virtually a member of the family: this was a certain Anna Shackleton, who years before had come from Scotland and had been the governess of Mme Gide when she was a girl. After the marriage of her charge, Anna had remained as a welcome guest and beloved companion. From the portrait which Gide has drawn of her, it is clear that she must have been extraordinarily attractive when young, and that she must have retained throughout her life a distinctive personal charm. But she was, as it turned out, an old maid of the Victorian era. Endowed with all the virtues of the Victorian old maid, she could not avoid the short-comings common to that species. Then there was also Aunt Claire, a sister of Mme Gide, a paragon of respectability and conventionality who gave freely of her opinions and advice—always the most moral to be sure.

These three good women, all well meaning, had on their hands a very difficult problem. Gide himself has told, almost complacently, what a nasty little boy he was at that time; how he would slyly and for no apparent reason trample on the sand castles built by other children in a public garden [8]—how he once savagely bit the beautiful bare shoulder of a cousin who wanted to pet him [9]—how he was a tell-tale, repeating conversations he had overheard [10] and, what perhaps explains everything, how at

8. *Si le Grain ne meurt*, Part I, Chap.I, p.33.
9. *Ibidem*, Part I, Chap.I, p.34.
10. *Ibidem*, Part I, Chap.VI, p.198.

an unbelievably early age he contracted vicious solitary habits.[11] Good will and high morality were of absolutely no avail in a perverted case like his.

To make matters worse, the life of the family after his father's death was almost perpetually nomadic. For years Mme Gide kept moving from place to place. She was agitated by a restlessness easily to be understood in a person whose whole existence had been thrown out of balance by a harrowing and unexpected loss. She found a multitude of reasons for a continual change of residence. A sense of family obligation would carry her from one end of France to the other to visit some relative; concern for the health of her precious son would send her in quest of a milder climate or a health-giving spa; the lure of intellectual splendour and possibilities of education for the boy would bring her back to Paris. So every few months there was a change; but not much pleasure in it, for the same restrained family atmosphere was to be found in every lodging. As a result of this unsettled life, André Gide for many years did not know the stability and steadiness of a home. The more or less fixed centres of the family's numerous migrations were first the region of Uzès, where young André came in contact with the stern, poor, and virtuous Huguenots on the Gide side of the family; secondly, the two estates belonging to the Rondeaux—La Rocque and Cuverville, in Normandy,— where he met a crowd of little cousins of that branch of the family. One winter, however, was spent in Montpellier, near his uncle, Charles Gide, the famous economist; ten months at Lamalou and Gérardmer in the Vosges Mountains; some time also on the Riviera. Finally Paris became more or less their permanent place of abode.

André's schooling during that time was as erratic as

11. *Si le Grain ne meurt*, Part I, Chap. I, p.32.

his home life, and even more disorganized. He went from
one institution to another, and in between he received
some sort of instruction at home from an ever-changing
set of eccentric tutors. He was not happy at school, and
was frequently subjected to cruel teasing by his school-
fellows. At the age of twelve, when just recovering from
smallpox, so upset was he at the prospect of returning to
the hated Lycée de Montpellier that he fell ill again, this
time with a nervous complaint. Gide himself said later [12]
that he could not tell exactly how much of his suffering
was real, and how much imaginary or mere pretence. He
actually had very acute headaches, but the little actor
also knew how to fool the doctors and to display to his
anxious family a regular show of most alarming symptoms.

Gide sums up the whole situation when he says that
he could perceive in that period of his life nothing but
'darkness, ugliness, deception.' [13] Yet through that darkness there shone, though but faintly, a few hopeful rays.
On several occasions the child felt himself suddenly shuddering, as if on the threshold of some tremendous discovery—the discovery of the deep reality of life in contrast to the superficial and conventional pattern constantly held out to him. In describing that trance-like
state into which he fell occasionally Gide uses the German word 'Schaudern,' for want of an adequate French
expression. [14] This experience occurred to him rarely—
sometimes for no apparent reason—sometimes linked
to a definite emotion, as when one day he was told of the
death of a little cousin,—a cousin practically unknown to
him. [15] It was a sign that his innermost being instinctively

12. *Si le Grain ne meurt*, Part I, Chap.IV, pp.149–151.
13. *Ibidem*, Part I, Chap.I, p.32.
14. *Ibidem*, Part I, Chap.V, p.172.
15. *Ibidem*, Part I, Chap.V, p.171.

craved something more genuine, more intense, than the cold, conventional world which his environment offered.

Another partial revelation of his own strange personality came to him at the age of thirteen. Of all his cousins and playfellows, the reserved and retiring Emmanuèle Rondeaux was perhaps the most lovable. André was genuinely fond of her, but his affection was perfectly calm and unemotional. One day, however, in Rouen, he happened by chance to discover a family secret—the cause of a great sorrow that was eating up the soul of the idealistic young girl—namely, the misconduct of her mother. Instantly filled with admiration for the quiet stoicism of Emmanuèle and above all stirred with pity for her unfathomable distress, the purpose of his life became clear to him: he would devote his existence to her and would protect her from the wicked world—he would heal her wound and worship her eternally because she was so good and so unhappy. 'Je découvrais soudain un nouvel orient à ma vie,' wrote Gide forty years later.[16] It was not 'love' but the germ of a supremely exalted sentiment which he was to cherish throughout his life.

At about the age of sixteen or seventeen a sudden change took place in him. Before then, he had been sunk in lethargy; now he woke up. The completion of the adolescent period no doubt accounts mainly for the transformation, but the spiritual accompaniment of the change throws an unexpected light on his character at the time.

Now his feelings for Emmanuèle turned into something which both called love. But their love remained on an ideal and ethereal plane. They had both been trained to consider everything pertaining to their bodily nature as

16. *Si le Grain ne meurt*, Part I, Chap.v, p.164. Gide had even written originally 'Je découvrais soudain le mystique orient de ma vie.' *Si le Grain ne meurt*, Nouvelle Revue Française, Paris, 1926, I, 5, p.129.

impure and repugnant. In their contempt for the flesh and in their horror of carnal sin they could imagine a personal union only for mutual spiritual encouragement towards purity and virtue. There was in that youthful enthusiasm a rare and sublime quality. Many years afterwards, in writing of the walks the two of them used to take hand in hand in the morning at La Rocque, he expressed himself thus: 'Eblouissement pur, puisse ton souvenir à l'heure de la mort vaincre l'ombre! Mon âme, que de fois, par l'ardeur du milieu du jour s'est rafraichie dans ta rosée. . . .' [17] 'Oh, rapture pure and dazzling, in the hour of death may thy memory dispel the darkness! How oft in the heat of the day has my soul found refreshment in thy dew. . . .'

For these two idealistic adolescents—their youthful ardour untroubled by doubts—mere virtue was not enough. Sanctity was the ultimate and common goal which they sought. Their love developed along parallel lines in a glow of mystic, religious enthusiasm. The time came for their first communion. Gide, it is true, found the honest, dull Pastor Couve, who was in charge of his religious instruction, somewhat unsatisfactory and uninspiring; but his own ardour made up for the deficiencies of his teacher. In order to mortify the flesh he used to get up at dawn and plunge into a cold tub, filled the evening before with icy water. Sometimes he would sleep on a wooden board or get up in the middle of the night to kneel and pray. Then he felt that he had been able to 'reach the extreme limit of happiness.' [18]

This happiness was not without its counterpart of restlessness. Nature cannot be suppressed altogether and many times Gide was aware of unsatisfied longings from

17. *Si le Grain ne meurt*, Part I, Chap.VIII, p.262.
18. *Ibidem*, Part I, Chap.VIII, p.267.

another stratum of his being. These did not point in the
direction of his ideal Emmanuèle and were in themselves
disconcerting and perplexing.

For a while these longings found an outlet and a certain
amount of justification in an entirely different field. Gide's
nervous condition had improved and he was now able
to attend school regularly. He was in attendance at the
'Ecole Alsacienne,' a private school in Paris, run on
humane, modern, and intelligent lines. For the first time
he developed an interest in his studies—in literature
above all. The Greek poets were of decisive importance in
his mental evolution. In them he found a picture of life
entirely different from that which had been drawn for
him by his mother, by Anna Shackleton, by Pastor
Couve, or even by Emmanuèle. By the Greek poets he
found that Nature was not condemned but glorified, and
her aspirations were held to be legitimate, not shameful.
Gide himself was carried away with a thoroughly pagan
love of beauty. Curiously enough that pagan ardour
co-existed with his Christian religious enthusiasm without
in the least disturbing the latter. They were merely for
the time being in two separate compartments. One of his
school friends, Pierre Louis, later famous as a novelist
and poet,[19] shared his admiration for poetry; and the
two of them, full of expectation, were waiting for the
great, rich world to open before them.

Music took on at the same time a preponderating importance in Gide's life. He had for many years been required to have piano lessons from teachers as eccentric
as his other tutors. Finally he was entrusted to the care
of a M.de la Nux, who was a true musician and an intelligent man. Under his direction, Gide's progress was amazing. Musical problems became clear and obvious to him;

19. Under the pen name of 'Pierre Louÿs.'

it was a real initiation into this difficult field. Bach and
Schumann won his early allegiance; later Chopin took
first place in his admiration. Henceforward music was an
essential element in his spiritual life. He even went so far
as to say that Chopin more than anybody else taught him
his technique as an artist.[20] His style indeed is filled with
musical resonances. Gide, essentially a pianist, is less
sensitive to the rich harmonies of complete orchestration
than to the actual quality of a melody, to the almost imperceptible quivering which gives an aria its moving
power, to tonal inflexions suggesting rather than expressing a hidden world of mysterious shadings. But the world
suggested by music is far removed from the clear-cut,
bald, somewhat prosaic world of Gide's puritanic education. Gide himself, however, did not at first suspect the
contrariety and simply enjoyed music for its own sake as
an expression of the confused and tumultuous feelings
which at the time were surging up within him. After all,
perhaps Mme Gide was right in condemning Chopin as
the enemy.

Nevertheless Gide could not help being aware of the
struggle going on within himself between his suppressed
lower instincts and his absolute moral principles. This
conflict was the subject of his first book, *Les Cahiers
d'André Walter*, published in 1891. For, after gaining his
baccalauréat, Gide had decided to become a writer. His
mother did not object to the plan, and he had sufficient
independent means to wait until success came. Success
did not come to him with *André Walter*, however; and he
was so disappointed with his failure that he had practically
the whole edition destroyed immediately. Shortly afterwards he asked Emmanuèle to marry him; but the girl

20. Ch.Du Bos: *Le Dialogue avec André Gide*, Au Sans Pareil, Paris, 1929,
    Troisième entretien, p.69.

was faithful to her lofty ideal of sainthood, and it was obviously impossible to remain a saint in marriage. So, for Gide's sake as well as for her own, she refused.

Then began for Gide a long period of distressing mental confusion. The decision taken by his cousin did not put an end to his love for her; on the contrary it increased if not his love certainly his respect. At the same time he realized more and more that in him a struggle was taking place; his mature instincts were challenging his early ideal. There was no prospect of a solution to the problem, because while he wanted to be himself and to live a full, rich life, he nevertheless was loath to give up the ideals which to his way of thinking gave his life its very meaning. At that time he was determined that if a sacrifice had to be made, it would not be his ideals that would be surrendered.

In this respect he found encouragement and precept in the then flourishing literary school of the Symbolists. Most of the Symbolists were people who had become disgusted with the realities of life, had turned their back on them and were trying to find in poetry an ideal refuge even though it were only an imaginary one. In this there was a certain similarity to Gide's own personal experience. So when his friend, Pierre Louis, took him to gatherings of the leading literary persons of the day he found there a congenial atmosphere and a sympathetic welcome. For a while he was a regular guest at the receptions given every Tuesday evening by the poet, Stéphane Mallarmé, and on Saturday afternoons at the house of J.M. de Heredia. There he met many Symbolists of note: Henri de Régnier, F.Viélé-Griffin, F.Hérold, Paul Valéry; he also made the acquaintance of Oscar Wilde, then at the height of his literary vogue, but without for the moment suspecting the idiosyncrasies of the man.

At this period Gide was a thin, pale young man, who generally appeared in public wearing a dark romantic cape. He allowed his hair to grow long and retained his brown beard. His lips were thick and sensual, but his mouth was straight and firmly closed. He spoke very little as a rule, for he was incredibly timid in company, modestly retiring, almost elusive, though not from any sense of inferiority, because he was perfectly conscious of his own ability and was by no means lacking in pride. He was emphatically chaste. Apparently as an affectation he always carried a small Bible in his pocket, ready to produce it any moment. Nevertheless, he was inwardly burning with desire and consumed with inexpressible longing for 'forbidden' pleasure.

He wrote several books, *Le Traité du Narcisse*, *La Tentative Amoureuse*, *Le Voyage d'Urien*—all of the Symbolist type—without attaining success or progressing towards a solution of his problem. The moral crisis under which he was labouring began to tell on his health. His nerves went to pieces again; in a physical examination preliminary to his military service, he was pronounced unfit—on account of tuberculosis. In view of this medical verdict something drastic would have to be done, if he was not to come to a premature end as his father had before him.

. . . .

Gide decided that he must leave Paris and his family and acquaintances, in order to try and be himself. One of his friends, Paul Albert Laurens, a painter, had just obtained a travelling scholarship and was going to North Africa. When he left in October 1893, Gide accompanied him. The small pocket Bible was left behind.

The beginning of the trip was difficult for Gide. He became feverish, feeling very ill and miserable. The two

friends struggled through Tunisia and finally reached the
Algerian oasis of Biskra on the edge of the Sahara desert.
There they stopped. Gide was very weak indeed. Was
he to die without ever having lived? He wondered. However, the beneficent climate and the interest which he
felt in the new and wonderful spectacle of life surging
strongly in the oasis and perhaps even more his will to
live—all had a curative effect upon him. Soon he began to
recover, and in the feeling of well-being natural to con-
valescence, he discovered a savour in life a thousand
times more enthralling than he had ever suspected. There
seemed to well up within him a new found delight in the
sheer joy of living, in the love for this gorgeous, splendid
earth. Life was good. Man had a right to enjoy it to the
full. All superimposed 'duties' became hateful to him—
and were simply cast off. When his mother, alarmed on
account of the state of his health, and even more because
of the altered tone of his letters, came to Biskra to look
after him, she found him with a native girl, Mériem
ben Atala. Madame Gide fled in horror.

Returning subsequently to Europe, Gide brought back
with him his new revelation—'the secret of a resurrected
man.' [21] But what a contrast was the north after the
glorious Algerian sunshine! People seemed so banal, with
their little interests and their petty quarrels. A doctor
sent him to the Jura Mountains, in Switzerland, and he
stayed at a little village called La Brévine. There his
health was definitely restored, and there too he wrote his
satirical book, *Paludes*, in which he expressed his disappointment with society as he found it in Europe.

His one desire was to return to Africa, and soon he did
so. This time he went to Algiers, and then to the lovely
little city of Blidah. There he encountered Oscar Wilde

21. *Si le Grain ne meurt*, Part II, Chap.I, p.386.

again. The latter was travelling with Lord Alfred Douglas. On several occasions during the course of his previous trip, Gide had entertained grave doubts about his own tendencies. Through Oscar Wilde's influence, he came to realize fully that his fundamental nature was not like that of normal men. This discovery brought him such a strange sense of peace that he had the feeling of being at last absolutely himself. The whole moral structure of his early years, or what was left of it, was now perforce entirely swept away. There was no longer any problem confronting him. He had found complete liberation.

. . . .

When he returned to France, he found his mother dying. For a long time the two had been almost estranged. Though Mme Gide did not realize the change that had come over her son, she felt that he was lost to her; she fought against his own strong resistance to win him back, a struggle marked by an occasional temporary reconciliation—which Gide himself spoke of as a 'truce.' [22] Yet he was still deeply attached to his mother, and when she came to die he confessed that he 'felt all his being sink into an abyss of love, distress and freedom.' [23] He was free now, completely free.

Soon afterwards, on 8 October 1895, he married Emmanuèle. Why she reconsidered her decision, is easy enough to imagine. Years had passed. She was not so young now. Like the rest of the family too, she may have realized that her cousin, left to his own devices, was not, after all, following the path which would lead to sanctity. His reasons are more difficult to diagnose. The death of his mother may have awakened temporarily his religious and moral feelings. He may have felt, when she died,

22. *Si le Grain ne meurt*, Part II, Chap.II, p.436.
23. *Ibidem*, Part II, Chap.II, p.443.

that he had lost his last anchor, as it were; that he was
completely adrift; and he may have wanted almost instinctively to grasp the only strong, sure thing within
his reach. He still loved Emmanuèle ideally—perhaps he
thought he could make her share his newly discovered
enjoyment of life. Gide in his book, *Si le Grain ne meurt*,
reviews all these possible causes of his own action, finds
them all unsatisfactory, and concludes: 'Our most sincere
actions are those which are least calculated. The explanation that we seek for them afterwards remains empty. It
was fate that was driving me.' [24]

Fate was indeed driving him on to a moral tragedy. He
returned to Algeria almost immediately, accompanied by
his wife. There he finished a book which he had begun to
write a few years before, *Les Nourritures Terrestres*, in
which he expressed his enthusiasm for the earthly realities
in which his being now delighted. The book, published in
1897, was a failure, and caused a break between Gide and
his Symbolist friends, who hated and despised reality.

At the same time a serious rift had occurred between
Gide and his wife. He loved her more than ever, but in a
spiritual way only. When she came to understand his
moral perversity, she shrank from him and 'took refuge
in God.' Gide many years later, writing impersonally in
his *Journal des Faux-Monnayeurs*, seems to have put the
drama succinctly in this way: 'The surprising part of it
is, he feels that he still loves her desperately—I mean with
a desperate love, for she will not believe in his love on
account of his previous unfaithfulness . . . of a purely
carnal order. But precisely because he loved her without
sensuality (at least of a bodily kind) his love is preserved
from every cause of destruction. He is jealous of God, who
steals his wife from him. He feels that he cannot fight,

24. *Si le Grain ne meurt*, Part II, Chap.II, p.444.

having been defeated in advance; but he conceives a hatred for this rival and everything that is connected with Him.' [25]

So he began a course of questionable behaviour in defiance of all God's commands, not exactly out of spite, but in order to assert himself more strongly. Yet he still believed in God. His was not simply one of those fairly common cases of loss of faith after a moral-sensual crisis. The idea of God was too deeply rooted in him to be so easily eliminated. At the time of Gide's first trip to Algeria, life and nature had merely claimed their due, in spite of the restrictions of the moral code. In the wild exuberance of youth, moral chains had been suddenly and violently broken. He had considered himself free. The promptings of the flesh had been openly avowed, accepted as a self-justifying reality and permitted to seek satisfaction. Now, in Paris Gide could not help hearing the divine voice telling him that there *was* a Law. The very presence of his wife, who in spite of everything always remained for him a faithful and devoted companion, the mute reproach of her suffering, were a constant reminder to him of his moral obligations. The two voices, of God, and of Satan, would alternately be raised in argument within him. The dialogue continued torturing him for years.

His health once more broke under the strain. He suffered from headaches and insomnia, and his nerves tormented him relentlessly. He tried to find escape in travel. For years he rushed hither and thither, visiting Germany, Spain, Turkey, Austria, Italy, Greece, going again several times to Algeria, but never remaining anywhere for long. Erratic, unstable, elusive, he seemed to be constantly on the wing. His face wore a tormented look. The tragedy

25. A.Gide, *Journal des Faux-Monnayeurs*, Nouvelle Revue Française, Paris, 1927, 2 Janvier 1921, p.38.

of Oscar Wilde's end added to his anxiety and restlessness. In Paris itself he led a notoriously wild life, amid a few of his friends, among them Henri Ghéon. He even went so far as to import an Algerian native boy, Athman, whom he had known during his second trip to Africa. There was in this attitude of his a note of defiance: he was daring to be himself.

Three foreign writers had at that time an outstanding influence on Gide—Nietzsche, Dostoievsky, and Goethe. In Nietzsche he found a thinker who had resolutely cast off the conventional rules of morality, advocating the glorious principle that the individual should live fully, intensely, dangerously, glorifying the present moment and singing a lyric hymn to vital and intoxicating joy. 'Yes, Nietzsche demolishes; he undermines—not as one discouraged but fiercely, nobly, gloriously, superhumanly, as a new conqueror violates things grown old. The horror of rest, of comfort, of all that threatens life with diminution, torpor, sleep, that is what makes him rend asunder walls and arches. . . . He undermines outworn structures and fashions no new ones himself—but he does more: he fashions the workers. . . . The wonderful thing is that, at the same time, he fills them with joyous life and laughs with them amidst the ruins.' [26] This is but one phase of Nietzsche's philosophy but it is the one which had the greatest significance for Gide, as it crystallized in formal expression what he himself had felt more or less unconsciously. 'I was waiting for him before I knew him—before I knew him even by name. . . . Reading him, it seemed to me that he was stimulating *my* thought. . . . Without him many generations perhaps would have spent themselves in timidly insinuating what he affirmed with boldness,

26. A.Gide, *Lettres à Angèle*, Œuvres Complètes, Vol.III, Nouvelle Revue Française, Paris, 1933, XII, pp.230–231.

with mastery, with madness. Even we, personally, were running the risk of allowing all our work to be encumbered with formless movements of thought—thought which has now been expressed.' [27]

In Dostoievsky the central point, as Gide saw it, was the relation of the individual to God. All Dostoievsky's books written after he accepted the Gospel in Siberia are suffused with the evangelical doctrine of humility, resignation, and renunciation. Nevertheless Dostoievsky still retained much of his previous outlook, some of it evil, some of it impure, but blended with the new fundamental aspiration after Christian ideals. He did not sacrifice to theoretical unity and simplicity the rich and sometimes disconcerting complexity of the human soul. In him Gide found an example of conscience in distress, laden with a feeling of sin—of unavoidable sin—and yet at the same time a truly noble conscience longing for salvation.

Goethe showed Gide a possible way to acquire a more balanced mental equilibrium. In the early part of his life Goethe himself was far from having attained the Olympian serenity which he possessed in his old age. In fact he had known for a long time—during his years of 'Sturm und Drang'—all the extremities of moral restlessness. He was in search of his own conception of the truth, and many a time, in face of the incomprehensible, he would stand shuddering, full of expectancy, anxiety, and hope. Considering this 'Schaudern' to be an indication of a man's great personal worth, which held a promise of noble fulfilment, he came to think that it represents the best that is in man.[28] Gide himself had experienced more than once this very 'Schaudern' when brought face to face with the

27. *Lettres à Angèle*, XII, p.236.
28. 'Das Schaudern ist der Menschheit bestes Teil.' Goethe: *Faust*, II, Act I, Finstere Galerie, l. 6272.

reality of life. If he hailed it as one of his most precious possessions, and adopted the German word to designate it, it is certain that he did so because the example of Goethe was hovering in his mind. Goethe however went a step farther, and in the course of a trip to Italy finally discovered in art the solution to his problem. Thus he became aware of his true personality; as an artist, he had found himself at last.[29] Through his art his various inner difficulties and conflicts harmoniously resolved themselves. Gide, even at a time when he was still seeking his own salvation, experienced on contact with Goethe, the artist, a strange and blessed peace, very similar to Goethe's own tranquillity—a foretaste of the serenity that would be his once the secret had been revealed to him. In 1905, under the date of Tuesday, June 5th, he wrote in his diary:[30] 'Il pleut à torrents. Enfermé dans la serre avec les poésies de Goethe, entouré de calcéolaires jaune d'or, sans fièvre, sans soucis, sans désirs, je goûte une

PARFAITE FÉLICITÉ.' [31]

Such spells of perfect happiness were not of frequent occurrence during this period of Gide's life. His fundamental restlessness allowed him little leisure for repose or for work. During these many years his literary productions were few and far between. The two books *L'Immoraliste* (published in 1902), in which he expresses a pagan enthusiasm for life, and *La Porte Etroite* (published in 1909), in which are expressed his aspirations after holiness, represent the two main aspects of the great dilemma under

29. 'Ich darf wohl sagen, ich habe mich in dieser anderthalbjährigen Einsamkeit selbst wiedergefunden, aber als was?—Als Künstler!' Letter from Goethe to Karl August, Duke of Saxe-Weimar, 17 March 1788.
30. A.Gide, *Journal*, Œuvres Complètes, Vol.IV, Nouvelle Revue Française, Paris, 1933, Cinquième Cahier, p.528.
31. In Gide's original text the two words PARFAITE FÉLICITÉ are printed as above, in capital letters on a line by themselves.

which he was labouring at the time. In addition, he published a number of less important writings: articles in magazines, such as *Lettres à Angèle* (1898–1900); short plays like *Philoctète* (1899); *Le roi Candaule* (1901); *Saül* (1903); accounts of his travels, for example, *Amyntas* (1899); and a satirical tale, *Le Prométhée mal enchaîné* (1899).

It is noteworthy that even these secondary works are concentrated into a few short years, and that after a while Gide withdrew into almost complete silence. These publications as a rule found little favour with the general public—except *La Porte Etroite*. Yet now and then, one or another of them would throw a sudden and revealing light on the path of some unknown young man, struggling to find his way in the darkness and confusion of his own puzzling and conflicting tendencies. Grateful or anxiously questioning letters were sometimes received by Gide and were always faithfully answered. And so, by and by, without any display, Gide unexpectedly found himself the spiritual guide of a number of young men scattered throughout France. They were not very numerous at first, but they must all have been interesting personalities and mentally very much alive.

Gide could not but be aware of his growing influence, even when it did not take the form of personal relationship. The realization that he was understood by some—and moreover, that his writings had an effect upon them—contributed more than anything to pacify him and to give him new confidence with which to face his own problems. He grew less agitated. He spent a great part of his time in the country, at Cuverville; and at times it seemed that calm was almost within his reach.

However, real activity was necessary to enable Gide definitely to extricate himself from the slough of his depression and achieve some measure of progress. For many

years he had written articles for a literary magazine called
L'Ermitage; he had also procured for the review the collaboration of several of his personal friends, all of them
men of considerable ability. But the magazine, born under
the sign of Symbolism—now completely out of date—
could not rid itself of its old associations. By 1908 *L'Ermitage* had passed out of existence. Among the former con-
tributors, however, there were still the makings of an
excellent team, if only some elimination could be effected
and a thorough literary and artistic discipline established
and maintained. The best of them felt this; but it was
André Gide who actually put the idea into execution. In
February 1909 the first number was published of *La Nouvelle Revue Française*. The name of Gide did not even appear among the members of the ' Comité de direction,' but
he really was the mainspring of the movement and the soul
of the whole group. The best known of his early associates
were Jean Schlumberger, Henri Ghéon, Alain Fournier, Paul
Claudel, Jules Romains, Jean Giraudoux, Jacques Copeau.

They all of them had a common ideal of artistic sincerity and morality. They wanted to fight against the com-
mercialization of literature, against syndicates of writers
for reciprocal praise and advertisement; they were for
directness and simplicity of expression, and against artificiality and over-sophistication. In practice they criticized
one another freely—in fact there was a mutual exchange
of candid criticism among them! Art was put before friendship and even before personal interest or vanity.

The spirit of self-abnegation and devotion to art, expressed in this new movement initiated by Gide, met
almost immediately with unqualified success. In 1911, a
publishing enterprise was begun in connexion with the
magazine, and soon became one of the most thriving and
influential centres of literary life in France. In 1913 Jacques

Copeau decided to introduce into stage production the qualities of simplicity, sincerity, and expressiveness which were the keynote of the group, and he founded the theatre of 'Le Vieux Colombier.'

All this meant for Gide much more than mere activity— it was action in the best sense of the word. Now he was creating—and his creation was genuine and worth while. The doubts and inner conflicts he had felt so acutely in the preceding years lost their tormenting aspect. A dialogue was still taking place in his conscience; it was impossible for him to adopt one point of view to the exclusion of its opposite. He would waver alternately from one to the other; but this he did now almost with tranquillity. He was thoroughly convinced that he had the right to enjoy life in his own way. In this spirit he wrote the daring *Corydon*; but fearing a scandal, had it published anonymously in Belgium (Bruges, 1911). He allowed only a few copies to be printed and those for private circulation only. At the same time his religious preoccupations were finding an outlet in a controversy with Paul Claudel. Claudel was trying to convert Gide to Catholicism. In this he was entirely unsuccessful, however. Yet the attention of Gide had been powerfully drawn to some aspects of the Roman Catholic faith; and shortly afterwards he directed his irony against certain Catholic circles in *Les Caves du Vatican* (1914).

Gide was now attaining a sort of dual philosophy of life. He recognized two irreducible elements, both equally precious, which he would henceforth contemplate and cherish separately and in turn, since they could not possibly be reconciled—namely, earthly reality and spiritual aspiration. Yet it must be said that during this period Gide turned more often, and more willingly it would seem to the earthly than to the heavenly side.

. . . .

The Great War broke out. Like all his fellow-country-
men, Gide was deeply stirred by this upheaval. *La Nouvelle Revue Française* ceased publication for the time being. Gide's friends went to the trenches. He himself worked
for a year and a half in a 'Foyer' for French and Belgian
refugees, and witnessed suffering and misery a plenty.
All over the country there was a spirit of exaltation and
sacrifice. Gide's friend, Rivière, passed over into the Catholic fold; as also did Henri Ghéon. They wrote to him about
their conversion, urging him to follow their example.

For Gide, the great spiritual crisis had come. He turned
back to religion. Satan, he thought, was responsible for his
errors of the last few years. Up to now he had been convinced that there was opposition between Life and God—
and he had been deliberately neglecting God. Now he
came to the conclusion that there was no such opposition.
True religion—that is to say, Gide's religion—contained
no fundamental hostility towards the various claims of
the body. It was possible at the same time to worship God
and to enjoy life to the full. Gide's former dualism resolved itself into a mystic unity of love both for the Creator and for His creation. While for him the two remained
distinct, there was, he now felt, no real conflict between
them. Not only has man an absolute right to live his own
bodily life; but he may do so, in whatever way he chooses,
and yet be perfectly acceptable in the eyes of God. In this
frame of mind Gide brought out simultaneously a little
book of exalted religious mysticism, *Numquid et tu?* and
an amazing confession and vindication of his most private
experiences before his marriage, *Si le Grain ne meurt*,
printed in Belgium in a very limited edition. Shortly afterwards but still in the same spirit, he produced *La Symphonie Pastorale* (1919). The war had given Gide both a
creed and a balanced perspective.

In the years immediately following the war Gide felt a surge of vitality such as he had perhaps never before experienced. He was now sure that his life in its entirety was justifiable and, according to his view, in the highest sense, moral. There was no longer any problem for him to solve, nor any embarrassment whatever. He mixed freely with the young literary iconoclasts of the day, the 'Dadaïsts,' encouraging them in their efforts after emancipation. He started writing what he hoped would be his masterpiece, a compendium of his views on the world: *Les Faux-Monnayeurs*. The *Nouvelle Revue Française* which had resumed publication, was enjoying unprecedented success. Having the collaboration of Marcel Proust, Paul Morand, Jean Giraudoux, and Paul Valéry, Gide seemed to have organized a literary 'brain trust.'

The inevitable reaction followed. Some people were jealous of his sudden and remarkable success—others were sincerely anxious concerning the nature of his influence on the younger generation. Even though the public at large did not know the truth about Gide's private life, some unpleasant rumours were filtering through into literary circles. The attack came from two sides. The Rabelaisian Henri Béraud openly accused him in 1923 of having achieved his success through political influence—Jean Giraudoux, then an official in the Ministry of 'Affaires Etrangères,' being directly implicated in the matter. Shortly afterwards in 1924 the Roman Catholic Henri Massis thundered an indignant protestation against Gide, that perfidious moral corruptor of youth. Gide replied by throwing on the market thousands of copies of *Corydon*, (1924), *Si le Grain ne meurt*, (1926) and *Numquid et tu?* (1926).

This manœuvre was considered more than a scandal; and it was greeted with an ominous silence. Gide was almost

completely deserted. The *Nouvelle Revue Française* as a
going concern did not suffer much, it is true, but after the
abnormal revelations of *Corydon* and *Si le Grain ne meurt*
André Gide was shunned, even by former friends, as
being dangerously compromising. No voice was raised in
his defence. Gide did not seem to regret what he had done,
but he was filled with bitter disgust. He sold part of his
library—especially the books sent him by former admirers—as a sort of symbolic gesture, and set off for the
Congo in Central Africa.

Meanwhile in his absence an amazing reversal of opinion was taking place. The books of Proust, then in the
course of publication, were gradually educating the public
to look with different eyes on certain sexual subjects which
up to then had been strictly taboo. The founder of the
Freudian school of psychology was working in the same
direction. Many people, too, though not taking personally
the same stand as Gide, could not help admiring the heroic
sincerity which had made him dare to affront and challenge public opinion. Gradually public opinion veered
round again, and Gide found himself once more accepted
and praised.

In the interval, however, Gide himself had undergone a
marked change. In the course of his long trip in Equatorial
Africa, he had witnessed only too often the harsh and
cruel treatment inflicted upon the natives by officials of
the colonial administration and by the agents of the great
rubber companies. There he was practically powerless to
interfere, but he returned to Paris filled with indignation.
He was firmly convinced that there was something wrong
in a world which tolerated such abuses towards fellow human beings and was determined to do all in his power to
put an end to these evils. In his *Voyage au Congo* (1927)
he denounced scathingly the appalling abuses he had seen,

audaciously printing the names of the responsible persons, together with a detailed account of the incriminating facts. A public scandal followed. The Chamber of Deputies conducted an investigation of the charges, but little if anything came from it. Gide found all his sincere and generous efforts of reform very cleverly and effectively blocked in an unobtrusive way by the capitalistic companies he had attacked. So he was led to consider this question—which at first had had for him a purely humanitarian interest—from a political and social angle. The whole system that made such inhuman outrages irremediable now seemed to him more than ever fundamentally wrong.

At the same time Gide became further aware that he had lost contact with his countrymen. The public now accepted his peculiarities as a matter of course. He was universally recognized as a great writer and an artist, but, of his old personal influence over young men, scarcely a trace was left. Though he had definitely established his own moral balance, Gide suffered in remaining thus ineffectual or negligible.

In 1932 he officially informed the world that he had become a Communist. This raised a fresh scandal! At the basis of his conversion to the Soviet creed there undoubtedly lies the sincere belief that a different social organization would bring better material conditions to the working classes; but there are also moral and psychological reasons for his change of principles. André Gide made his motives quite clear at the 'Congrès international des écrivains,' held in Paris in 1935. Since his open repudiation of the accepted rules of public morality it has been impossible for Gide, a *bourgeois* by extraction and tradition, to maintain any real communion of spirit with his own social class. On the other hand, in the France of today, to establish a close contact with the people, lacking as they are in intellectual and artistic refinement, is also an utter impossibility for a man of Gide's subtle and delicate culture. In his isolation, Gide turned his eyes towards the future; he began to hope that eventually Sovietism will give the masses genuine culture and intellectual freedom. Then, he thinks, communion between the people and an artist like himself will become a reality.

A trip, however, that Gide undertook in 1935-36 to the U.S.S.R. failed to fulfil his almost boundless expectations. In that respect, indeed, he had imagined that Russia was 'a land where Utopia was about to become a reality.' [32] He came back to France still a Communist, yet obviously disappointed. What does this disappointment mean if not that Gide, once more, after observing one aspect of things has turned to look at the other side of the picture, and considering alternately the merits and the drawbacks of the system, in his utmost sincerity, wavers, hesitates, and feels at a loss how to come to a decision?

2. Outlook Upon Life

In the course of Gide's moral evolution, the love of life and the respect for Christian ideals have sometimes been the cause of bitter conflict, but finally they have been united in a subtle and complex harmony. It is easy to trace throughout his works a similar duality of divergent or convergent aspirations.

In Gide's passionate love of life there is something fundamental and even primitive. It expresses itself spontaneously in a feeling of inexhaustible and irrepressible joy. 'La joie en moi l'emporte toujours,' says Gide.[33] This joy does not necessarily accompany a particularly pleasant

32. A.Gide, *Retour de l'U.R.S.S.*, Nouvelle Revue Française, Paris, 1936, Avant-Propos, p.15.
33. *Si le Grain ne meurt*, Part I, Chap.VIII, p.257.

incident. It springs simply from the vital contact with reality, and is in all probability the pure expression of the great vitality of the man himself. As such it does not call for explanation, but is none the less an essential factor in his way of living. If he is cast down by trials and tribulations, it is never for any length of time. His natural resilience causes him to react almost at once, though rarely with violence; and in most cases he shows a subtle tenacity in the face of misfortune. He first reconnoitres the difficulty and then attacks it; he will perhaps retreat for a while, in order to gather his forces, but will then return again and again to the attack, until the obstacle is finally overcome.

This obstinacy of Gide's implies an unbounded confidence in himself. Although he passed through periods of depression he was always at heart a decided optimist. He is firmly persuaded that what happens to him—to all of us—is invariably for the best. Certain aspects of things may not please us, but that is because we do not look at them in the proper spirit; in the long run they usually prove to be what is good for us. 'In the worst adversity, I instinctively look for anything that might afford me amusement or instruction. I even push the *amor fati* so far that I feel loath to consider that perhaps some other event, some other issue might have been preferable. Not only do I like things as they are, but I hold that they are for the best.' [34] At the age of fifty, he is of the same opinion. 'So eager is my joy, so strong in me is the assurance that the event which at first appears most unfortunate is, on reflection, the one which may best instruct us, that there is some profit to be gained in the worst experience . . . that if we do not recognize happiness more often, it is because it comes to us with another face than

34. *Si le Grain ne meurt*, Part i, Chap.x, pp.315–316.

that which we were expecting.' [35] This active acceptance of life in its completeness is not at all in keeping with the Christian ideal of resignation to the will of God and of trust in His providence. Gide's complete acquiescence in life as it is arises from the fact that he feels intensely that life is good and he loves it as a pagan would.

Yet no man was ever more deeply imbued with Christianity than Gide. He believes implicitly in God—not an abstract, philosophical God, but the definite God of the Bible; and he has never ceased at any moment or under any circumstances during his whole life to believe. Every one of his books implies belief in God. In his works he does not discuss the existence of God, because for him there can be no question about it. The great problem is how to approach God, to reach Him, to enter into communion with Him. In that respect Gide's attitude is full of complexities. He has a deep-seated reverence for religion; it is for him a permanent source of inspiration. When he was seventeen he had the unforgettable experience of sublime spiritual rapture and then knew perfect joy. Even after the climax of his exaltation had passed, something of it remained with him; he knew what heights religious fervour could attain. At the same time, however, he harboured a very definite resentment against his early religious training. The religious austerity of his family had all but crushed him during his childhood. Later his own religious scruples had totally warped his early experiences during adolescence. He had suffered tortures of moral anguish for the sake of religious principles—or religious people. Even after he cast off all the shackles, a sort of vague anxiety remained with him. The pains he had endured were not to be forgotten—they might even return. His own sincere belief in God was an ever-present threat

35. *Si le Grain ne meurt*, Part II, Chap.I, p.346.

to his peace of mind. Thus his religious feelings were a strange mixture of absolute faith and profound veneration on the one hand, combined with what amounted to almost hatred and concealed fear on the other.

It was only by means of a thoroughly personal conception of religious life that Gide could reconcile these apparently antagonistic elements within himself. This was possible because he was a Protestant. The fact that he was a Protestant explains to a large extent his whole attitude towards life and religion. Whether as the result of heredity or of education Gide was endowed to the full with the Protestant spirit of independent, personal thought in religious matters. He always considered that it was his right and also his duty to go freely in search of the truth, even to combine conceptions that were seemingly antagonistic in order to discover a doctrine sincerely and profoundly satisfying to himself. Moreover, he had an instinctive disinclination to be one of the herd. He wanted to be entirely himself and definitely distinct from others. Gide's Protestantism is psychologically at the root of his individualism.

This Protestant conception of the religious life in Gide's case has been at the same time both a source of weakness and of strength. It gave his feeling of religion a remarkable pliancy and endurance. Had it been bound to more rigid tenets, his faith might have been broken and perhaps destroyed comparatively early. As it was, it could adapt itself to the evolution of his personality and keep pace with all the transformations which he underwent in the course of his life. Many people try to find in religion, or in abstract principles, as the case may be, a sure and permanent foothold in the midst of the universal flux; and religion, with its associated ideas, is often the only continuous basis of a man's existence. Gide, always faithful to the original concept of Protestantism, refuses to see in religion anything rigid, definite, and unchanging. So his personality, without prop or support of any kind, is apt to bend and sway in every direction.

Thus Gide's conflict with his mother appears in a somewhat new and different light. It must be remembered that Madame Gide, though herself a Protestant, came of a family which was originally Catholic. She seems to have retained the Catholic ideal of one 'Truth' and one only, which since it is 'the Truth' cannot be subject to interpretation and must not be critically examined. Gide's revolt against religion, as represented to him by his mother, was much less a revolt against religion itself than against a special form of it, which it was not in Gide's nature to accept. Gide once declared, 'I am neither a Protestant nor a Catholic; I am a Christian, that is all.' [36] But in truth the spirit of Protestantism guided him in all his personal interpretations of the Word of God.

However personal and adaptable Gide's interpretation of the teachings of religion might be, one point could not escape his earnest examination. The abnormal tendencies, which were his, are in several passages of the Scriptures the object of most emphatic condemnation. Morals and public opinion are alike unanimous on that point. It was difficult to discover an explanation that would condone or absolve this failing.

Now these failings were an integral part of his personality. They were of his very being, his own world. He was no more able to rid himself of them than to change the constitution of his body. So the conflict between his physical desires and his religious ideal became really tragic for him; and apparently there was no possible solution to the prob-

36. A.Gide, *Numquid et tu?*, Œuvres Complètes, Vol.x, Nouvelle Revue Française, Paris, 1936, 'Avant-Propos de l'Edition de 1926,' p.344.

lem. The antagonism between the two opposite sides of
his nature became a sort of obsession with him until his
keen and reflective mind, brooding over its own difficulties, discovered that his was only a particular case of the
general antagonism that exists between flesh and spirit,
body and soul, reality and idealism. So Gide was led to
face a problem of much broader, almost universal bearing—a problem which is not confined to morals, but extends into the field of æsthetics and even of metaphysics—
a problem which must confront every man without exception at some time of his life.

Many men live happily without trying to find an original solution to the enigma; they merely follow their
impulses without troubling themselves about the eventual
contradictions which their behaviour implies. Gide could
find no comfort in this form of self-deception or hypocrisy.
He was incapable of lying to himself. His actions and his
ideas had to be in agreement. 'It was not acceptable to me
to live without principles and the claims of my body could
not dispense with the approval of my mind.' [37]

In his particular case two solutions appeared to him to
be possible. After his African experience he simply took
up his stand *against* the moral rules which until then he
had accepted as his own. It was an implicit acknowledgement of their existence. One does not fight something
which does not exist. At that stage, Gide identified himself
more or less with his 'Immoraliste': 'Mon seul effort,
effort constant alors, était donc de systématiquement
honnir ou supprimer tout ce que je ne croyais devoir qu'à
mon instruction passée et à ma première morale.' [38] He
could break the moral rules, but he could not possibly

37. *Si le Grain ne meurt*, Part ɪɪ, Chap.ɪ, p.347.
38. A.Gide, *L'Immoraliste*, Œuvres Complètes, Vol.ɪv, Nouvelle Revue Française, Paris, 1933, Part ɪ, Chap.vɪ, p.56.

ignore them; and in breaking them he experienced the malicious enjoyment of one who strikes a blow at an enemy.

That solution, of course, was not a satisfactory one, and could hardly be permanent. Very soon Gide came to question whether the relations between the Divine Will and human life were in truth what his education and his environment had taught him to believe. Was the puritan doctrine an adequate expression of true morality? Had God really intended man to lead such an austere and drab existence as the sectarians preached? So much in Gide's nature protested against the puritan point of view that he could not help doubting; but to decide definitely against it was by no means easy.

In fact a tremendous task was now facing him. In order to make up his mind in all sincerity, he would not only have to meditate but also actually to explore and to test in detail all his views concerning man and life—man's place in the scheme of things—his relations with his environment—the moral rules, their value and bearing. Gide never would accept a ready-made opinion on any of these points; rather would he investigate, experiment, and decide for himself and by himself. Only after drawing a personal conclusion on each and all of the various aspects of man's life and ideals, could he have a genuine and individual outlook on the world as a whole, and hence on the part man is supposed to play in it. The moral programme which Gide set for himself was no less than a complete and exhaustive exploration of life, always keeping his attention centred on two main points: the earthly reality of our environment and the moral imperativeness of our ideal. If he could succeed in establishing the relation of all facts and thoughts falling under his investigation, to these two major elements he would discover the meaning of life.

This is indeed the great point of general, human interest in Gide's endeavours. Here is a man who refused to accept the ready-made ideas which are proffered to us and even urged upon us from every side, and who decided to see for himself, think for himself, and then draw his own conclusions. After his explorations he would have a thoroughly personal conception of the world, from both the material and the spiritual standpoint.

But what is 'culture' if not a personal interpretation of our environment, and an original, coherent manner of reacting to it? The person who accepts ready-made, standard views as the guide for his own thinking and his own behaviour may be—and frequently is—an excellent citizen, but he is not necessarily a cultured man. Gide may not be a model citizen—and many people are of that opinion—but model citizen or not he had reached the highest degree of culture by thinking for himself. From a purely intellectual and cultural standpoint few modern writers are more instructive and interesting to study.

The road he took was by no means easy. To begin with, he had cast out all the superimposed ideas which had been gathering on his mind like a thick crust—the work of his mother, his teachers, friends, and acquaintances even. He was helped in ridding himself of this foreign accumulation by his natural reactions as a convalescent in Africa, while recovering from the dangerous illness which had threatened his life. For a convalescent the past is pain and suffering, the present is hope, the future is new life and joy. In his mind the past recedes into darkness, fades, and is forgotten. Of course the past is not altogether abolished. The essentials of the personality remain intact but all that had been artificially added to the original being by education or convention is often left behind, lost sometimes so irretrievably that an entirely new person completely unexpected seems to spring fresh and new from the ordeal. 'The accumulation on the mind of all acquired knowledge peels off like cosmetics on a face and in spots exposes the bare skin, the "authentic" being that was concealed underneath. . . . It was henceforth that "authentic" being whom I intended to discover . . . whom all around me, books, masters, parents, and even I myself had at first endeavoured to suppress. . . . These added layers had to be shaken off.' [39]

But even after the layers have been cast off, the task is by no means definitely completed. Under the continuous influence of one's social surroundings, they tend to form again, and to grow as life goes on, and are perhaps even more firmly fixed towards the end. The combined effect of the pressure exerted by society and of one's own indifference allows conventional ideas to settle surreptitiously like a coating, as it were, on the mind and there to become set. Constant scraping away is necessary; and it can be performed only by a constant attitude of very alert criticism. Gide's critical attitude is not merely a temporary expedient used for a definite purpose at any particular stage of his mental evolution. It is a permanent necessity and he is always on the watch in order that the mind may be kept free and not be overgrown with conventional notions. Even in his most constructive periods, Gide has at hand the ready weapon of sharp criticism to combat any threatening invasion of adventitious untested ideas. The existence of a critical tendency side by side with an affirmative disposition is perhaps the most original part of Gide's way of thinking. The cause of this apparent contradiction is his instinctive distrust of anything ready-made, and his predilection for personal discovery.

Indeed Gide sets out to rediscover on his own account

39. L'Immoraliste, Part I, Chap.6, p.55.

all the elements of our culture. His work appears as a gigantic piece of experimentation. He must taste of life in all its various aspects, ideal and material, high and low, with a completely unprejudiced mind or, as he said himself, as 'un esprit non prévenu.' [40] Personal contact with all sorts of conflicting realities is indispensable if the appreciation is to be sincere. The progress is very slow; it took Gide twenty years to come to a conclusion. And the pace was not by any means uniform. There were alternating periods of advance and regression. After taking for a while a direct and firm hold on some part of reality, he would draw back into a more abstract mood in order to be at some distance and so better able to judge the whole. After considering some matter well from one angle, he would turn to observe it from the opposite point of view. These apparently disconcerting jumps from one point of view to another are thoroughly characteristic of the Gidian method. They may be psychologically connected with the man's restlessness. They have been mentioned often by his critics as evidence of inconsistency. In fact this perpetual balancing is an absolute necessity for his purpose, which is to grasp and to understand the whole of every fact or question. After studying one side he realizes that there is another side also, which looks contradictory but is really one complementary. The desire to see only one side of things may give one the reputation of being 'logical' and 'good'; but for the man who wants to know things from all sides, it is an unbearable limitation, since it prevents the development of his natural personality into a complete whole.

The full development of personality is the ultimate step in the evolution of the Gidian programme. The personality which makes contact with all aspects of reality successively, has the best chance of realizing all its own po-

40. A.Gide, *Un Esprit non prévenu*, Ed. du Sagittaire, Paris, 1929.

tentialities. In fact when all these potentialities have been developed to their utmost, we know all that we can possibly know of reality. So the problem of knowing the world is practically identified with the problem of developing one's personality. According to Gide, the great duty and the unimpeachable right of every individual is *to be himself*. Yet the difficulty of this is almost insuperable because education, family, society, all conspire to mould a man to a conventional pattern. But if a man accepts this pattern unquestioningly, he betrays the will of the Creator whose plan it was that he should play in this world a certain definite and original part—and not another. Gide, once called upon to give the 'formula of his life' answered: 'Nous devons tous représenter'—which he explains in the following way: 'I persuaded myself that every being, or at least every one of the elect, had a part to play on earth, which was definitely his own and resembled no other, so that every effort to submit to a common rule became in my eyes an act of treason, yes, treason, which I compared to the great sin against the Holy Ghost "that shall not be forgiven." ' [41] Thus Gide's theories imply an unbounded and almost mystic individualism. It is to be noted, however, that this individualism is not a hot-house product requiring protection and selfish isolation from contemptible surroundings. It is an individualism which involves complete communion with the world at large, knowledge and even experience of all its varied aspects; because it is only when these aspects and their mutual relations are intimately understood that the proper place of the individual in the general plan can be ascertained and satisfactorily filled.

This triple programme which Gide set himself—systematic criticism and elimination of ready-made conventional

41. *Si le Grain ne meurt*, Part I, Chap.x, pp.332–333.

ideas, thorough and impartial examination of each aspect of reality, self-realization implying complete assimilation of all experiences humanly possible in this world—this trilogy accounts for the classification of Gide's writings into three divisions, which Gide himself calls *'sotie,' 'récit,' 'roman.'*

A *sotie*, properly speaking, was a sort of satirical play very popular in France in the Middle Ages. The players (called the *Sots*), under a more or less grotesque disguise, would ridicule the solemn and venerable pillars of society of the day: the bishop, the judge, the king, and so on. The satire was generally so gross and exaggerated that it was possible to consider the whole piece merely as a grotesque farce, thus saving the feelings of the victims. Gide applies the word *sotie* to such books as *Paludes, Le Prométhée mal enchaîné, Les Caves du Vatican*, in which he gives free play to his devastating criticism. His attacks are not sarcastic in the style of Voltaire; he follows rather the lines of the medieval plays, putting the objects of his derision on the plane of the ludicrous and absurd. There is nothing intrinsically comic in them, but they are made to appear so utterly stupid and impossible that they almost cease to be real. Gide achieved his aim by a strange and deliberate mixture of definite realism and extravagant fancy. The mixture is so well blended that after a while the reader wonders what is true and what imaginary, and finds himself no longer able to take seriously that part of reality which has been presented to him.

A *récit*, or tale, is the name Gide gives to the account of an actual experience—or life seen from a definite angle. It generally involves two main characters—the protagonist and the necessary partner, usually of the other sex—along with a number of secondary, unimportant figures. It represents reality as perceived by a certain type of person and often takes the form of a confession. Sometimes the partner, in compliance with Gide's instinctive desire to examine the other side of things, gives the counterpart of the main point of view in an abbreviated form. *L'Immoraliste*, *La Porte Etroite*, *Isabelle*, *La Symphonie Pastorale*, *L'Ecole des Femmes*, are all examples of that typically Gidian representation of one side or another of a complex reality.

When the complex reality can be grasped as a whole, simultaneously, and taken from every side, then, and then only, thinks Gide, is the writer mature enough to write a novel. To Gide the *roman* is the highest possible achievement of literary art. In attempting it the artist signifies that he thinks himself capable of perceiving not only one aspect of reality, but reality in all its complexity,—of accounting for a multiplicity of characters and their mutual, moral relationships. It shows each individual in relation to all the others, and *vice versa*. Gide has only attempted one such ambitious creation: *Les Faux-Monnayeurs*.

Generally speaking, these three types of works correspond to the successive stages of Gide's mental evolution,—the critical *soties*, having been written mostly at the beginning, the exploratory *récits* in the middle, and the constructive *roman* towards the end of his life experience. Nevertheless they do not all come in that regular order. It is typical of Gide that he has never continuously followed a straight and unchangeable line. He likes, after an advance, to retrace his steps and make an almost completely fresh start; so that in the chronological order of composition and publication *soties*, *récits*, and *roman* are mingled indiscriminately. As a result, some of these works do not correspond entirely to the type to which they are supposed to belong. For instance, the *Caves du Vatican* is essentially a *sotie*, but the book was written rather late in Gide's career, at a time when a definite conception of the world in general was beginning to take shape in the writer's mind, so that in its construction this *sotie* is almost like a *roman*. *La Porte Etroite* was begun in the form of a *sotie*, a satire on puritanism, but by and by Gide became so impressed by the serious aspect of the subject that the book finally became a *récit*. *Isabelle* is a *récit*, but it was written fairly early, when Gide was launching an attack on a certain conception of literary art which was then the fashion. He adopted the plan of constructing his tale on the model of the books he wanted to criticize and then after holding the reader in suspense, disappointed him purposely in order to expose the emptiness of the whole conception—which is a characteristic process in his *soties*.

The trend of Gide's evolution may best be understood by following the main periods of his life. He began his career as a writer with the publication of a set of Symbolist books. This was at a time when he was still under the influence of his puritan education and shrank in disgust from the lusts of the flesh and from all worldly realities— for which nevertheless he was craving unconsciously. He was then endeavouring to find in pure idealism a satisfaction that ever eluded him. The *Cahiers d'André Walter* shows Gide under the name of André Walter soaring upwards after perfection, but secretly longing for voluptuous pleasures and finally losing his beloved Emmanuèle. Strangely enough, the Emmanuèle of the book refuses to marry André Walter just as a little later the real Emmanuèle was actually to refuse to marry André Gide. Was it premonition? Death comes to André Walter when he is on the verge of insanity, bringing the book to an end, but not to a satisfactory conclusion: no satisfactory conclusion, no real solution of his difficulties was possible—revolt was the only course open to one facing such a dilemma.

Gide's own revolt took place at the time of his first two trips to Africa. *Paludes*, a *sotie*, bears witness to the efforts he made to extricate himself from the morass of orthodox morality and mediocrity. So eager is he to escape from the general stagnation that he is ready to overthrow and destroy everything that stands in his way. But under the passion of his satire is bubbling the joy of a new discovery—the discovery of the sheer delight of living. This exultation fills *Les Nourritures Terrestres*. Here in a kind of lyrical outburst Gide celebrates the pleasures of the senses, their luscious and intoxicating voluptuousness. He feeds on them greedily. For the taste of the average reader they may seem perhaps too rich, like the sweetmeats sold at native stalls in Algeria, where the book was conceived.

With Gide's marriage there began a long period of crisis which was to continue until the Great War. For nearly twenty years Gide explored reality, scanning first one and then the other side of every question. The two mutually antagonistic *récits*, *L'Immoraliste* and *La Porte Etroite*, are the most outstanding landmarks of these audacious investigations. They represent the positive aspects of his search for truth; but the two *soties*, *Le Promethée mal enchaîné* and *Les Caves du Vatican* were written at the same time and show that his critical mind was still on the alert. *Promethée*, written shortly after his marriage, is far from comic; it is almost tragic. Prometheus, the Titan of the Greek legend, has landed somehow in modern Paris. He goes to a café, but his eagle follows him. Prometheus, who has grown to like the bird, starts to feed it with the liver which is its due—his own liver, that is to say. Imagine the commotion on the *Grands Boulevards*! But the eagle here stands for remorse of conscience gnawing at a man's vitals. Prometheus finally kills the bird, and turns it over to a cook to be served at a dinner with his friends. The dinner goes off well and no one feels the worse for it. In much the same way Gide was trying to dispose of his own *conventional* conscience. He could not make a 'dinner' of it, so he tried to laugh it away.

In *L'Immoraliste* Gide relates with almost embarrassing definiteness his experiences as a newly-wed and as a convalescent. An intense love of life is throbbing all through this work, less sensually but more convincingly and more profoundly than in the *Nourritures*. Gide depicts, with marvellous minuteness as well as subtlety the feelings of the young man, Michel, who, stricken with consumption, recovers almost by a miracle. Convalescing he gradually becomes aware of the powers that have lain dormant and inert within him; he learns with increasing wonder and pleasure to bring these into play; and he worships all the more passionately this gorgeous gift of life which he had nearly lost without ever having experienced it fully. Michel, however, is not alone. His young wife, Marceline, who has nursed him back to health, cannot share completely his impressions and experiences. She is, as it were, an unassimilable element that cannot be incorporated into the new personality that Michel is developing. She feels this and suffers in consequence. As in his own way he loves her, he suffers also; a subdued strain of sorrow accompanies, as on muted strings, the glorious lyric of his resurrection. This gives to the book a tender and human appeal, yet does not alter its meaning; and *L'Immoraliste* on the whole sings a hymn of praise to life and joy.

La Porte Etroite considers the opposite view of things. Here we find ourselves among stern puritans and idealists. Jérôme is in love with his cousin, Alissa. They are both very young and their affection has a mystic quality of

158 ANDRÉ GIDE

ideal purity. Juliette, Alissa's younger sister, also falls in love with Jérôme, and Alissa in a spirit of pure sacrifice, is ready to efface herself in order that her sister may marry the man of her choice. Juliette, however, in emulation of Alissa's self-abnegation, renounces her dream and gives her hand to an elderly suitor. Nothing now stands between Jérôme and Alissa except Alissa herself. She has been deeply stirred by the crisis; and she shrinks back from Jérôme's singularly pure advances. She appears cold and unromantic. She seems indeed to have set herself to destroy the ideal, poetical vision he had conceived of her. Jérôme does not wish to importune her. He goes off to Greece to study archæology, and when he returns after three years, Alissa is scarcely recognizable—she is dying. When Jérôme again proposes marriage, she refuses—in the sure hope that life after death for her in her purity would be the beginning of true happiness. After her death her diary reveals her secret. She was in love, passionately in love, with Jérôme; but her religion had persuaded her that merit is to be acquired by resisting one's spontaneous impulses and desires. Anxious to attain perfection and saintliness, she had crushed her own inclinations for love and life—instead she had chosen purity and death. In this she was not thinking of herself alone. She was seeking salvation also for the man she loved. So she had renounced all hope of happiness in this world mainly for his sake—in order that he might be kept free from secular attachments, and that he might progress towards that 'porte étroite,' through which, as the Scriptures tell us, two cannot pass at the same time.

The heroic sacrifice of Alissa is represented not as the outcome of cold and abstract theories, but as the vibrant and desperate endeavour of a soul thirsting after righteousness. Underneath the restrained and dispassionate surface of the book there is a deep quivering emotion impelling the reader, however foreign to him that type of emotion may be, more than once to feel profoundly touched. This is probably because Gide here evokes the most poignant of his own experiences. Alissa is a combination of Emmanuèle Rondeaux and of Anna Shackleton.[42] Jérôme has many of the features of Gide himself at the time of his engagement, a similarity which explains the otherwise puzzling attitude of Jérôme, when he remains so unnaturally calm and unmoved in the presence of a woman who loves him deeply and sincerely. This is only a suggestion, however, as the whole work breathes such a fine spirituality untainted by bigotry, such an elevated dignity without hardness, that it is probably to be reckoned as Gide's masterpiece.

André Gide nevertheless seems to have entertained a personal preference for *Les Caves du Vatican* above all his other works.[43] The book is founded on an almost unbelievable rumour which actually spread through France at the close of the nineteenth century. For many years the Roman Catholic Church had shown little sympathy towards certain modern political institutions and especially towards the republican régime in France. When the liberal Pope, Leo XIII, advised a reconciliation of the Catholics with the government, many people were dumbfounded. Subsequently it was rumoured that the real Pope had been kidnapped by Freemasons and was being held prisoner in some underground prison connected with the Vatican; further, that the man who now sat on the throne of Saint Peter and issued such disconcerting mandates was nothing but an impostor. Unscrupulous persons were not

---

42. *Si le Grain ne meurt*, Part I, Chap.IX, p.278.
43. Léon Pierre-Quint, *André Gide*, Delamain et Boutelleau, Paris, 1933, Part I, Chap.IV, p.87.

wanting who took advantage of the credulous. Devout and unsuspecting folk were approached, in all secrecy, and persuaded to contribute their mite to start a crusade to deliver the true Pope.

In Gide's book, among the innocent victims of this scheme, was the Comtesse Guy de Saint-Prix. Asked to keep the plan secret she could not refrain from blurting it out to her sister-in-law, who, in turn, revealed it to her husband, the shallow and harmless Amédée Fleurissoire, a dealer in religious images of papier mâché. Amédée decided to go to Rome and investigate the matter for himself. We are told how on reaching Rome he was decoyed into an only too hospitable house. We learn what happened to him there. We see him fall in the clutches of Protos, one of the confederates in the scheme. On Protos's suggestion, Amédée Fleurissoire decided to take the night train to Naples. As it happened, in the same compartment travelled Lafcadio Wluiki.

This Lafcadio was born in Bucharest. He knew nothing of his father. His mother, a courtesan, had brought him up indulging him in all forms of luxury, thanks to the generosity of his various 'uncles,' usually members of the diplomatic corps. Sent away to school he managed to escape from its uncongenial discipline; and his mother having died, he went off to Paris and for a while lived there on his wits. This was a matter of no great difficulty as he was more than ordinarily good-looking; while at the same time he was clever and crafty, agile and strong, endowed with an extremely attractive personality. Moreover, he was totally lacking in morals.

Quite unexpectedly Lafcadio learns that he is the natural son of a certain Comte Juste-Agénor de Baraglioul, who dying bequeathes him a fortune. What is Lafcadio going to do with it? He first establishes contact with his

half-brother, Comte Julius de Baraglioul (who happens
also to be the brother of the Comtesse de Saint-Prix) and
further with the count's daughter, Geneviève, in whose
eyes, after rescuing two children from a fire in unusually
melodramatic circumstances, he appears as a romantic
hero. Then he proceeds to Italy, vaguely intending to
push his adventures into Java. As fate would have it, on
the journey between Rome and Naples, he encounters
Amédée Fleurissoire in the railway compartment. For no
reason at all, Lafcadio throws the harmless little fellow out
of the speeding train. Amédée is killed outright. Lafcadio
has meanwhile lost his hat in the scuffle. Protos, who is
on the same train, finds it and cuts out the compromising
trade-mark. He prepares to blackmail Lafcadio, but before he can put his intentions into effect he is seized by the
police, in mistake, for the murderer. Lafcadio contemplates
surrendering himself to justice; but Geneviève, throwing
herself at him, becomes his mistress, after which he does
not feel so eager to give himself up. . . .

The character of Lafcadio aroused extraordinary enthusiasm among the young men of the post-war period. Gide
portrays him as being full of abounding health and vitality,
of love of life for its own sake, of contempt for the shackles
of convention, of desire to be heroic or else very bad, but
at all events to do something exciting; in fact, he is the
very embodiment of a schoolboy on a holiday. All this
appealed strongly to a youth that had been thwarted by
years of repression and suffering. At the same time Lafcadio manifests absolute scepticism towards all laws and
creeds, and a readiness to experiment freely with any new
and interesting sensation. Both of these traits coincided
with the characteristics of the Western world which Gide
conveys to the reader in this book: a world that was undergoing a complete change, whose accepted rules had lost

their value, and from which something new must come into being though its shape had yet to be defined. These various trends of ideas—full appreciation of life, contempt for the conventions of a society which has outlived its time, free search for novelty—are typical of Gide at this period of his life. They also show clearly the direction in which he was moving.

The moral crisis precipitated in Gide by the war expressed itself essentially in two books—*Numquid et tu?* in which he explained his new religious mysticism, and *Si le Grain ne meurt*, which is the most daring confession French literature has seen since J.-J.Rousseau. About the same time appeared *La Symphonie Pastorale*, containing clear forecast of his ultimate view of life.

This little tale is presented in the form of a diary, kept by a certain Swiss Protestant clergyman. This pastor in the course of his visits, discovers in the remotest corner of his mountainous parish a secluded cottage in which a very old woman has just passed away leaving her niece of about fifteen, alone in the world. The girl has been blind from birth; and since the old aunt who reared her was deaf, she had never learned to speak. Her mind was a complete blank, and her body, though shapely enough, was covered with vermin and dirt. The pure-hearted and charitable pastor takes her to his home. Notwithstanding the grumblings of his nagging but clear-sighted wife, he decides to keep her in the hope of awakening her mind and soul. With infinite patience and ingenuity—using, for instance, the 'Pastoral Symphony' of Beethoven as an initiation to Nature and beauty—and carefully preserving her absolutely pure soul from all knowledge of evil, he eventually succeeds in his efforts. The young Gertrude grows into a most attractive and intelligent girl. The pastor's son, Jacques, is well aware of her charms, and frankly though timidly tells her of his admiration. But the young woman loves only the man who has made her what she is—the pastor—and she says so. Why should she not? She knows no evil. Her affection is pure and innocent and the candid pastor has no difficulty in persuading himself that *his* affection for *her* is no less innocent and pure. Then it is discovered that the girl can acquire the use of her eyes if she submits to an operation. The operation is successful and at last she is able to see. Then comes the catastrophe. She now realizes how sinful it was to centre her affection on a married man and at the same time discovers that Jacques, whose young face was the one she had really imagined and worshipped when thinking of the pastor, is the man whom she actually loves. But it is too late. Jacques, rebuked by his father, has turned Catholic; he is taking holy orders, and embracing perpetual celibacy. Gertrude, completely distracted, throws herself into an icy river and dies soon afterwards.

The idea underlying this tale is that enlightenment, knowledge, and intellectual understanding are the source of all unhappiness. Just as Adam and Eve before tasting of the fruit of knowledge were in a state of perfect innocence and bliss, so Gertrude before she gained her sight could perceive no evil in anything and was absolutely pure and happy. She was almost incapable of committing sin. As the Gospel says, 'If ye were blind ye should have no sin.' [44] Sin is possible only when man can see clearly and reason out the bearing of his behaviour, when he can conceive a law, set it down—and break it. The feeling of guilt—nay, guilt itself—arises from a conscious infringement of certain more or less conventional rules laid down by man in accordance with his conception of right and wrong. As Gertrude herself said, when at last she could

44. St. John, 9.41.

see: 'What I saw first of all was our error, our sin . . . I
remember a verse from St. Paul which I repeated to myself during a whole day, "For I was alive without the law
once; but when the commandment came, sin revived and
I died." ' [45] Light, knowledge, and law mean inevitably
sin, unhappiness, and death.

Happiness and innocence could be ours if it were possible
for us to return to the soul's primitive virginity. It was in
that blessed state that Gertrude had been placed by a combination of extraordinary circumstances. By a miracle of
candid simplicity the pastor also had for a while been rendered absolutely 'blind' and innocently happy. Under such
conditions man may be truly himself without concern as to
what should or should not be. His personality freely ex-
pands and blossoms, and joy pure and unadulterated is his.

The conflict between the moral and the physical world,
the spirit and the flesh, then simply ceases to exist. They
meet and blend harmoniously without any clash. In various phases of their mutual interraction they resemble the
different instruments of a perfectly balanced orchestra;—
each separately has a value of its own; collectively, they
melt together into a supreme and enchanting harmony.
For Gertrude in her innocence, for the pastor also, there
was no moral problem to be solved, no tragedy of the
ideal warring against more worldly aspirations and desires. That is why the pastor could so well take the Sixth
Symphony of Beethoven as an illustration of the earthly
reality as it is perceived by a pure and candid soul like that
of the sightless and innocent Gertrude.

After the views set forth in *L'Immoraliste*, and the very
antithesis of these arguments presented in *La Porte Etroite*,

45. A.Gide, *La Symphonie Pastorale*, Œuvres Complètes, Vol.IX, Nouvelle Re-
    vue Française, Paris, 1935. IIe Cahier, 29 mai, pp.84–85. Cf. St. Paul,
    Romans, 7.9.

the *Symphonie Pastorale* is in the nature of a synthesis or
a reconciliation of the two opposing points of view. There
is indeed no fundamental antagonism between flesh and
spirit, the real and the ideal. Man will be aware of their
essential harmony if he is content with being simply and
unreservedly himself, just like a little child; for 'except
ye become as little children, ye shall not enter into the
Kingdom of Heaven.' [46] But once that genuine simplicity
is destroyed through moral 'enlightenment,' good and
evil will immediately rise up and contend against each
other, bringing only suffering and doubt in their train.

Having reached this conclusion and come into possession of a general philosophy in relation to the world at
large, Gide sought to give an objective picture of the
world, as he saw it, in the novel, *Les Faux-Monnayeurs*.
In this attempt he was not altogether successful, for the
book, though possessing great interest and originality,
did not fully justify the hopes of its author. Also it is somewhat disappointing to the reader.

In this novel the centre of the stage is held by a group
of Parisian schoolboys, their parents, relatives, friends, and
confederates. The episode from which the book derives its
title is the association of some of these boys with a gang
of crooks who make use of them in order to put counterfeit
money into circulation. This is, however, only a minor
incident in the midst of many other more or less loosely
connected happenings. The systematic lack of continuity
and the dispersion of interest was intended by Gide to
depict a feature of actual life that is generally distorted
by intellectual novel writers. Most novels trace the development of some plot from the beginning through various stages of evolution to the end. In real life, however,
we see the beginning only of some events, the intermediate

46. *La Symphonie Pastorale*, IIe Cahier, 3 mai, p.63. Cf. St. Matthew, 18.3.

part or perhaps only the end of others; seldom do we witness their developement from start to finish. All sorts of things happen round us concurrently, usually with the merest casual link between them. Gide tries to depict this manysidedness of life by presenting a number of occurrences almost simultaneously. So in *Les Faux-Monnayeurs* Bernard Profitendieu discovers by chance that he is not the son of his supposed father, and runs away from home to lead a free, adventurous life. His brother, Vincent, forsakes everything for the love of Lady Griffith, a siren, abandoning even Laura—the wife of a poor school-teacher —whom he had led astray. Count Robert is hovering with most questionable intentions round young Olivier Molinier. An old music teacher, La Pérouse, fallen on evil days and unhappy in his home life, lives only for the ideal grandson he has never seen; while little Boris, his grandson, a neurotic child, is induced by some fiendish boys of his own age at school to shoot himself in the classroom.

Some unity is given to this variety of episodes by the presence of 'Edouard,' a novelist, who is more or less connected with all these happenings, and who is engaged in writing a novel on—*Les Faux-Monnayeurs*. Edouard has very much the appearance of Gide himself; and since he puts down in his diary, which is included in the book, the progress he is making with the book itself, we see the book being written almost before our eyes as we are reading it. At the very moment we are offered a piece of fiction, we are shown how the creation was made; we are even treated to some criticisms of it, by Gide himself. This most unusual procedure is only another expression of Gide's utter sincerity; yet to the reader, it must be confessed it is somewhat disconcerting.

Gide, as he said himself, wanted to write 'un roman pur' [47] which, according to his own conception, should

47. *Journal des Faux-Monnayeurs*, 2ᵉ Cahier, 1ᵉʳ nov. 1921, pp.72–73.

depict the direct contact with every side of reality. To quote the words of Edouard in the book: 'I should like to bring everything into this novel. No cutting with the scissors to limit its substance in one place or another. For more than a year I have been working at it; everything that happens to me I pour into it . . . everything that I see, that I know, all that I learn from the lives of others and from my own.' [48] Everything that life teaches him is to be found in this book but absolutely nothing else; no descriptions, no systematic psychological studies, no lyrical outbursts, no general moral idea, no thesis, nothing by *pure* experience.

So the characters are not analysed carefully nor with any minute detail, but simply outlined like so many sketches or musical themes on which the imagination may perform endless variations. Reality is grasped not as a logical continuity but in conformity with Gide's own mental rhythm—through alternating movements of approach and recoil; again not as an uninterrupted development in time, but through concentration of attention on isolated moments, so as to extract from each its content of life and emotion. Thus Gide's own personality attains its fullest and richest expression, but the mind of the reader remains unsatisfied and perplexed.

3. *The Gidian Thought Process*

THE most interesting part of Gide's work is not the general conclusion that he reached but rather the long winding road he followed for so many years in an effort to discover and formulate his own point of view. Gide set himself the task of rediscovering for himself the world in which we live and its culture. Each one of us has to face more or less the same problems, and anyone not disposed to ac-

48. *Les Faux-Monnayeurs*, Part II, Chap.III, p.271.

cept conventional solutions, believing himself entitled to his own personal opinions, may arrive at a conclusion very different from Gide's—since every person builds upon unique original data; but Gide's attitude in his search at all events offers an example of undeniable sincerity and thoroughness.

In Gide's case the search after truth was so sincere and so thorough that it left an indelible stamp on his personality. His questing attitude became an almost permanent characteristic; even after he reached a conclusion, Gide went on investigating, as if condemned for ever to criticize and doubt. Thus one can scarcely speak of a Gidian solution of difficulties; but it may certainly be said that there is a Gidian method of approaching them.

The most momentous, decisive step in Gide's life was his throwing away, in his early twenties, all the ideas, all the intellectual conceptions which had been imposed on him by his environment. This gave his true, spontaneous self, buried beneath these intellectual conceptions and in danger of suffocation from them, freedom to exist and to expand. The process, however, involved so much moral effort that Gide was permanently affected by it. Throughout his life he retained a characteristic distrust of everything intellectual. His anti-intellectualism was at first violent and almost iconoclastic. 'Il faut, Nathanaël, que tu brûles en toi tous les livres.' 'You must, Nathanaël, burn up within yourself all books.' [49] Such is the advice given to the disciple in the *Nourritures Terrestres*. Gide pondered the matter well as time went on, but in no way retracted his opinion. We cannot, he believed, grasp the whole of reality but only catch a few scattered fragments of it. Logic essays to establish some connecting link be-

---

49. A.Gide, *Les Nourritures Terrestres*, Œuvres Complètes, Vol.ii, Nouvelle Revue Française, Paris, 1933. i, 3, p.74.

tween the fragments and to create out of them a consistent
ensemble. These fragments do not naturally fit together.
Logic, however, forces them to do so by planing off a
minute, protruding detail here, or filling up a little hollow
there, or again by entirely reshaping an unadjustable element. Life, as we perceive it, is not logical. To make it
seem so, the intellect is obliged to do violence to reality;
this is what Gide opposes with all his might. Reality is all
too precious to be placed on a Procrustean bed and cut or
stretched according to our own logical concepts. Scientists
profess to be interested only in generalities; they are eager
to discover laws which can be applied to a whole set of
natural phenomena. But in the case of an individual person, is this possible without overlooking those peculiar
elements that make the individual different from all
others—that make him absolutely and uniquely himself?
Gide refuses to concede the point. He wants to perceive
the whole of reality, or at least as much as can be perceived, unaltered by intellectual rearrangement, keeping
all its original flavour and quality intact. In fact, the more
different from all others a person appears, the more vitally
real, and therefore valuable, he seems to Gide's enquiring
mind; and Gide will preferably give his attention to those
very aspects of reality which are the most peculiar and
which fall least under the circumscribing influence of
intelligence.

This line of reasoning seems to imply a fundamental
contradiction. Gide set himself with all the strength of his
intelligence to break the power of intelligence. But is not
that very contradiction a challenge to intelligence? It is
admirably suited to Gide's avowed purpose—the overthrow of intellectualism. Contradiction thus comes to be
an integral part of his mental attitude. When Gide has
considered any one aspect of things, and made some point

definite and clear, almost at once he feels the urge to consider exactly the contrary. This tendency sometimes gives an impression of hopeless inconsistency, though actually it is only the outcome of his intense feeling for the rich complexity of the universe. He is persuaded that any one positive statement does not exhaust the total content even of a fragment of reality, and that the corresponding statement in the negative is at the same time profoundly and equally true. By positing contradictory views on a subject, Gide was better able to give a really complete account of a matter in question. From an intellectual standpoint, however, two contradictory statements equally true are an absurdity. One or the other must be rejected. Yet Gide would like to retain them both; that is perhaps why he has always refused to offer a logical solution of the problems he attacks. Nevertheless, if formal contradictions clash irreducibly in the world of intellect and logic, they *do* coexist in the realm of actuality as it is conceived by Gide, just as they coexist, and agree for instance in the world of music; and so Gide's conclusions appear not as a selection of definite elements to the exclusion of others but as an harmony in which all contradictions blend, complementing and mutually enriching each other.

Gide has shown himself to be more than simply the convinced exponent of a clever theory. He tried to carry his anti-intellectualism into the practice of life—to put it into action. Gide's essential aim is to make possible the realization and development of a man's innermost personality—if this has not been completely obliterated under the weight of ideas alien to its nature. In the ordinary course of life a man's actions are generally conditioned by many different considerations, some of them perhaps obscure, but many of them perfectly apparent and well defined. The more intelligent a man is, the more he will

weigh pros and cons in his judgments, carefully considering where his interest lies, what dangers may be encountered, what consequences will ensue. On the basis of these
he may be prompted to act, or he may be deflected from
his initial purpose, or even turned from it altogether. All
these motives are not really part of a man's personality.
They have been forced on him by education, tradition,
ruling prejudices, considerations of family, or technical
calculations, as the case may be; but they are not the
expression of his true self.

A man is truly himself only when he acts spontaneously
—not on second thought but quite impulsively, almost
without thinking at all. If intelligence is not permitted to
come into play, if no control of any kind is exerted over
the fundamental impulses, a man's actions are the complete and genuine expression of his own innermost nature.
Such actions occur only when no time is allowed for intellectual deliberation. Ever since the time when he definitely adopted this view, as Gide says, 'the quickest, the
most sudden action seemed to me to be the best. It appeared to me that my action was all the more sincere in
that I was sweeping away before it all those considerations
with which I attempted to justify it at first. Henceforward,
acting haphazardly and without giving myself time to reflect, my slightest actions appear to me more significant
since they are no longer reasoned out.' [50]

Spontaneous, unpremeditated actions are indeed more
common than the casual observer would be inclined to
think; quite often they mark the most important and decisive steps in life. 'Have you not noticed, Hildebrant then
said, that the most decisive actions of our life, I mean those
that are most likely to decide our whole future, are very

50. A.Gide, *Pages inédites*, Œuvres Complètes, Vol.x, Nouvelle Revue Française,
Paris, 1935, I, p.26.

often actions to which we have given no consideration? [51]
Referring to the motives which led him to marry, Gide
years afterwards admitted his failure to discover a sensible
explanation for his behaviour.[52] At the beginning of 1912,
when he served as a member of the jury in several criminal
cases, he noted that some offenders stated they could give
no accountable reason for their action. There was a workman, for instance, who was found guilty of arson, and
who kept on repeating to the judge, 'Monsieur le Président, je vous dis que je n'avais aucun motif.' [53]

Gide called such deeds 'actes gratuits'—gratuitous actions, and under that name they have become a frequent
and controversial topic among French writers. The theory
was formulated in the *Prométhée mal enchaîné* thus: 'A
gratuitous action? How can it be? And you must understand that this does not necessarily mean an action which
yields no profit, because otherwise. . . . No, but gratuitous—that is an action that is motivated by nothing—
do you understand?—no interest, no passion, nothing.
This is the disinterested action, born of itself; the action
that is without an aim, therefore without a master—the
action that is free.' [54]

A famous example of gratuitous action is to be found in
Les Caves du Vatican. Lafcadio is alone in a compartment
of the night train *en route* from Rome to Naples. Enters
Amédée Fleurissoire, who sits down in the corner opposite
him next the door. Lafcadio begins to doze but cannot get
to sleep. Fleurissoire is constantly fidgeting, struggling
with his new collar, taking off his coat, adjusting his cuffs

51. *Les Faux-Monnayeurs*, Part III, Chap.XV, p.508.
52. *Si le Grain ne meurt*, Part I, Chap.II, p.444.
53. A.Gide, *Souvenirs de la Cour d'Assises*, Œuvres Complètes, Vol.VII, Nouvelle
Revue Française, Paris, 1934, II, p.29.
54. A.Gide, *Le Prométhée mal enchaîné*, Œuvres Complètes, Vol.III, Nouvelle Revue Française, Paris, 1933, Chronique de la moralité privée, I, p.105.

or his tie. Lafcadio looks out of the window; the countryside is black except for the squares of light cast on the
ground outside from the various compartment windows of
the moving train. In the middle of one of these squares
dances the grotesque shadow of Fleurissoire; the others
are empty. Then thought Lafcadio, 'There, quite close to
my hand, right under my hand, is this double lock, which
I can open and shut easily; this door which, if it suddenly
gave way, would let him topple forward; a slight push
would do it; he would fall headlong into the darkness;
not even a cry would be heard. . . . Who would know
anything about it? . . . A crime without a motive . . .
what an embarrassing case for the police! . . . Hullo!
. . . we are on a bridge now, I think; a river . . .' The
window-pane had turned black and the reflections appeared in it more distinctly. Fleurissoire bent forward to
straighten his tie. 'There just under my hand, that double
lock . . . by heaven! it opens even more easily than I
thought. If I can count to twelve without hurrying before
I see a light burning in the countryside the chap is saved.
I'll begin: one, two, three, four (slowly, slowly!) five, six,
seven, eight, nine, ten—a light!' [55] Fleurissoire did not
utter a cry.

This is not a 'thrill murder.' A thrill murder is usually
thought out and carefully planned in advance. Lafcadio's
deed is just the translation into action of a spontaneous,
irrational impulse—the kind of impulse that each of us
may experience at times; but the majority of us have the
sense to suppress it immediately, without making any
outward sign. Yet such deeds are, or would be, the true
reflection of ourselves. Moreover, these impulses are not
always criminal. The example cited is selected merely be-

55. A.Gide, *Les Caves du Vatican*, Œuvres Complètes, Vol.vii, Nouvelle Revue
Française, Paris, 1934, V. 1 and 2, pp.336, 337, 338.

cause it is typical and striking. At all events the 'gratuitous action' has this quality: it gives a man the only real freedom he can know—freedom to be himself. Rational motives exert an external pressure on the mind, limiting and restraining its absolute liberty. Absolute liberty is possible only when all rational motives are eliminated; it is a manifestation of the original and genuine personality. When the original personality finds complete and adequate expression, all scruples about good and evil must vanish *ipso facto*. Is it not right to be true to one's own nature? 'Je me délivrai du même coup du souci, de la perplexité, du remords,' says Gide, and so he could reach 'cet état de joie qui me faisait connaître mon acte pour bon au seul plaisir que je prenais à le faire.' [56]

Gide has always refused to organize the fundamental tendencies of his nature into a moral or logical system. A system implies preference and selection. Gide shrinks from the prospect of sacrificing anything of value. 'The necessity of making a choice was always intolerable to me. To choose appeared to me not so much to select something as to reject what I did not select.' [57] It is because there is no coherent system in his thought that contradictions can coexist there without clashing. This does not imply any obscurity or confusion. In fact every idea explored by Gide's keen intelligence is outlined with perfect clarity and delicate precision; but every principle thus determined stands independently by itself and is not arbitrarily or artificially welded into an uncongenial setting.

Yet sometimes that state of suspense seems difficult to maintain and a solution by elimination or compromise appears to be the unavoidable conclusion. Gide evades the

56. A.Gide, *Pages inédites*, Œuvres Complètes, Vol.xi, Nouvelle Revue Française, Paris, 1936, i, p.26.
57. *Les Nourritures Terrestres*, iv, i, p.111.

difficulty by refusing to formulate a definite conclusion. This evasiveness is one of the characteristics of his general attitude. Gide himself uses the English word 'desultory' to describe this idiosyncrasy of his.[58] He nimbly eludes any hold that might paralyze his ever alert curiosity, shifting his standpoint and skipping about according to the dictates of his wandering interests.

These changes are facilitated by the constant criticism he brings to bear on everything and everybody—especially himself. Whenever Gide makes a statement, even in deadly earnest, he cannot help thinking that the contrary is at the same time possible, and even probable. That instinctive habit of facing both sides of the problem simultaneously, which is not duplicity but the acme of sincerity, frequently manifests itself in the almost imperceptible tone of subdued irony which permeates Gide's writings. One of the best examples is the character of the pastor in the *Symphonie Pastorale*. The pastor, who expresses many of the theories which are closest to Gide's own heart, has about him an air both of candour and of stiffness, suggesting that the good clergyman is almost mimicking himself. The suggestion is very slight, but it gives a certain half-humorous turn to an otherwise deeply tragic situation. It is not a warning that the clergyman's position should not be taken seriously. Gide's is not the type of irony that sneers at things just for fun. It is merely a discreet reminder that no matter how much truth there may be in a statement, it can never contain the whole truth.

Gide's *penchant* for stating both sides of a question cannot but be extremely disturbing to those who have accepted a certain truth and would like to ignore that which is not in conformity with it. By clever thrusts in all direc-

---

58. A. Gide, *Pages du Journal de Lafcadio*, Œuvres Complètes, Vol. XI, Nouvelle Revue Française, Paris, 1936, II, p.18.

tions he indisputably shows that whatever stand a man may have taken, there is always something to be said in opposition. Every man should be compelled to doubt whether he has reached an absolute and unshakable standpoint and induced to question and revise his ideas—as Gide himself did on his own account. Gide never provides an answer for others to repeat after him. Everyone must work out his own interpretation of the world, instead of taking things for granted. Gide does not want to supply ready-made solutions for people's problems; his aim is to oblige the reader to study for himself these problems for which there can be no solution but a particular and personal one. 'So much the worse for the reader who is lazy; I want readers of another kind. To disturb—that is my function. The public always prefers to be reassured. There are those whose business it is to do so. There are only too many of them.' [59] It might be added that he seems to experience a secret joy in destroying people's lazy serenity, in compelling them to wake up and become restless with anxiety and doubt. Was this not what had befallen Gide himself? He seems to have retained a personal hatred for traditional, commonly accepted ideas, probably on account of the absurd moral restraints under which he had suffered in his youth. Years after ridding himself of these fetters, he finds an equivocal pleasure in 'corrupting' the people round him.

He does it moreover with a perfectly easy conscience—nay, with the conviction that he is being highly moral. Morality usually implies strain and exertion. Now it had been a very hard struggle for Gide to cast off the thick crust of religious and moral traditions which had been laid upon him by his family and his education. So the incessant effort which this involved had given his emanci-

59. *Journal des Faux-Monnayeurs*, IIe Cahier, La Bastide, 29 mars 1925, p.111.

pation a character of difficulty which is normally associated with the achievement of morality. He had to exert
all his will-power in the process, 'so that,' as he says, 'I
never appeared to myself more moral than at the time
when I had decided to be moral no longer—I mean, nor
longer moral except in my own way.' [60]

Gide's deliberate intention of disturbing the moral confidence and peace of others, so strangely combined with
the oft-repeated affirmation that his own conscience is
absolutely at rest, has led some critics to see in him a
demoniacal influence. 'Il n'y a qu'un mot pour définir
un tel homme,' writes H. Massis, ' . . . c'est celui de
démoniaque.' [61]

4. *Earthly and Heavenly Themes*

THE various points of view presented by Gide in his
stories cannot be considered as progressive steps in a
definite argumentation. They can best be compared to the
themes of a musical composition, each of which has a
value of its own, and expresses its own intrinsic meaning;
but each is open to variation and also to free association
with similar or contrasting motives. They are not presented once and once only, but may recur again and again
either increasing by repetition the impression they are
intended to convey, or enriching it with new shades of
feeling by a multiplicity of ever-renewed combinations.
The Gidian 'themes' can be conveniently arranged into
two groups—earthly themes and heavenly themes—corresponding more or less to the two great aspects of life,
the material and the spiritual. Indeed, the two sides have
been pursuing a dialogue in Gide's soul all through his life.

60. *Pages inédites*, Œuvres Complètes, Vol.xi, 1936, i, p.25.
61. H.Massis, *Jugements*, ii, Plon, Paris, 1929, André Gide, i, p.21.

The fundamental earthly theme according to this scheme of grouping is 'la ferveur.' The first advice given to the disciple in the *Nourritures Terrestres* is: 'Nathanaël, je t'enseignerai la ferveur.' [62] By fervour Gide means the eager acceptance of every sensation or emotion in all its fulness and intensity. Everything is good in life except apathy and indifference. One must love 'without troubling whether it is right or wrong'; [63] seek 'an emotional existence . . . rather than tranquillity'; [64] experience 'every passion and every vice.' [65] Yet Gide does not advocate wild and reckless living. A riotous life bruises and spoils the precious content of almost every impression except the harshest and most crude. Gide holds that a man should enjoy to the full, but delicately, almost reverently, all the sensations that come to him. Thus sensation becomes almost a religion. 'Mes émotions se sont ouvertes comme une religion,' [66] says Ménalque in the *Nourritures Terrestres*.

This religion affirms that joy is to be found not in a more or less hypothetical future but in the present moment. Man must learn to make the most of every instant. 'Nathanaël, je te parlerai des instants. As-tu compris de quelle force est leur présence?' [67] It is useless to live in the dead past. 'I don't want to remember. . . . I should be afraid that, in doing so, I might prevent the future from happening and make the past encroach on the present. It is from complete forgetfulness of yesterday that I create the freshness of every new hour. . . . I don't believe in dead things and to me being no more and never having been are just the same. . . . If only our poor minds knew

62. *Les Nourritures Terrestres*, I, 1, p.64.
63. *Ibidem*, I, 1, p.64.
64. *Ibidem*, I, 1, p.64.
65. *Ibidem*, I, 1, p.67.
66. *Ibidem*, I, 1, p.66.
67. *Ibidem*, II, p.90.

how to embalm memories! But memories keep badly; the
most delicate fade away; the most voluptuous decay on the
spot. . . . Regrets, remorse, repentance are joys of yes-
teryear, seen in retrospect.' [68] Nor will it serve any good
purpose to live in the future, not even if it means preparing for happiness that is perhaps to come, still less if
it means wearily anticipating the results of our present
actions. Things always turn out differently from our expectation of them. The future reveals itself in its own good
time. Happiness is fortuitous and may accost us at any
moment like a beggar on the road.[69] The novelty of every
instant is infinitely precious because it is absolutely unlike
anything that has been before or ever will be again. Let
man enjoy to the fullest extent and possess without sur-
mise or afterthought the priceless and unique wonder of
the present moment.

Every possession enriches its owner—for a while; but
after a time the owner himself is possessed by what he
has. Habit, laziness, comfort seize and hold him, and
very soon he finds himself, as it were, in a rut. The mental
drowsiness into which he falls is difficult to shake off, and
if allowed to become settled rapidly turns into complete
torpor. So before lethargy sets in one must change, says
Gide; it may be a change for the worse, it does not matter.
A man must turn away from what is mellow, satisfying,
dull. 'Ne *demeure* jamais, Nathanaël—never remain at a
standstill, Nathanaël. As soon as an environment has
come to resemble you or you have made yourself similar
to your environment, it is no longer profitable to you. You
must leave it. Nothing is more dangerous to you than your
family, your room, and your own past.' [70] All the latent

68. *L'Immoraliste*, ii, 2, p.114.
69. *Les Nourritures Terrestres*, ii, p.84.
70. *Ibidem*, ii, p.90.

potentialities of a man's soul cannot attain full development except in special and varied surroundings. In order
to give every inherent possibility within ourselves the opportunity to thrive and expand, it is necessary to expose
every side of our personality in turn to the fertilizing influences of varied circumstance.

A man must therefore live in a state of perpetual expectation. There is indeed nothing more stimulating than
the feeling that something is about to happen, whatever
it may be. Expectation must not be understood to imply a
definite and particular wish. It is rather the joyful acceptance of every sensation or emotion that each moment may
bring—and not the hope of something else. 'Nathanaël,
may every expectation in you be indeed not a desire but
simply a disposition to welcome. Expect all that comes to
you; but desire only what comes to you.'[71]—'Nathanaël,
je te parlerai des attentes.' [72]

Constantly expecting something new, a man must keep
himself in a state of permanent receptivity. He should not
involve himself so far in one direction so as to be unable to
draw back and face another aspect of things at the call of
circumstance. Be always on the alert lest the opportunity
of some valuable experience should slip by and vanish
for ever. All through his life Gide resolutely refused to
take sides, to commit himself—not out of timidity but
because he wished to be always in readiness to greet any
possible new phase of the rich motley of reality.

This attitude, while offering unlimited possibilities of
adventure, exposes a man to danger. Gide is well aware of
this and is ready to take the chance. In his opinion these
unavoidable risks give life an added zest and flavour. He is
too moderate, and has too keen and delicate a sense of pro-

---

71. *Les Nourritures Terrestres*, i, Chap.iii, p.73.
72. *Ibidem*, i, Chap.iii, p.72.

portion, to advise anyone to 'live dangerously' just for the sake of the excitement that this brings; but he accepts and welcomes danger as he does any other intense aspect of life.

Nevertheless, the most intense experiences a man may have are found not in selfish and solitary sensations, but in the complete and intimate communion with another being. Gide himself possesses that capacity of communion to the highest degree. In the 'Journal d'Edouard,' which forms part of the *Faux-Monnayeurs*, there is mention of 'the singular faculty of depersonalization which enables me to feel other people's emotions as if they were my own.' [73] In the still more confidential *Journal des Faux-Monnayeurs* one reads: ' . . . In life, it is the thoughts, the motions of others that dwell in me; my heart beats only in sympathy. That is what makes any discussion difficult for me. I abandon my own point of view at once. . . . This is the key to my character and to my work. The critic who has not grasped that will make a poor show.' [74] When in a state of perfect sympathy with the deep emotion of another, he feels himself carried away in a transport of mystic ecstasy. 'I have often felt that, in moments as solemn as this, all human emotion in me may be transformed into an almost mystic trance, a kind of enthusiasm, whereby my whole being has the sense of becoming magnified or rather liberated from all selfish attachments, as if dispossessed of itself and depersonalized. Those who have never experienced this will certainly not understand me.' [75]

It is at all events easy to understand that in Gide's estimation this is by far the most intense feeling a man can ever experience on earth and therefore the greatest thing that life can offer. Out of this arises the last and most

73. *Les Faux-Monnayeurs*, Part i, Chap.xii, p.148.
74. *Journal des Faux-Monnayeurs*, IIᵉ Cahier, 15 nov. 1923, pp.87–88.
75. *Les Faux-Monnayeurs*, Part i, Chap.xviii, p.239.

unexpected of Gide's 'earthly' themes: abnegation carried
as far as complete forgetfulness of self—'Pousser l'ab-
négation jusqu'à l'oubli de soi total.' [76] Abnegation is not
the thwarting of life but the choice of the exalted path by
which we attain its richest and most sublime expression.

From here the transition is easily made from 'earthly'
to 'heavenly' themes. The kernel, as it were, of Gide's religious ideas is the conception of a fundamental antagonism between Christ and Christianity, between Jesus and
St. Paul. According to Gide the Gospels do not present any
definite commands or prohibitions. They are not written
in the imperative mood. But they are full of wise and truly
divine advice as to the way of reaching perfect happiness.
They illuminate the path leading towards ideal bliss. They
do not command or threaten. 'Je ne trouve pas précisé-
ment de défenses et de prohibitions dans l'Evangile. Mais
il s'agit de contempler Dieu du regard le plus clair possible.' [77] The commands and threats have been introduced
into the Christian doctrine, first by St. Paul, then by a
series of unauthorized commentators. The central theme
of Gide's religious thought, which recurs again and again
throughout his books, is that it is necessary to rid Christianity of St. Paul and his successors, and to return to the
Gospel.

'It is more and more apparent to me that many of the
ideas which constitute our Christian faith are derived not
from words of Christ himself but from the commentaries
of St. Paul. . . . If I have to choose between Christ and
St. Paul, I choose Christ . . . I search the Gospel, but I
seek in vain for commands, threats, prohibitions. . . . All
these originate from St. Paul. . . . Is it betraying Christ,

76. *Journal des Faux-Monnayeurs*, IIe Cahier, 15 nov. 1923, p.87.
77. A.Gide, *Les Nouvelles Nourritures*, Œuvres Complètes, Vol.ix, Nouvelle
    Revue Française, Paris, 1935, ii, pp.98–99.

is it slighting or profaning the Gospel to discern in it above all *a method of attaining a life of blessedness?* The state of joy which our doubts and our hardness of heart prevent us from realizing, is a condition that is obligatory upon every Christian.' [78]

The secret of supreme joy and indestructible happiness is revealed in the Gospel; it is self-forgetfulness, sacrifice, and renunciation. From a purely earthly standpoint, Gide had already learned by experience that self-forgetfulness brings a man the highest and fullest joy life can possibly provide. This divine message is in harmony with Gide's own human conclusion. By self-abnegation and whole-hearted sacrifice man enters into communion with the Deity, and attains the Kingdom of God. Gide points [79] to the passage of the Gospel containing the words, 'he that loveth his life shall lose it, and he that hateth his life in this world shall keep it unto life eternal.' [80] As Gide explains, whoever cares greatly for his own fortune in this world, and centres his interest in himself will find nought but disappointment and wretchedness. A man must renounce this world, if he desires the supreme happiness of communion with God. 'I find from experience that every earthly object I covet is darkened by the very fact that I covet it, and simultaneously the whole world loses its transparency—or my vision loses its clarity—so that God ceases to be perceptible to my soul, and that, in abandoning the Creator for the creature, my soul . . . loses possession of the Kingdom of God.' [81] It is impossible to be materially prosperous in this world and at the same time spiritually happy in God. Possession of the other world is attained by renunciation of this world.

78. *La Symphonie Pastorale*, II*ᵉ* Cahier, 3 mai, pp.62–64.
79. *Numquid et tu?* 4 mars 1916, p.322.
80. St. John, 12.25.
81. *Les Nouvelles Nourritures*, II, p.99.

The *other world* does not lie beyond the grave. The eternity of the Kingdom of God is not to be considered in the light of the human conception of time. 'Eternal' means without beginning or end. Nothing in our experience of time can give us any idea of the meaning of this. In place of the common conception of eternity as a measureless extent of time must be substituted a purely spiritual and qualitative idea. Eternity may be the attribute of any particular moment. Gide notices that in the Gospels there is no definite promise of a future life; on the other hand, he interprets [82] certain passages (for instance, St. John, 13.17) as the unequivocal affirmation that it is given to man to enjoy Eternity here and now, 'et nunc.' When man immolates himself, he is living in God—he is in the Kingdom of God, in Eternity. 'Celui qui aime sa vie . . . la perdra; mais celui-là qui en fera abandon, la rendra vraiment vivante—lui assurera la vie éternelle: non point la vie futurement éternelle—mais la fera déjà, dès à présent, vivre à même l'éternité.' [83] Gide does not altogether dismiss the possibility of a future life; but he thinks that it is at best a fond hope, perhaps only a pious illusion. However, Eternity in the present is for Gide an absolute certainty.

Whoever experiences the realization of Eternity in the present comes into possession of a strange peace. All doubt, all hesitation, all anxiety must vanish before this overwhelming happiness. Every real or imaginary stain or guilt or sin must be washed away,[84] and one's early innocence restored. Gide thus embraces a type of mysticism not very different from the 'quietism,' dear to Fénelon, which flourished in the seventeenth century. 'Quelle

82. *Numquid et tu?* 18 fevrier 1916, pp.317–318; 15 juin 1919, pp.339–340.
83. *Ibidem*, 4 mars 1916, p.322.
84. *Ibidem*, 23 avril 1916, p.327.

tranquillité! Ici vraiment le temps s'arrête. Ici respire l'Eternel. Nous entrons dans le royaume de Dieu.' [85]

That blessed state of perfect peace and joy is not reached without effort. It is only with the greatest difficulty that we learn to carry out the Gospel injunction to 'die to ourselves.' [86] Renunciation must not be just the outcome of weakness, indolence, or passivity; it is the fruit of superlative energy and activity and of a strong and sturdy attitude towards life. Man must be himself. He must not try to attain sanctity by clamping upon his own personality obligations that are foreign to his nature. Sincere abnegation is the normal outcome of one's highest tendencies when developed in the right direction, following one's own bent, but always upwards. 'Que chacun suive sa pente . . . mais en montant.' [87] Life should be a constant endeavour fully to realize oneself, in the highest sense of the term, even to surpass oneself, but only in harmony with one's natural endowments.

So the deep harmony between two seemingly opposite themes becomes manifest if they are considered as one whole. They truly represent the various aspects of the same reality seen from different angles. The idea of abnegation may be considered as constituting a bridge between the earthly and the heavenly themes, since abnegation is at the same time the superlative form of human experience and the way of approach to the Kingdom of God. Moreover, the typically Gidian precept of perpetual change, of continual disruption of the ties of comfortable habit on the one hand, and on the other the Christian idea of renunciation, are but two sides of the same conception of abandonment of worldly things. The

85. *Numquid et tu?* 18 fevrier 1916, p.318.
86. *Ibidem*, 18 fevrier 1916, p.317.
87. Léon Pierre-Quint, *André Gide*, I, 3, p.49.

present moment is all-important; it is the only reality
from which man can extract genuine and profound earthly
joy. Eternity is to be found therein as far as it can be
apprehended by man. Lastly, just as Gide urges us to
live in our sensations with an almost religious fervour,
similarly he advocates and extols intense striving after
complete realization of the sublime.

In this symphony of thoughts, where the motives are not
organized in any definite system but have free play, blending and harmonizing with each other, Satan stands out as
the great discordant element. The words, 'le démon,'
'le diable,' come with disconcerting frequency from Gide's
pen whenever anything goes wrong in what he considers
to be the normal course of things. When the unexplained
or inexplicable appears and exposes unsuspected flaws in
his argument, Gide attributes it all to the Devil. In the
Journal des Faux-Monnayeurs an imaginary interview is
described wherein Gide clearly explains his views on the
subject: 'To be perfectly frank, I do not believe in the
devil. I use him as far as possible as a childish simplification and apparent explanation of certain psychological
problems. . . . None the less, in spite of all I say, this
remains: the instant I admit his existence—and this
happens with me sometimes, even if only for a moment—
from that instant, it seems to me that all becomes clear,
that I understand everything; it seems to me that I
suddenly discover the explanation of my life, of all that is
inexplicable and incomprehensible, of all the darkness in
my life.' [88] But if everything that is inexplicable, incomprehensible, and evil in life is attributed to a hypothetical
Devil, the Devil threatens ultimately to have the lion's
share, in the case of a great many people and perhaps of
Gide in particular. Massis forcibly expresses that view

88. *Journal des Faux-Monnayeurs*—Identification du Démon, pp.141-143.

when he calls Gide 'démoniaque.' [89] Gide does not seem
to be much disturbed by the accusation; he appears to be
almost proud of it. 'Vous savez ce que disait Goethe? Que la
puissance d'un homme et sa force de prédestination étaient
reconnaissables à ce qu'il portait en lui de démoniaque.' [90]

5. Gide's View of the World

THE powers of darkness have a favourite lurking place in
man's subconscious mind. Gide has a special predilection
for hunting them out, not in order to destroy them, but
mainly for the sheer interest of discovering them and
bringing them to the light. He experiences a strange
pleasure in exposing in the most respectable and even
most saintly people unsuspected and reprehensible phases
of mentality. Quite often these workings of the subconscious mind are hidden, even from the person in whom
they occur, behind a sophistry of well reasoned arguments.
For instance, in the *Symphonie Pastorale*, when the pastor,
who is passionately in love with young Gertrude, though
he is not aware of it, understands that Jacques is about
to propose to her, he emphatically disapproves on purely
moral grounds, and succeeds in sending away his too
obedient son and rival. Almost every man, according to
Gide, has a definite ugly strain in him, perhaps limited to
subconscious longings, or displaying itself in imagination
only—more often finding an outlet in a secret life of shame,
carefully concealed from all but his partner in guilt. Gide
loves to pry into these most private affairs, not so much, as
in the case of Proust, in order to study the intricate
psychological mechanism involved but rather because he

89. Cf. p.177.
90. *Journal des Faux-Monnayeurs*—Identification du Démon, p.144. Cf. Goethe,
    Dichtung und Wahrheit, Part IV, Book 20.

finds a specific moral—or immoral—interest in the cases themselves. A man whose life is devoid of these complications must, he thinks, have a very poor and empty personality. Has not Goethe said, as Gide remembers only too well, that the power of a man is recognizable by what he has of the Devil in him? Thus Gide is interested particularly in turbid and heavily burdened souls. In *L'Immoraliste* Michel shows small liking for the good little boys who are his wife's special pets. On a certain occasion, however, he sees one of them steal a pair of scissors and immediately he is greatly attracted to him. Gide presents an insinuating picture of these tendencies in people. He seldom states facts plainly. He merely makes suggestions, awakening suspicions by implications and hints; he stirs the reader's curiosity and often sends the imagination wandering along forbidden paths. So he succeeds in conveying a half-veiled but all the more convincing impression of the hideous festering larvæ that are bred at the bottom of man's soul.

Yet love, according to Gide's experiences, appears to be singularly free from these unsavoury elements. He has retained a perfectly pure and almost immaterial conception of love, a legacy of his idealistic education and the youthful enthusiasm of his adolescence. Real love is for him a spiritual longing, which springs up, often at first sight, between two people of noble character. It has its source in the innermost recesses of the human soul—in fact, is part of the very soul and therefore should live and endure as long as the soul itself. Its ethereal nature places it out of the reach of disappointment and decay. Such a pure and exalted sentiment naturally precludes any possibility of defiling relationship; and indeed the very idea of combining ideal love with physical pleasure appears to Gide to be a sort of profanation.[91] Between the two there

91. *Si le Grain ne meurt*, Part ɪɪ, Chap.ɪ, pp.375–376.

can be no compromise. Woman as an ideal of moral devotion fills him with respect and admiration. Woman as an
object of desire inspires him with loathing and disgust. In
the *Faux-Monnayeurs*, young Olivier, speaking of his
first experience of physical love, says to a friend: '"It is
disgusting. It is horrible. . . . Afterwards I wanted to
spit, to be sick, to tear my skin off, to kill myself,"—"You
are exaggerating!"—"To kill *her*."' [92] Was this the last
remnant of Gide's puritanical abhorrence of the sins of the
flesh?—or just the result of his own idiosyncracy? At any
rate the ending of *Le roi Candaule* clearly shows his position. 'That face of yours, so beautiful, Madam, I thought
it should remain veiled.'—'Veiled for you, Gyges. Candaule has torn my veil.'—'Well, then, sew it up again.' [93]

Gide does not deny that pleasure is permissible, even
right; but it belongs to an entirely different type of experience from love. Just as sensuality would besmirch true
love, love would hamper the free play of healthy sensuality. 'I had made up my mind to dissociate pleasure from
love; and it even seemed to me that this divorce was
desirable, that in this way pleasure was rendered purer,
love more perfect, if heart and flesh were not entangled in
each other.' [94] A man will attain more harmonious fulfilment of his divergent desires and aspirations by not
confining them all to one other person alone; his ideal
longings may expend themselves in more or less distant
worship of one ideal being, and his earthly passions will
best be satisfied by a variety of ephemeral adventure.

There is an obvious connexion between these theories
and Gide's own personal experiences. In this matter
Gide has stated very frankly—almost defiantly—what he

92. *Les Faux-Monnayeurs*, Part I, Chap.III, pp.52–53.
93. A.Gide, *Le roi Candaule*, Œuvres Complètes, Vol.III, Nouvelle Revue Française, 1933, III, 5, pp.395–396.
94. *Si le Grain ne meurt*, Part II, Chap.I, pp.349–350.

believes to be the truth. Whereas Proust draws a gloomy picture of abnormal people, as suffering from a real nervous disease, on the contrary Gide claims that that abnormality is to a certain extent 'natural.' According to Gide, the nature of 'abnormal' people is not the nature of 'normal' people, but it is no less a part of the natural scheme of things; and hostile public opinion is solely responsible for the mental distortions and deformities of unfortunate victims who are for ever obliged to make a pretence of being what they are not. He is persuaded that, should they be allowed to conduct themselves with complete freedom, they would, like the Greeks of old, attain a harmony of existence in no way inferior to that enjoyed by others. This partly explains why Gide felt it his duty to speak what he considered to be the whole truth. He did so at the cost of a terrible scandal, and with the realization that he was sacrificing his own personal reputation in order to eradicate what he considered a cruel prejudice, and to secure the enfranchisement of many sufferers.

'Familles je vous hais! foyers clos; portes refermées; possessions jalouses du bonheur.' [95] Gide's view of the family seems to have been almost entirely conditioned by his own personal experiences. He has little liking for the institution of the family which in his own case kept him in bondage during the days of his youth, and which later on following his marriage shackled him with new ties and obligations, without affording him the compensation of children of his own. The family appears to Gide like a prison. In the following quotation from the *Faux-Monnayeurs* there is a significant play on words, which emphasizes this view. 'La famille . . .,' says Bourget, the Roman Catholic and conservative writer, 'cette cellule sociale.'—'The family, the cell of society.' One should

95. *Les Nourritures Terrestres*, IV, Chap.I, p.116.

rather say, retorts Gide, 'the régime of the cell—the prison-cell (le régime cellulaire).' [96] In point of fact, Gide's criticisms apply more to the forms of family life as they existed before the war, in European countries under the influence of French culture, than they do to forms of family life as we see them in the present day. Yet despite the evidence of a definite trend in a more liberal direction, many features of the old order are still frequently to be seen; and they bear a striking resemblance to the picture presented by Gide. Gide evokes the stuffy atmosphere of those narrow family circles where man and wife, living year after year in close proximity, never losing sight of each other, become in spite of that—or perhaps because of it—relentless, mutual tormentors, or at best indifferent strangers. If either shows a more than customary forbearance—if the man strong-minded and commanding in public meekly submits at home to all the capricious demands of his wife, it is rarely due to affection or even to natural weakness. 'Nine times out of ten, if the husband gives way to his wife, it is because there is something for which he has to be forgiven. A virtuous woman . . . takes advantage of everything. Let the man stoop down for an instant, she leaps immediately on to his back.' [97] Adultery is rampant perhaps because it affords a means of escape from the unbearable oppression of that confined existence. Most couples are kept together only by a tacit acceptance of unpleasant facts, which has its source not in a genuine and tolerant broad-mindedness but in the fear of complications, of material losses, of public censure, all of which resolves itself into hypocrisy.

The authority of parents over their children is theoretically almost absolute; actually in most cases children

96. *Les Faux-Monnayeurs*, Part I, Chap.XII, p.168.
97. *Ibidem*, Part III, Chap.I, p.328.

continue in a state of complete dependency until they are grown men and women. As soon as they can, girls begin to look about them for a suitable 'parti.' If they do not exert themselves sufficiently, or if they fail in their efforts to capture a husband, they have nothing in prospect but to wither away in saintly or sour-faced spinsterhood. A few may attain freedom; but with what difficulty and often at what a price! The boys are either crushed under the parental yoke or live in a state of more or less latent revolt; liberation comes to many only after a struggle which consumes the best of the energy of their young manhood.

Fortunate is the youth who can free himself;—still more fortunate is he who does not need to free himself, who on account of circumstances has not to breathe the stifling atmosphere of a too well regulated family life. All his youthful strength may be dedicated to the glorious experience of life. Most fortunate of all is the natural child, who is without family ties and so from the outset can lead a natural and untrammelled existence. 'L'avenir appartient aux bâtards. Quelle signification dans ce mot: "un enfant naturel"! Seul le bâtard a droit au naturel.' [98]

Feminine devotion is usually the cement of family life. Yet women do not seem generally to have the best of the bargain. It appears to be their proper and normal lot to be sacrificed. Most of them—the best of them—are impelled instinctively to immolate themselves for the sake of another. This is the whole philosophy of the book, *L'Ecole des Femmes*. Eveline writes in her diary: 'Before I met you, it made me suffer to feel that my life was without any purpose. . . . A life without some devotion, without object, could not satisfy me. . . . It is only since that conversation in the garden of the Tuileries that he opened

98. *Les Faux-Monnayeurs*, Part I, Chap.XII, p.169.

my eyes to the part a woman plays in the life of great men. . . . I keep in mind this that my whole life must henceforth be devoted to enabling him to accomplish his glorious destiny.' [99] However, it is not only great men who may enjoy the privilege of such devotion. Women bestow it almost indiscriminately on the most unworthy. This devotion is admirable as it is astonishing. Yet if a woman is merely following the dictates of an irrepressible instinct, should she be considered so meritorious? And should the man who is the object of the devotion feel so proud of it? After all he is nothing but a convenient pretext; if he had not chanced to present himself, the very same devotion would have been bestowed automatically and without distinction upon somebody else. In the *Faux-Monnayeurs* Laura, who was ready to pour out all her love on Edouard, is disappointed in her expectations; she then proceeds to marry another man, a school teacher, not out of spite but with all the sincerity of her genuine soul. 'How admirable is woman's propensity to devotion! The man she loves is generally to her only a kind of peg on which to hang her love. How easily and sincerely Laura had made the substitution!' [100]

In 1912 Gide was for some time a member of the criminal jury in Rouen. The way in which justice was dealt out left him aghast. He often saw poor innocent wretches bullied or tricked into making admissions technically implying their guilt simply because a conviction would mean a little triumph for the police who reported cases, for the magistrate who investigated them, or for the presiding judge. The real facts in the statements wrung from the prisoners were so distorted by intimidation or by cun-

99. A.Gide, *L'Ecole des Femmes*, Nouvelle Revue Française, Paris, 1931, I, 7 Oct. 1894, pp.14–16.
100. *Les Faux-Monnayeurs*, Part I, Chap.XII, p.145.

ning that the truth became barely recognizable. He saw
the members of the jury divided among themselves,—
divided within themselves even,—some of them coming
to the trial with rigid principles and ready-made verdicts;
others physically incapable of concentration and of giving
hours of sustained attention to minute and intricate details; most of them utterly devoid of psychological intuition; and all reaching a unanimous decision made up of
compromise, contradictions, and ignorance. At any rate
the motives of the criminals were in Gide's estimation
often completely puzzling even to a penetrating mind.
Many had acted for no accountable reason. His ideas concerning 'gratuitous actions' thereby received complete
confirmation. Obviously so many of the phenomena of the
subconscious mind still escape our knowledge that it is
difficult for us to pass a clear judgment on unbalanced
people, as criminals generally are. Criminals should not
merely be put in jail—as the insane were in the seventeenth century—but they should be treated in some other
way—exactly how, Gide does not say, for he does not
know. Apparently nobody knows yet. Gide, however, could
not help realizing and, with his usual sincerity, proclaim-
ing that justice in its present form is a grotesque and almost barbarous parody of what it should be.

The Church does not escape Gide's criticism. In the
spiritual field Gide had already noted an antithesis between Christ and Christianity. In the field of action also
the Church, according to Gide, has failed in its original
mission, because it has not accepted the words of Christ in
their true spirit and has misinterpreted and distorted them
to suit its own worldly interest. Jesus Christ constantly
and consistently blessed the poor and adjured the rich to
dispose of their wealth. Yet the Church today is the strongest ally of the capitalistic order. 'The day that the Church

evaded and put to one side the simple teaching of Christ, "Sell all that thou hast and give to the poor," it seriously compromised its prospects. By entering into a compact with what the Gospel called Mammon, which is the very spirit of capitalism, it thereby exposed the weak point of Christianity.' [101] Gide believes that Christ cannot be held responsible for this. Indeed there never would have been any such weakness in Christianity if Christ's own doctrine had been followed—that is, put into practice, and not merely 'interpreted' by the Church. As it is, wealth, in the eyes of certain so-called Christians, appears no longer as 'an obstacle against entrance into the Kingdom of God, but on the contrary as a mark of the Lord's approval; so that the most prosperous bank seemed to be the most blessed.' [102]

Similarly the gospel of peace has been turned, says Gide, into a weapon of war. The holy writ has been distorted so as to defeat the very purpose of the Master and to justify the oppression He desired to relieve. 'Do you think that Christ would recognize himself today in his Church? It is in the very name of Christ that you ought to fight the Church. . . . He preaches resignation. This doctrine of submission—those wanting to oppress others use it— an abominable misuse. Religion is bad because by disarming the oppressed it delivers them up to the oppressor. But the oppressor in allowing the oppressed to be delivered into his power betrays Christ.' [103]

Yet are not the family, the law, and the Church the very foundations of our society? Gide turned rather late to the criticism of social institutions. His own individual problems had absorbed his interests for many years and

101. A.Gide, *Pages de Journal*, Nouvelle Revue Française, Paris, 1934, Feuillets, I, pp.179–180.
102. *Ibidem*, p.175.
103. *Ibidem*, 18 avril 1932, pp.155–156.

it was only after he had achieved the deep harmony of his various personal aspirations that he began investigations in this other field. He did so reluctantly. He realized only too well that he was treading unprepared on a ground full of pitfalls. 'I feel only too well how incompetent I am. These political, economic, and financial questions belong to a field where I enter only with fear urged on by an ever increasing desire to know.' [104] He felt an imperious need to explore—all the more urgent on account of the European situation which was becoming every day more critical.

Gide first approached social problems from the colonial angle. On his trip to the Congo he was forcibly struck by the cruel treatment of the natives. These conditions are unquestioningly accepted as a matter of course by the whites long familiar with colonial life; but for others this brutality is so remote that, though they may be informed as to the facts, they are not touched by the horror of their reality. When suddenly the actual facts were thrust upon Gide, he was deeply moved by the horrible and apparently quite unjustifiable sufferings of the natives, which he could only witness helplessly. He then began to scrutinize the colonial system, and found it to be at the very basis of our present-day civilization. Small numbers of white people from the little peninsula of Europe have more or less completely subjugated, dispossessed, or in some cases exterminated, most of the coloured inhabitants of the rest of the globe. They have annexed the world, and are now exploiting it. They have drawn huge profits for themselves and built up a seemingly powerful civilization—but at what price, Gide had just been able to see. Ominous rumblings seem to be indicative of so much resentment on the part of the victims that the end of this civilization may not be very far distant. Gide would be one of the

104. *Pages de Journal*, 5 mars 1932, pp.147–148.

first to rejoice at the collapse of the enterprises of colonization, as he has seen only too closely the selfishness that inspires them and the unbelievable cruelties that they inflict.

The main organisms of the system are, according to Gide, the large capitalistic stock companies. They have enormous tentacles, sucking up the vitality of the places which come within their grasp, and which are left exhausted and empty. They have almost unlimited power on account of their huge financial resources. They take no moral responsibility, because an anonymous 'board' directs and controls all their activities. Gide learned this at his own expense. When he came back to France, he violently attacked the rubber company which he thought responsible for the worst excesses he had witnessed in the Congo. His attack was countered with an apt though elusive retort; he was himself slandered, his protests hushed up and rendered innocuous, and very soon he was completely outplayed. 'La Forestière' succeeded in thoroughly quenching him. Gide was intelligent enough not to persist in a hopeless fight. Nevertheless, this probably more than anything else convinced him that the whole structure of modern society must be destroyed and society rebuilt after another plan.

In 1932 Gide officially proclaimed his sympathy for the Communist party. He has given his reasons for so doing; they are two-fold. On the one hand they are of a purely general almost sentimental nature; 'Because I suffer to see injustice. . . . Because the régime under which we still live seems to me nowadays only to protect abuses, which are becoming more and more distressing. Because, on the conservative side, I see nothing today that is not dead or dying; . . . because I believe in progress.' [105] But Gide also believes that the individual will have a bet-

105. *Pages de Journal*, Autres Feuillets, p.194.

ter opportunity of freely developing all his potentialities within a communistic than within a capitalistic society. It has been argued that such is not the view generally accepted on this point; it is ordinarily supposed that Communism implies complete subordination of the individual to the group. Gide nevertheless insists, 'I remain a convinced individualist. I consider the attempt that is usually made to establish an opposition between Communism and individualism to be a grave error.' [106] However since he does not give us a more precise explanation as to the way a harmony between the two can be effected, one may suspect that Gide merely projected his ideals and his fond dreams into a better world of his imagination. At any rate he is quite categorical on the subject: 'Pourquoi je souhaite le communisme? Parce que je crois que c'est, à présent, par lui que l'homme peut parvenir à une plus haute culture.' [107] Shortly after his arrival in Moscow, he even stated publicly 'Le sort de la culture est lié dans nos esprits au destin même de l'U.R.S.S.' [108]

Yet in the course of his trip throughout Russia he was compelled to alter his view. Though still 'déclarant . . . son amour' for the U.S.S.R. and for 'la cause qu'elle représente à nos yeux,' [109] though fully acknowledging the value of the material achievements he had witnessed, he could not help feeling alarmed at the monotonous uniformity and the *petit bourgeois* 'conformism' [110] which, according to him, threaten to stifle, under the present soviet régime, every individual effort towards a genuine, original culture.

106. *Pages de Journal*, Autres Feuillets, p.192.
107. *Ibidem*, p.194.
108. *Retour de l'U.R.S.S.*, Appendice, I, Discours prononcé sur la Place Rouge à Moscou pour les funérailles de Maxime Gorki, 20 juin 1936.
109. *Ibidem*, VI, p.92.
110. *Ibidem*, III, pp.66–67.

So the conception of culture which one met with at the beginning of Gide's search also concludes the cycle of his investigations; and it is now possible to reach a better understanding of his views on the subject. He does not approach the problem of culture as a philosopher. In fact he seems to have an instinctive distrust of philosophy. 'Alexandre,' as he says in *Paludes*, 'est un philosophe; de ce qu'il dit, je me méfie toujours; à ce qu'il dit, je ne réponds jamais. . . . Quand un philosophe vous répond, on ne comprend plus du tout ce qu'on lui avait demandé.' [111] This sally is the satirical expression of a permanent attitude of his. He feels loath to organize his feelings or ideas into a regular system. He looks at the world spontaneously, like an artist. Art for him embraces the whole of life; in fact he does not separate art from life in any respect. Life and art involve the same process; the true perception of some part of the richness of reality. In his writings Gide has done nothing else but transpose his own intimate experiences. As he expresses himself in the *Journal d'Edouard*, 'my tastes, my feelings, and my personal experiences all went to feed my writings; in my best turned phrases I felt again the beating of my heart.' [112] Our very actions and all the moral problems they imply are in the same way closely related to our view of the contrasts or harmonies we discover in the checkered world displayed before us. In an imaginary dialogue Gide has made it very plain what his ideas are in this respect: 'Les questions morales vous intéressent?'—'Comment donc! l'étoffe dont nos livres sont faits!'—'Mais qu'est-ce donc, selon vous, que la morale?'—'Une dépendance de l'esthé-

---

111. A.Gide, *Paludes*, Œuvres Complètes, Vol.i, Nouvelle Revue Française, 1933, 'Jeudi,' p.408.
112. *Les Faux-Monnayeurs*, Part i, Chap.xi, p.138.

tique.' [113] Life, morals, æsthetics, are only different aspects of the same fundamental identity, in which æsthetics or art sounds the dominant note.

It is Gide's belief that the first step in art is the accurate delineation—just as in life it is the true perception—of some fragment of reality. This is approximately as far as the human mind can go. For Gide there is no hope of ever attaining the absolute, notwithstanding the hopes of certain philosophers or the promises of some religions. This is no reason for not holding as infinitely precious this little fragment of truth, which may be considered in the light of an endeavour after that absolute which for ever escapes us and yet draws us irresistibly.

Such fragments of reality as we can grasp must find simple, concrete, and adequate expression. They must not be distorted for the sake of argument. In fact, they must not be used to prove anything whatever. They are what they are, and in the field of art, to alter them is almost equivalent to dishonesty in the field of morals. 'I have always had the greatest difficulty in embellishing the truth. Even to change the colour of a person's hair, when writing of it, appears to me like trickery which in my estimation makes the truth less probable.' [114] As he says also 'I have never been able to invent anything.' [115] A scrupulous objectivity is one of the most essential duties of the creative artist.

The natural tendency of almost anyone who has discovered some little piece of truth is to boast about his find and to make the most of it. Gide has a real aversion for all emphasis and exaggeration. He feels annoyed as a man and ruffled as an artist at any overflow of feelings or of words beyond what is strictly in keeping with the

113. A.Gide, *Chroniques de l'Ermitage*, Œuvres Complètes, Vol.iv, Nouvelle Revue Française, Paris, 1933, i, p.387.
114. *Les Faux-Monnayeurs*, Part i, Chap.xi, p.135.
115. *Ibidem*, Part i, Chap.xii, p.169.

actual nature of the facts. He prefers even to be over-reticent than to give adequate expression to his ideas, leaving the imagination of the reader to complete the picture and so to participate in the emotion inherent in it. Gide very well understands the suggestive power of restraint in art as well as in life. 'If effusiveness embarrasses me, if exaggeration of feeling annoys me, nothing contrarywise was more apt to touch me than this restrained emotion.' [116] Throughout his writings there is an almost imperceptible vibration due to a constant checking of the full display of emotion or thought.

Various fragments of truth, all clearly defined and self-contained, might in many cases be assigned places at opposite extremities of a logician's or moralist's system. Yet, according to Gide's conception of life and art, they may just as easily remain side by side. That situation which Gide himself calls 'la cohabitation en moi des extrêmes' [117] would mean for many people real suffering or hopeless incoherency. Gide is not in the least disturbed by it. On the contrary, the dialogue between the various elements stimulates his mind, as it were, and urges him towards the attainment of balance, the creation of harmony—which is the highest point of creation in art, as well as in life, since the two are inseparable. 'This *state of dialogue* which to so many others is almost unbearable, became for me a necessity. That is because, for those others it cannot but be prejudicial to action, whereas for me, far from resulting in sterility, it was on the contrary leading me on to a work of art and it immediately preceded the act of creation, and ended in balance, in harmony.' [118] The aspiration towards balance and harmony

116. *Les Faux-Monnayeurs*, Part III, Chap.XII, p.478.
117. *Pages inédites*, Œuvres Complètes, Vol.XI, 1936, II, p.27.
118. *Ibidem*, II, p.27.

is fundamental in Gide's nature. It was the origin of the first revolt of his thwarted personality against a too rigid and narrow discipline. It is the final achievement of his life as well as of his art. In the intervening period all his writings have been impregnated and permeated by it.

For that reason, and also on account of the sheer clarity of his thought, of the dignified restraint of his expression, Gide's artistry has sometimes been compared to that of the great writers of the French Classical School of the seventeenth century. Gide's 'classicisme' confers on his writings a permanent and compact solidity. Had they been more showy, his works would perhaps have attracted public attention earlier. As they are, they have a universal and lasting quality that assures them of a permanent place in literature.

Gide's style forms the most typical characteristic of his art and is closely related to his general attitude towards life. Perhaps the most obvious feature of practically all his writings is the occurrence of sudden and unforeseen breaks in many of his phrases. Sometimes a sentence that the reader was unconsciously expecting to go on, stops short abruptly. Quite often a sentence which had begun in a certain rhythm halts and pauses, and then continues in another rhythm. Or again the grammatical sequence may be interrupted and the sentence may end with a different construction from that with which it began. All these abrupt changes seem to be connected with Gide's natural aversion to conventional, expected developments of thought—in short, to what might be called his hatred of eloquence. The constant break in the sentence serves to keep the attention of the reader from wandering, and prevents him from being lulled by the rhythm of regular phrases as by the hum of well oiled machinery. This peculiarity shows that the author never permits himself to be carried away by the thoughts he is expressing, or tied down by a formula for rhythmic or grammatical reasons—or indeed for any other reasons—but that he is always on the alert, thinking independently and with continued freshness and vigour. This is the stylistic counterpart of Gide's refusal to submit obediently to the demands of conventional logic.

These sudden interruptions do not make for a limitation of outlook; on the contrary, they are a subtle invitation to the reader to let his own imagination pursue a direction hinted at occasionally by Gide. The same end is served by Gide's constant use of very simple and unpretentious terms, which however imply more than they actually express. This moderation in vocabulary and this conciseness in the combining of words, are but two aspects of the fundamental restraint which is one of the principles of Gide's conception of art. The aim is always to set the reader thinking for himself in order to complete, or perhaps simply to continue, the half-uttered thought. Another impulse in the same direction is given by the typically Gidian habit of placing the verb at the end of the sentence. A phrase which ends with a verb has the effect of incompleteness, and remains open, so to speak, for the development of a train of unexpressed, but none the less real ideas in the mind of the thoughtful reader.

Gide's prose, as the most tangible part of his art, remains very close to real life. There is nothing theoretical or artificial about it, especially nothing conventional or ready-made. The sentences are not modelled on a set pattern, are not specifically well turned and displayed for our admiration in full and splendid array. They give the impression of being formed and of taking shape under our very eyes. The reader, watching the sentences being formed, feels that he is taking part in an exploration of reality. It is impossible after the first few words to guess even vaguely where the rest is going to lead, whether it will develop along a straight line, or turn sharply to right or left, rise or fall, or merely stop short before an obstacle. So it is hardly possible to read Gide rapidly. One must grope along through the windings of his phrases. Yet there is no obscurity in them; all is perfectly clear. Progress however can be made only step by step. There are circumlocutions, hesitations, advances and retreats, disappointments, and marvellous finds. Reading a sentence of Gide's is a miniature adventure. Just as his attitude towards life was one of curious and interested investigation, his style is a combination of perpetual inquiry and discovery.

Thus it may be understood why Gide's style is both critical and poetical. It is critical inasmuch as it proceeds cautiously, never hurrying blindly forward, but always taking stock of its position, examining the ground ahead, sometimes wandering in search of a better path, stopping, or even retracing its steps. It is poetical because it keeps in close touch with reality, never allowing abstract intelligence to interpose a veil between human personality and the essence of things. Sometimes the brightest jewels are found in privileged moments of complete communion between mind and reality. Purely poetical moments are as rare in Gide's prose as they are in ordinary life; but a sort of dim poetical colour suffuses all his writings, precisely because he never loses sight of the actuality of things and never wanders into the theoretical or the conventional.

That sincerity towards himself and towards reality appears on the whole to be the fundamental feature of Gide's personality and his work. He is a sincere man, seeking his own interpretation of the world. He refuses to accept the ready-made images that are offered to him, and resolutely rejects those that are forced upon him. He wishes to dis-

cover his own truth. All his writing bears testimony to
the manner in which he has achieved this; it sets an example of how the discovery may be made by any one of
us. In fact it must be made, to some extent, by all those
who do not want to be merely one of the herd, who refuse
simply to repeat words and formulæ that have been taught
them, who desire to live a life of their own. 'J'écris pour
qu'un adolescent, plus tard, pareil à celui que j'étais à
seize ans, mais plus libre, plus hardi, plus accompli, trouve
ici réponse à son interrogation palpitante.' [119] To such
Gide is an inspiring example though he has insisted that,
as for others, he was never an advocate of his own views.
His truth is not everybody's truth; his conclusions apply
to himself alone. Gide is never eager that other people
should adopt his own ideas, but he would have them go
forth and seek the truth for themselves. 'Nathanaël,
throw away my book. . . . Do not think that *your* truth
can be found by someone else; be ashamed of that more
than anything. . . . Throw away my book; say to yourself that this is only one of the thousand possible attitudes
towards life. Search out your own. . . .' [120]

119. *Les Nouvelles Nourritures,* Fragments du Ier livre, p.96.
120. *Les Nourritures Terrestres,* Envoi, p.223.

JEAN GIRAUDOUX

III. JEAN GIRAUDOUX

1. *Giraudoux's Life*

JEAN GIRAUDOUX, so far, is little known abroad. In France, however, there are very few people who do not evince a strong and definite reaction towards him, one way or another. Many believe him to be one of the greatest contemporary masters of French literature; others there are who regard his works as the quintessence of exasperating artificiality. These variations of opinion, and even the heated controversies which have arisen from time to time about his place in French literature, may be attributed to a number of causes: the difficulty of access to his art; the many formal complications which mask or hinder the approach to his thought; the very subtlety of his ideas and feelings, which, to be appreciated, call for the exercise of delicate and assiduous ingenuity and sympathetic understanding on the part of the reader. The effort necessary for penetrating through the intricacies of Giraudoux's imaginative creations is, however, well repaid by the enjoyment of the poetical charm, the keen wisdom and the light fantasy which are so harmoniously mingled and blended in all his writings.

Jean Giraudoux was born on 19 October 1882, in Bellac, a small town of less than five thousand inhabitants in the old province of Limousin. Apart from its association with Giraudoux, the town seems to have no particular claim upon our admiration or interest. Though Bellac is of some antiquity, its history does not recall any especially heroic deeds or important political events. It is picturesque enough, but not more so than a hundred other French provincial towns. The climate is harsh and damp, and in winter very cold. The surrounding country, it is true, shows some attractive scenery: the rolling hills are crowned with thick, dark woods; patches of brown fields or green meadows deck the lower slopes; down in the valleys, swiftly flowing streams and lively brooks bubble over mossy stones and rounded pebbles—yet an atmosphere of seriousness, almost of melancholy, seems to pervade the whole landscape.

For Giraudoux, however, Bellac—'*c'est bien la plus belle ville du monde.*' [1] Throughout his works he has never tired of expatiating upon the quaint charm of his native town and the beauties and attractions of his beloved Limousin. Both town and province strongly influenced his development and left their indelible stamp upon him. Giraudoux grew up in Bellac within the peaceful atmosphere to be found in almost any secluded French provincial town at the close of the nineteenth century. His family belonged to the lower middle class; his father was an engineer, in the public service, being in charge of the numerous small bridges of the region. So Giraudoux from early childhood was acquainted with all the familiar types of a small, old-fashioned French community: *le pharmacien*, the chemist—*l'agent voyer*, the road surveyor—*le percepteur*, the tax-collector—*le controlleur des poids et mesures*, the controller of weights and measures, and many varieties of *inspecteurs*, all deeply imbued with a consciousness of their own importance in the petty officialdom of France.

To these good folk life did not present many complications or problems. Their ideas rested upon an old and

1. J.Giraudoux, *Provinciales*, Emile-Paul, Paris, 1927, ii. Allégories. A l'Amour, à l'Amitié, p.133.

firmly established yet mellow tradition; they had simple
and definite notions of good and bad; their merits as well
as their defects were moderate and normal; they led a
dull but well regulated and well balanced existence. 'Small
towns are not mirrors which distort. The prevailing qualities of life in general, its ebb and flow, were reflected
in Bellac only in such a well ordered way and so patently
that they were quite inoffensive. January there was always cold, August always torrid; each of our neighbours
had but one virtue or one vice at a time; we learned
to know the world, as is fitting, by spelling out each
season and each sentiment separately. Each of the well
plastered houses in the street played, as it were, one
musical note—avarice, vanity, gluttony: no sharps nor
flats; no miser-glutton, no modest-wanton. . . .' [2]—So
speaks one of Giraudoux's heroines, who had been brought
up in Bellac—very much as was Giraudoux himself. No
doubt many of these queer *petits bourgeois* were open to
ridicule—but always in a rather pathetic sort of way.
After all they were not missing the essentials of life, since
they enjoyed their home town, their family, their occupa-
tion or their trade, in fact their whole existence, quietly,
sincerely, earnestly. 'We tasted life . . . in all its full-
ness.' [3] This simple but wholesome conception of living
became and remained the foundation of the whole development of Giraudoux's personality, sometimes arousing in
him nostalgic memories in later years.

In the Limousin countryside closely surrounding the
little town and within easy reach even of a child, Giraudoux early learned to understand and appreciate Nature.
Nature did not reveal herself here in her most spectacular
aspects; but contact with a subdued, delicate type of

2. J.Giraudoux, *Suzanne et le Pacifique* Emile-Paul, Paris, 1930, I, pp.22–23.
3. *Ibidem*, I, p.16.

scenery, whose charm depends essentially on seasonal impressions and fine hourly shades, sharpened Giraudoux's perception of its most subtle and elusive manifestations. From his native Limousin he derived an instinctive and lasting taste for the disciplined lines of an old French landscape, with an acute awareness of the rarest and most fleeting elements of beauty in the play of line and colour under a changing sky.

These influences, which his town and his province exerted on Giraudoux, have been extended by—and probably to some extent mingled with—other childhood experiences. His father, being unable to endure the damp climate of Bellac on account of his rheumatism, removed to the village of Cérilly, in Auvergne, where he had been appointed collector of taxes. Cérilly was less prepossessing than Bellac, though the moral atmosphere was almost identically the same. It is likely that the picture of a sleepy provincial town, which Giraudoux has evoked so often under the name of Bellac, actually combines the features of Bellac itself and of little Cérilly, to which the boy regularly returned for his school holidays.

Giraudoux's schooling had already stretched over a number of years. At first he went to a primary school in the village of Pellevoisin; then he was sent as a boarder to the *Lycée* of Châteauroux. Of the town of Châteauroux itself—'the ugliest city in France' [4] and banal as Giraudoux always felt it to be—he retained little else than a wistful memory. But the *lycée* was the influence that really moulded his mind in the way it was to remain for the rest of his life.

He always stood first in his class in every subject; for he was already displaying a keen and brilliant intelligence

4. J.Giraudoux, *Adorable Clio*, Emile-Paul, Paris, 1920, Nuit à Châteauroux, p.79.

and was working with a zeal and enthusiasm which far exceeded, not only the requirements of the curriculum, but even the wishes of his teachers. 'O work, beloved work,' he wrote reminiscently twenty years later, 'thou who overthroweth shameful laziness! O work of a child, generous as the love of a child! It is so easy, however watchful the teachers' supervision may be, to work unceasingly. In the refectory whilst the mail was being distributed, since I never received any, I took advantage of the opportunity to review my notebooks. On Thursdays and Sundays, in order to avoid going for a walk with the other pupils, I used to slip stealthily into the studyroom. . . . During recess between classes, I did not even trouble to conceal my book, but moved slowly round and round a pillar, according to the position of the supervising master, who was pacing up and down the courtyard. I used to get up every morning at five and joyfully retrieve from my desk a half-constructed composition, the scattered sheets of an essay. . . .' [5] Giraudoux absorbed with eagerness all that his teachers were able to offer him. Latin, Greek, and French classical literature were then the fundamental subjects taught in the French secondary schools. Latin especially played a decisive part in his mental development. He himself declared afterwards: 'I could almost say that the first language I wrote in a literary way was Latin.' [6]

He not only assimilated the linguistic husks of the classics, but also soon felt active within himself the spirit which they are supposed to inspire. Every human thought or action, past or present, became in his eyes tinged with the splendid and noble glow of eternal beauty. All that

5. J.Giraudoux, *Simon le Pathétique*, Grasset, Paris, 1926, i, pp.18–19.
6. F.Lefèvre, *Une heure avec . . . Quatrième Série*, Nouvelle Revue Française, Paris, 1927—Jean Giraudoux, p.119.

was mean and contemptible in life disappeared from view in the glorious pursuit of disinterested grandeur. Giraudoux, under the transparent disguise of one of his characters, reviews his indebtedness to his first teachers. 'I owed them,' he says, 'a broad outlook on life and a limitless soul. I owed it to them that, when I saw a hunchback I thought of Thersit, and when I saw a wrinkled old woman I thought of Hecuba. I knew too many heroes to conceive of anything but beauty or ugliness on an heroic scale. I owed to them any belief that I had in inspiration. . . . I owed to them my belief in those sentiments that one experiences within a sacred wood, during a night in Scotland, amidst an assembly of kings—a belief in mystic exaltation, in horror, in enthusiasm. . . . We knew by heart all the noble lines, all the sublime utterances. . . . How sweet is the sublime to a boy reading after his lessons are done, in the ill-lighted study, while the thunder rumbles outside. . . .' [7]

This moral idealism, this epic transfiguration of the universe, was but one side of Giraudoux's mental development during his school years. At the same time, a rigid intellectual discipline of the kind with which in France most university men become deeply imbued, was laid upon the docile student by the joint efforts of scores of teachers, all ardent devotees of *La Raison*. A strictly rationalistic method, implying careful analysis of problems, precise accounts, symmetrical statements, clear distinctions, and consistent deductions, became, temporarily at least, a part of his personal way of thinking. Later on, ironically apostrophizing an imaginary character who stands for one of his former teachers, Giraudoux has referred in the following manner to this professorial craze for explaining everything logically. 'How sweet it

7. *Simon le Pathétique*, I, pp.31–32.

was to tread the ground, how sweet to live—you declared—when you explained all that comes to pass by
reason! These mechanical birds in this tower were singing
by the grace of reason. . . . By virtue of reason, as soon
as winter had fled, spring returned, and as long as the
pole star looked blue, by virtue of reason, one was ready
to die. How lovely the Seine appeared, in the neighbourhood of Les Andelys, when, by reason, it traces twelve
curves, each of them containing a railway station and
a church!' [8] Yet willy-nilly—and whatever his ulterior
reactions may have been—Giraudoux was too good a
student not to allow himself to be impregnated with the
fundamental doctrine of his masters, the mark of whose
influence he has carried all through his life.

After obtaining his *baccalauréat* with great distinction,
he was awarded a scholarship in a Parisian *lycée—Lycée
Lakanal*—where he was to prepare for the entrance examination to the *Ecole Normale Supérieure*. The *Ecole
Normale Supérieure*, on the Rue d'Ulm in Paris, is officially a centre of training for higher university posts, but
in point of fact it has become to a large extent an institution for intellectually outstanding young men, who
eventually scatter and sometimes distinguish themselves
in the most diversified fields—in literature, politics, scientific research, diplomacy, and even in the world of business. The majority of the *Normaliens* do of course become professors, but even then it is more often than not
because an academic career is the only course open to
them. . . . The *Ecole Normale* is a kind of intellectual
hot-house. Candidates for entrance are subjected to a
very rigorous process of selection. An intense intellectual
activity is maintained by the extremely high standard of

8. J.Giraudoux, *Juliette au Pays des Hommes*, Emile-Paul, Paris, 1924, VI,
Prière sur la Tour Eiffel, pp.184–185.

scholarship required—also by the free intercourse of keen, young minds, all of them original, all of them different, enriching one another by the stimulation of their mutual reactions. Yet the *Ecole Normale* lacks the invigorating breath of fresh air. It is sometimes referred to mockingly as the *monastère de la rue d'Ulm*; indeed, in its secluded and confined atmosphere there is much that is abstract and artificial. Among these gifted young men, who as a rule have learned a great deal from books, but know little of actual life, it often happens that a few independent spirits will experience the irrepressible longing to break away and plunge into the rough and tumble of reality.

Jean Giraudoux entered the *Ecole Normale* in 1903. The training that he received there continued on the same lines as the schooling that had been given him previously at the *Lycée de Châteauroux* and at the *Lycée Lakanal*, both of which had inculcated in him a lofty moral ideal, a subtle dialectic ability, a thorough classical culture, but at the same time a secret desire to get away from it all. Of course, as he himself intended to become a professor, his studies were infinitely more advanced and more specialized than before, but their general trend remained approximately the same.

Giraudoux, however, did not become a professor; the prospect of a life of bookish erudition was too much for his natural vitality. When the time came for him to decide finally whether he would enter on a university career or not, he chose instead to take what the world might offer him and went abroad. He was not throwing off his intellectual past in disgust or in anger; his intellectual habits had become too much an integral part of his personality by now. But he was well aware that culture and learning represent but one small facet of the great motley universe; he did not want to remain restricted within the narrow confines of a bookcase; he felt an urge to explore the world.

He did explore the world for nearly five years, with the careless joy of a schoolboy playing truant—often on foot, with a *rucksack*. Sometimes he had casual employment; sometimes he was entrusted with an official mission; generally he went without much money, but always he trusted to his luck, which brought him frequently a picturesque adventure. At one time he became the tutor of a German prince (the Prince of Saxe-Meiningen); at another he did some newspaper work for the French daily paper *Le Matin*. Meanwhile he was sending in short stories to the literary magazines—*La Grande Revue, L'Ermitage, La Nouvelle Revue Française*. In the course of his peregrinations he visited hurriedly the greater part of Europe —Germany, Holland, Norway, Austria, Italy, the Balkans; he even took a short trip to the United States, Canada, Mexico, returning *via* the Azores.

Of all the countries he saw, Germany was the one which had the most decisive influence upon him. While still at the *Ecole Normale*, he had carried his study of German literature far enough to receive the *Diplôme d'études supérieures d'allemand* from the University of Paris; he was able to speak German fluently, and the encounter with the actual spectacle of German life and culture aroused in him a medley of conflicting reactions. Up to then the realities he had known—those pertaining to French life, of course—had fitted more or less easily into the framework of his French mental categories, formed in the course of his school training. Naturally, he must have suspected that reality extended, in many of its aspects, far beyond the range and reach of any merely rational system. Yet he had not been conscious of any

definite incompatibility between ideas and facts. Now, in
Germany, he was brought into contact with a whole set
of new facts—facts which refused to conform to the pattern of his French classical culture. He was too clear-
sighted not to perceive the tremendous intrinsic interest
and value of these facts; on the other hand, his mind had
been too definitely moulded by his own intellectual training for him to be able to discard this training without
ceasing to be himself. Before this, indeed, a rift had become perceptible within his personality at the time when,
for the sake of a broader existence, he gave up the university career for which he had been preparing throughout
his youth. But this rift widened into a real dualism when
personal contact with a reality different from the one
which had hitherto surrounded him revealed to him the
presence of a checkered universe, passionately interesting
and entirely independent of the rules of rational logic
which had been presented to him at school and college as
the supreme law of all reality.

Giraudoux's numerous journeys all over Europe and
his trip to America strengthened the impression—which
Germany had primarily been responsible for fostering in
him—that, quite apart from the realm of theoretical
ideas, there is a richly variegated world which must be
enjoyed with a direct and spontaneous naïveté. For
Giraudoux had experienced neither pessimism nor despondency in connexion with this dislocation of his general
outlook. He was young then. He enjoyed excellent health;
during his school-days he had been devoted to athletics;
he had even achieved some very creditable performances
on the running track; the wholesome out-door life he
was now leading most of the time was invigorating and
exhilarating. The whole world seemed prosperous; life
was easy everywhere; no passports were required from

the traveller; international suspicions were temporarily dormant; in spite of some distant but ominous rumblings, optimism was the keynote of Europe about the year 1910— and in this optimism Giraudoux fully shared. Sometimes he would take hard, bright fragments of this newly discovered reality and try to string them together on the guiding thread of his old ideals, but this was done in a spirit of jest and without any pangs of anxiety or remorse. So came into being the short stories which were later collected under the title of *Provinciales* and *l'Ecole des Indifférents*—but very few people noticed them at the time of their original publication.

The years were passing and Giraudoux could not continue indefinitely leading this enjoyable but decidedly erratic existence. It was time for him to settle down. Yet he both wanted to go on travelling and at the same time to retain a foot-hold in Paris, to which he was strongly attached through the charm of its rare culture and by other influences as well. These diverging aspirations— clear reflections of his dual nature—he was able to hold together through the prospect of a diplomatic career. In 1910, thanks to some influential connexions, he was appointed *élève vice-consul* in the French Ministry of Foreign Affairs.

Actually, for four years, there was little alteration in his mode of life. A great part of his time was spent in travelling on more or less important diplomatic missions. In the course of these he visited both Russia and the Orient. When not abroad, he remained in Paris, working in the office of the Ministry of Foreign Affairs, and attending to his own private interests in his leisure time. It was then that he wrote the reminiscent and wistful *Simon le Pathétique*, which was in the course of publication when the war broke out.

In the war Giraudoux took an active and gallant part. He fought with distinction on the Marne, in Alsace, at the Dardanelles, and was three times cited for bravery. Having been wounded and temporarily disabled for infantry service, he was sent to Portugal. Later he accompanied Marshal Joffre and Bergson on a mission of good will to America.

The war does not seem to have changed Giraudoux's general philosophy of life to any marked extent. In 1914 he was thirty-two years of age; his personality was then too strongly fixed to be transformed easily or swayed by external events. Of course, as a civilized human being, he deplored the wanton destruction and slaughter of the war; but precisely because he found himself in the thick of action, because he accepted all his responsibilities with a calm heroism, he was less struck by the hideous and sordid side, than stimulated and inspired by the epic aspect of the great struggle. In his little book *Adieu à la Guerre*, in which he sums up his war impressions, he says: 'Comment la guerre se passa? En réveils, en réveils incessants. Tous mes souvenirs de guerre ne sont que des souvenirs de réveil.[9] The word *réveil*, 'awakening,' must be taken here as having a symbolic as well as a literal meaning. War revealed to him human realities much deeper and wider than any afforded by his previous adventures, and he enjoyed the experience to the full. This explains the seemingly strange epigraph which appears at the beginning of the most important of his war books, *Adorable Clio*: 'Pardonne-moi, ô guerre, de t'avoir—toutes les fois que je l'ai pu—caressée. . . .'[10]—'Forgive me, o war, that—whenever I could—I have caressed thee. . . .'

The most direct consequence of this new and intense

9. J.Giraudoux, *Adieu à la Guerre*, Grasset, Paris, 1919, p.13.
10. *Adorable Clio*, Epigraphe.

vision of reality vouchsafed to Giraudoux was that it brought to a climax the latent problem always present in his mind concerning the dissociation of classical culture and the modern world. Before the war, he could still throw fragile and elegant bridges across from one side to the other, as if in play. War for him forced a grim reality into the foreground, obscuring his idealism, which was relegated, temporarily at least, to a position of secondary importance.

For Giraudoux the post-war period was not a time of trouble and anxiety, as it was for so many of his countrymen. After a short interlude he resumed his duties at the Ministry of Foreign Affairs, eventually qualifying for the French civil service. He was greatly helped in his career by the appreciation and friendship of Philippe Berthelot, son of the illustrious scientist, Marcelin Berthelot, and at that time head of the political department at the Quai d'Orsay. Though Giraudoux still retained his fondness for travelling, he was no restless globe-trotter like his colleague and friend, Paul Morand. As a place of residence he definitely preferred Paris to any other spot in the world. The eminently civilized life of the capital, and the calm and peaceful atmosphere of a happy home—for he was now married and the father of a family—constituted for him the strongest of ties and exerted on him a most steadying influence.

Nevertheless, as a diplomat—though a diplomat stationed in Paris—he was keenly interested in foreign countries. Until 1924 he was attached to the *Service des Œuvres Françaises à l'Etranger*—that is to say, the department of the Ministry that supervises and fosters the development of French intellectual influence abroad. So it was possible for him—indeed it was one of his official duties—to observe from a particular angle the movements and the trend of public opinion throughout the world. The great problem which he felt lay at the foundation of the reconstruction of Europe after the upheaval of the war was the question of the future relations of France and Germany. He was well acquainted with Germany and he knew only too well the difficulties which stood in the way of a reconciliation between the two countries. He remembered how deeply impressed he had been several years before, when he had realized the profound disagreement existing between the French classical ways of reasoning and the German fundamental views of reality. Yet the desirability of an understanding between the two countries was obvious and Giraudoux's book *Siegfried et le Limousin* (1922) may be considered as a sympathetic, though perhaps pessimistic, exploration of the possibilities of achieving a Franco-German mutual understanding. The book proved an enormous success and brought to its author, who up to then had been only the favourite of a small *élite*, wide and general recognition.

Giraudoux meanwhile had found himself involved in a feud which for a time profoundly agitated the *Ministère des Affaires Etrangères*. Personal antipathy brought Philippe Berthelot into conflict with Raymond Poincaré, then Prime Minister and one of the leading statesmen in the field of French foreign policy. Though Berthelot was a follower of Briand, Poincaré's rival, the differences between them seem to have been more a matter of individual incompatibility than of disagreement on political principles. After an open breach had occurred as a result of some dealings connected with the failure of the *Banque Industrielle de Chine*, among the directors of which was a brother of Berthelot, the latter had to retire. This was in 1922. Giraudoux's sympathies were all on Berthelot's side—

as everybody was aware. In 1924 he was 'exiled' from his beloved Paris by being appointed to the staff of the French Embassy in Berlin. When the Poincaré ministry was overthrown, which happened in the course of the same year, Giraudoux was able to return to Paris. He was then placed in charge of the Press Bureau at the Ministry of Foreign Affairs.

The struggle, however, was not by any means over. To relieve his feelings and to vindicate his friend Berthelot, Giraudoux attacked Poincaré in a virulent diatribe entitled *Bella*. The attack missed fire to a large extent because the book was brought before the public precisely at the time when Poincaré, once more Prime Minister, was putting an end to the disastrous system of inflation and was being hailed all over the country as the 'saviour of the franc.'

Shortly afterwards Giraudoux joined the Commission appointed to settle the differences between Turkey and her opponents during the late war—especially France. Both in Constantinople and in Paris his work as Commissioner brought him for a long period of time into close contact with Turks and other Orientals of all sorts and conditions. Later on, when Briand—also a friend of Berthelot—became one of the leaders in the international peace movement, Giraudoux was privileged to observe at close range the pathetic efforts of the French statesman to bring about a measure of pacification in the field of European diplomatic relations. A reflection of these events is clearly apparent in *Eglantine* (1927) and *Combat avec l'Ange* (1934), in which Giraudoux has recorded his political experiences and impressions of this period in a fictitious and romantic setting.

Meanwhile Giraudoux had emerged, quite unexpectedly,

as one of the leading French playwrights of the day. In 1928 a dramatized version of the book which first brought him recognition—*Siegfried et le Limousin*—was produced on the stage, under the shorter title of *Siegfried*. Overnight it was revealed that Giraudoux possessed an instinct for the theatre that almost nobody had suspected in him. Up to then he had been regarded as a subtle humorist, a writer of delicate fantasies, an imaginative poet—none of which characteristics seemed to qualify him for the drama. The 'hit' made by *Siegfried* marked a turning point in his development. After *Siegfried* he continued writing intricate novels as before, and he retained his connexion with the Ministry of Foreign Affairs; but the lure of the public's applause, also the realization of his own dramatic capacities, the conviction that he had definitely found his most adequate vehicle of expression, led him to devote more and more of his time and his activity to the theatre. His *Amphitryon 38*, produced in 1929, proved a great success; *Judith*, staged in 1932, did not arouse so much enthusiasm; but his later productions—*Intermezzo* in 1933, *Tessa*—a French adaptation of *The Constant Nymph*, the play by Margaret Kennedy and Basil Dean—in 1934, and *La Guerre de Troie n'aura pas lieu* in 1935—were received with general approbation.

The essential aspects of Giraudoux's talent have not been altered by leaning towards drama; on the contrary, they assert themselves perhaps more clearly and more sharply than before. But it is difficult to decide whether this change in orientation—this clearer and sharper mode of presentation—is due to the influence of the stage or to the growing self-confidence of a writer who has gained universal recognition just at the time when he has reached a state of well balanced maturity.

2. Ideals and Reality

'Do you remember the day that you ordered me to choose between the stoic and the epicure and I couldn't obey you, for I liked both?' [11] This apostrophe which Giraudoux addresses to one of his symbolic professors gives the key to the main problem which is evoked under one aspect or another in practically every one of his writings. Stoicism and epicureanism, moral ideals and earthly reality have met throughout the ages in many a bitter conflict as well as in frequent intercourse. The works of Giraudoux offer only another instance of their irreducible antagonism and their ineluctable association.

On the one hand, Giraudoux became imbued during his school years with a clear and noble conception of existence, either derived from the books he studied or infused into him by the eloquence of his idealistically minded instructors, who illustrated their teachings with inspiring examples of real or imaginary heroes from the past. He was to cherish this 'vision splendid' all through his life, and he clung to it and maintained it stubbornly in spite of all its apparent contradictions with reality and his own personal disappointments. On the other hand, he was also alive to the existence of an external world that was not unpleasing to the senses—a world that was richly coloured, variegated, mysterious, enormous, sometimes immoral, often inexplicable and disconcerting, voluptuous or crude, violent or restrained, but always of supreme and engrossing interest. He enjoyed this reality, accepted it as it was, and gave it his fullest and most sincere allegiance. Now a moral conception of life and an intense perception of reality cannot possibly

11. *Juliette au Pays des Hommes*, VI, Prière sur la Tour Eiffel, p.188.

subsist side by side, in separate and distinct compartments as it were, without ever coming into contact. Sooner or later they must confront each other. All Giraudoux's work bears witness to this confrontation.

On the whole, the case of Giraudoux is not an exceptional or even an uncommon one. The majority of men find themselves at one time or another in the same state of mental dualism, torn between a pure and revered ideal and an attractive, overpowering reality. Hence the almost universal appeal of Giraudoux's writings. His originality, however, has lain to some extent in the special terms in which his particular problem was set—in the peculiar nature of the ideal he nurtured and the sort of reality he met with. But it is essentially in the way he disposes of the problem itsel' that he has displayed the true originality of his nature. Whereas most men make a clean-cut choice and develop into either inveterate dreamers or disgruntled realists, Giraudoux by an amazing *tour de force* has succeeded in retaining the essentials of the opposing elements of his personality and built up for his own use a fragile and graceful structure, which he invites the reader to visit and admire.

Giraudoux's ideal comprises several distinct aspirations or tendencies. The most obvious and perhaps the dominant feature is a constant preoccupation with moral ends and purposes. 'A mon avis,' he says, 'le but d'un livre, l'idée dominante d'un auteur au moment où il écrit un livre, doit être une idée morale. . . .' [12] And speaking of modern French literature—or rather of *his* conception of modern French literature—he remarks: 'French literature today is distinguished chiefly by moral and poetical qualities, which far exceed its value as mere entertainment. That is why it does not seem entertaining

12. F.Lefèvre, *Une heure avec . . . Quatrième Série*, J.Giraudoux, p.118.

to everybody, and why more than ever it attracts the
attention of the literary public in countries demanding in
their reading elevation and consolidation and not mere
pleasantries.' [13] Giraudoux loves and praises all the high
and noble sentiments—friendship, patriotism, generosity,
self-control, abnegation. Good and evil have a positive
meaning for him and he is always definitely on the side of
virtue. Yet his idea of virtue does not conform to the
Christian idea of virtue. He is not over-fond of weak and
humble feelings such as pity. 'Pity is what takes the place
of love in selfish people.' [14] There is a certain amount of
hardness, of pride, of tension in his ideal; man is constantly reminded of his eminent dignity and exhorted to
try and surpass himself. If any influence is to be assigned
as the source that has inspired these tendencies in Giraudoux, it is certainly that of the stoicism of the Ancients.
'There is a philosophy which I have always appreciated,
and that is the philosophy of the Stoics.' [15] The word
'sublime,' which so often recurs throughout his writings,
most adequately describes the goal towards which he
consistently strives.

This striving after the 'sublime' does not imply any
extraordinary or supernormal achievement on Giraudoux's part; it is just an endeavour to picture the world
more as it ought to be. In a well regulated universe everything should be in its proper place, every attack against
the general order should be punished, real merit should
be rewarded, virtue should finally triumph. Giraudoux
has been so deeply imbued with the classical idea of a
sovereign order ruling the whole world that the existence

13. F.Lefèvre, *Une heure avec* . . . *Première Série*, Nouvelle Revue Française,
Paris, 1924, J.Giraudoux, p.148.
14. J.Giraudoux, *L'Ecole des Indifférents*, Grasset, Paris, 1922, Jacques l'Egoïste,
p.20.
15. F.Lefèvre, *Une heure avec* . . . *Première Série*—J.Giraudoux, p.150.

of that order has acquired in his mind the value and power of a logical postulate. This order he conceives not as an arbitrary and external dictate imposed on Nature but as the expression of the eternal reason which, from within Nature itself, has brought order out of chaos. The influence of French classical rationalism is easily discernible in this belief that there are logical rules and laws which constitute the framework of reality, and that, through the understanding of these rules the whole process of the creation becomes obvious, simple, and clear. Yet this rationalism of Giraudoux's is in no sense theoretical and abstract; it is deeply human, being closely linked to tradition and heavy with the thoughts—and sometimes the passions—of generations of men. It is not a mere framework without solid content, but the concrete result of centuries of human effort to discover within man's confused experience the outline and shape of duty and truth.

Nevertheless, Giraudoux must have perceived long before he left college that in real life things are not as they should be, and that the supposed sovereignty of reason is not the only power controlling the world. But this conception, at once moral and rational, was so noble and so satisfying that he retained it against all the contradictions of brute facts, giving it a place in the privileged realm of his adolescent day-dreams. A sublime moral ideal and a logical rational order may after all be little else than beautiful figments of the imagination, yet they are instinct with tremendous spiritual force and deserve to be carefully nurtured. They cannot be treated as mere fictions without losing their efficacy as conditioning motives of behaviour. But they can very well stand being surrounded with a conventional, imaginative, poetic atmosphere—in fact, they cannot survive without it, as Giraudoux indicated when he spoke of 'la fantaisie qu'exigent les humanités.' [16] So in order to protect them from the corrosive action of reality, Giraudoux has deliberately enveloped them in an aura of free, airy, but indestructible fancy. This does not mean that they should be lost in the midst of vague and indefinite clouds. He is too much a lover of classical precision to save them at that price. But, while retaining their solidity and vigour, he allows them to be transfigured and transposed on to a higher, more ideal plane in the way that human actions become transfigured and transposed in epic poetry. Hence his thoroughly personal judgments and opinions on literature: 'My idea has always been that the supreme epoch of French literature was that of the *Chansons de Geste*. . . . Great poetry is always epic. . . . The novel in France is precisely what remains of that epic poetry.' [17]

So the ideal of Giraudoux, with its triple aspect of 'sublime' moral aspiration, rational intellectual discipline, imaginative poetical fantasy, is seen to be a complex but perfectly coherent and normal growth. Its roots are deeply embedded in classical culture of the kind that he received at school; but its luxuriant foliage has too often concealed the essential unity of the different shapes and divergent aspects that it presents.

Giraudoux's vision of reality stands in intimate connexion with his own life experiences. The contacts which he made with the external world during the formative years of his life fall naturally into two categories. His first experiences embraced all the early impressions that he garnered, respecting his family, his native town of Bellac, his beloved province of Limousin, and also to some extent his sojourns at Châteauroux and Cérilly.

16. *Simon le Pathétique*, ı, p.27.
17. F.Lefèvre, *Une heure avec . . . Quatrième Série*—J.Giraudoux, p.118.

The second round of experiences came to him years later, when after leaving the *Ecole Normale* he went travelling through Europe. From these two periods there remained with him two distinct sets of images, tinged with entirely different emotional colours. In the course of time the two sets mingled together in his mind, but they never melted completely into one another to form one indivisible whole. So a picture of reality drawn by Giraudoux usually combines elements from these two sources, not placed in separate compartments but generally intermingled like the pieces of a colourful and intricate mosaic.

The essential elements of his provincial experience are as a rule simple and matter of fact. They are mostly the sights, noises, and smells of a friendly little town; thus Giraudoux calls up the scene of the good people hurrying about their business or gossiping in a *café*, the bustle in the street and the din of the fair, the far-off sounds from the surrounding country, and the savour of the evening meal partaken of at home with the family. . . . 'On market days I had only to turn in my chair in order to shut out the sight of the market-place and see before me the empty countryside, denuded of its flocks. I had acquired the habit of making this half-turn on every occasion, directing my glance from the parson perhaps or the *sous-préfet*, as each passed by, over to the hills with their emptiness and silence by way of contrast and compensation as it were; and it was scarcely more difficult to change the kingdom of sounds—I had but to change windows. From the side facing the street one might hear children at a game of trains, or a phonograph, perhaps the trumpets of the newsboys, and the noise made by the ducks and the young goats that were being borne off to the kitchens. . . . From the side looking towards the mountain came the sound of the real train and of the animals whose bellowings and bleatings could be guessed at in winter, before they actually reached the ear, because of the white cloud of vapour about their muzzles. There we dined in summer, on a terrace. Sometimes it was the week when the acacias exhale their fragrance and we ate them in our fritters; or the time when the larks shot up into the sky and we ate them in our pies.' [18] All these simple, unpretentious details possess a strong and pungent quality. One feels they are associated with some of the most powerful impressions that have at any time imprinted themselves on the consciousness of our author. The familiar objects are penetrated with an atmosphere of sentiment and the little world they constitute is charged with a thousand imperceptible memories, all very homely and yet deeply affecting. Nevertheless this little world, for all its emotional content, presented few mysteries or problems. The good folk in Bellac were not puzzled about the meaning of life; their thoughts were clear and their actions all had a definite purpose. Yet in spite of this there was nothing harsh or discordant about them, for a mellowness, the result of age-old tradition, softened all the asperities and gave unity of tone to the divergent manifestations of their lives.

The other side of reality with which Giraudoux came into contact—in Paris, in Germany, in America—contrasted sharply with the first intimate impressions he had kept from Bellac. This new world that opened before his eyes was infinitely more brilliant, attractive, and picturesque. To the enraptured gaze of Giraudoux there was unfolded a glittering pageant of new faces, strange costumes, outlandish manners, unfamiliar tongues, incomprehensible sentiments, unexpected adventures. Naturally

18. *Suzanne et le Pacifique*, I, pp.2-3.

it would not be easy for the mind to grasp at once and to understand this motley reality. Everything appeared mysterious, unreasonable, incomprehensible. It was impossible in the intricate maze of apparently unrelated events to trace the logical sequence of cause and effect. Without any warning before his very eyes good would turn into evil, or *vice versa*. In fact the issue between good and evil seemed to be of little consequence anywhere. Immorality seemed to be rampant. But it was difficult to gather a general impression of any kind. How was one to compare Bavaria with Mexico, Paris with Norway, Holland with the United States? Reality, as it revealed itself to Giraudoux, was composed of small, irreducible fragments, richly coloured, but all of them self-contained and hard, and having no common measure. Everywhere ambition, voluptuousness, pain, jealousy, love, selfishness, curiosity, passion, were parcelling mankind out into separate and intense emotional units. There was in this spectacle an intriguing beauty to which Giraudoux could not but be profoundly sensitive.

He welcomed the variety of impressions that the world was offering to him, with all the ardent fervour of his rich, vital nature, and soon he found himself longing to feel the embrace of earth's manifestations in all their inexhaustible diversity. Every aspect of reality—material or spiritual, past or present, high or low, familiar or strange—whether from Bellac, from Paris or from the Pacific Ocean, appeared to him to be equally worthy of eager, personal interest. A flower, a bird, a river, a smile, a glance, a tear, the clouds, the stars, the woods, anger, gaiety, caprice, friendship, love or war, were one and all accepted indiscriminately by him as integral parts of the wonderful experience that is life, to be enjoyed with the utmost sincerity and frankness. That attitude of universal curiosity, of complete and positive acceptance of all the gifts of Nature, bespoke a natural optimism springing from a vigorous and powerful personality. Yet Giraudoux never indulges in any outbursts of passion, nor does he ever display any marked enthusiasm for any of the objects of his enjoyment; he tastes their flavour and expresses his appreciation, but always with so much discretion and restraint that his attitude sometimes seems quite casual and unconcerned, as if he were merely amusing himself.

In fact, the objects in themselves have little importance in his eyes. He never tries to penetrate their essential nature and to give an account of their objective reality. Giraudoux is almost exclusively interested in Giraudoux. His art is entirely subjective; he himself is directly or indirectly the sole subject of his writings. As he once declared, 'On opening a book, the reader says to himself, "I am going to have a fine story." I would like him to say as he opens one of my works, "I am going to get into touch with a living soul."' [19] His soul is singularly vibrant and sensitive. This is expressed in the title, *Simon le Pathétique*, which he gives to an obviously reminiscent book about Bellac, about the *Lycée de Châteauroux* and a few delicately elaborated early love affairs. *Pathétique* should here be taken as having its original etymological meaning of 'feeling intensely.' Yet again, however intensely he may feel, Giraudoux, perhaps as a result of his classical training, always exercises the utmost restraint in the expression of his feelings. He never pours out his emotions intemperately. He merely suggests them—often only by vague allusions which are not always obvious to the reader. He is not generally addicted to deep, intimate introspection, preferring his own reaction towards the external world.

19. F.Lefèvre, *Une heure avec . . . Première Série*—J.Giraudoux, p.150.

So the material of Giraudoux's art will be found to lie precisely where his sensibility meets the external world. They meet so constantly that it seems difficult at first to distinguish and dissociate them. Yet there is little blending, and still less fusion between the two elements; they remain distinct but they reflect one another like a set of reciprocal mirrors. Giraudoux's soul takes on the colour of the landscape; the landscape becomes tinged with the same hue as Giraudoux's soul. It is impossible to say on which side the play of light starts—often it would seem to have started simultaneously on both sides. One of his characters, a young girl, named Suzanne, who has been living alone on a small island for several years, says: ' Here, as I gaze upon this island that has become a mirror for my soul, so that I cannot distinguish my soul from the mirror —when confronted with these *dalaganpalangs* that resemble some wish of mine, this hill of Bahiki, with its red and black hollows, which is the exact replica of some little trouble that I feel, these *gnanlé* birds that imitate to perfection the dust of thought that swirls round about my own thinking, I, the queen, am suddenly overwhelmed by my own perfection. . . .' [20] This is a comparatively simple case; but when Giraudoux stands in the very centre of his multi-mirrored universe, the images are tossed back and forth as in a dizzy and bewildering play of battledore and shuttlecock. Then, as Giraudoux says, 'Il y a trop d'écho pour moi en ce monde.' [21] The words 'miroir,' 'reflet,' which insistently recur throughout his works are in keeping with this.

Such an outlook obviously precludes any attempt, any desire even, to penetrate beneath the surface of things. Giraudoux is content to enjoy their purely external as-

20. *Suzanne et le Pacifique*, IX, pp.224–225.
21. *Adorable Clio*—Nuit à Châteauroux, p.63.

pect—their colour and shape—which from his standpoint
are much more important than their internal structure.
The internal structure of a thing can be perceived only
by analysis and often at the price of the dislocation and
disintegration of the most essential and the loveliest elements of reality. Giraudoux, even if he does sometimes
venture upon an analysis of himself—though with extreme
caution—always surveys the world around him with deliberate superficiality of outlook as a pure artist. The
remark of one of his characters might easily have been
made by himself: 'I find the surface layer of the world is
quite thick enough. To me every living thing, and every
object, assumes reality more from its colour than from its
skeleton.' [22]

Jean Giraudoux is loath to drill inquisitive holes into
reality for fear of detracting from its charm and dimming
its brilliancy; he likes to take any object he may be considering and by turning it over quickly to examine it on
all sides. So, spurred on by his curiosity, he perceives in
rapid succession, all sorts of different and sometimes even
contradictory aspects of the same character or fact. Nothing is more typical of him than the almost simultaneous
presentation of contradictory features, apparently antagonistic, yet often associated, in the motley spectacle of
the universe. In *Amphitryon 38* the Greek princess, Alcmena, says to her husband, Amphitryon, whom she believes to be Jupiter in disguise: 'A very good imitation
indeed. An ordinary woman would be deceived by it.
Everything is there. These two sad wrinkles for smiling,
and this comical little hollow for tears.' [23] And later on
Jupiter says to Alcmena: 'Since this morning, I have been
admiring your courage and your obstinacy, how you de-

22. *L'Ecole des Indifférents*—Jacques l'Egoïste, p.69.
23. J.Giraudoux, *Amphitryon 38*, Paris, 1929, Act II, Sc.7.

vise your stratagems with loyalty and your lies with sincerity.' [24]

An ordinary observer is usually inclined to analyse, and upon the basis of his analysis to interpret what he sees. Giraudoux's method of observation, however, is direct and unspoilt by intelligence. This faculty in a man is an exceptional gift, almost a touch of genius. Ever since Adam tasted the fruit of the tree of knowledge, man has been unable, so thinks Giraudoux, to see the world except through the veil of human reasoning. He sees a meaning and a purpose in a thing instead of the actual thing itself. Now this pragmatic, rational and conventional interpretation of reality, which has become almost second nature to man, robs the world of all its original freshness and colour. What man perceives is merely a set of practical signs of danger or of utility. Giraudoux—resembling in this respect a few of the poets—seems to have been exempt from the hereditary curse, arising from Adam's original vice of curiosity. He can look at things with an unsophisticated eye just as if he had been born during the period between the Creation and the catastrophe of the Fall of Man. 'I still live . . . in that interval which separated the Creation and the original sin. I have been excepted from the universal curse.' [25] Adam's Fall, which introduced the knowledge of good and evil, and hence reason and intelligence into the world, distorted the vision of all mankind; nobody since has ever seen the world and all that it contains—its grandest as well as its meanest objects—as Adam saw them in their primitive, entrancing poetical setting—no one, that is, save Giraudoux! 'I see the age-old furnishings of the world, as Adam saw them, the trees, the pools, without their first stain, and its mod-

24. *Amphitryon 38*, Act III, Sc. 5.
25. *Juliette au Pays des Hommes*, VI, Prière sur la Tour Eiffel, p.188.

ern furnishings, the telephone, the cinema, . . . , in all
their divinity.' [26]

Behind this seemingly strange assertion lies the actual
background of Giraudoux's mental development. The dissociation which took place in his mind between scholastic
rationalism and the spontaneous perception of the universe enabled him to see the world with a genuine freshness of outlook, unhampered by the conventional associations and the practical interpretations which mar the
direct vision of the average thinking being. So Giraudoux
had on one side of him his intellectual equipment with its
rich cultural tradition, and on the other, entirely separate, an almost childlike innocence and intensity of perception whereby he was able to absorb the poetry of the
universe.

Yet it may be questioned whether that direct perception
of the universe is as childlike and candid as Giraudoux
would apparently have us believe. Beyond all doubt it is
unspoiled by any rational, conventional interpretation.
But to what extent is the organ of perception itself, Giraudoux's own eye, allowed to perceive, to see things under
normal conditions? How alarming and revealing is a statement such as this: 'It is noon. A light wind stirs the plan-
tain trees; if you press your finger against your eyes,
everything will appear radiant with fanciful colours.' [27]
Very often one gets the impression that Giraudoux purposely presses his fingers against his eyes in order to see a
rainbow which does not exist in reality. His images of the
world are not distorted, it is true, by any intellectual, conventional interpretation; but they often appear to be distorted at the very origin of their perception by a *parti-pris*
of vision. This creates, sometimes, the loveliest of effects,

26. *Juliette au Pays des Hommes*, VI, p.189.
27. *Adieu à la Guerre*, p.26.

but effects which many consider the outcome of the most exasperating habit of deliberate self-delusion.

This is, however, but a minor difficulty in the understanding of Giraudoux's art. The major problem for the reader is the resolution of his fundamental dualism—pure reason and passionate reality. Giraudoux has insisted often on their apparent irreducibility. He makes Helen of Troy say: 'I confess I do not spend my nights reflecting on the fate of mankind, but it has always seemed to me that there are two kinds of men: those who are, if you will, the flesh of human life—and those who represent its organization and its contour. The first have their laughter and their tears. . . . The others have gestures, deportment, command. If you compel these two to form a single race, it will not work at all.' [28]

Giraudoux did not endeavour to compel them to form one race. The two elements are too antagonistic ever to fuse into one homogeneous whole. Yet even though they are naturally distinct and in many ways incompatible, they constantly interfere and mingle with each other. Both sides retain the marks of such encounters, emerging bruised but at the same time enriched by the struggle. Since these encounters are inevitable—also beneficial though generally painful—the best plan to follow is to look for a measure of harmony, since conciliation or identification is definitely impossible.

Giraudoux does not try to solve the problem by engineering a combination of idealism and reality. In fact, he never tries to solve any problem at all. Whether he is discussing questions of a general nature—such as the relations between France and Germany, as in *Siegfried*—or a more particular matter, like the quest for a suitable hus-

28. J.Giraudoux, *La Guerre de Troie n'aura pas lieu*, Grasset, Paris, 1935, Act II, Sc. 8, p.144.

band in *Juliette au Pays des Hommes*—he never offers a definite, 'cut and dried' solution. He is content to point out subtle resemblances which may—or perhaps may not —help the reader to discover unsuspected affinities. Many of these resemblances are simply associations of images and ideas: 'The sight of a bird sets him longing to go off to Brazil without a moment's delay . . . a hat in a shop-window makes him confess to an irresistible desire to look at a woman and to be in love . . .' [29] Sometimes his comparisons rest upon rather far-fetched analogies. Thinking of an elderly lady who is dying of consumption, and of a young and attractive American girl he has just met, one of his characters says: 'Great similarities are splashed across the world and show their light here and there. They bring together, they match what is small with what is immense. . . . To my imagination Madame de Saint-Sombre's handkerchief, with her initials on it, seems like the wreck of a ship with the name almost obliterated; to me Miss Spottiswood, whose Christian name I don't know, is like a large basket of flowers whose handle I cannot grasp.' [30]

Besides this rather simple process of association between external images, Giraudoux often uses another much more original method, in order to illustrate the interplay of ideals and reality. This typical method of his offers two distinct, yet complementary forms: At times, under some thoroughly modern aspects of every-day life, seemingly prosaic, crude, vulgar, he is able to discern traces of an old, noble ideal which to the more casual observer would seem completely obliterated. Yet, as Giraudoux explains, the old ideal is still there, perhaps deeply embedded, nevertheless as actual and present as the surface facts that alone

29. *L'Ecole des Indifférents*—Jacques l'Egoïste, p.8.
30. *Ibidem*, pp.69–70.

are perceived by the ordinary man. Conversely, at other times behind the myths and legends of classical antiquity, which to so many scholars appear as mere abstractions, fanciful imaginings or theoretical concepts, Giraudoux proves that a very warm human element can nearly always be detected. He even believes this human element in old classical tales to be closely related, nay almost identical, to the human reality that we know today. So, according to the case, either a noble ideal is revealed behind present stark reality, or intense living reality is made to surge from an old ideal.

As an instance of the first case, in *Amica America*, Giraudoux shows how, underneath the outer crust of financial greed, ruthless competition, and soulless efficiency which seems to overlie the modern American nation, there still lives in the hearts of the people the generosity, the disinterestedness, the capacity for genuine enthusiasm which, since the days of George Washington, all French schoolboys have been taught to consider as the American ideal. Again, in *Siegfried et le Limousin* Giraudoux makes it clear that, notwithstanding the unpleasant impression created by Teutonic ruthlessness during the war and afterwards, Germany still possesses a potent, captivating charm and a deep reserve of culture that will not disappoint those who have retained from their studies a high appreciation and regard for the ideals of Goethe, Heine, and Wagner.

As an example of the second case, in *Amphitryon 38*, the mythological princess, Alcmena, the future mother of Hercules, is pictured receiving the advances of the mythological god Jupiter. This seems to carry the reader, as a matter of course, into an imaginary realm of classical reminiscence and fantasy. Yet, in Giraudoux's play, Alcmena deports herself in such a natural manner that, amid the setting of a purely mythical Antiquity, we see in her essentially a dutiful and loving wife, not altogether exempt from coquetry, making the best she can of an embarrassing and puzzling situation—exactly as an actual, living woman would do today. Similarly, in *La Guerre de Troie n'aura pas lieu*, Giraudoux shows that the events presented in the *Iliad* are not merely episodes of an ancient Greek legend; they have a general human bearing. The emotions gripping the city of Troy when the outbreak of the war appears inevitable, the frantic and useless efforts made to avert the impending catastrophe, have—we can easily imagine it— an exact counterpart in our own contemporary anxieties, fears, and forebodings. The mythical heroes of Homer are shown by Giraudoux as behaving—*mutatis mutandis*— exactly in the manner of our modern diplomats and 'patriots.'

So present-day reality and ancient myths, facts and ideals, explain and mutually complement each other. Their relationship is not conceived by Giraudoux as a fast and binding union. He never tries to weld abstraction and reality strongly and immutably together. He simply suggests, as if in play, parallelisms, equivalences, between these two independent aspects of life. His suggestions, always new and original, often possess an illuminating value. They are not, however, founded upon careful analysis. Fantasy, humour, imagination, are for Giraudoux the best way to reach and seize the most elusive, subtle, and yet all-important affinities.

Generally speaking, Giraudoux appeals more to the imagination than to the reasoning power. One must not study and examine his writings critically but rather follow them with the sympathetic attention one gives to poetry. His whole work appears like a curious day-dream in which fragments of reality, viewed directly and in all their original freshness, are surrounded by an idealistically sublime atmosphere. The complicated patterns thus evolved are sometimes merely a joy to the eye of the artist; but very often, like mystical hieroglyphics, they hold a deep meaning—then they may be difficult to decipher and perhaps open to different interpretations according to the fancy of the reader. Giraudoux rejoices at these possibilities and variations. As he said himself: 'Je ne considère tout ce que j'ai fait que comme une espèce de divagation poétique.'[31] 'I consider everything I have written merely as a kind of poetical divagation.'

3. *Evolution of Giraudoux's Interpretation of Life*

THOUGH a consistent and definite manner of envisaging the ideal and the real, and of viewing their mutual relationship, is to be found in all Giraudoux's writings, it would be quite inaccurate to regard his thought and art as fixed and unvarying throughout the twenty odd volumes which so far constitute his works. Giraudoux's mind has passed through many changes; it is as difficult to follow these changes of outlook as it is sometimes to follow his elusive personality in his successive or simultaneous variations. Yet it is possible to distinguish five different periods in his evolution and to divide his works accordingly into five different groups. The various trends shown in his works may be placed roughly in chronological order according to a definite sequence in the course of his life; nevertheless, the groups so obviously overlap one another that it is absolutely out of the question to assign dates marking the beginning or the end of each one of them.

The first group includes all the books composed before the war as well as a few written afterwards. These correspond to the time when Giraudoux, freshly emancipated

31. F.Lefèvre, *Une heure avec . . . Première Série*—J.Giraudoux, p.149.

from his studies and just beginning to get acquainted with the world, was starting to compare the moral and logical rules which he had always been taught to revere with the rich and motley spectacle which was now being presented to his gaze. At this stage, amusement and irony clearly predominate. Giraudoux then is young, careless, optimistic; and he finds it supremely entertaining to juggle with brilliant fragments of reality. He is charmed with the reality he already knows; he retains a wistful attachment to his dearly beloved Limousin and Bellac; also he is drawn to the vast, picturesque, frivolously gay, amusing, and youthful world which has just been revealed to him. He does not take the world very seriously and yet he appreciates keenly all the many possibilities of light enjoyment it has to offer. Towards the moral and logical rules he shows the playful disrespect of a schoolboy on holiday; but he cannot bring himself to discard them altogether. He is constantly being put in mind of classical quotations or anecdotes—and this by modern every-day incidents. Often these involuntary classical recollections are all the more heroic and sublime, the more commonplace and banal are the existing facts which have evoked them. Giraudoux finds these contrasts exceedingly diverting. For him there are no grave problems. Life is a wonderful and fantastic game. His writings at this period faithfully reflect this light-hearted attitude; they can hardly be said to follow any definite line or to treat of any particular subject; they are more like casual rambles. Digressions, humorous remarks, clever annotations, lyric passages, hang together more or less loosely on the thin thread of an insignificant or undeveloped story. The general idea is not always easy to grasp; the charm, which is considerable, is derived from a multitude of delightful but unconnected details.

To this category belong: *Provinciales, L'Ecole des In-différents, Simon le Pathétique, Suzanne et le Pacifique, Juliette au Pays des Hommes. Provinciales* (1909) is a collection of thumbnail sketches of French provincial life. For example, the short story 'De ma fenêtre' describes a little boy's vague imaginings, when he is kept indoors by some childish ailment, about the good towns-folk he sees from his window. 'La Pharmacienne' tells of the wiles and manœuvres used by a respectable matron and her two marriageable daughters to entice the road-surveyor away from the chemist's wife, whose charms set all male hearts aflutter. *L'Ecole des Indifférents* (1911) presents three characters freely sketched—Jacques l'Egoïste, Don Manuel le Paresseux, et Le Faible Bernard—all of which appear to be partly actual and partly fanciful reflections of certain sides of Giraudoux's own personality.

In *Simon le Pathétique* the original is more plainly recognizable. The bulk of it was written before 1914; the war interrupted its publication, and in an altered version it saw the light of day in 1918. Giraudoux later changed a number of the episodes, the final text not appearing until 1926. Nevertheless the book is typical of his first period; it is a discursive and imaginative account of a sensitive adolescent's first view of the world. It describes young Simon's earnest application to his studies at the provincial *lycée*, the generous enthusiasm aroused in him by the classical humanities, the mediocrity of his teachers who read the lessons of the past not as providing a philosophy of life but as a pretext for notes and lectures, the young man's disillusionment at the prospect of such intellectual degeneracy, his emancipation from college and from books, and his first eager sally into the world. Then there appear on the scene the graceful images of several *jeunes filles*: Gabrielle, Hélène, Anne, Geneviève. He envelops them all in the delicate web of his delightful and affectionate fancy. The mutual attraction between Anne and himself seems about to blossom into a stronger attachment. Simon wavers and hesitates—until one day Anne comes to him with the great news that she is engaged to somebody else. . . . The many allusions to Giraudoux's own personal experiences are easy to discern, although they are not presented in any methodical or consecutive manner. The various episodes are set in a poetical atmosphere, which imparts to them the charm and remoteness of a desultory day-dream about the past.

Suzanne et le Pacifique (1921) and *Juliette au Pays des Hommes* (1924) are late manifestations of the free and whimsical spirit which was a characteristic of Jean Giraudoux before the war—a spirit which was not stamped out altogether by that great ordeal, for it put forth these two odd flowers of exuberant imagination in the midst of productions of a markedly different order.

Suzanne et le Pacifique is a variation on the theme of Robinson Crusoe. An Australian newspaper holds a competition in which prizes are offered for the best maxim on boredom. The first prize—a trip round the world—is won by Suzanne, a girl from Bellac, with the following entry: 'Si un homme s'ennuie, excitez-le; si une femme s'ennuie, retenez-la.' [32] Suzanne sets off on her trip, going first to Paris, where by chance she meets Simon (*le Pathétique*) and his friend, Anne. She sails from Saint-Nazaire across the Atlantic and through the Panama Canal to the South Seas. During a storm in the middle of the Pacific the ship sinks, and out of all the passengers and crew, Suzanne alone by some miracle is saved. She clings to a raft and is cast up on a small desert island.

32. *Suzanne et le Pacifique*, I, p.26.

The original Robinson Crusoe, marooned in somewhat similar circumstances, had set out immediately to rearrange the order of Nature. 'This Puritan, weighed down as he was by reason, though certain that he was Providence's particular plaything, did not put his trust in Providence for a single minute. For eighteen years he was busy all the time fastening strings, sawing stakes, nailing planks. . . . He had to have a table to eat off, a chair for writing, wheelbarrows, ten different kinds of baskets . . . three varieties of sickles and scythes, and a sieve and grindstones and a harrow and a mortar and a sifter. . . .[33] So much so that one would have liked to say to him: 'Now do sit down; lay aside your gun, your parasol and your stick. . . . Don't work for three months making yourself a table— just squat. . . . That tree that you want to cut down so as to plant barley—shake it, it is a palm-tree; it will give you your bread ready baked. And that one you are pulling up in order to sow peas—gather those yellow snakes growing on it, called bananas.' [34]

This is in fact what Suzanne does. Giraudoux draws a most humorous and whimsical picture of Suzanne's lazy, happy life in the bountiful bosom of tropical Nature. But after a while, a care-free life in the midst of plenty grows tedious. She longs for the human traits which in Europe have been stamped upon raw Nature by an age-old civilization. She contrives to fabricate make-up for her face. Being a woman she misses sin and tries to provide herself with it, resorting to her European memories for a fresh and abundant supply. 'I would take the recollection of one day in Europe, from the time of rising to the time of going to bed, sure that I would only have to tilt it, to shake it, just as if it were a prism, in order to have sin appear

33. *Suzanne et le Pacifique*, IX, pp.229–230.
34. *Ibidem*, IX, p.231.

therein.[35] But it is rather difficult to achieve a full-grown sin all by oneself. . . . She writes letters to Simon, and also writes Simon's supposed replies. Further she begins to give names to different parts of her island, names drawn from the little district of Bellac or from the cultural history of France. The French Academy and French literature provide her with scores of names, from Racine down to Paul Claudel, for which she finds plenty of bizarre applications. The island now seems quite human and thoroughly habitable, and Suzanne enjoys complete happiness and balance.

She keeps up the game until one day an English ship puts in at the island, picks her up and brings her back to Europe. When she sets foot at last on French soil and is again face to face with real French people and French surroundings, she is overcome with emotion. The extravagant but delightful tale ends abruptly with the unexpected words of a new and unexpected character, the embodiment of reason and common sense, which now comes into play: 'I am the Controller of Weights and Measures, Mademoiselle; why are you crying?' [36]

Notwithstanding the fanciful development of the plot and quite apart from Giraudoux's evident enjoyment of the romantic atmosphere of the South Seas—an enjoyment shared by the reader—*Suzanne et le Pacifique* is replete with significant intentions. In the first place, it represents a definite reaction against the aggressive and contentious attitude towards life, symbolized by the authentic Robinson Crusoe. Giraudoux has little sympathy for those who try by hard work and sheer obstinacy to force their own will upon reluctant reality. It would be so much easier, so much more harmonious, to follow Nature and conform to

35. *Suzanne et le Pacifique*, VII, p.171.
36. *Ibidem*, x, p.297.

reality! Giraudoux does not believe that reality is hostile
to man; he enjoys it as he finds it—as did Suzanne—in its
variety of contradictory aspects, and his optimism is always ready to see the best side of everything. Nevertheless, to him stark reality is but the raw material of life.
Reality by itself is shapeless and in the long run meaningless and dull. Reality must be fitted into the framework of
human ideas and culture. That is why Suzanne applies
to the abundant but simple products of tropical nature
which Providence hands to her the forms and outlines of
French classical civilization. As she remarked when she
left her island, 'In the foliage, in the shapes of the hills,
there was that harmony—brought there by me alone—
that harmony which forty millions of French people have
only just succeeded in imposing on their mountains and
their forests.' [37] This problem of the adaptation of raw reality to a system of elaborate ideas and principles is the
main problem in Giraudoux's writings. However, he does
not treat the problem seriously here. With the humour
typical of his first period he is content to state his general
position, leaving the adjustment of details to the vagaries
of unbridled imagination. The last words of the book—
which are put in the mouth of that worthy official, *le
contrôleur des poids et mesures*—are a warning to us that all
our dreams must come to an end, just like Suzanne's.

Juliette au Pays des Hommes does not exhibit the same
originality and boldness of conception as *Suzanne*. Juliette, a young woman of Limousin, is about to marry Gérard, a young man of the district. She loves him, and she
loves her native Limousin, but she also longs to see something of the world. She keeps a diary in which she has
noted down the names and addresses of all the possible
husbands who have crossed her path during the last few

37. *Suzanne et le Pacifique*, x, p.275.

years. So she goes off suddenly by herself to Paris with the intention of finding out what has become of them. She visits as many as possible, and also a few others into the bargain, and this sentimental review gives Giraudoux a pretext for satirical pictures of contemporary life. Juliette first traces a young assistant in botany at the *Ecole Normale Supérieure*, who is forgetting the world for the sake of a few minute and completely unknown plants; then she visits an archæologist who is lost in equally abstruse and apparently useless researches; also a well known writer who tries to initiate her into the mysteries of the *monologue intérieur*; lastly a frantic and passionate Russian. . . . Finally she returns to Gérard, who by this time is none too sure of being able to hold for long the affections of such an elusive person as his *fiancée*.

The only really important passage in the book is the famous 'Prière sur la Tour Eiffel.' In the course of her peregrinations, Juliette is supposed to call on the narrator of the story, who reads her an essay he has just composed. This essay begins with a delicate invocation to the city of Paris, as seen from the top of the Eiffel Tower, then proceeds with an outline of Giraudoux's own theories and conception of art. This piece, of course, has no connexion whatever with the rest of the plot; in fact it had been published separately the year before, in 1923; but it deserves particular mention for its poetical charm, also on account of its value as a literary document which has led certain critics [38] to call it the *Art poétique* of Giraudoux.

The second group includes books written under the direct influence of the war: *Lectures pour une Ombre* (1918), *Amica America* (1918), and *Adorable Clio* (1920). *Amica America* is a record of Giraudoux's mission to the United States. *Lectures pour une Ombre* and *Adorable Clio* are made

38. F.Lefèvre, *Une heure avec . . . Première Série*—J.Giraudoux, p.150.

up of short sketches, some of which, such as *Retour d' Al-sace* (1916) and *Adieu à la Guerre* (1919), had been pub-lished separately. They recount his actual fighting expe-riences or his impressions during the intervals between periods of campaigning. None of these sketches is really a masterpiece, except perhaps the 'Nuit à Châteauroux' in *Adorable Clio*. It chanced that Giraudoux had been taken far behind the front to a base hospital, situated in Châteauroux where he had spent so many years as an eager schoolboy at the *lycée*. In this sketch he recalls with wist-ful emotion memories of a past contrasting so oddly with the present. In a melancholy mood he bids a final good-bye to his childhood.

The tone of his writing in these war-books is markedly different from the tone of the books of the preceding pe-riod. Stern reality was now claiming recognition. Imagina-tion, fantasy, humour, were relegated to the realm of mem-ory or anticipation for occasional future use. Not that Giraudoux painted a realistic picture of the horrors of war—rather he portrayed its familiar aspects without any particular emphasis but with the true ringing note that could be sounded only by one who knew. Sometimes he mentions the elevating and purifying effects of danger, but without any declamations or obnoxious displays of heroism or of suffering. For him the war constituted above all a rich and deep human experience; the realization of this fact dominates his whole outlook and his account of the events he records.

The sudden intrusion into Giraudoux's life of the tre-mendous, overwhelming reality of the war had a double consequence on his mental evolution. On the one hand, ideals and fancies were compelled to recede under pressure of facts which were imposing themselves by the sheer force of their intensity. All Giraudoux's war books and practi-

cally all his subsequent writings present much more continuity and consistency of narration than his previous
works. On the other hand, the relations between ideals
and reality, which in the books of the first group were
treated with ironical amusement and inconsequential fancy,
tended to acquire in his eyes a seriousness which they
completely lacked before. Reality had already made very
dangerous inroads into his idealism. If he was to keep any
of his ideals at all—and Giraudoux, with his classical education, could not possibly do without them—the problem
of adapting them to facts was becoming important.

The problem was not so urgent as to claim Giraudoux's
entire and immediate attention. The fact that after the
war *Suzanne* and *Juliette* appeared as revivals, so to speak,
of the spirit of fantasy that was his before the war, shows
that he was not in any hurry to discover a solution. However, as his post-war impressions in that respect only confirmed his war-time experiences, the matter at first grew
upon him probably unconsciously; then it manifested itself in a series of works all obviously and definitely marked
with the same preoccupation.

This third group comprises *Siegfried et le Limousin*
(1922), *Siegfried* (1928), *Aventures de Jérôme Bardini*
(1930), *Fugues sur Siegfried*, *Visite chez le Prince* (in *La
France Sentimentale* [1932]), *Fin de Siegfried* (1934). All
these books are merely variations upon the same theme—
that of a man divided within himself and in quest of his
true personality. The very fact that Giraudoux took the
typical case of his 'Siegfried' and returned to it again
and again, considering it under many different aspects,
throughout a comparatively long period of years, proves
that the problem persisted in his mind in a most direct
and definite form. The dualism of ideals and reality is no
longer considered vaguely as in the books of the first cycle

—it is now squarely set forth and systematically examined from all possible angles.

In *Siegfried et le Limousin* Giraudoux supposes that a French soldier—the writer, Jacques Forestier—who has been wounded in the head, is picked up in no-man's land by the Germans. When he recovers consciousness, his memory has completely gone. Since his uniform has been torn completely from his body, it is impossible to tell to which nationality he belongs. The Germans, giving him the benefit of the doubt, re-educate him as a German, and he is given the name of Siegfried Kleist. Notwithstanding the amnesia his faculties are all intact; his mind has merely been emptied of all its contents; but his logical framework and his original reasoning power have remained exactly as they were before the shock. So he learns very quickly all that his instructors have to teach him, and within a few years he becomes a prominent man in Germany. Indeed Siegfried possesses what no other man has ever had before—the clear and lucid mind of a cultured Frenchman, plus a knowledge of the opulent and multifarious substance of German history and civilization. So he is able to organize after an orderly and logical plan a rich but somewhat tumultuous conception of reality—of Teutonic reality. Especially in the field of politics, his critical judgment reveals to his German compatriots the right position to take amidst the confusion and the troubles of the post-war period.

It happens that a former friend of Jacques Forestier, who believes the French writer to be dead, notices a striking similarity of thought and expression between the publications of Siegfried Kleist and those of Forestier. At first he thinks it is a case of shameless plagiarism. Then, his suspicions becoming thoroughly aroused, he goes to Germany to make enquiries, in the company of one Zelten,

who is a German of the sincere, intelligent, broad-minded
type, though neurotic, unbalanced, and much demoralized
by the upheaval of the war. The young Frenchman, pre-
tending to be a French-Canadian of the name of Chapde-
laine, is accepted by Siegfried Kleist as a teacher of French.
He immediately recognizes Kleist as his old friend. But
how is Siegfried to be made to realize and to feel that he is
French himself? Here many divergent influences come into
play. There is Eva, who was his nurse when he was
wounded during the war and who taught him to speak
German; she may be considered as the female incarnation
of Germany. In contrast to her we have Siegfried's erst-
while fiancée, the French sculptress Geneviève. She, however, can hardly be regarded as a flattering embodiment
of *La France*, as she is the divorced wife of Zelten and
moreover has had a very questionable past. Nevertheless,
it is amusing to see Siegfried's affections vacillating between these two women. Then we are treated to the ludicrous spectacle of one of these local and short-lived *coups
d'état*, which were by no means rare in post-war Germany.
This one is staged by Zelten himself, and his dictatorship
lasts only four days. Siegfried Kleist is among his opponents, and Zelten in a rage reveals the fact that Siegfried is of foreign origin—indeed that he was born a
Frenchman. So Siegfried gradually comes to feel that he is
really French. The feminine element plays practically no
part in his transformation, as Geneviève rather unexpectedly dies in hospital after an operation. It is essentially when he is brought up against the innumerable
trivial yet significant elements that compose every-day
reality in his native Limousin that Forestier's dormant
memories at last awake. Then quickly, and practically
without any difficulty, the French side of him displaces
the German, and the French conception of reality resumes

its natural and normal place within this Frenchman's
rational mind.

In his stage version of this novel Giraudoux has altered
considerably its purport and bearing. The framework and
setting of the plot are the same, but the political importance of Siegfried has increased to such a point that in the
play he is represented almost as the saviour of Germany.
Zelten is plotting to overthrow Siegfried, and, suspecting
the latter's true identity, he has brought Forestier's
former *fiancée*, Geneviève, from France. Geneviève is still
the artist, but as a character in the play is presented as
thoroughly respectable—no reference is made to her past,
and she is quite ready to incarnate the French nation with
all due decorum. She does it so well, in fact, that the
struggle between the French and the German elements in
the soul of Forestier-Siegfried takes the form of an amorous
tourney between Geneviève and Eva. Limousin is left out
entirely. The *coup d'état* devised by Zelten brings matters
to a climax and Kleist leaves Germany, with Geneviève
on his arm—French by nationality, it is true, but convinced that within himself 'Siegfried and Forestier will
go on existing side by side.' [39]

Another version of the ending (*Fin de Siegfried*) makes
Siegfried the victim of a patriotic German secret society,
anxious to spare the Fatherland the shock of the scandal-
ous discovery. He is shot, and the bullet, which hits him
precisely in his old war-wound, liberates, as it were, all his
old memories of France, which come crowding back during
his last moments, making his death poetical—in a manner
somewhat reminiscent of the death of Cyrano de Bergerac.

All these variations of the ending of the Siegfried story,
show conclusively that, though Giraudoux had definite
ideas about the way in which the problems were stated,

39. J.Giraudoux, *Siegfried*, Grasset, Paris, 1928, Act IV, Sc.3.

he was much more uncertain as to how they should be solved. Two different problems are discussed in this 'Siegfried' cycle. The most obvious is that of the relations between France and Germany. Giraudoux seems to have tried to investigate the possible foundations on which a collaboration between French and German cultures could be established profitably. He shows that each of these nations is richly gifted in certain respects and evidently deficient in others. The shortcomings and the strong points of the two parties are not coincident but complementary. If the French clearness and nimbleness of thought could be united with the intense and mystic affinity with nature that is characteristic of the Germans, what a powerful combination would be thus effected! Giraudoux seems to intimate that such an association is theoretically not impossible; he is more indefinite as to the practical outcome of the efforts that have been made in that direction. At all events the elements of the problem —namely, the contrasts in the fundamental moral and intellectual characteristics of France and Germany—are presented with an intelligence, penetration, and breadth of view which are sufficient to endow each of the books with a permanent and engrossing interest.

The second question which appears throughout the 'Siegfried' cycle is that of the dissociation of mental categories from reality. Siegfried is a man who has retained the classical French way of thinking, with its logical, critical, ideal forms; but he has been deprived by circumstances of the natural content which ought normally to fill the mind of such a man. His problem is concerned with the adaptation of some sort of plastic reality to the empty but solid framework of his original culture. This adaptation is not a simple or an easy matter. In fact, as presented under its most striking aspect, it is the problem which

Giraudoux had to face on his own account, when he went to Germany and found himself, with his classically moulded type of mind, in contact with a strange, new, heterogeneous world. But, whereas in his previous books Giraudoux had only given more or less humorous and fanciful hints as to the possibilities of an accord between the two, here he frankly faces the question and clearly indicates several alternatives. In *Siegfried et le Limousin* he seems to assume that the French conception of reality can fit perfectly well into the logical mind of the Frenchman, provided that different and foreign perceptions of reality be effectively expelled or kept out. In the play *Siegfried* he suggests that such expulsion is hardly possible; and he allows the reader to infer that a state of instability must almost inevitably ensue. In the *Fin de Siegfried* he definitely evokes a catastrophic ending. But whatever the final result may be, and it will vary with circumstances, the necessity of a solution is very clearly asserted.

In the *Aventures de Jérôme Bardini* Giraudoux has taken up a similar case, but in very much modified terms. Jérôme Bardini abandons his wife and disappears from home; his reason for doing so is not definitely stated—the reader is left to infer that he might be suffering from partial amnesia or is perhaps driven by some obscure pathological craving for freedom. He goes to the United States. Although he retains all his faculties and his intelligence, his past life seems to drop away from him as if it had never been. In New York he meets a girl named Stephy. who eventually marries him in order to escape from the banal reality of her own family surroundings. When Bardini in turn grows too banal, she leaves him also. Thereupon he 'adopts' a 'kid' [40] who, also a victim of amnesia, has strayed from home and ever since has been leading a

40. The English word 'kid' is used in the French original.

free, vagabond life. As the result of a mental and physical shock, the boy recovers his memory, and is restored to his parents. Bardini eventually recovers too and is taken back to France by a friend.

The three main characters, Jérôme Bardini, Stephy, and the 'kid' are in a way thorough, sane, and rational persons. Their thoughts are logical and their behaviour perfectly co-ordinated. Yet they all feel an irresistible desire to change their lives, to alter, as it were, the material provided for them by reality—in order to replace it with some other set of experiences, about which they seem to be very vague. But in any case they all face a problem fundamentally similar to that of Siegfried, with, in addition, the craving to escape. On the one hand, their mental faculties are in good working order, but their minds have been virtually emptied of their store of past experience. On the other hand, they find themselves placed in a motley, complicated universe. The aspects of it which had filled their consciousness in the past having proved unsatisfactory, they discarded these either involuntarily or of their own free will, and then set out to obtain an adaptation of reality that would better suit their mental requirements.

Jérôme Bardini as a study, however, is far from reaching the same high standard as *Siegfried*. None of the characters possesses a distinctive personality; Jérôme, Stephy, and the 'kid' seem to be mere reflections of one another; perhaps, through the interplay of 'multiple mirrors' in the characteristic style of Jean Giraudoux, to be also reflections of some of the author's own personal traits. Then, *Siegfried* owed much of its interest to the picture of present-day Germany, which the author knew so well. Giraudoux, however, knew very little of the United States. He tried to overcome this difficulty in part by placing Stephy in a German-American environment; but this notwithstanding, the evocation of American realities seems dull, colourless, and inadequate. In general, the book is valuable as evidence of an idea which has preoccupied the mind of Giraudoux for many years.

Even though *Jérôme Bardini* is closely related to the Siegfried books by the similarity of the main theme, yet by reason of its date, and of several other features, it belongs to another group of works, which began with *Bella* (1926) and comprised *Eglantine* (1927), *La France Sentimentale* (1932), and *Combat avec l'Ange* (1934).

Bella is by far the best known book in this group, not so much on account of its intrinsic value as of the sensation caused by the many personal allusions it contains. *Bella* is a thinly disguised record of the rivalry between Poincaré and Berthelot, who appear under the fictitious names of Rebendart and Dubardeau respectively. Giraudoux even broadens the rivalry into an almost epic struggle between their two families, which are considered as representing two opposite sides of the French character and temperament. The Rebendarts—those at least who participate in public life—have cold, clear, keen, and calculating minds; they are emphatically honest and abstinent in private life, and yet avid of official honours and dignities; most of them have become either lawyers or politicians, or both. The Dubardeaus are spontaneous, generous, versatile, broad-minded, human, endowed with imagination; some of them are artistic yet with a strong sense of reality; they have given to France a series of inventors and scientists of mark. Bella de Fontranges, the widowed daughter-in-law of Rebendart, falls in love with Philippe, the son of Dubardeau. The two young people find themselves in a dilemma, being torn between their feelings of reciprocal affection and the fact of the hereditary family feud. Finally Bella burns the comprising paper which Rebendart was about to make use of in order to have Dubardeau unjustly convicted, and she makes a desperate attempt to bring about a reconciliation between the two enemies. Her attempt is in vain; and realizing that she has failed in her object, she meets her death, being overcome by the violence of her emotion.

The story of Bella possesses undoubted dramatic power, and the character of Rebendart stands out in strong and bold relief. Yet, in spite of the symbolic importance that is given to the two rival factions and of the discreet charm of Bella herself, the sensibilities of the reader are apt to be offended by the tone of caustic—and sometimes un-fair—sarcasm which pervades this masterpiece of bitter personal polemic.

Eglantine—though full of episodical, topical allusions—is devoid of the aggressive element found in *Bella*. Eglan-tine, the young foster-sister of Bella, and a beautiful and attractive girl, receives attentions from two elderly suit-ors—Moïse, the Jewish director of a great international bank, and Bella's father, the Baron de Fontranges himself. She falls in love first with the one and then with the other. The unusual situation of this young girl, beset by two admirers well on in years, provided Giraudoux with the opportunity of presenting a subtle and diverting portrayal of love, self-consciousness, and jealousy in two elderly rivals. The attitude of Eglantine would be puzzling, and her *penchant* for men of advanced years rather surprising, if it were not definitely stated that the characters of Moïse and Fontranges have a symbolical meaning—Moïse representing the Eastern character and culture, and Fon-tranges the Western. If they are pictured as no longer young, it is because in fact these two aspects of the world are likewise not young. Giraudoux, since his contact with the Turks in the course of his official duties, had obviously been tempted by the desire to draw a comparison between Western and Oriental mentalities. His own personal choice seems to be embodied in Eglantine herself, who after showing partiality for the attractions and merits of Moïse—the East—finally casts in her lot with Fontranges—the West.

La France Sentimentale is a composite book, made up of eleven independent episodes, recalling several themes already discussed by Giraudoux. Siegfried, Bella, and her twin-sister Bellita, Fontranges, Simon, and Anne are involved in new 'sentimental' entanglements against a background of contemporary political events. The events themselves are of secondary importance only, and the same may be said of the book itself.

Combat avec l'Ange describes two distinct sets of events proceeding along parallel lines. On one side we have the record of the last months of the life of Brossard, a Prime Minister of France; on the other we have an attempt to elucidate the psychological obsessions of an Argentinian girl, Maléna Paz. The only link between the two is Jacques, secretary to Brossard, and lover of Maléna. The character of Brossard has many of the features of Briand, and in the background the troubled political atmosphere of Europe is evoked by a mass of suggestive detail; more original and more amusing perhaps is the satirical and obviously true inside picture of the every-day existence of a French Prime Minister—one who finds no difficulty in disgracing a chief of police or a colonial governor, but who cannot obtain the dismissal even of an usher. Being about to die, he has little care for the great cause of Peace, to which he is supposed to be devoted body and soul, but can only think of a young woman of whom he caught a glimpse a few days before. That woman happens to be Maléna. Maléna is so morbidly jealous that she will not

believe the plain and simple truth—that Jacques, whom
she loves, also loves her. She pursues him with extravagant
suspicions, and in order to justify to herself the mistrust
which she entertains about Jacques and a certain Gladys,
whom she imagines to be her rival, she goes so far as to
lock them up together in two communicating hotel rooms.
She is cured of her obsession in a most singular way. One
night, after a fitful crisis, she wakes up and tells her nurse
that she has been attacked by an angel, shaken and bruised
and finally vanquished. Who was that angel? The angel
of death? No, she says, it was a being 'qui avait l'ordre
de me vaincre vivante,' [41] or in other words to compel her
to cease inflicting on herself torments of her own creation.

All the works of Giraudoux belonging to this group are
constructed on the same plan; they have as their basis a
strong, solid, consistent presentation of actual facts, of
which he had obtained a first-hand knowledge in the
course of his professional duties—such as the conflict between Poincaré and Berthelot, the mental outlook of the
Oriental, the various activities of Briand. The account that
he gives is a free literary version of the actual facts; yet
the essential features have been retained and can be recognized without much difficulty. They are of real dramatic
interest and engross the attention of the reader whenever
they are introduced. They are not presented in continuous,
uninterrupted succession, but are divided and cut into
separate episodes; each episode constitutes a single whole,
which can be grasped and retained easily by the reader.
Intermingled with these episodes there runs a love-story
of a purely imaginary and sometimes quite fantastic kind.
Its various incidents are presented without much of a
preamble or indeed justification. The constancy and devotion of Bella, the fickleness of Eglantine, the insane passion

41. J.Giraudoux, *Combat avec l'Ange*, Grasset, Paris, 1934, IX, p.291.

of Maléna, may have actual counterparts in the still very mysterious field of feminine psychology; but they are difficult to understand from the point of view of practical common sense. The reader is confronted all the time with actions or ideas of which no clear explanation is given, and which he may sometimes hesitate to attribute to spontaneity of nature or to incoherency of mind. Yet the rather disjointed tale is always told with infinite delicacy. Its very elusiveness generally carries with it great evocative and poetical power; it launches the imagination into realms unknown and leads to discoveries which, it is true, are sometimes disturbing, but are always unusual and often thoroughly original; for Giraudoux never allows himself to get lost in the clouds, and his most indefinite evocations are invariably punctuated with subtle yet keen remarks which nail the web of his fancy to the strong framework of reality.

And indeed all the books of this group correspond to a period of Giraudoux's life when his attention was centred more firmly than at any other time on reality. After the fanciful period of youth, after the dramatic but in some respects unreal experiences of the war, after the subsequent period of moral restlessness which found expression in the 'Siegfried' cycle—the necessity of pursuing a career, the normal interest of a man in his daily work, the obligations and cares of the father of a family, closed in upon Giraudoux, making him more conscious of reality than ever before. For a while the fundamental problem which had been the main topic of consideration in *Siegfried* was set aside. At least its underlying presence is manifested only by casual allusions scattered here and there; also by the periodical reappearance of the old theme, as exemplified in *Jérôme Bardini* or in *Visite chez le Prince*. But, on the whole, *Bella, Eglantine, La France Sentimentale,* and *Com-*

bat avec l'Ange form a group of works in which facts decidedly take precedence over imagination; whenever imagination asserts itself, it has not the same fine quality that made Giraudoux's earlier works little masterpieces of delightful fancy.

Nevertheless, Giraudoux was gradually finding his balance and his own definitive formula. With advancing years the difficulties connected with a career and with family preoccupations became less acute, loosening their grip upon him, as it were. By and by he was able to view things with an aloofness and distance allowing him to form a new perspective in which ideals and reality were at last harmoniously blended.

Giraudoux took his first step in this direction as early as 1919 with *Elpénor*. Elpénor is one of the sailors of Ulysses, and one of the most insignificant characters in Homer's *Odyssey*. This very insignificance—the fact that we know practically nothing of the original Elpénor's thoughts or actions—left Giraudoux absolutely free to represent Elpénor's life and personality exactly as he pleased. The book seems at first sight to be written in the same vein as *Suzanne et le Pacifique*, giving vent to an almost intemperate flow of unbridled imagination. Yet *Elpénor* is almost the exact converse of *Suzanne*. In *Suzanne* Giraudoux had imposed upon the motley spectacle of tropical nature on a small Pacific island the framework of an organized and regular conception of life—that of French classical and traditional culture. In *Elpénor*, conversely, he filled the more or less bare, theoretical framework of a classical Greek legend with the richness of modern life. He indulges unhesitatingly in the most startling anachronisms in order to infuse life into abstract classical concepts. Not only Elpénor but also Ulysses, the Cyclops, the Sirens, from being purely intellectual entities, become warmly human and incredibly near and akin to ourselves.

With the success of his play *Siegfried* in 1928, a new period seemed to be definitely inaugurated in Giraudoux's works. *Amphitryon 38* (1929) shows distinctly the direction in which he was moving. The strange title of the play constitutes in itself a programme. A well known classical legend explains how Jupiter, having fallen in love with Alcmena, the chaste and beautiful wife of the Theban General, Amphitryon, and despairing of being able to overcome her virtue with the ordinary wiles of the seducer, took on the human semblance of Amphitryon, and, so disguised, visited Alcmena while her husband was away campaigning against the enemy. Complications set in when Amphitryon himself returned unexpectedly and Alcmena was suddenly confronted with the two men, indistinguishably alike. Some time afterwards the infant Hercules was born. . . . Many French dramatists, including Molière, have been tempted by this curious legend, and numerous plays—say thirty-seven at least—have been written upon the same theme—so much so that any new and original treatment of the subject seemed well nigh impossible. In composing a thirty-eighth *Amphitryon* Giraudoux had to depart radically from the hackneyed versions of the plot, if he was to achieve a play of any interest at all. By deliberately making the character of Alcmena that of a modern, living woman—instead of the unreal and conventional legendary figure she had been heretofore—he made a success of this venture. Once again, as in *Elpénor*, Giraudoux infused into the statuesque, rigid lines of the antique, a warmth and richness from modern life as he knew it. But whereas *Elpénor* was just an entertaining exercise, fantastic and extravagant at times, *Amphitryon 38* was a revelation of the many human truths that may be contained in the mould of a seemingly outworn classical tradition. Anachronisms of expression, allusions to contemporary events or facts, references to modern ideas or feelings are freely used in order to create the atmosphere of actuality which constitutes the most striking and original feature of the play. At the same time, they are presented with so much tact and discretion that they never create an impression of grotesque parody. Still less do they degenerate into an offensive realism. With marvellous virtuosity and ingenuity Giraudoux hovers between the stately ideal of classical antiquity, with its regular beauty, its poetical charm, its mythical remoteness, and the reality of broad human experience packed with emotion, humour, sorrow, and laughter. He passes insensibly from one to the other, hinting at affinities, alluding to resemblances, sometimes almost playfully letting his imagination soar for a while and then without effort coming back to earth again. Thus modern reality becomes animated and poetical under the influence of an older ideal; thus again abstract, classical forms are filled with a new and throbbing life coming from an intense, present actuality.

Giraudoux applied the same procedure to the story of Judith and Holofernes. Perhaps because he was not so much in his element with Biblical tradition as with Greek mythology, his *Judith* is scarcely equal to his *Amphitryon* in vital and poetical conception.

Intermezzo—as the title itself indicates—marks an interlude in the regular progress of Giraudoux's dramatic development. Yet this interlude is perfectly in keeping with the spirit of his other plays, and expresses perhaps even more clearly than most of them the position that Giraudoux had reached. *Intermezzo*, however, is not usually considered a 'clear' play, perhaps because its form differs notably from what the public expects to see on the stage. It is not an antique play with a modern atmosphere; it is a modern play with a fairy-tale atmosphere.

Isabelle, a young school teacher in a small town in Limousin, applies most unorthodox methods of pedagogy to the little girls entrusted to her care. Instead of stuffing them with the dry and conventional notions of the official programme, she tries to awaken in them an ideal, optimistic, sincere, and genuine appreciation of life; and she obtains from them an enthusiastic response. Further, she longs to educate the inhabitants of the little town in the same way. She wants to destroy some of their prejudices and create among them the harmonious order which, according to her idealistic views, ought to reign everywhere. Prompted by this noble intention, though forced to act secretly, she would send anonymous letters to various persons, not of course in order to disturb the peace of happy families but, for instance, to draw the attention of a husband to the virtues of his wife, which otherwise he would certainly have overlooked. By and by, the atmosphere of the whole district is completely transformed, thanks to her mysterious influence. Nay, a supernatural power seems to exert a beneficial, though most unusual action on all the happenings, small or great, in the region. So when a lottery is drawn, the first prize is won not, as could be expected in this illogical and stupid world of ours, by a millionaire but by a poor man who needs the money badly. Similarly, a motorcycle is won, not as usually happened before by a person who could never use it, as, for example, the Mother Superior of the Convent, but by a boy who had coveted the thing eagerly. Further, even the persons who die now in the town are not the youngest and the kindest, as a blind and absurd fate so often in the past decreed. Death seems to choose dis-

cerningly, selecting the oldest or the wickedest individuals. . . . Public opinion is aroused by these occurrences;
they seem too intelligently and too ideally planned to belong really to the irregular and crazy world that we know.
The influence of Isabelle is strongly suspected, and soon
a strange rumour spreads about the town: Isabelle, they
say, is in communication with a spirit. And indeed she is.
But there is nothing horrible or frightening about this
spirit. To Isabelle he manifests himself as a handsome, pale,
young man, draped in a romantic black cape, friendly,
though elusive and remote. He represents all the Dead,
whom in her youthful, mystic, all-embracing love for the
universe, Isabelle would associate even with present-day
life. He also represents the 'Ideal' handed down to living
generations by generations past—abstract and pure, in-
accessible and invisible to the vulgar crowd, but revealing
itself sometimes to an ardent and candid soul.

An inspector comes to investigate these fantastic rumours that are circulating; after attending one of her
classes he suspends Isabelle immediately, replacing her,
temporarily at least, by the Controller of Weights and
Measures. This is apparently the same Controller of
Weights and Measures who had already made a fugitive
appearance at the end of *Suzanne et le Pacifique*, and as
in the former work so in the present he personifies common
sense. But the Ghost still continues his manifestations in
the neighbourhood, and everything goes on in a supernat-
urally satisfactory manner in the little town. The inspector
hires some 'executioners' to dispose of the Ghost . . .
thus do vulgar and practically minded people always try
to destroy what they cannot understand. Meanwhile the
Controller of Weights and Measures has fallen in love
with Isabelle—he even goes to the length of proposing to
her—but he has no fancy to share her affection, even if

only with a Ghost. What he, the Controller, has to offer the girl is the warm and full reality of life; he has no difficulty in driving away the Ghost, who is nothing but an unsubstantial, mystic dream. When the Ghost finally vanishes, Isabelle faints away; but soon she comes to life again, hearing the joyous concert, made up of all the happy noises of the little town: bugles, bells, the whispering of women, the sing-song of the schoolgirls reciting their lesson. She fully regains her senses when the words *velours* and *crêpe de Chine* reach her ears.

It is easy to recognize and to follow here the familiar themes which run through all the works of Giraudoux. What Isabelle pursues at first is the generous ideal of life as it should be lived—life as Giraudoux himself dreamt of it when he was at school—life as all high-minded adolescents dream of it, when the heroic figures of the past inspire them with a mystic enthusiasm, and they cannot conceive why justice, order, and reason should not rule the universe. This ideal is the ideal of schoolboys and schoolgirls, and Isabelle, the little school teacher, does not seem very far removed from her pupils. The most abstract and sublime aspect of this ideal is embodied—if such a word may be used in this connexion—by the Ghost, himself a figure from the past, somewhat cold and unsubstantial, but pure and alluring by reason of his very elusiveness. The Controller represents reality—plain, simple, but dense and resistant earthly reality—full of the good things, the small trivialities of life. The Controller is in love with Isabelle. Reality seeks to join the Ideal. In the mind of Giraudoux, there are no longer any insurmountable obstacles between them; eventually Isabelle will marry the Controller. It only remains for them to rout the Ghost, the most unreal part of the ideal, and to realize in themselves a harmonious union of spirituality and humanity.

But the Ghost will not be 'dead.' He will appear again, fifteen years hence, to the children of the Controller and Isabelle.

In *La Guerre de Troie n'aura pas lieu* Giraudoux returns to his original combination of modern reality in an antique setting. The setting is that of the city of Troy on the eve of the famous siege. Helen has just eloped with Paris, and if she is not returned to her husband the Greeks will declare war. All those who will be called on to play an active part in the war, or those who realize they will suffer directly from it—that is to say, the great majority both of Greeks and Trojans—are opposed to a conflict. And undoubtedly matters might be amicably arranged if the diplomats, such as Hector and Ulysses—or Giraudoux—could be left alone to settle the differences of the two nations. But there are others, those who believe they have nothing to fear—also the dangerous, excited ideologues. They are a mere handful, it is true, but they are capable of rousing the stupid herd passions of the crowd. Employed perhaps but as the simple instruments of an inexorable Fate, they will bring about a great conflagration at the very moment when the danger seems to have been definitely averted. It is strangely easy for us to discern at the bottom of this plausible Trojan problem the same preoccupations which were besetting modern statesmen about the year 1935, and which are still exercising all the European nations.

Then there is the question of Andromache and of Helen herself. Helen embodies the instinctive and vital element of reality. That which is orderly, reasonable, lawful, holds no appeal for her. It pleases her to submit, not to her legitimate husband but to a lover. What are her real feelings towards Paris? Why should she try to analyse them? She has only to follow her instincts, which are in

accord with rhythm of the Universe. Should she remain
in Troy or return to Greece? The Universe will decide
for her. But the prospect of returning home—a move
which would ensure peace—appears unattractive and
colourless to one who prefers life highly coloured. If war
comes, she will not shrink from hardship, hunger, insults,
suffering, any more than her beauty shrinks at the prospect
of decrepit old age. Are not the unpleasant as well as the
pleasant aspects of reality but integral parts of the variegated life she loves?

In contrast to Helen, Andromache personifies pure virtue and clear intelligence. In her eyes good and evil
are separate and distinct; spontaneously she chooses the
good and rejects the evil. In the light of such a clean-cut
conception of right and wrong, every problem becomes
simple and its solution obvious; in order to avoid war let
Helen give up her Paris, whom in fact she does not really
love. And so logical is the mind of Andromache that when
she realizes that a conflict is unavoidable, she beseeches
Helen to try to love Paris so that the war may at least
have a sufficient cause.

The fundamental dualism of passionate reality and rational idealism is further illustrated by the way in which
the question of the return of Helen is presented to the
Trojans. Iris, the Messenger of the Gods, carries these
two messages to the Trojans: 'Yes, Aphrodite charges me
to tell you that love is the law which governs the world.
Everything that pertains to love becomes sacred, whether
it be falsehood, cupidity or lewdness. She takes care of
every lover, from king to shepherd. . . . She forbids you
two, Hector and Ulysses, to separate Paris from Helen.
Disobey her and there will be war.' [42] And when Hector
asks if there is any message from Pallas, the Goddess of

42. *La Guerre de Troie n'aura pas lieu*, Act II, Sc.12, p.175.

Reason, Iris replies: 'Yes, Pallas charges me to say to you that reason is the law that governs the world. Everyone who is in love . . . is out of his mind. . . . She orders you, Hector, and you Ulysses, to separate Helen from this curly-headed Paris. Disobey her and there will be war.' [43] For many years Giraudoux had been content to let that antinomy remain unsolved, or to hint at solution by humorous comparisons or poetical parallels. Now his attitude is more definite and positive. Iris expresses this point of view in her third message: 'Zeus, the Ruler of the Gods, sends you this message, that those who only perceive love in the world are as foolish as those who do not perceive it at all. It is wisdom . . . sometimes to make love and sometimes not to make love.' [44]

This may seem to be a purely verbal solution of the difficulty. As a matter of fact, it implies merely that Giraudoux has attained a degree of harmony and balance. All his works—his general outlook on the universe in its broadest aspects, as well as in its most humble details—display the means by which such harmony and balance can be attained.

4. *The World of Giraudoux*

THE view of the universe implied in the works of Giraudoux is in no sense organic or systematic. It is impossible to discern in these works any fixed and definite idea as to the interrelations of the various aspects of life. Sometimes contradictory statements are made about the same person or object, presenting in rapid succession opposing aspects of the same reality. Sometimes widely divergent impressions are recorded side by side; the reason for such an

43. *La Guerre de Troie n'aura pas lieu*, Act II, Sc.12, p.176.
44. *Ibidem*, Act II, Sc.12, pp.176–177.

association is left to the imagination of the reader. Nevertheless, an undoubted unity of tone is maintained throughout all this diversity and apparent disorder—so that definite tendencies and leading trends of thought may be
more or less isolated and studied.

One of the ideas which recurs most persistently throughout the works of Giraudoux is that life is controlled by
a superior, guiding fate. The words *La Providence*, *La
Destinée*, are used—indifferently, it seems—whenever it is
necessary to assign a cause to unexpected and surprising
events. Since Giraudoux refuses to link logic and reality
together, but most of the time keeps them separate and
distinct, he finds it difficult to associate one set of human
events with another. To attribute them to 'Fate' is a normal and easy way of explaining facts whose logical ante-
cedents are not immediately perceptible. Yet Giraudoux's
Providence is entirely unrelated to Christian doctrine;
his *Destinée* does not imply a belief in fatalism. Fate is
considered in rather a familiar way, as a force or a multiplicity of forces, acting irregularly and capriciously upon
human actions and movements. His conception recalls to
some extent the conception that the ancient Greeks and
Romans had of their numerous Gods and Goddesses. Yet a
gradual evolution is discernible in his ideas in this respect.
In his early writings, he seems to toy somewhat irrever-
ently with the word 'destiny,' as if it were merely a convenient term without much objective reality behind it.
Later on, he comes nearer to an appreciation of fate resembling the ἀνάγκη of the Greeks—a supreme, irresistible,
impersonal power, controlling men and Gods alike—from
which it is idle to expect either consideration or mercy.
Whether this change of attitude on the part of Giraudoux
is traceable to his war experiences, or to the constant
steady pressure of new impressions obtained during the

years of his maturity, is difficult to tell, as the transition is a gradual one, though clearly discernible particularly in his latest productions.

In the works of Giraudoux life is considered from several apparently different and yet correlated positions. Its more permanent and established aspects, such as the fundamental elements of human nature, are deliberately overlooked. On the other hand, the most external and fleeting manifestations—the changing of the seasons, elusive shades of thought, a glance, a smile, the racing of the clouds across an autumn sky—are recorded with subtlety and yet with precision. Giraudoux looks upon himself as a 'journalist of mankind,' not attempting to set forth eternal laws or to determine unalterable verities, but simply recording, as they occur, the multitude of trifles which constitute our daily lives. 'What I am chiefly to be credited with is the publication of that newspaper which gives detailed news, not of men themselves, who are by definition unchangeable, but of everything that in relation to them is ephemeral—that is to say, the seasons, the feelings, the elemental wonders of the universe—and which keeps one in constant touch with the variations . . . affecting, for example, honour, autumn, or the perishable constellations.' [45]

This deliberate superficiality is closely related to a very delicate and penetrating sense of morality. Giraudoux is perfectly well aware that in the depths of every human mind hideous uncontrollable thoughts are stirring. Modern psychologists seem to have made it their business to bring them to the surface and expose them to view, thus permitting them to infect and spoil everything around them. Giraudoux believes that the best plan is to keep them buried out of sight. It is sometimes stated that these un-

45. *Juliette au Pays des Hommes*, vi, Prière sur la Tour Eiffel, p.190.

lovely things constitute the essence of reality. He denies this, believing that they are merely certain elements of a complex whole and assume an undue importance only if they are artificially developed beyond their normal size and proportion. The slimy worms that creep underground are no more essential and infinitely less interesting than the flowers that grow on the surface. So in the name of clean thinking and moral, wholesome living, in the name of idealism, Giraudoux would banish from conscious attention and consideration the monsters that constantly threaten to emerge from the depths where they lurk. The true art of life consists in keeping in check, by the exercise of strict self-control, all the repulsive thoughts, the impure cravings, the unlovely desires that might besmirch our moral nature. And the best way to achieve this aim is to ignore them resolutely and systematically. Juliette, having caught a glimpse of all the unpleasant tendencies that were lying latent within her, comes to the following conclusion: 'Juliette suddenly perceived lying motionless in the depths of her being, all these monsters that are unleashed when the mind becomes confused, all of them contrary to what she thought she knew and loved, monsters lying dormant but nevertheless existent—the reverse side of her love for Gérard, of her affection for her uncle, of her taste for pancakes, of her modesty. She felt conscious of all the things that a human being guards and protects by keeping silence with himself; and she realized that anyone who does not carry within him an internal replica of himself that is both deaf and dumb, constitutes a trapdoor by way of which evil may flood the world.' [46]

This suppression of these evil tendencies within ourselves should not require a great display of energy nor

46. *Juliette au Pays des Hommes*, v, p.156.

imply superhuman effort and strain. It should be accomplished easily, modestly, smoothly by intelligent and tactful adaptation to the natural conditions of life. Giraudoux likes life as it is, yet he is in no sense its dupe. He is generally optimistic yet not unduly or blindly confident. Life is not perfect; it is wise not to attach too great a value to its gifts—which more often than not are bestowed out of season. 'Tous les biens de la vie me sont venus une année ou une heure trop tard.' [47] We may even despise life a little if only to assure our mental freedom; but to grapple with life, to struggle against Nature, in order to improve or to dominate either, is a dangerous procedure foredoomed to failure.

Giraudoux's attitude is one neither of revolt nor of resignation, but of courteous understanding and politeness. The word 'politeness' recurs as a *leit-motif* whenever he tries to define his attitude towards human existence. This may be owing to the influence of his diplomatic environment; more probably it is the manifestation of an inborn disposition. At all events, although life may often prove deceptive and disappointing, a man must go on behaving well from the standpoint of pure good breeding. There is no question of prospective punishment or reward, nor of supreme devotion to an ideal and an absolute. Just as a polite man retains his manners even amidst unsatisfactory surroundings, so a self-imposed discipline will enable him to accept what life has to offer. He will not ask for more, associating with his fellow-men kindly and unassumingly, acting always, for his own personal satisfaction, as if— which is unfortunately rarely the case—life were generous and fair and other men dependable and friendly. Such a man, thinks Giraudoux, is really a civilized man. 'Civilization . . . is a state of personal modesty which leads

47. J.Giraudoux, *Siegfried et le Limousin*, Grasset, Paris, 1922, v, p.177.

civilized man to make the course of his life run parallel to
Nature (thus incidentally avoiding a meeting with that
pitiless person), to attach . . . the smallest possible value
to life, to pay to its opposite, death, a certain amount of
deference . . . and, on the other hand, by reason of that
mild contempt for life, not to complicate it on earth by
demands exceeding human needs; to practise—but without making oneself a nuisance to others and through self-
discipline—the qualities which would be necessary if life
were just, pleasant and eternal, qualities such as courage,
activity, some moderation, and kindness.' [48]

Such a philosophy, if generally accepted, would result
in a world of perfectly free and independent people, con-
ducting themselves with tact and respect towards each
other, exercising self-restraint, never incurring obligations
or perpetrating intrusions, never cruel, though somewhat
formal and cool. A sincere contentment would pervade a
clear, transparent atmosphere. Then we should have 'a
humanity in which every man would be distinct from the
rest, in soul as well as in body, as a star is distinct from
other stars,—in which the relations between human beings
would always consist only of inflexions, assents, transpar-
ences; and in which silence by itself would be a common
good and pleasure . . . in which the human atmosphere
would constantly have a limpidity a thousand times lighter
even than the limpidity of evenings in early spring . . .
when every creature in the rays of the setting sun, still
fresh as morning, resembles the big, sexless shadow that
precedes or follows him as he goes.' [49] It would be 'a world
where one owes no accounts, no smiles, no tears to any
person, where desire is replaced by continual satisfaction,

---

48. *Siegfried et le Limousin*, VII, p.251.
49. J.Giraudoux, *Aventures de Jérôme Bardini*, Emile-Paul, Paris, 1930—The
    Kid, II, p.194.

and the religion offered to Our Lord replaced by politeness towards His creation.' [50]

This conception has very much the semblance of a dream, and it is indeed a poetical dream like so many of the products of Giraudoux's imagination. Yet it clearly indicates the orientation of his thoughts, which tend to a half-indifferent, half-pantheistic acceptation of the universe as it is. One of his first books bears the title, *L'Ecole des Indifférents*, and Giraudoux remained faithful to his own 'school' throughout his other works. Indeed every human being, every living creature in the world, being enveloped in a cloak of 'politeness,' is individualized and isolated to such a point that reciprocal influences cease to be markedly perceptible. The universe resolves itself into a collection of independent units, all of which are equally interesting. Why then prefer one to another? A man, a plant, or an animal, all are equal under the law of Giraudoux's all-comprehensive politeness. He loves them all, singly and collectively, indifferently, just as they are. This all-embracing love and spontaneous confusion becomes actually an appreciative pantheism; and Giraudoux, very much after the manner of his 'Juliette,' is affected by the 'disease which consists in treating objects as human beings, as if they were Gods and Virgins, the Gods like cats or weasels—a malady which is caused not by a life spent in libraries but by personal relations with the seasons and with small animals, excessive pantheism, and politeness towards all creation.' [51]

But then if the whole of creation is 'politely' accepted, why should one not also welcome death, which is just one aspect of the universal flux and change? Indeed Giraudoux shows a special predilection for death. What would be the

50. *Aventures de Jérôme Bardini*—The Kid, III, p.221.
51. *Juliette au Pays des Hommes*, VIII, pp.229–230.

ideal death? Again, it would be an act of politeness, such
as the death of Eglantine as it is pictured by the imagination of Moïse: 'She was simply becoming less and less pink
and lively every day. She reached the state of supreme
immobility by self-restraint, by a politeness towards nothingness that increased hour by hour.' [52] In Giraudoux's
works the dead play an outstanding part. They are not
referred to with sorrowful regret but provide a ductile and
supple material on which Giraudoux's imagination can
work. Whereas living characters, even if fictitious, offer a
certain amount of opposition, and sometimes bring disappointment even to their creator, the dead are completely
flexible, and through them life may be given the ideal
complement of perfection in which it is naturally lacking.
That is why Giraudoux chooses to live in familiar association with the dead. 'Death? The dead? I go into mourning
a thousand times—mourning which is not really my own.
Young men, young women, whom I have met once or
twice, and of whose death I have suddenly heard, appear
to me and become familiar acquaintances. I dream about
them almost continually. . . . Thus can insignificant
shadows bring me all that is missing in life, in friendship,
in love . . . I have only to press their warm shapes to
my heart, and they invade it and dilate it. A living person
who smiles, who weeps, even on our account, reveals
within himself an ocean of joy or sadness beside which we
count for very little indeed. My vanished ones, modest
and perfect, are my slaves. So distinct is my vision of
them, that they belong to me, as would a dead man
whose picture was in my possession, while his family
had none.' [53] For Giraudoux death holds neither horror
nor fear. 'The prospect of my own death, of the death

52. J.Giraudoux, *Eglantine*, Grasset, Paris, 1927, III, p.99.
53. *L'Ecole des Indifférents*, Jacques l'Egoïste, pp.23, 29–30.

of my friends, did not arouse in me any care, any anguish.' [54]

Giraudoux pictures the existence beyond the grave somewhat as the Greeks of the Homeric period conceived it—as an existence without tortures or bliss, similar to the life on earth and yet attenuated, phantasmagoric, simplified, and evolving without material obstacles in a vague, greyish, shadowy atmosphere. '"Is everything different where you are, Edith?"—"Everything is the same. Except that we have sovereign command over all the things that with you are hostile. We can catch the birds and the sunbeams. Our shadows do not revolve round about us like a compass measuring out life. They are always the exact length of our bodies and never go before us. What has been said about the asphodels is true; the meadows are covered with them, and with cowslips as well."—"Do you gather them?"—"We never stoop down. We always walk erect."—"Edith! Edith! so it is true? Your ankles, your knees are all in one?"—She leans against my shoulder, sobbing, and I comfort her passionately. Tearing herself away from me, she plunges, still erect, into the wall; now only her hand is extended from the tapestry. I kiss it, but it is like imprinting a caress on the hand of one engulfed in a quicksand.' [55] Being dead is not a torment; it implies a sort of immaterial laziness. '"What pleases me in the prospect of death," says Isabelle to the Ghost, "is the laziness of death, that rather heavy, numb fluidity whereby people in fact do not die but are only drowned."' [56] Nevertheless the dead are not eternal. 'There comes a time when they are seized with fatigue; a plague of the dead blows over them, a tumour of annihila-

54. *Combat avec l'Ange*, IX, p.265.
55. *L'Ecole des Indifférents*, Jacques l'Egoïste, pp.24–25.
56. J.Giraudoux, *Intermezzo*, Grasset, Paris, 1933, Act I, Sc.8, p.77.

tion gnaws at them. The beautiful grey of their shadow becomes silvery and oily. Then the end is near, the end of everything.' [57]

This conception of the universe where all the forms and aspects of reality, including death, are indiscriminately absorbed in joyful acceptance is closely akin to pantheism. Giraudoux looks on Nature as one whole; 'gods' and animals, plants and human beings, living or dead, are but partial manifestations of a supreme totality. Each element within that *ensemble* retains a measure of individuality, but all are so firmly linked together by strong similarities and affinities that it can be said that each unit reflects the others and is reflected by them.

What then should be man's attitude towards Nature? Man is a part of Nature; Nature, as is shown in *Siegfried et le Limousin*, forms an integral part of a man's personality. Man reflects Nature; Nature reflects man. That man is wise who adapts himself to Nature, who follows Nature consciously and deliberately. Even if he attempted to fight against her—like Robinson Crusoe—he would fail to disrupt the harmonious relations prevailing between the various elements of the world, and he would wear himself out by his own fruitless efforts. There is indeed no necessity to fight; Nature is kind to man, when man takes care to conform to her wishes and her moods. But it is not always easy to perceive Nature's demands. They can hardly be detected by intellectual research, as an investigation is always limited in its scope, and every man has willy-nilly to face the whole of reality. They cannot be grasped through intuitive, lyrical communion with the whole universe, as the universe is parcelled out into a multiplicity of isolated though interrelated elements. The best course is to gain firsthand knowledge of as many of these elements as possible.

57. *Intermezzo*, Act i, Sc.8, p.78.

Giraudoux's relations with Nature may be compared to
a series of confidential conversations carried on in a subdued voice. They contain a mixture of intimacy, polite
reserve, discreet appreciation and distant respect, which
confers on them a charm and a tonality all their own. In
Giraudoux one finds no spectacular descriptions of land-
scapes, nor outbursts of enthusiasm over shapes or colours,
but only a few modest notes which are sufficient to create
an atmosphere and to establish a subtle bond of communion between man and things. For instance, some autumn
impressions are presented thus: 'You must not think that
dead leaves fall suddenly, like ripe fruit, or noiselessly like
withered flowers. . . . There are leaves which fall at
night, brushing against a branch and pausing anxiously,
then starting again, and in fear lest they awaken the tree,
making more noise than ever. Only the aspen leaves are
shed all at once, silvery no longer. . . . From my bed I
could see and hear them falling. Autumn was spreading
under the lime trees like a silken net, softening the fall of
the leaves. I wondered how the birds could reach the
ground.' [58] Here is a variation on birch trees: 'I have seen
the birch trees quivering in the winter by the shores of the
Caspian, against the snow, with their rings of black bark
which seemed to be separated by empty space; one wondered what was supporting the branches. And I have seen
them in midsummer, by the channel near Astrakhan, with
their white rings, like fine mushrooms, alongside the
water. . . . And when, perched on top, you have one of
those big grey and black crows, the whole tree trembles
and bends as if ready to break; and I would throw stones
at the bird until it flew away, and then all the leaves
would talk and signal to me. And seeing them shivering,
golden above and silvery underneath, you feel your heart

58. *Provinciales*, De ma Fenêtre, I, pp.3-4.

filled with tenderness.' [59] It is clear that Giraudoux in
his early years must have become deeply imbued with
the charm of the countryside and that in most of his descriptive notes he is recalling some aspect of his beloved
Limousin.

Human characters, however, play by far the most important part in Giraudoux's writings. He in fact is much
more interested in the personages themselves than in their
adventures. In his novels or plays the plot is generally
outlined in rather a casual manner, but the feelings and
reactions of the characters are related in minute detail.
Yet Giraudoux is not an adept in psychology; he could
not in any sense be compared in this respect to Proust, for
instance. He does not pretend to any new and personal
discoveries about the workings of the mind and heart. He
does not probe very deeply in his analysis of human sentiments. Of course, many clever and penetrating observations are met with in his works; but as a rule he is content
to pass lightly over the well explored field of normal
reactions, occasionally indicating some delicate and elusive shade of thought, or perhaps adorning the sober pattern of plain facts with arabesques conceived by his fertile
imagination.

Nearly all Giraudoux's characters are endowed with
extraordinary sensitiveness. As a rule their emotions are
not very deep and do not display any marked degree of
intensity or violence; but they are liable to assume all
sorts of shapes and forms and they go through the whole
gamut of capricious feelings. Giraudoux sets down a great
variety of impressions; some are but lightly touched upon,
others are allowed to vibrate with subtle and delicate inflexions and an amazing richness of tonality. These modu-
lations are to be found almost exclusively in the realm of

59. *La Guerre de Troie n'aura pas lieu*, Act III, Sc.12, pp.173–174.

sentiment. Giraudoux's works are practically devoid of passion and sensuality; references to purely intellectual problems are few and far between. Yet the inner life of his characters is far less rich than might be inferred from their capacity to receive impressions. They do not indulge in introspection and self-analysis; there are among them no tormented souls, no victims of complexes, no anxious hearts. They look exclusively outwards. They are wide open to the influences of the external world, constantly changing from moment to moment.

They are so sensitively receptive that each individual, separate element of a total impression exerts on them its own separate and distinct effect; so their personality seems to become diffused in a multiplicity of fragmentary feelings concerning the most casual and insignificant happenings. Important facts and trifling details seem to occupy the same place in their consciousness. In *Juliette au Pays des Hommes*, when Gérard learns, while shaving, that his fiancée is deserting him and going to Paris, he cannot repress a start, which makes him cut himself. 'One cannot imagine how much moral anguish it takes to outweigh the hurt from just one clumsy stroke of the razor. In such a predicament the first care in the world that a man will have, even when he can hear the whistle of the train that is carrying his fiancée away from him, is not to run to the window but to run to the mirror and stop the bleeding.' [60] What were soldiers in the Great War thinking about at the moment when they were killed? Were they filled with hatred towards the enemy, with idealistic confidence in the justice of their own cause? Not at all! 'If they had been allowed . . . to express a regret, it would have been perhaps that they had not been rid, during the month, the week or at least the day preceding their death, of their

60. *Juliette au Pays des Hommes*, I, p.27.

toothache, their colic, and also of that General Antoine who forbade them to wear mufflers.' [61]

Hence Giraudoux's characters display a certain lack of moral unity and consistency. They do not reason out and co-ordinate intellectually the various aspects of their mental life. They cannot be brought into line with any general or central idea; they are full of contradictions; they live from moment to moment. It is impossible to foresee what they are likely to do next—not because we are not well enough acquainted with them but simply because their actions are unpredictable. Besides, they are not given to activity. Most of them are passive, hesitant, irresolute—they waver between several decisions and are unable to take a definite stand. They accept almost with indifference the events which are brought their way by circumstances or 'Fate' or 'God.' There are among them no real heroes, fighting energetically, pursuing a lofty ideal with determination. The few who have attained glory—like Judith—have been impelled by motives very different from those attributed to them by fame.

The most usual motive activating them is love. Giraudoux does not present a new version of the traditional picture of love. He simply offers a number of clever variations on the age-old theme. His characters accept love as it comes, without calculation, for its human and poetical value; they accept it with its retinue of cares, joys, sorrows, hopes, and disappointments. True, they are never carried away in a rapture of overpowering bliss—their sufferings always appear to be quite tolerable; but there is a pure and delicate quality in their emotions which confers on these moderate pleasures and pains a captivating charm such as a display of unleashed passion would not possess for the reader.

61. J.Giraudoux, *Bella*, Grasset, Paris, 1926, II, p.38.

Nevertheless, these half-real, half-imaginary beings lack the robust and vigorous substance of reality. Their physical aspect is generally presented with adequate precision, by means of a series of little touches of detail which are more clever than striking; but their moral personality seldom stands out in clear and strong relief. They seem vague and indefinite. Their very elusiveness may be considered a merit, for it leaves free scope to the imagination of the reader. On this account also it is difficult to form an impression of them as concrete, living human beings, seeing that they are but little more than semi-abstract conceptions of the mind. However, in this respect Giraudoux's plays differ greatly from his novels. In his novels, the outlines of the characters are often lost in a haze of subtle, ingenious, and even contradictory details; in the plays the exigencies of the stage setting have compelled Giraudoux to concentrate and simplify his presentation to a marked degree, so that, though his characters are still fundamentally the same, they are more clean-cut in design with the essentials more easily grasped.

The cause of this almost shadowy quality and lack of substance in Giraudoux's creations is that most of them—the *Indifférents*, Suzanne, Juliette, Siegfried, Philippe Dubardeau, Hector—are but reflections of Giraudoux's own personality—or rather of certain sides of his personality, each of which projects itself into a set of lively but superficial and unco-ordinated images. Those of his characters which have been modelled directly on some other person are even less life-like. He himself admits this, not without some surprise, it seems. 'The only characters I have really copied are those which are considered by one and all to be imaginary and fictitious.' [62] The explanation may perhaps be found in the fact that Giraudoux con-

62. F.Lefèvre, *Une heure avec . . . Quatrième Série*, J.Giraudoux, p.121.

siders the universe merely as a collection of material for stimulating his own sensibilities, where the other human beings are scarcely more than amusing puppets providing him with a show. 'Il est vrai . . . à mesure que j'examinais mes amis, que l'univers me semblait peuplé de fantoches.' [63]

Special mention must be made, however, of the way in which Giraudoux has presented young women throughout his writings. Obviously he has always been especially attracted by them; as he himself puts it, 'les jeunes filles seules m'attiraient.' [64] In the whole of nature and humanity they are the mirror in which he has always liked best to see his own reflection. They appear, all of them, like creatures seen in a dream. They radiate the airy charm of the characters in plays by Musset or Marivaux. They seem to be endowed with a spontaneous and indestructible purity; they may have a past, like Geneviève—they may have been married, like Bella—they may be thoroughly emancipated, like Eglantine—they may, like Juliette, make excursions into *le pays des hommes*, or, like Suzanne, travel as far as the Pacific—they nevertheless possess a natural innocence that apparently keeps them free from all stain and blemish. Even Helen of Troy manages to be 'remote' and 'distant' [65] in love! Yet they are not absolutely cold in their preternatural candour. Giraudoux has noted the revolutionizing change that takes place within the souls of pure young women on their first approach to human reality. Before the great initiation, the world appears to them as an abstract, cool, and almost transparent entity. They themselves look so graceful, so immaterial, that they scarcely seem to belong to the coarse, average

63. *L'Ecole des Indifférents*, Jacques l'Egoïste, p.39.
64. *Simon le Pathétique*, III, p.63.
65. *La Guerre de Troie n'aura pas lieu*, Act I, Sc.4, p.32.

earthly things we know. ' "But suddenly Man arrives on
the scene. Then all of them contemplate him. . . . They
quiver before him in hypocritical admiration, beset by a
fear such as even a tiger could not inspire in them. . . .
Then the mischief is done. All the walls of reality, through
which they could see a thousand heraldic symbols, a
thousand delicate traceries, become as it were darkened,
and all is over."—"All is over? If you are alluding to
marriage, you mean to say that life is just beginning." ' [66]
Life begins anew on a different plan; it may be a cheerful,
homely comedy, as experienced by Isabelle when she
marries the *Contrôleur des Poids et Mesures*—It may be a
poignant and tragic revelation, such as comes to Judith
after she meets the powerful and overwhelming Holofernes. In any case the *jeune fille* has become a woman.

Woman is depicted by Giraudoux as essentially kind and
weak. In most cases and almost always she wants really
to be good. But circumstances, and her own inborn coquetry, constantly play tricks with her; half-passively,
half from curiosity, she finds herself involved in adventures
which later on she will look back to with perfectly charming remorse. Woman is not perfect, however men may like
to imagine her so. ' "You must have met women who as
far as you could see seemed to personify intelligence,
harmony, sweetness."—"Yes, I have seen some like that."
—"What did you do then?"—"I approached nearer and
that was the end." ' [67] In the case of women as with all the
rest of the universe it is wiser—and more tactful—to look
on the pleasant surface than to pry into the secrets hidden
underneath. A woman herself ought not to attempt to go
out of her way to seek happiness but must find contentment in a superficial existence. ' Women commit a sacrilege

66. *Intermezzo*, Act iii, Sc.4, p.194.
67. *La Guerre de Troie n'aura pas lieu*, Act i, Sc.5, p.47.

when they go in search of happiness . . . they must wait for it without complaining and without suffering. Have they not, in order to beguile the time of waiting, innumerable play-things and distractions: nooks in lozenge-paned windows, kitchens, the summer-time with its travels? They have but to apportion to each week a little hope, to each month a little happiness: the purchase of a novel, a game of tennis, a passage in a quartet played by a favourite musician. So they will be satisfied, like the gipsies who keep travelling on and on along the road, and yet rejoice at every milestone.' [68]

This evocation may not correspond to any actual living type—it seems rather to be a blending of features taken from reality with the more or less fanciful imaginings of Giraudoux the man. But the blending is so skilfully achieved that it is very difficult to tell where the junction takes place, and Giraudoux's female characters derive from that double origin the warmth and spontaneity of nature and also the remote and almost immaterial charm that only unreal creatures can possess.

Human beings appear in Giraudoux's works not only as individuals but also as representatives of many different nations. People from France, Germany, England, North America, South America, from the modern Orient, from ancient Greece and from Judea pass through his works in a motley, cosmopolitan procession. Yet his writings contain nothing that even faintly recalls the showy international display to be found in the works of Paul Morand, for instance. Giraudoux is essentially French; and foreigners with all their sensibility and thought are approached by him from the outside and without much sympathy. He may not himself at first sight seem so typically French, but it must be remembered that his

68. *L'Ecole des Indifférents*, Don Manuel le Paresseux, p.123.

adolescent days—that is to say, the formative period of
his moral development—coincided with the time when the
Symbolist School in literature and the Impressionist
School in painting had just produced their most sensa-
tional masterpieces and were at last arousing the attention
of the general public, before they disappeared from the
scene. Thus it is evident that Giraudoux's attitude is related to one definite period and aspect of French sensibility. France and French culture positively fill his writings
from end to end. His points of view, his feelings, the allusions he makes, the manners he describes are entirely
French; to the French reader very few French writers
give the impression of being so thoroughly at home as
Giraudoux in a French atmosphere and on French soil.
This is undoubtedly one of the reasons why he has gained
comparatively little recognition abroad.

Yet he does not very often speak explicitly of France—
perhaps because France is implied, taken for granted, as
it were, in all his writings. Occasionally, however, and
especially when he is comparing France with her neigh-
bour, Germany, he makes some clear-sighted and pungent
remarks on French mentality. Thus, 'no other nation
enjoys more thoroughly what it possesses and limits itself
more completely to what is in its possession than the
French people . . . which is a sign of peace. No other
nation attaches its desires more firmly to what it does not
possess than the German people—a sign of war.' 69 In
Siegfried et le Limousin the narrator has a dream. In this
dream Siegfried Kleist is being transmuted from a German into a French character and expresses himself in the
following manner: 'Kleist was exclaiming to me that the
atmosphere for him was becoming clearer, that his reason-
ings were being provided with proper dialectical hinges,

69. *Siegfried et le Limousin*, IV, p.142.

and his passions with adequate articulation, that the insects appeared smaller and more slender, that the singing of the birds, the meaning of which he had understood up to then, was to his ears now nothing but a mere warbling . . . and finally that he felt an ungovernable desire for absinth and economies.' [70] But even when Giraudoux indulges, as above, in mild criticisms of France, his strictures never have the caustic appropriateness that marks the satire of Paul Morand.

In writing of foreign countries he practically never depicts their external features for the sake of picturesque effect. In his portrayal of Germany he refers only to the most obvious—and often in themselves insignificant—details of every-day life which contrast with his French ways and habits; as for example the German custom of hanging 'mottoes' on the walls or placing them indiscriminately on household objects. When in *Jérôme Bardini* he carries his hero to the United States, he refrains from giving the slightest suggestion of American local colour. His representation of ancient Greece is reminiscent in many respects—*mutatis mutandis*—of the discreet and modernized version given by Racine in the seventeenth century.

The moral characteristics of foreign nations interest him somewhat more. Germany, however, is the only country of which Giraudoux has painted a full-length portrait. He obviously found Germany attractive—at least the old Germany—and without her he is bewildered and confused 'like a dog that has had all its feeler-whiskers cut off on one side of its face.' [71] He likes Germany because it is 'un grand pays poétique et humain.' [72] 'Germany is a great country—industrious and ardent—a country resounding

70. *Siegfried et le Limousin*, v, p.150.
71. *Ibidem*, i, p.18.
72. *Ibidem*, i, p.18.

with poetry, where the singer who sings out of tune reaches the hearts of her listeners more often than the singer who sings in tune in other climes, but it is a brutal and blood-thirsty country, merciless to the weak. . . .' [73] 'Whenever the German has tried to make a practical edifice of her [Germany], his work has collapsed within a few decades. Whenever he has believed in his country's peculiar gift for transforming every great thought and every great deed into a symbol or a legend, he has constructed something that will endure for eternity.' [74] 'Paroxysm, not orderliness, is the rule in Germany.' [75] All such statements are possibly one-sided and debatable, but at least they show that Giraudoux in his effort to understand the German people displayed a fairness, a sympathy, and at the same time a penetration which are seldom encountered in contemporary French writers.

His references to other nations, however, are rather disappointing. The United States is very indistinctly sketched in *Amica America* and in *Jérôme Bardini*. The conflict between East and West—which purports to be the main theme of *Eglantine*—fails to portray the characteristics of the oriental mind in a striking and arresting manner. There is little beyond the mere suggestion that the Oriental has introduced into modern life a good deal of brutality, recklessness, and nervousness. Other casual remarks about England, Russia, modern Greece are often pointedly clever but do not as a rule convey the impression of a new light being thrown on a worn-out subject.

Giraudoux never, in fact, attempted didactically to offer information about the outside world. Objects, persons, nations interest him only in so far as they constitute

73. *Siegfried*, Act ii, Sc.2.
74. *Ibidem*, Act i, Sc.2.
75. *Siegfried et le Limousin*, iv, p.140.

a medium in which his own personality can reflect itself, or as they provide him with material for his imagination and a rich field for his art.

5. *Giraudoux's Art*

THE art of Giraudoux is extremely elaborate and complicated; it is in many respects perplexing to the general reading public. The uninitiated and unprepared reader is constantly wondering whither he is being led—and even frequently loses sight of the point from which he started. In Giraudoux's works there is no trace of any logical, regular, well constructed plan such as is usually to be found in French novels and plays. He seems to proceed at random, impelled by his tireless and ever-changing fancy. His intentions are not always clear; his remarks, too, seem often to have little connexion with the facts to which they are supposed to refer.

In the course of an interview given in 1924 Giraudoux offered an explanation for this apparent incoherency of his, to this effect: that most of his books were written very hurriedly, his professional duties not allowing him time to polish and perfect his original conception. '*Siegfried et le Limousin*' he said, 'required twenty-seven days; I take a blank sheet of paper and I begin to write; the characters are born as I proceed; after five or six pages, I can see the way clear. . . .'[76] He also admitted that 'as a rule, it is a very bad thing to write a book too quickly; but one would require to have time, a great deal of time, and it happens that nowadays most writers, besides their literary profession, have another profession which is often entirely different.'[77]

76. F.Lefèvre, *Une heure avec* . . . *Première Série*, J.Giraudoux, p.149.
77. *Une heure avec* . . . *Quatrième Série*, J.Giraudoux, p.120.

But it would be too simple just to accept the idea of improvisation as a satisfactory explanation of all the difficulties and obscurities to be found in Giraudoux's writings. He is too much of an artist to express himself inadequately merely on account of his own remissness. If he is continually improvising, it is apparently because by this process he preserves as much as possible of the spontaneity and freshness of his inspiration. After stating that for many an author writing is a relaxation, a real holiday, he adds: 'If one can spend one's holidays enthusiastically writing, it would perhaps spoil them to be scratching out words, attending to the smallest details, and constantly striving for perfection.' [78] A work of Giraudoux hardly ever presents a continuous logical development of ideas; it is more like a casual, desultory talk, sometimes emphasizing insignificant particulars, sometimes summing up rapidly culminating catastrophic events, sometimes even evoking, in retrospect, happenings long over and done with. But in every case the bulk of the work is made up of a collection of concrete statements concerning facts. Intermingled with these are allusions, remarks, and commentaries, sometimes intended to link the facts together, sometimes merely suggested by association. In the latter case the remarks may be only remotely connected with the general topic under discussion.

The facts presented are generally in themselves unimportant, and yet they possess a curious power of evocation. If Giraudoux has to describe an individual or a bit of scenery, he does not stress their most striking features. He will mention instead a few minor details—a little mannerism in a man, the slant of a roof, the glittering of a shop-window in a street—and, as if by magic, the person or the village in question will take shape in the mind's

78. F.Lefèvre, *Une heure avec . . . Quatrième Série*, J.Giraudoux, p.120.

eye and stand forth complete with vivid clearness. His method reminds one of the technique of those artists who with a few, deft strokes, representing a cane, a monocle, and a hat, conjure up the whole aspect and personality of the man they have to portray. On purpose he leaves out the seeming essentials; but the imagination of the reader is cleverly challenged and re-creates the picture with more life and intensity than any exhaustive description could have done. Thus, through this form of art, living things and inanimate objects are endowed with a peculiar, weird existence; as they are never directly portrayed but are forcibly suggested to the mind, they almost partake of the nature of hallucinations; they are tremendously real and yet actually absent; and the phases both of their reality and their absence alternate according to a rhythm which confers on Giraudoux's creations a vibration all their own.

It must be added that every descriptive remark made by Giraudoux has but a very limited scope. Very seldom does he try to characterize with one broad sweep the general tone of an *ensemble*. He considers all the fragments of reality separately and distinctly and assigns to each one of them its proper colour. He does not like to mix or combine shades. Though he avoids bright colours and prefers subdued tones, he is moved spontaneously to give clear and pure expression to each aspect of the universe that he is considering. Every point touched upon comes out in its actual and original hue. So Giraudoux's vision of the world evokes a multiplicity of coloured spots, all in juxtaposition but not blending, full of freshness and luminosity but spread over the surface of reality and hardly ever revealing what may lie underneath. This view of the world is brilliant and amusing; but in the long run it tends to become tiresome on account of its very diversity and lack of any unifying principle.

In this general picture Giraudoux inserts a variety of short personal remarks, the object of which is generally to hint at a similarity or an affinity between some fact presented by him and another fact belonging either to classical antiquity or to the most up-to-date aspects of contemporary civilization. These constant references to such widely divergent realities bewilder and distract the attention of the reader; at the same time they enable him to perceive subtle relations between seemingly unconnected sides of life, which otherwise he never would have noticed, and they furnish for Giraudoux's somewhat superficial presentation of facts a background of traditional culture and vivid actuality. The contemporary allusions are numerous and often mystifying. An initiated Frenchman, especially if he is familiar with the political and diplomatic affairs of the day, will relish the veiled and malicious references to modern celebrities and contemporary events. To the layman they are sometimes puzzling; to the foreigner often quite incomprehensible. Fifty years hence readers of Giraudoux will be unable to understand many of his works without the aid of a glossary. The allusions to classical antiquity are of real interest to the scholar; to the ordinary reader they are likely to prove at times so enigmatic that Giraudoux himself finds it necessary to explain, within brackets, exactly what he means. For instance, he alludes to the heroism of a doctor who had both his hands amputated one after the other because they had been dangerously affected while he was giving radium treatments to cancer sufferers; he then proceeds to compare this brave doctor with the Athenian soldier who at the battle of Salamis, in order to prevent a Persian ship from escaping, seized hold of the vessel with his right hand; when his right hand was severed by the blow of an axe, he caught hold with his left hand; and when his left

hand also was severed, he held on by his teeth. The similarity between the two situations may not seem obvious,
but the passage is rendered even more obscure by such an
elusive and concise form of presentation as the following:
'This one-armed man, who had had his fingers, then his
hand, then his other hand cut off while holding close to
radium the vessel (if you will, and if you have grasped the
allusion to this battle of Salamis)—the vessel of our
sufferings.' [79]

Side by side with these contemporary or classical allusions, which are so typical of Giraudoux, one finds through
all his works a delicate vein of satire. When he is depicting
a character or expressing his own personal views, or simply
stating plain, unadorned facts, one can imagine him doing
so with a slightly ironical smile, as if to show that he is not
the dupe of anybody, not even of himself, and that he is
inviting the reader not to take any of the human actions
or ideas too seriously. Except in the case of *Bella* his irony
is not as a rule definitely directed against anything or
anyone in particular; it is more a general attitude of nonchalant amusement towards the whole comedy of life.
Undoubtedly he has the knack of catching the caricatur-
ist's side of things, as when he speaks of the peace having
been signed 'by Lloyd George who looks like a poodle,
Wilson who looks like a collie and Clemenceau who looks
like a mastiff. Europe sets its highest hopes upon this
peace which has been signed by men resembling dogs.' [80]
His humour is hardly ever biting or profound; it is rather
of the harmless and entertaining variety, though generally
arresting by reason of the very singularity of his ideas and
comparisons.

The literary style of Giraudoux reflects the fundamental

79. *Juliette au Pays des Hommes*, VI, Prière sur la Tour Eiffel, p.177.
80. *Suzanne et le Pacifique*, X, p.290.

tendencies of the man. He does not carefully polish in order
to attain definite literary effects. Improvisation is the
main source of his originality. He allows each sentence to
take shape spontaneously—not seriously and with an
effort, but casually, even playfully. 'There is an element
of gambling, of luck, in every sentence of prose as much
as in any line of verse. It is that important element of
improvisation which gives to a work life and above all
poetry.' [81] Of course improvisation does not go hand in
hand with perfection of form or with lucidity; indeed
Giraudoux's style is far from being either perfect or even
clear. The grammatical construction is frequently in-
correct. Sentences lacking a verb are plentiful. The logical
articulations are deficient. The syntax is so twisted—
ordinary words so often forced to mean something other
than their usually accepted sense—that the general import of many passages is only too frequently doubtful or
even genuinely puzzling. This is far removed from the
ideal of clarity and precision which is sometimes considered the most typical characteristic of pure French
prose. Giraudoux is well aware of the possibility of such
criticism, and retorts: 'In French style, simplicity and
clarity together constitute only one of its characteristics.
The French soul is too complex and—fortunately or unfortunately—too much linked up with poetical or philosophical considerations for the language, which according
to certain critics is considered the only true French, to be
sufficient for its needs.' [82] Consequently Giraudoux, when
necessary, will deliberately discard clarity and correctness
in order that he may express the more adequately the
complexities of his elusive thoughts and feelings.

One of the most typical features of Giraudoux's style is

81. F.Lefèvre, *Une heure avec* . . . *Quatrième Série*, J.Giraudoux, p.117.
82. *Ibidem*, pp.126–127.

the predominance of plain statements of fact, and a direct
presentation of persons or of things. Quite often a sentence
will open with a 'c'est' or 'c'était,' but not infrequently
the verb is omitted and the noun or nouns thrown helter
skelter and quite abruptly at the reader. Adjectives are
scarce, and as a rule subdued and even colourless. On the
other hand, his metaphors, that is, the comparison or
assimilation of one subject or fact with another, are extremely numerous. Indeed, it is this richness of imagery
that really confers on Giraudoux's style its peculiar and
original colour. The images employed are seldom striking,
vivid, or powerful; they are, instead, strange and far-
fetched, and not likely at first sight to appear natural; after
due reflection however they often reveal to the reader affinities which would not ordinarily have been suspected.
Giraudoux likes to consider a rapid succession of antitheti-
cal aspects of reality, looking at things first from one point
of view and then from another; the result in a sentence is
the juxtaposition of contradictory elements—the adjec-
tive belying the noun, for instance, or the adverb the verb.
He loves to make joy appear sad, sorrow cheerful, to make
things that are natural appear strange, and things that are
perfectly simple appear very complicated. He obviously
delights in these literary *tours de force*, much as a musical
virtuoso likes to display his technical skill. In many respects he is a virtuoso in literary style. He launches
impromptu into fanciful variations on a theme, not so
much with the idea of conveying any definite impression
as for the pleasure of combining difficult figures and em-
bellishments—all for his own instinctive enjoyment as a
sincere and consummate artist. For Giraudoux is really a
great artist. He possesses a keen sense of the external
value of words, of the cadence of a phrase; his sentences
even though they may be irregular from a grammatical

standpoint lend themselves always to a well modulated rhythmical rendering.

On account of its fanciful quality the style of Giraudoux has often been compared to that of the French humorist, Jules Renard. Giraudoux himself has protested against this comparison and has made it clear that in the matter of style the most decisive influence brought to bear upon him has been the example of certain Latin writers. 'The language to which I am most indebted is Latin. Do you follow me? I do not refer to the Latin of Cicero or Quintilian—the language of argument and exposition—but to the Latin of those wonderful writers, Pliny, Tacitus, and above all Seneca, whose language is so racy, so full of comparisons and singularities, and in whose style improvisation plays a considerable part.' [83]

The very fact that he acknowledges such a writer as Seneca to be his model and guide, illumines two essential aspects of Giraudoux's art and personality. On the one hand, Giraudoux is certainly fond of a brilliant play on words, of piquant verbal effects, of pointed epigrams, antitheses, and unexpected comparisons. He even carries that love of acrobatic subtlety into the field of thought and sentiment. On the other hand, his sentiments and thoughts possess at the same time a noble, classical elevation, similar in many respects to that of his favourite Stoic philosopher.

Very frequently the one aspect of Giraudoux's talent obscures the other. Some critics can find nothing in his works but a display of artificial virtuosity. The word *précieux* has often been used to qualify his art. And it is true that he is not far removed morally from *Préciosité* —that seventeenth century cult of over-refinement and stilted affectation in manners, style, and ideas. He likes so much to draw clever and fantastic arabesques that one

83. F.Lefèvre, *Une heure avec . . . Quatrième Série*, J.Giraudoux, p.119.

feels tempted to apply to him the remarks he makes about one of his own characters: 'Bernard endeavoured to achieve a complete stylization of each action performed by him during the day, each landscape, each emotion. In the same way certain hives of bees construct their honeycombs with cells of superior workmanship. But they never fill them up with honey.' [84]

Honey is decidedly to be found within the light and fragile edifices of Giraudoux's literary art. This honey is his contribution to the solution of the problem of the relations between ideality and reality. The problem is considered by Giraudoux from a particular and definite angle —that of a confrontation between classical culture and the modern world. At first sight the two seem to consort ill together; many people hold that any attempt to reconcile them must end in reciprocal mutilation or even in utter failure. Not a few are resigned to abandonment of the classics and are disposed to build a brand new civilization on a fresh foundation. Giraudoux belongs to those who adhere to the classics and who yet realize the relative incompatibility of the classical conceptions with certain important aspects of modern life; therefore he scrutinizes reality, endeavouring to discover in what way it can be assimilated to his ideal. He has not formulated any ambitious plan for a universal and comprehensive solution of the difficulty. He merely considers those few elements of the universe which come within his reach, and is content when he finds that the contradictions so loudly advertised often conceal secret affinities. He points out these affinities, similarities, identities, discreetly—often with a smile —and through these multiple identifications he creates for himself amidst the anxieties and disturbances of modern life a delicate and poetical harmony.

84. *L'Ecole des Indifférents*, Le Faible Bernard, p.197.

PAUL MORAND

IV. PAUL MORAND

1. *Life and Person of Paul Morand*

THE figure of Paul Morand is surrounded and obscured by a strange and persistent legend. His writings have such a vivid and convincing quality that the general reading public in France has come to believe the author himself to be possessed of the moral and even sometimes the physical characteristics of his fictitious heroes. With the publication of each new book more features have been added by the imagination of his readers to the popular conception of him that has evolved out of the most heterogeneous and contradictory elements. Paul Morand himself has good-humouredly analysed some aspects of this fanciful caricature of himself that has become established in the public mind. 'That cynical mouth came into being after *Tendres Stocks*, that pallor after *Ouvert la Nuit*; that heavy jaw characteristic of the businessman was imposed on me after *Lewis et Irène*; that sleek hair of the noctambulant grew after *L'Europe Galante*; the slanting eyes are those of *Bouddha Vivant*; and after *Magie Noire* my photographs even, O shade of Dorian Gray! began to take on a negroid look.' [1] In vain did Morand repeatedly protest that he was not at all the 'monster' [2] so many people believed him to be. Notwithstanding his denials the French public continues to picture him as a cynical globe-trotter, 'agité et brutal,' [3] always 'running after a train, a suitcase

1. P.Morand, *Papiers d'Identité*, Grasset, Paris, 1931, Ma légende, pp.10–11.
2. *Ibidem*, p.10.
3. *Ibidem*, p.10.

in his hand,' [4] selfish and hard, yet flighty and superficial; they think of him as a specialist in love—or rather in the sexual extravaganza that goes by that name in certain cosmopolitan circles—and finally as a snob. The reality seems to be more complicated and at the same time less strikingly romantic.

Paul Morand—born March 13, 1888—received from his family, either directly or by way of spontaneous reaction, strong and determining influences. His father, Eugène Morand, was endowed with an unusual variety of natural gifts and talents. He is known essentially as a painter; but he also attained recognition as a playwright, and he was by no means ignorant of musical technique and art. Moreover he was a good English scholar, specializing in Elizabethan literature as a hobby. In collaboration with Marcel Schwob he made a translation of Hamlet which was staged in 1900—with Sarah Bernhardt taking a leading part. One of his own plays *Grisélidis* was well received at the *Théâtre Français*. Also he wrote a number of libretti for Pierné, Massenet, and a few other composers. To these achievements in art and letters, he added natural steadiness, balance, and a sense of efficiency which qualified him to pursue an official administrative career in which he won great success. He was placed in charge of the storeroom in the Louvre for statuary not on exhibition, as 'Directeur du Dépôt des Marbres'; then he became and remained for twenty years (1908–28) Director of the important 'Ecole des Arts Décoratifs.'

Personally, Eugène Morand was laborious and earnest, by no means narrow minded or dull, yet happy within his own definite sphere. He was not over fond of travelling, and sports he regarded with suspicion. 'You must leave sport to the idle, my boy,' he once said to his son then aged

4. *Papiers d'Identité*, Ma légende, p.16.

twelve, 'to people who ride on horseback. Sport engenders lazy habits.' [5] The boy accordingly was forbidden henceforward to buy *L'Auto-Vélo*, a newspaper devoted to accounts of sporting events. Theoretically something of a radical in his political opinions, Morand's father was nevertheless in practice a deliberate conservative.

His very unusual combination of inspiriting artistic talents on the one hand,—of solid, steady *bourgeois* qualities on the other, influenced in these two opposing directions the activities of the whole Morand family. The atmosphere of the home was exceedingly respectable and proper. The life of the household was punctuated by the ritual of French family tradition in which the unspeakably stiff and wearisome institution of Sunday dinner has always ranked paramount. Morand confessed that the effect that weekly ceremony had on him was enough to decide him in the choice of a career. 'I intended, above everything,' he says, 'that it should take me far away from the Sunday evening family dinners. I was fond of my parents, but I detested the gloomy dinners which in their solemnity recall those of the last years of Louis XIV, as described in Saint-Simon—occasions on which so many French families call a Sunday evening truce.' [6] In truth the abhorrence in which Paul Morand held those Sunday dinners was but the symbol of his deep reaction to the family circle of which he was a member. Even as a child he longed to run away from the monotony and uniformity of his environment. The desire to travel, to mix with strange people in strange lands, which appeared early in his life and was to remain one of the salient features of his character in later years, seem less of a positive craving for excitement and adventure than a means of escape from

5. P.Morand, *1900*, Editions de France, Paris, 1931, IV, p.140.
6. P.Morand, *Mes Débuts*, Denoël et Steele, Paris, 1933, pp.12–13.

oppressively dull and respectable surroundings. 'Travel, the colonies, the great open spaces appealed to me simply because they would take me far away.' [7]

Yet the 'wanderlust' had been strongly felt by one at least of Paul Morand's ancestors. In the middle of the nineteenth century his grandfather, an expert bronze smelter, had been induced to go to Russia. He had settled in St. Petersburg as a director of the Imperial Bronze Foundry. Paul Morand's own father was born there, but he ultimately returned to France and was married in Paris. As a result of that long stay in Russia, the Morand family tradition had acquired some special features. By way of spontaneous reaction against a foreign environment, as it happens to most exiles, certain national characteristics of the family had become intensified to the point that the Morands appeared in some respects more profoundly French than the average Frenchman. So they were led to display the firmest attachment to the typical conventions of French family life. At the same time, their temporary uprooting had severed many links with their original French surroundings, particularly with the more conservative and solid elements. They had developed an interest in foreigners and an understanding of things and ideas alien to their own, such as are often considered queer and suspicious by the orthodox members of the social class to which they were supposed to belong. So the family, though coming of genuine old French stock and still very conventional in some respects, was no longer deeply and firmly implanted in French soil.

On account of this interest in foreigners, and also because of Eugène Morand's vocational and professional association with the artistic world, many of the guests and friends of the family were not of the kind that would

7. *Mes Débuts*, p.13.

ordinarily foregather in an average French *bourgeois* home. Amongst them were theatrical folk, like Sarah Bernhardt,[8] artists and poets belonging to the Symbolist and 'Décadent' schools, such as Mallarmé and Marcel Schwob.[9] A few Americans, such as Vance Thompson, a few English—some of them of the most unconventional type—like Oscar Wilde, Lord Alfred Douglas,[10] or the journalist Frank Harris[11]—found a welcome within the family circle. These unusual people brought into the otherwise conventional and well regulated Morand home, a special atmosphere of their own. They represented much freer, more interesting and colourful aspects of life than those which ordinarily prevail within the strict and narrow limits of French family tradition. They afforded young Paul Morand glimpses of a queer, alluring, exciting outside world which he must have felt eager to explore.

At school Paul Morand was not a very proficient pupil. According to the decision of his parents, who were conservative and lovers of the classics, he was assigned to studies in which dead languages form the main discipline of the curriculum. To the great dismay of his father, the boy found sports more interesting than lessons. He was not a great athlete himself, though he did some running and played rugby occasionally; but he loved to follow the exploits of the famous prize-fighters of the day, and still more to watch the performances or merely to read about the speed records periodically established and broken by the then recently invented automobile. Referring to himself and his school-fellows, he says, 'Notre

8. *1900*, v, pp.190–191.
9. *Papiers d'Identité*, Interview, p.24.
10. *Ibidem*, p.24.
11. P.Morand, *Rond-Point des Champs-Elysées*, Grasset, Paris, 1935, ii, pp.167–174.

grand amour, ce fut le moteur.' [12] There was of course no question of his acquiring a car of his own, but his youthful imagination revelled in fantastic day-dreams about this new mechanical device.

This first great enthusiasm of his was to leave its mark on him for the rest of his life. The love of speed, the sympathetic understanding of the machine, the instinctive perception of a strange beauty in practical and powerful efficiency stamped him as a thoroughly modern boy. The generation to which he belonged did not seek their ideal in the mirage of a glamorous and romantic past, believing the present to be full of a more real and vivid poetry than any other period known—the poetry of stupendous natural forces harnessed by the master-mind of the engineer, forces that are still jostling each other in the rush to create a bustling new world, but also shaping the lives of men along harder, swifter, and stronger lines than could ever have been imagined before.

Every summer young Morand was sent to England in order to learn English. In 1908 on the advice of Lord Alfred Douglas [13] his father agreed to let him spend one full year at Oxford. He did not do much actual studying there, but as he was then at the time of life when a young man's personality begins to take definite shape and his ideas to tend in one direction or another, this sojourn abroad, in an English environment, was of the utmost importance for his ulterior development. He learned to observe things and people at a different angle from that to which he was accustomed at home. The wonderful achievements of Great Britain, viewed from London and Oxford, inspired him with admiration and respect. Thus he realized that France was not the whole world, nor even

12. *1900*, IV, p.143.
13. *Papiers d'Identité*, Interview, p.24.

the centre of the world, as many French people fondly believe. He heard French ideas and manners freely criticized—sometimes even ridiculed. He suffered on that account, yet he was intelligent enough to realize that in many cases the criticism or mockery was not without point.

So his outlook gradually underwent a change. His views were broadened and enlarged far beyond the limits of his original surroundings. But this did not develop in him any sharp antagonistic reaction to his early French environment, nor any anger nor bitterness. He realized that there lay outside the boundaries of France a rich world full of engrossing interest, and he was attracted by it and wanted to know it better. At the same time he retained a secret wistful attachment to his own country—not sufficiently pronounced to prevent him from travelling abroad but strong enough to make him feel an exile when away from France and to give the tang of *dépaysement* to any sojourn in another country.

Having completed his year's study in England he returned to France and eventually decided to follow a diplomatic career. As a child he had cherished the dream of becoming a naval officer because he might thereby escape from the dull, narrow family circle. But a stiff examination requiring a considerable knowledge of mathematics guards the entrance to the commissioned ranks of the French navy. Morand, as he himself says, more or less humourously, knew nothing whatever about mathematics,[14] so he chose diplomacy as a makeshift; it would serve the same purpose of taking him abroad to strange and distant lands.

After doing his military service he entered the great French diplomatic school, *Ecole Libre des Sciences Po-*

14. *Mes Débuts*, pp.13–14.

litiques. The course of instruction there does not include a profound study of any special subject, its purpose being not to turn out experts in definite, particular fields, but to impart a wide general knowledge of all the varied questions that may confront the statesman in our motley and complicated modern world. There all the great contemporary problems, with their historical, geographical, racial, political, psychological, and economic backgrounds, are reviewed by professors of recognized competency and explained in the light of the most up-to-date scientific methods. These studies are of engrossing interest and attract a large number of students including foreigners; but the ground covered is necessarily very extensive, and it is often impossible, owing to lack of time, to probe the depths of any given question. Hence certain characteristics which are more or less common to all students who have passed through the school. Most of them exhibit a predilection for the great problems that exist today rather than for abstract, classical, and theoretical questions. They are in close contact with human, living reality—not always with the most joyful and pleasant sides of it, but often with its most stirring or dangerous aspects. They are able to discourse intelligently on all these problems, because they possess a large fund of ideas or facts regarding each and every question. Frequently they appear brilliant, as they have been trained to display whatever they may know in a clever and arresting way; but frequently again, they may give an impression of superficiality, which is not always unfounded, because their information, being spread over such a large surface, is likely to be thin in any one definite spot. In addition they are generally notable for their polish of manner, with its careful blending of friendliness and aloofness, of composure and outwardly engaging

kindness—sometimes also for more than a hint of snob-
bishness; all of which tendencies stamp them as very
different from the ordinary run of French university
students. Morand was strongly marked with the imprint
of the school. Many characteristics to be found in his
writings—the genuine interest in international problems,
the broad understanding of different human factors, the
pointed cleverness, the dazzling though perhaps somewhat superficial virtuosity of expression—all seem to be
traceable to that essential stage in his early professional
training.

After a short preliminary stay in the Department of
the 'Protocole'—which takes charge of official political
and diplomatic functions in Paris—Paul Morand was
sent abroad. He was destined to remain abroad for the
next seven years. During that period an unusual variety
of circumstances spread before his eyes a kaleidoscope of
strange sights, queer people, and striking events. These
early checkered experiences contributed perhaps more
than anything to determine Morand's original view of the
world and of reality.

First he went to England as an 'Attaché' at the French
Embassy in London and remained there for nearly four
years (1913–16). With England and London he was
already fairly well acquainted. However, in the course of
these four years, which according to himself [15] were
among the most important years of his life, he found
opportunities for widening and deepening his knowledge
of the people, the country, and especially the great city—
a knowledge that was to unfold, as he says, 'secrets
which books and professors had never let me glimpse' [16]
before. There he saw extremes of abject destitution on

15. P.Morand, *Londres*, Plon, Paris, 1931, v, p.327.
16. *Ibidem*, v, p.330.

the one hand and of security and luxury on the other. He
mingled, by virtue of his office, with the most brilliant
representatives of English high society, a curious race
which has since almost completely vanished—'une race
à peu près disparue' [17]—but which all unconsciously was
then flashing out in final effulgence before it waned. For a
while Morand revelled in these lofty associations. 'Aussitôt après avoir quitté Paris et m'être installé à Londres,
je fréquentai des duchesses. En un mot, je fus snob.' [18]
Morand later outgrew that snobbery, but at any rate he
retained a vivid picture of this wonderful social pageant
in all its dazzling splendour. In London also Morand
learned what he calls 'le sens de la terre'; [19] there he
began to grasp the organic complexity of this tremendously vast and yet disconcertingly small universe. That
conception was to grow and develop in him along original
lines in the course of his subsequent travels. Yet his ideas
in that respect were always to bear the mark of his first
experience of the world which he had seen from the centre
of a great Empire.

When the war broke out, regular diplomatic work was
everywhere complicated by a multiplicity of unofficial
dealings, underground intrigues, and clandestine negotiations. A throng of secret agents, informers, adventurers,
and go-betweens had gravitated to the main diplomatic
centres of Europe. Thus was Paul Morand initiated into
a *milieu* entirely different from any he had previously
known. He was brought into contact with a medley of
human wrecks, shady characters, powerful personalities,
idealists, and desperadoes, all caught by the fever of
action, and in the eyes of a young man, transfigured and

17. *Mes Débuts*, p.52.
18. *Ibidem*, p.50.
19. *Londres*, v, p.330.

rendered romantic by the glamour of mystery and the
ever-present threat of danger. This was Morand's first
contact with a world of underhand intrigue, a world with
which he was to become much more familiar in the years
that followed, and in regard to which he felt throughout
his early life a keen and searching curiosity.

In 1917 Morand was sent as 'Attaché' to Rome and in
1918 he was attached temporarily to the staff of the
French Embassy in Madrid. In both these places he found
himself in an atmosphere similar to that which he had
known in London. In addition to a growing knowledge
of the world of diplomacy, Morand acquired in Italy
and in Spain entirely new perspectives of people and
things. Up till then his experience had been confined to
the familiar aspects of France and England, to which
were subjoined more or less theoretical views on the rest
of the world. Now he was confronted with altogether
different realities in obvious contrast to all that he had
known before. Morand did not see Italy or Spain from
the point of view of the dilettante or the artist. He went
to these countries to perform a definite task, that of a
diplomat during war time. As he was naturally a keen
observer of character and of conditions, he eagerly studied
and carefully noted the individual and typical features
of each race and nation with which he came in contact.
Being a young man and a bachelor, Morand was able to
mix with all kinds of people in every variety of circumstance and to penetrate intimately into the national characters of the peoples among whom he lived. Thus he
could grasp all the sharp and subtle differences which distinguish an Italian from an Englishman, a Frenchman
from a Spaniard. He understood these contrasts and
accepted them, without desiring to abolish them, rejoicing rather in their colourful variety. When the war ended,

thanks to these many and frequently changing contacts
with a variegated, checkered reality, Morand's outlook
had become truly cosmopolitan.

. . . .

For several years after the war (1919–25) Morand
remained in France, being engaged in duties of not too
exacting a nature at the Ministry of Foreign Affairs in
Paris. This was probably the most fruitful and most
significant period of his whole life. He was then in his
early thirties and the possessor of an unusually rich fund
of miscellaneous experiences; although quite mature in
many ways, he was still receptive and open to outside
influences of all sorts.

Paris was just then the Mecca of a strange medley of
people. Refugees of many different nationalities—from
Russia, from Central Europe, from the Balkan states,
even from the East—were flocking to the French capital
in order to find shelter in their distress or to further their
hopes and ambitions. International revolutionaries and
agitators of every hue were busy gathering money, re-
cruiting supporters, intriguing for help, and plotting to
gain power. Adventurers, eager to prey on that amorphous
multitude, having marked down their victims, would
often rise to sudden heights of wealth and influence, only
to collapse and be swallowed up in the maelstrom of woe,
disaster, and shame. Foreign tourists, attracted by the
lure of a depreciated currency were having a glorious
time in 'Gay Paree' and keeping up a ceaseless round of
wild revelry and artificial jollity. The French, exhausted
and impoverished by the war, shrank back in disgust
from that invasion, barricaded themselves behind their
prejudices and took refuge in their homes, leaving the
field clear for a while to the host of wretched or triumphant

aliens who had boldly established themselves in their
midst.

The state of affairs in Paris then was but a particular,
if accentuated example of what was happening at that
time throughout Europe. All over the Continent, as an
aftermath of the war, large numbers of individuals had
been uprooted from their original environment, and for
many years these homeless ones shifted restlessly from
place to place, seeking to adapt themselves to new surroundings, demoralized by the sudden change of conditions, and causing demoralization wherever they came.
People of different nationality were thrown together who
had no common ground in the matter of language, religion, or manners, and who had widely different hopes
and aspirations. This abrupt intermingling of opposite
mentalities was prolific in colourful contrasts, sharp antagonisms, and moral clashes,—the idiosyncrasies of each
side being exaggerated by its reaction and opposition to
the other. This unusual mixture of heterogeneous national elements was a typical feature of post-war Europe,
and was for a while one of the most striking aspects and
most urgent problems of European civilization.

Meanwhile a wave of wild craving for immediate
pleasure was sweeping Europe from end to end. This was
but a spontaneous, and on the whole normal reaction
after years of strain, repression, and suffering. As a result,
the barriers of traditional respectability were carried
away before an overwhelming tide of desire for material
enjoyment and extravagant luxury. Millions of women
had been either deprived of their husbands or robbed of
the prospect of ever obtaining one. Some gave themselves up to a more or less disgruntled state of resignation,
but not a few others, discarding ordinary standards of
accepted morality, set out to wrest from life whatever

chance or luck might throw in their way. Unprincipled men were not averse to seizing what pleasure or profit they could extract from the situation. Thus did many people launch themselves recklessly upon an orgy of immorality and adventure. In that spirit of mad abandon, all the moral rules which in ordinary life afford a measure of protection to the weak were of no avail. So the weak, who were mostly women, fell the first victims, and were trampled ruthlessly underfoot, while the cunning, brutal, or merely lucky scoundrels gloated insolently in their success. The number of persons engulfed by this wave of immorality was actually comparatively small, though it appeared at the time to be tremendous because of the shameless notoriety of the affairs. Nevertheless, even if the masses were not affected by that superficial agitation, some profoundly disturbing influences were at work among the general population.

The great upheaval of the war and the subsequent revolutionary outbreaks that occurred in some countries had put a great strain on people everywhere and rendered then abnormally sensitive. Their nerves would quiver and react intensely in response to the slightest anomalous stimulation, and there was no dearth of such occasions at that time. What with the difficulty people had in readjusting their own changed views to a world that was continually changing before their very eyes, what with the uncertainty of the future, the distracting fluctuations of the various currencies, inflation with its train of feverish activity, extravagant speculation and depressing misery, conflicting ambitions, frustrated hopes, and political unrest,—the morale of the European nations was indeed shaken to the depths. The sense of an impending catastrophe worse even than the one that had just occurred, and a foreboding of the approaching end of existing civilization, were in everybody's mind. This was due less to any clear intellectual perception of coming changes in the structure of society than to a profound despondency resulting from the racking experiences which had been the lot of European peoples during five years of ordeal and distress.

Yet the years of trial were over now and the feeling of discouragement and despair was in many strangely mingled with the exhilarating, intoxicating impression of having escaped from the gory nightmare of war—a sense of liberation, of intense joy, of returning vitality. From the ruins, brand new life was springing up everywhere, effervescing with fresh ideas, tingling with novel sensations. The heart of youth was throbbing in an almost lyrical mood. The past was dead, the present was here, hard and raw, but its very hardness filled the young with excitement and glee.

That strange mixture of black despair and zest for life was one of the typical features of post-war Europe. Though it could easily be explained by circumstances, it was in itself illogical and absurd, and more than anything else perhaps contributed to stamp that period as reckless and mad. In the midst of hopeless contradictions people felt that the world was completely out of joint, and wondered apprehensively what the future would bring forth.

When Paul Morand arrived in Paris in 1919, he was well able to understand that turbid society, exhibiting the heterogeneous traits of a crowd of exiles from many lands, and distinguished by rampant immorality and universal restlessness. He belonged to a family which had been in voluntary exile for nearly half a century, and he himself had been abroad during the most decisive years of his life; moreover, he had been associated with all kinds of queer and interesting characters in London, Rome, and Madrid; he had witnessed at close range a number of events of a most questionable nature; also, since by instinct he was a thorough-going modern, he fully shared in all the stirring emotions that were rocking the world. So with his keen understanding and receptive sympathy he found himself in complete accord with the anxious spirit of that time.

Morand seems then to have gone through a phase of profound moral depression. This period of despondency was apparently not connected with any definite personal disappointment or grief. It was probably but an individual instance of the widespread feeling of gloom and dejection which was at that time affecting practically the whole of Europe. The idea of suicide was in the air, just as it had been after the Napoleonic wars—in similar circumstances though in a much more marked degree— during the early despairing, morbid period of French Romanticism. It was partly to escape from that obsession that Morand sought refuge in writing. In his case, as in that of many others, the sense of moral decay was curiously coupled with an unusually pronounced imaginative activity. Writing afforded him a means of giving vent to his intellectual effervescence; also it enabled him to recover a measure of personal equilibrium. 'My life,' as Morand himself said, 'is a continual struggle against my feelings, which lead me far afield. . . . Books or suicide, which? But suicide is out of the question. There remained books. Writing enables the blood to circulate. So I wrote.' [20]

Morand was then haunting the most advanced literary circles in Paris. Some of them, like the 'Dadaïsts,' were ultra-modern and provokingly audacious in their verbal innovations; others, such as those which centred round

20. *Les Nouvelles Littéraires*, Paris, 8 fév. 1930.—Article by Nino Frank on 'Rien que la Terre' contains the above declaration made by P.Morand.

the 'Nouvelle Revue Française,' were sincerely striving
to attain a genuine artistic expression of their own original feelings and views. Morand was influenced by both
groups—for the two were not absolutely separate and
distinct at first. His first publications—*Lampes à Arc*
(1919) and *Feuilles de Température* (1920)—were collections of short poems, most of them referring to circumstances or impressions of the war and the armistice period,
many being obviously inspired by Morand's own experiences in England, Italy, and Spain. They all bore the
stamp of a fundamental pessimism and of a restless
imagination; with their jerky, syncopated style they
sounded an unmistakable note of challenge to *bourgeois*
common sense and the rational conception of things.
Morand was then in the vanguard of the young artists
who thought that the old civilization was dying and that
a hard, cold, shoddy, industrial, banal new system was
about to take its place. Between the two worlds, one
already moribund and the other yet to be born, these
young artists were striving to create a strange new language of their own to express their agony and their forebodings.

Tendres Stocks (1921) was conceived somewhat in the
same spirit. The three short stories about three young
women, drifting in war-time London, were but a pretext
for an indictment of the precarious state of contemporary
morals; yet the style was less frantic and dislocated than
in Morand's previous writings, and his evolution in the
direction of the ideals of 'La Nouvelle Revue Française'
was clearly marked.

Ouvert la Nuit (1922) and *Fermé la Nuit* (1923) brought
Paul Morand instantaneous and lasting fame. In these
two collections of short stories, he conjures up with haunting intensity the very atmosphere of some typical social

groups in turbid, post-war Europe. *Lewis et Irène* (1924), a full-length novel in similar vein, was not an unqualified success. *L'Europe Galante*, though not published until 1925, belongs to the same group of works; in it the themes previously presented in the *Nuits* were repeated in a more daring key, fully justifying the translation of the title used in the English version, 'Europe at Love.'

At this stage of his moral and literary evolution, Morand appeared as the most typical representative of the fascinating though unbalanced post-war period and also as its most genuine and adequate interpreter.

. . . .

In 1925 Morand's life took a new turn; the Ministry of Foreign Affairs sent him to Siam to assume charge of the French Legation in Bangkok. To reach his new post, Morand crossed the Atlantic, raced over the American continent from New York to Vancouver, traversed the Pacific to Yokohama, skimmed along Japan, saw Peking, Shanghai, Hong Kong, Macao, touched Singapore and finally arrived at his destination—Bangkok. He remained there only for a very short time. The tropical climate affected his health and he decided somewhat abruptly to return to France that same year, by way of Ceylon and the Suez Canal.

This trip round the world was for Morand the starting point of a new life and the beginning of an almost entirely different outlook on people and things. Up to 1925, he had travelled to and fro all over Europe, but in most cases these journeys had been made as rapidly as possible from one capital to another, and the main experience gathered from these various trips was a thorough knowledge of the ways and uses of international trains and of the comparatively small steamers which threaded the narrow

European seas. The girdling of the earth afforded him entirely fresh revelations—the powerful poetry of distance,
the lure of the great open spaces, and the spell of the colourful pageant of a world full of rich contrasts. He discovered new problems, broader, more compelling, than the
questions of morals or of maladjustment amongst Europeans which had, until then, claimed the greatest part of
his attention. As a matter of fact he had begun his acquaintance with these world problems at first in England,
and later at the *Ecole des Sciences Politiques*; but it was
not until after his journey round the world that they became a living reality to him. Ideas that he had imbibed in
the course of conversations or of lectures, or from books,
at last took on their full meaning, so that Morand came
to acquire all of a sudden, as it appeared, though in fact
as the result of long preparation, a genuine 'sense of the
earth.'

The way in which he had had to travel seems to have
determined definitely the trend of his new ideas about
'the earth.' Receiving orders to proceed at short notice
to his legation at Bangkok, he could not roam leisurely
about but was obliged to rush headlong to his destination,
meanwhile snatching impressions as best he could. The
speed with which oceans and continents flashed across
his vision forced on him the impression that the earth
was very small indeed. Again, his contact with coloured
peoples, especially during his sojourn in Siam, caused
him to realize the supreme importance of racial even
more than national problems at the present day. Henceforward the two questions—the influence of speed of
transportation upon contemporary life, and the puzzling
considerations of ethnical psychology were to be the
main preoccupations of his mind.

When Morand got back to France, he found the country

undergoing a startling transformation. After years of
restlessness following the war, a period of comparative
prosperity and equilibrium had begun. In 1926 Poincaré
put an end to the disastrous system of inflation, restored
the gold standard, and brought back confidence and
stability. Soon afterwards the Locarno treaty was signed.
The clouds seemed to be lifting everywhere. The general
belief that European civilization was in an advanced
stage of decay lost ground, if it did not vanish altogether.
Life was easier for many, and more hopeful for everyone. Money was plentiful, literature flourishing. So Paul
Morand, without altogether severing his connexion with
the Ministry of Foreign Affairs, asked for leave of absence.
In 1927 he was placed on the unattached list. Not long
after his return from Siam, he had married a Roumanian
lady of the princely and illustrious family of the Soutzo.
He established his residence—it proved to be a very comfortable one—in Paris; but for several years he spent a
large part of his time travelling, devoting the rest of his
energy to writing.

His travels no longer consisted of rapid dashes from
one point of Europe to another, but took the form of
extensive and costly journeyings to distant countries,
such as the United States, the West Indies, and even
Central Africa. His writings during this period were of
two kinds. Some were direct accounts of his travels up
and down the earth; *Rien que la Terre* (1926), *Le Voyage*
(1927), *Paris—Tombouctou* (1928), *Hiver Caraïbe* (1929).
Others were more elaborate studies of the moral characteristics of the large human groups, with which Morand
had come into contact in the course of his travels outside
Europe, and which seem to hold within themselves the
future of mankind: the yellow races in *Bouddha vivant*
(1927), the black in *Magie Noire* (1928), the American

people in *Champions du Monde* (1930). In these ethnical studies which are presented in the form of novels, Morand did not try so much to expound theories or to make predictions as to offer an objective picture of the most typical aspects of the modern world. Appropriately he gave to this series of studies, recording the outstanding features of contemporary civilization, the collective title of *Chronique du XXe Siècle*. The book *L'Europe Galante* is included in the series, though in truth this selection of short stories concerning the ways and byways of love in post-war Europe, belongs to an anterior and different stage of Morand's outlook on life, and seems to have been linked rather artificially to the three other volumes of the *Chronique du XXe Siècle*, perhaps merely for the sake of symmetry, in order to include Europe along with Asia, Africa, and America.

The world-wide economic depression, which started with the slump of 1929 on the American stock market, was not immediately felt in Europe. When its effects eventually penetrated to France, the moral atmosphere of that country once more became overcast, its political structure was shaken, and the personal life of practically every citizen was affected. In particular, the crisis upset the whole mode of existence that Paul Morand had organized for himself, consequently altering his views and modifying the character of his writings to a large extent. However, the change came gradually and the foundation of his general ideas was not radically disturbed; his conception of life had been built up in the course of many years of rich experience, and it could not be altogether transformed in a man already approaching a mature and settled age. His impressions and judgments merely took on a somewhat different tinge and new preoccupations and interests appeared, scattered throughout his most recent works.

On account of his personal connexions—especially his marriage with Princess Soutzo—Paul Morand had important financial interests in Central Europe. As this area suffered most severely from the economic depression, Morand's own income was all of a sudden very markedly reduced. In 1932 he asked to be placed on active service under the Ministry of Foreign Affairs and became the head of the official Tourist Bureau in France, a position for which he was eminently fitted on account of his experience in travelling and his first-hand knowledge of so many different types of possible foreign visitors. Furthermore, to add to his income, he lectured extensively and wrote innumerable articles for magazines and newspapers. He produced book after book—frequently not so much because he felt driven to express his opinions and views, as because he had to fulfil some contract with a publisher. During this time he still managed to travel far and wide, sometimes in connexion with his official duties, sometimes on his own account. This feverish activity and productivity naturally did not allow him to give the same care and attention as before to the elaboration of his works. Some evidence of haste and even of negligence are definitely noticeable in his more recent writings. Yet such is the perspicacity of his observation, the originality and directness of his vision, and the natural artistic quality of his style, that his works, when they are published, never fail to arouse wide interest. Undoubtedly they will survive as documentary evidence of unusual value for the conditions and circumstances of our present-day world.

In the mass of miscellaneous writings produced by Morand since the depression, it is possible to distinguish four separate, different trends. First, his most original contribution to literature during this period is perhaps his *Portraits de Villes*, striking and penetrating studies of New York (1929), London (1931), and Bucharest (1935). New York Paul Morand scarcely knew at all, but as he himself explained in an interview: 'Un éditeur de Paris me commanda un *"New-York"* auquel je ne pensais nullement. Je l'ai écrit aussitôt avec ardeur et beaucoup de plaisir.' [21] He had become thoroughly well acquainted with London in his early twenties and he was personally linked to Bucharest by his marriage. In each case, thanks to his own very special *flair*, he achieved, though in different ways, original, and colourful masterpieces.—Secondly, Morand became for a while an aviation enthusiast. His air-travel impressions of South America, described in *Air Indien* (1933), and of Central Europe in *Flèche d'Orient* (1931), struck a shrill, modern note new to his work, though completely in harmony with his general conception of life.—Thirdly, the growing political and social unrest in France about this same time caused him to turn an anxious eye upon the internal troubles perplexing his own country. A retrospective view of *1900* (published in 1931) helped him to take a measure of the rate at which France had been changing since the days of his youth. In the ironical *France-la-Doulce* (1934) and in *Rond-Point des Champs Elysées* (1935) he examined more directly some of the disturbing problems and difficulties which beset contemporary French civilization.— Finally, in the reflective mood of a man in his forties, he began to turn reminiscent and to look back wistfully at his own past life in *Papiers d'Identité* (1931) and in *Mes Débuts* (1933).

These many different and sometimes quite divergent directions which Paul Morand's writings have taken in

---

21. *Les Nouvelles Littéraires*, Paris, 14 juin 1930. Article by Pierre Descaves: 'Confidences de M.Paul Morand.'

recent years have been a puzzle to the reading public and have made it difficult to determine the real import of his work. Yet his work does carry a meaning and possesses an original value of its own. Its unity does not lie in the formal similarity of the various subjects treated but in the identity of spirit which inspires all his books—the spirit of our modern time. Beyond any doubt Morand is the most typical representative and interpreter in French literature of the world of today, with its manifold and rapidly changing phenomena, with its over-intellectual culture, its crude and callous display of efficiency and power, its sharp and violent racial and national antagonisms, its fundamental restlessness, its moral frailty, and its fervent longing for a recovery of order and balance. All these complex and sometimes contradictory feelings and aspirations Morand has experienced within himself, because the circumstances of his life have moulded his personality in such a way as to make him particularly apt to understand and to express the idiosyncrasies of his time.

In appearance Morand is healthy, robust, usually tanned; he is fond of sports. His bearing is simple, open, and direct. He is very obliging and friendly, though a slight natural reserve successfully protects his personality from an indiscreet prying on the part of mere casual acquaintances. He possesses the perfect breeding of a man of good society with the manners of a diplomat. People have accused him more than once of being a snob, but he strongly protests against this imputation. Though usually active and even lively, he nevertheless has frequent bouts of listlessness amounting almost to indolence; the cumulative effect is to create an erroneous impression of complete serenity.

Yet, inwardly, Morand is highly emotional and sometimes passionate to the point of violence. This natural intensity of feeling may account to a large extent for the striking lack of any shading in his works. Morand likes hard and vivid colours, sharp contrasts, frank and even brutal assertions. The blending of delicate hues, the subdued rendering of half-tone impressions holds no appeal for his ardent nature. In the ordinary course of every-day life the ardour is kept under careful control. Occasionally the hidden fire flares up in a sudden, brief blaze, but it can nevertheless be felt perpetually smouldering deep down under the coldest of exteriors. He professes to hate and despise sentimentalism: perhaps he is more or less consciously aware of the overwhelming power sentiment might easily acquire over himself. This assumption of cynicism is probably but a spontaneous defence against the ever-present threat of an emotional conflagration.

The restraint which Morand has set upon himself is not merely the result of education or a triumph of strong will-power. It is to be attributed chiefly to his own clear-headedness. However disturbing circumstances may be, Morand's mind remains, as a rule, calm and composed. He has a keen intelligence. He is not a philosopher and he has little inclination for involved theorizing; yet by a bold thrust he often penetrates much more deeply into the very core of some crucial problem than any professional thinker with all his reasoning. Cold, bare facts are capital to him. He knows how to reach them, how to extract from an incoherent mass of facts those which are truly representative of a deeper reality, how to let them speak for themselves with a convincingness that no elaborate explanation could possibly attain.

Morand, however, is no mere collector of curious facts. There is nothing of the dilettante in him. His passion for

knowledge is genuine and sincere. He wants to know the
truth, and will allow no illusions, prejudices, or theories
to interfere with his direct perception of things. His
desire for adequate information often prompts him to
enter into very serious researches. In certain respects he
is decidedly a bookworm. This does not mean that he is
trying to look at reality through other people's writings.
But whenever bookish investigation is necessary for the
clarification of his own views, Morand does not hesitate
to plunge deliberately, and apparently with a certain
amount of pleasure, into libraries and archives. Yet there
is nothing abstract and, so to speak, external in Morand's
manner of studying life around him. An unusual capacity
for sympathy enables him to vibrate in unison—intellectually, of course—with almost any form of strong emotion or passion, with which he happens to come into
contact.

Hence his ability to understand profoundly and portray
with accuracy the characters of the queerest even of the
most disreputable kind. He is able to describe the drift-
wood and the refuse of our modern civilization without
having himself ever stooped to the level of the debauchee
or the rake. In fact, Paul Morand, though not a puritan,
leads a perfectly normal and balanced existence. He has
been happily married for many years, and his private life
does not correspond in the least to the fanciful and lurid
portrait which, on the evidence of his books, the lavish
imagination of many of his readers has drawn of him.

Yet Morand has undoubtedly been attracted by the
most unpalatable aspects of the modern world, and seems
to have had a special predilection for using the most
lamentable wrecks of society as chosen subjects for his
writings. This may be accounted for by some fundamental features of Morand's personality. He himself is a

striking instance of uprooted humanity. His family had
been transplanted long before he was born and he himself
was brought up in the midst of an uncertain, unsettled
tradition. The desire to escape from monotony and dul-
ness—or perhaps just a subconscious atavistic 'wanderlust'—drove him abroad during the decisive years of his
life. His marriage to a person of foreign nationality later
accentuated his cosmopolitanism. So he found himself
belonging properly speaking nowhere, being familiar with
almost every country in Europe but completely at home
in none. The subversions and disasters brought about by
the war and developing during the post-war period added
to his perplexities. A deep pessimism, which may have
been inborn in him, found a rich aliment in the spectacle
of a disintegrating world. The most desperate aspects of
modern society struck him as being the most typical.
His profound uneasiness manifested itself in an irrepressible craving for motion and excitement. He *had* to move
—he *had* to travel. Travelling satisfied his restlessness
and at the same time increased it. Nowhere could he
find definite contentment, as he was perpetually haunted
by vague, yet powerful aspirations towards an ever-
elusive moral home, an abode of self-realization and peace.

Nevertheless, Morand is not always despondent and
despairing. There is in him a vigorous strain of energy
and vitality. If he sympathetically shares in all the
anxieties of our time, he is also fully aware of the great
achievements of the present century. At an early age he
had perceived the powerful beauty of modern machines.
The amazing technical progress which has taken place in
the last twenty-five years could but increase his admiration and his enthusiasm. Yet he is no engineer; he is not
especially interested in the working of driving-rods or
cog-wheels. Morand is essentially an artist. Is this trait

in him inherited from his father, the painter? Or, does it result from his early contacts with an artistic milieu? At any rate, as an artist, he does appreciate and he does admire the tremendous pageant of the modern world, which has been shaped by the enormous forces set free by the will of man. These forces sometimes seem to escape beyond the will and the calculations of man himself; but in that tumultuous unbridling of power there is a deep poetry. Morand is keenly sensible of it, and throughout his works the various aspects of the contemporary scene are presented in the garish light that so well reveals their individual character.

2. *A Picture of the Modern World*

PAUL Morand pretends to be neither a thinker nor a philosopher but simply an artist—a painter of reality. He even goes so far as to say more or less humourously, 'I do not believe that an artist needs to have ideas.' [22] Many original ideas are indeed to be found in his writings, but no book of his was ever written merely for the sake of presenting or illustrating his ideas. Every one of his works offers primarily a picture of some aspect of the world as Morand himself saw it. Quite naturally definite ideas and conceptions came to him as the result of his experiences and appear as the normal outcome of the events or conditions recorded. Nevertheless, the description of reality is the basis of his art and constitutes the most original and enduring part of his literary production.

Two entirely different views of modern life are presented by Morand. They are not by any means contradictory nor even divergent; they simply correspond to two successive

22. *Les Nouvelles Littéraires*, 14 juin 1930. Pierre Descaves: 'Confidences de M.Paul Morand.'

stages in the author's life experience, and at the same time to two different periods in contemporary civilization. The first is a picture of post-war Europe, permeated by an atmosphere of confusion, immorality, and despair. The second embraces the whole world, in a somewhat steadier ambit, notwithstanding the trepidations caused by the rapid march of technical progress and the ominous tremors heralding the approach of major transformations.

The picture of post-war Europe is forcibly presented in the volumes published between 1919 and 1926, and is especially effective in *Ouvert la Nuit*, *Fermé la Nuit*, *Lewis et Irène*, and *L'Europe Galante*. To these may be added *Flèche d'Orient* in which a state of mind typical of the post-war period is curiously combined with air-travel impressions obviously of a much later date.

Ouvert la Nuit narrates episodes, some insignificant, others highly dramatic, in the lives of six women, victims of the moral and material disintegration of Europe. Each episode is named after a definite 'Night.' The first, the 'Catalonian Night,' centres round Doña Remedios, formerly the mistress of a Catalonian agitator who had been executed for his part in a revolutionary uprising. Returning from an international socialist congress in Lausanne held in his honour, she reaches Barcelona intent upon retaliation. A professor of history, who has been in love with her for many years, agrees for her sake to conceal a bomb inside a bouquet of her favourite flowers, and to hurl it into the King's carriage.

The aristocratic and refined Anna Valentinovna is living in the most sordid poverty among other White Russian refugees in Constantinople. After many gruesome and heart-rending adventures she has become a waitress in a cabaret. She had in her possession a few securities, which she had sewn into the lining of her fur coat, with the inten-

tion of holding them until she could escape from Constantinople. To her dismay the fur coat had been pawned in a most
disreputable part of the city by a poverty stricken relative
in order to obtain money for drink. By chance she meets
an old friend and admirer—now married—and with the
money she has saved goes under his escort to recover the
coat. She finds the securities still intact. What is she going
to do with them? Keep them in the hope that better times
will come? No! ' "I shall go to Paris alone for my own
purposes," says Anna. "This will be my one last happiness. For look," and pointing over the Golden Horn, and
beyond the Bosphorus and the sea, she indicated the route
she had followed in coming, "I shall never go back there.
I shall never see my own country again. . . . I am young,
but no longer very young, and I know what I am saying.
. . . In Paris I shall stay at the hotel on the Quai Voltaire, because the Louvre is truly regal in the evening
towards five o'clock at the end of the autumn; I shall settle some family affairs; I shall go and see the church in the
rue Pierre-le-Grand, where I was baptized. In the second
week following my arrival I shall be almost penniless.
Then I intend to hang myself and to have done with this
misery I know only too well. . . . Farewell." ' [23] And she
goes off into the darkness of the night—the Turkish night.

The attractive, eccentric Isabelle, who is a consumptive
and a neurotic, is determined to remain in Rome, ob-
stinately refusing to return home to France—nobody
knows why. She consorts with strange and questionable
people. She spends a great deal of time with an excessively
handsome cinema star, and then in the doubtful company
of a powerful mulatto. An aura of mystery surrounds her.
One day she disappears completely. Some of her friends

23. P.Morand, *Ouvert la Nuit*, Nouvelle Revue Française, Paris, 1930, La Nuit
    Turque, p.101.

going to look for her at the villa she has rented in a deserted suburb of Rome, find her there—this Roman night
—lying murdered on the floor, 'naked, motionless, with
black marks about her neck.' [24]

Then there is Léa, the thoroughly unprincipled yet
curiously sentimental lady-love of a bicycle racer, and her
sordid yet laughable adventures in the 'Six Day Night'—
also Zaël, the homesick, little Jewish dancing girl, who,
on returning to her native Budapest, is kidnapped by
anti-Semites and thrown into the Danube, in the 'Hun-
garian Night'—and lastly the blonde Aïno who has the
questionable distinction of being the secretary of a nudist
club, in the 'Nordic Night.' One and all drift helplessly
towards catastrophe or shame.

Fermé la Nuit is the counterpart of the above, presenting pictures of four men—all of them new 'vainqueurs,'
in the mad turmoil of the post-war period. O'Patah, an
Irish patriot and revolutionary agitator, after a life filled
with sordid adventures, violent struggle, and epic triumph,
descends into hopeless debauchery and is struck down at
last by general paralysis and insanity in his exile at
Portofino Kulm on the Italian Riviera. Baron Egon von
Strachwitz is a product of the era of defeat and demoralization in Germany. He is an aristocrat, who has been ruined
by the revolution. He is tied to an hysterical wife. He
indulges in many strange hobbies, one of the less abnormal
of which is to keep scores of live snakes in glass cages
attached to the walls of his apartment in Charlottenburg.
In 'Nuit de Babylone' a French politician is depicted who
enjoys life in his own particular French way, while the
Ministry of which he is a member is being turned out of
office. Lastly we have the Levantine, Habib Halabi, beauty
specialist and quack, who has skyrocketed to a position of

24. *Ouvert la Nuit*, La Nuit Romaine, p.124.

wealth and secret power among the élite of high London society. In a case of dangerous and suspicious hæmorrhage, when death threatens the sufferer, he is called in, rather than a doctor or surgeon, and amazingly succeeds in his most unorthodox cure.

Lewis et Irène is an ambitious attempt to show the demoralizing influence of a certain type of large scale business enterprise. Lewis, young, handsome, and wealthy, but a cynical blackguard in private life, is an exceptionally keen and ambitious business man—in fact, a regular shark. The prospect of profits to be made in connexion with a sulphur mine takes him to Sicily. There, in spite of his cleverness, he is completely outmatched by a young woman, Irène, who is also engaged in speculating and gambling on a grand scale. Irène, a member of the Apostolatos family and of the bank of the same name, represents a perfect type of Greek beauty,—cold, self-contained, intelligent, and chaste. Apparently she thinks only of shares and dividends, and lives exclusively for the carrying out of financial transactions and the manipulation of large combines. Lewis meets her again in London. The desire to possess her is aroused in him; she resists. But after the strongest urging on his part, she eventually consents to try matrimony with him. Then they discover that they are really in love with each other; and for a while love seems to be enough to fill their lives. Yet before long business creeps in surreptitiously between them. They have kept their financial interests separate and distinct. Irène is more successful in her enterprises than Lewis and a shade of jealousy—of rivalry almost—insinuates itself into their relations. By and by they drift apart. The accident of a wild and thoroughly immoral party into which Lewis has dragged his wife reveals how wide and deep has grown the breach between them. Irène runs away. However, circumstances, in the shape of business, almost at once bring them face to face again, but this time as competitors, almost indeed as adversaries. Eventually they are able to form a business partnership; but business itself has made love between them—and likewise a normal, happy life—impossible.

The characters and circumstances described in Paul Morand's books of this period should not be taken as representing the average general state of European society after the war. They are merely abnormal and extreme cases, valuable only as signs and symptoms of the underlying deterioration. The mass of European people, then seething and bubbling, as it were, with all sorts of internal ferments, was throwing up to the surface a scum of miserable and depraved individuals, in the same way as the froth rises to the surface of a liquid in fermentation, covering and concealing everything that lies beneath. Though the froth does not constitute the whole liquid, it is because the liquid is fermenting that the scum can form and spread; moreover, the scum alone is visible to the observer and from its nature and composition the kind and the degree of the fermentation going on beneath can be indirectly, but none the less surely determined.

In the same way, the world pictured by Morand was not the whole European scene but only a small fraction of it— a thin but obstreperous layer of disorderly people, adventurers and crooks, loose women, or just frail victims of circumstance, all of them falling an easy prey to abnormal vices, alcohol, cocaine, secret diseases, living recklessly in an atmosphere of perpetual excitement and feverish pleasure, lest they should sink at once into blind despair. Morand shows that many of them had been driven into exile by revolutionary outbreaks, by rank poverty, or by personal restlessness. Abroad their original national fea-

tures had often become accentuated—aggravated, as it
were, by the restraints put upon them through contact
with uncongenial surroundings. They flocked instinctively
to the great capitals, but occasionally some migrated to
the cosmopolitan seaside resorts, dwelling, according to the
vagaries of circumstance, either in wretched slums or in
luxurious hotels, haunting night clubs, gambling dens,
low dives, or nickel-plated modern bars. They lived on
caviar and champagne—when they were not starving. As
shown in *Ouvert la Nuit* and *Fermé la Nuit* many turned
night into day and spent the greatest part of their conscious existence under the garish lights of the big, fast-
living cities. They made up a world of their own, a world
of artificiality and brutality, of corruption and decay,
exhaling under the reek of cheap perfumery a perceptible
smell of 'high venison.' ' "Tu a vieilli, mûri . . ."—
" . . . Mûrir? On durcit à de certaines places, on pourrit
à d'autres: on ne mûrit pas." ' ' "You have grown older,
more mature . . ."—" . . . Mature? One becomes hard
in places, one rots in others: one does not mature." ' [25]
Among them, working for a living was a cross between an
exciting gamble and sheer robbery. 'Business certainly is
amusing,' says Lewis. 'Whether it is done with sea-shells,
with Bank of England notes or with depreciated paper
currency, it is all one. We are in this world for the purpose
of gambling.' [26] As Lewis also says, 'Les affaires modernes,
ce n'est pas du travail, c'est du pillage.' [27] Yet in most
instances it was much less a case of deliberate wickedness
than of desperate surrender in face of the crushing brutality of a hostile destiny. 'C'est une génération sacrifiée,
Madame: les hommes sont devenus soldats, les femmes

25. *Ouvert la Nuit*, p.6.
26. P.Morand, *Lewis et Irène*, Grasset, Paris, 1924, i, 4, p.32.
27. *Ibidem*, iii, 1, p.170.

sont devenues folles. Le destin y a encore ajouté un joli lot de catastrophes.' [28] Not infrequently the immoral abandon of their lives is relieved by some deep, and, to the onlooker, absurd yet touching sentimentality, while at the same time it may be absolved by their heart-rending distress and suffering. Since the war men had been at a premium and women had to fight for them. 'Je lui dis que depuis la guerre la situation est renversée et que ce sont les hommes qui deviennent une denrée précieuse pour laquelle les femmes doivent se battre.' [29] In this concert of misery and extravagance, the shrill notes of sensuality and sex, perpetually recurring like a maddening motif, compellingly suggest an acute, almost painful obsession of impurity and shame. Aïno, in 'La Nuit Nordique,' aptly though rather crudely sums up this impression when she says to her admirer—who is also the narrator of the story—'Vous êtes un cochon international.' [30]

Such unbalanced and picturesque characters have not been peculiar to post-war Europe. Similar characters did exist before, and even at the present day are not altogether lacking—though they display somewhat different features to be sure. Yet, immediately after the great upheaval, the universal uneasiness bred these people suddenly in such numbers, dramatic circumstances gave their lives such unexpected twists and turns, that they may be considered among the most typical manifestations of that period of moral confusion and unrest. Then extraordinary specimens of weird humanity stood out clearly against the hard, cold brightness that lit the sky after the storm. There was little that was beautiful and attractive in them, but

---

28. *Ouvert la Nuit*, La Nuit Romaine, pp.106–107.
29. P.Morand, *Fermé la Nuit*, Nouvelle Revue Française, Paris, 1930, La Nuit de Portofino Kulm, p.75.
30. *Ouvert la Nuit*, La Nuit Nordique, p.199.

they embodied the reckless and desperate spirit of an era, and they presented a rich display of vivid colours, sharp outlines, intense and striking contrasts, that might well tempt the brush of an artist like Paul Morand.

The morbidity characteristic of post-war Europe faded away after a few years. The picture Morand has drawn of that now vanished world remains as a most invaluable testimony to the final moral tragedy of a sacrificed generation. Meanwhile there had come into being a fresher and larger world, which Morand was eager to explore; and after 1925 his extensive travels became the new source of his inspiration. Some of his journeys carried him rapidly across continents and over the seven seas, enabling him to gain a broad general view of the whole world. On other occasions he studied more particularly some definite, arresting aspect of this same world which was now his domain.

It is perhaps in his accounts of rapid, hasty journeys that Morand's original qualities are displayed to best advantage. Whereas usually travellers prove most interesting when they have been able to proceed in leisurely fashion, taking time to observe, Morand strikes the deepest, most personal notes when he has been compelled for some reason or other to proceed with all possible speed. He is unrivalled then in his vivid rendering of the fleeting or acute impressions that the traveller experiences on a fast train, a great liner or an aeroplane. For example, he notes in the following way the sensations of a passenger in a plane taking off on a foggy morning and flying over the Rhineland. 'The earth unbending like a spring seemed to hurl the travellers far away. The plane which was floating on a bottle-green fluid, began to describe circles in the void. Those ogres, the factories on the Rhine, with their roofs like the leaves of so many unfolded screens, were sucking in whole suburbs into themselves, taking away the men and women. One could not hear the wail of the sirens, like the lamentations of the Jewish people, as they summoned the population to work, but the puff of white steam they sent forth was visible. The smoke belching from the chimneys as from a blunderbuss added to the darkness of the fog, now sticky as a mass of gluten. . . .' 'La terre parut se détendre comme un ressort et projeter les voyageurs loin d'elle. L'avion qui flottait sur un jus vert bouteille, se mit à découper des arcs dans le vide. Ogresses, les usines du Rhin, aux toits dépliés comme des paravents, aspiraient des faubourgs entiers, les privant d'hommes et de femmes. On n'entendait pas les sirènes, pareilles aux lamentations du peuple juif, qui appelaient cette population au travail, mais on voyait leur jet de vapeur blanche. La fumée des cheminées en tromblon obscurcissait encore le brouillard, maintenant visqueux comme du gluten.' [31] Morand knows how to conjure up the numberless fragments of impressions which go to make the charm and fascination of a distant sea voyage. 'No sooner have I landed than I begin to miss the Asiatic liners, the passengers in linen suits, in Chinese trousers, in Malay sarongs, the Annamite nursemaids, the orderlies of the Residents, the Quarantine flag,—that bit of jaundice, the engine-room furnace, the rattle of the ventilating shafts, the three sounds made by the water as it is rent apart at the bow, lashed at the stern and cast off at the side, the water bubbling under the stem of the boat, and forming those great, marbled, soapy patterns like Javanese batiks on the surface of the sea.' [32]

The very speed with which Morand accomplished most

31. P.Morand, *Flèche d'Orient*, Nouvelle Revue Française, Paris, 1931, III, pp.46–47.
32. P.Morand, *Rien que la Terre*, Grasset, Paris, 1926, Malle des Indes, pp.239–240.

of his travels made him acutely conscious of the contrasts between different countries, as well as of the most general and striking features of the regions through which he passed. Various aspects of the world occurring normally miles and miles apart but joined insensibly together by a multiplicity of things progressively changing and melting into one another, were suddenly, as it were, thrown side by side without transition of any kind. The abrupt juxtaposition, in the eyes of the traveller, of distinct, even opposite aspects of the world made it possible for him to capture their very essence. Of course, in such circumstances, many shades and details were bound to escape him, but could it possibly be otherwise when surveying the whole planet, as it were, at a glance? Moreover, the modern ways of living and thinking, as a result especially of the rapidity in transportation, make it imperative that the whole earth be conceived as a unit and that the relations between its different parts with their prevailing characteristics be understood simultaneously.

Morand's insight is exceptionally keen. When he has to pass through a country rapidly, his vision is thoroughly individual, reaching spontaneously the most typical features, presenting new and unexpected images of reality, and yet conveying the irresistible impression of truth. However, if his pace is slower, his view becomes normal, average, almost banal. His book *Rien que la Terre* is the most typical example of this. The chapters in which he describes his hurried trip round the world have a vivid and fascinating quality; those in which he deals with the customs of Siam—where he stayed for a few months—are reminiscent of the picturesque descriptions in a Baedeker guide-book. Morand is himself, his inimitable self, when he evokes in a few illuminating sentences the fundamental aspects, the irreducible antagonisms, the unsuspected affinities of nations, races, and continents—as seen by a man who really possesses a sense of the earth as one harmonious whole.

After his rapid bird's-eye view of the globe, Morand has tried to take a few more specific soundings in the less known regions of the world. *Paris—Tombouctou* and *Hiver Caraïbe* are but simple diaries of two trips to Central Africa and the West Indies respectively. *Air Indien* gives with greater originality the account of an extensive journey by air over South America along the Andes. In each case, the interest of these books—apart from their documentary value—is rather slight and on the whole they present much less original points of view than their antecedent, *Rien que la Terre*.

More ambitiously, Morand made an attempt in *Bouddha Vivant* to penetrate the mystery of the relations between East and West. Oddly enough, he took as the basis of his fictitious tale the great facts which tradition has handed down concerning the life of Buddha. According to the oldest sacred Buddhic records, the young prince Siddartha Gautama was brought up by the King, his father, amid great luxury and with such care that he was never allowed to witness even the slightest sign of suffering, decay, or death. One day, however, he went to the nearest town; on the way he saw in succession an old man, an invalid, and a corpse. The driver of his chariot tried to explain to him that such things as pain and evil did indeed exist on the earth. Siddartha, shocked by the revelation, decided to renounce his artificial happiness. He left his palace immediately and lived as a beggar and ascetic, while he sought for a divine revelation. But asceticism failed to bring him the mysterious knowledge for which he yearned, and he returned for a while to a more normal life. Then, suddenly illumination came to him, as he was sitting under

the sacred Boddhi tree; there he attained supreme en-
lightment, total knowledge, and entered into the perfect
state of 'Buddha.' Henceforward he went among men
preaching and showing them the way that leads to ultimate
deliverance and to the bliss of Nirvana.

Similarly in Paul Morand's book, Prince Jâli, son and
heir of the sovereign of Karastra—an imaginary kingdom
which greatly resembles Siam—has been reared by his
father in the ignorant and voluptuous isolation of an
oriental court. He comes unexpectedly into contact with a
young French adventurer, Renaud d'Ecouen, whom he
takes as his chauffeur and who—just as did the chariot
driver of the Buddhist tradition—tells him of the attractions and monstrosities of the external world—in this case
the achievements and miseries of Western civilization.
Prince Jâli leaves his father's kingdom and sails for Europe,
eager to learn. In Cambridge he begins frantically to
absorb a hodge-podge of scientific knowledge, which he
finds difficult to assimilate. On meeting with a ghastly old
woman, the mother of a *femme légère* he had known in
London, and with a cripple, the victim of a hideous disease,
and finally when confronted with a corpse—the body of his
friend Renaud, who has died from an abscess of the liver
—a complete revulsion of feeling takes place within him.
His native Asiatic mentality reasserts itself. Yielding to his
Buddhist craving for renunciation, he gives away all his
riches and goes about like a mendicant, burning with intense religious fervour,—and taken by everyone for a
tramp. He leaves England to go to France, but the French
like the English fail to respond to his eloquence.

Enlightenment was to come to him in a very unexpected
manner. In Paris he meets an American girl, Rosemary
Kent, whose interest is aroused by the strange personality
of this young man. He in turn is fascinated by the wonder-

ful specimen of womankind she represents. They call this reciprocal interest 'love.' It proves too strong for an ascetic like Prince Jâli. He follows her to New York. In addition to their individual disparities there is the irreconcilable opposition of race; and very soon the colour bar makes itself felt. All Jâli's beautiful Western dreams are shattered and the bitter truth now dawns on him. Meanwhile his father has died in far-away Karastra and Jâli returns there to live and reign as an absolute monarch of the East—in the East where he belongs.

The book presents a study of different though related problems, such as the influence of Western technique on an intelligent Oriental—the fundamental ineptitude of the Europeans to understand the religious mysticism which forms the very basis of the Asiatic soul—the spontaneous reciprocal attraction and curiosity and also the insuperable obstacles to a real communion between individuals of unconnected races, as exemplified by the relations of Jâli with Rosemary Kent. The concurrent treatment of such a diversity of subjects gives rise to some uncertainty in the reader's mind as to the point Morand wants to bring forward. Yet the very complexity of the situation presented creates a convincing impression of the manifold difficulties which lie in the way of a mutual understanding between East and West. Morand has not tried to give a representative picture of the oriental soul. He merely wanted to show simultaneously how the East appears to the West and the West to the East, and to disclose the gross and crude mistakes that each side is bound to make in the interpretation of the other on almost every point of contact. His conclusion seems to be that it would be better for both to keep apart, yet he is aware that irresistible attraction and compelling circumstances may disastrously draw them together.

Magie Noire represents an effort to grasp and to record some of the typical features common to all the representatives of the negro race at the present stage of world evolution. Morand's first important contact with negroes was made in 1927, in the course of a long itinerary through the southern part of the United States and also during a trip taken to the islands of the West Indies. In 1928 he went to Central Africa and found there what seemed to be the answer to certain psychological problems about the negroes which puzzle and disturb the minds of enquiring white men.

Two main aspects struck him as fundamental. Their relations with the white race are obviously a dominant factor in the life of all negroes but especially in the case of those belonging to the American group. Morand, as many others have done, endeavoured to show the elements of hatred and admiration, the internal conflict of the half-caste, and the sense of inferiority and inordinate pride, which enter as components of the complex emotions roused in the coloured people by the whites. He showed more originality and insight, however, when he set himself to study the manifestations of another, more mysterious, side of their soul—revealing itself in the mystic strain that runs through negro music, which all but conquered America and the whole modern world in recent years; in the compelling rhythm of negro dances; in the superstitious practices of witchcraft or 'Vaudou' in the Antilles; in the incomprehensible transports which sway the African soul; and above all, in the mystic link which, despite history and distance, still secretly unites all those who partake of negro blood. Morand shows the real unity of all these apparently different factors, and traces them to their source in the deep, atavistic spirituality of the race. He shows that among the blacks there exists a universal sympathy which resolves the individual existence of man, animals, plants, and even minerals, into a magic whole, and that it is from the intimate, all-embracing communion with Nature that the negro draws his power of appeal, and derives some of his amazing beliefs and the incentives for his extravagant actions. 'Fais la paix avec les animaux, les végétaux, les minéraux. Tous même famille. Reconnais tes parents. Sans eux on ne peut rien,' [33] says a master of 'Vaudou' to his disciple. In the words 'Magie noire' Morand finds a key to the soul of the race. 'La race noire, la plus matérielle du monde, est en même temps une race magique.' [34]

Eight short stories illustrate these mysterious impulses of the black race. The tales are not all of equal merit but some of them have intense dramatic power and almost symbolical value. In 'Le Tzar Noir' we find the character of Occide, a mulatto from Haiti, who, underneath a veneer of French culture, instinctively adheres to the darkest superstitions of the Antilles. Though cunning and crafty as a politician he is nevertheless childishly sincere; and he loathes the whites, while assiduously aping them. He becomes the dictator of his island and then introduces all sorts of absurd measures which seem to be a challenge to reason and common sense, and which actually spring from an inherited memory of primitive African life, that still haunts him subconsciously even though for generations the Atlantic has separated his own forefathers from the land of their origin.

In 'Adieu, New-York!' the refined and fascinating Mrs. Pamela Freedman is taking an African cruise on the luxurious and ultra-exclusive American liner 'Mammoth.'

33. P.Morand, *Magie Noire*, Grasset, Paris, 1927, i. Antilles—Le Tzar Noir, ii, p.36.
34. *Les Nouvelles Littéraires*, Paris, 23 juin 1928, P.Morand, 'Poésie Noire.'

She shows no desire to cultivate the acquaintance of any of her fellow passengers, with the exception of one young man, the son of a senator and the best-looking man on board. General curiosity and jealousy are aroused. Then a passenger who knew her mother reveals that Mrs. Freed-man has some coloured blood in her veins. A conspiracy is immediately hatched. Her cavalier is intimidated into shunning her. When the ship touches at a lonely spot on the coast of Africa, it happens that, on her copy of the printed notice informing passengers when the ship is due to sail, some unknown hand has altered the time of sailing from 10 A.M. to 10 P.M. Pamela Freedman takes a long trip into the jungle, and when she returns she finds that the boat has left. There is nothing for her to do but to seek the hospitality of the local French administrator. At first she is furious at the trick of which she is the victim, but gradually the spell of Africa works upon her, and she feels strangely at home, at peace. . . . Soon she feels the call of the blood. She finds herself irresistibly drawn towards one of the household servants, a supremely handsome and powerful specimen of manhood, who is in reality the son of a tribal chieftain and is being held prisoner because he is suspected of practising witchcraft. As if hypnotized, she runs away with him, follows him into the jungle, to be one of his wives, and there finds complete contentment. 'Elle se sentait rentrer dans le monde noir, elle se noyait en lui. . . . Elle en avait assez d'être une fausse Blanche! Pourquoi s'enorgueillir d'un progrès emprunté? Son progrès à elle, c'était de revenir, par une étonnante et harmonieuse union, à la terre ancestrale. . . .' [35]

The tale of 'Le Peuple des Etoiles Filantes'—the People of the Shooting Stars—offers an impressive picture of a village in Central Africa. All the inhabitants of the village

35. *Magie Noire*, III, Afrique, I. Adieu, New York, IX, p.239.

are seized by a superstitious frenzy of destruction; they burn the stores, the plantations, their own huts, in the belief that inexhaustible plenty will magically follow the annihilation of all that has been so painfully created and carefully organized under the direction of civilized whites. How such a conception could come into the minds of simple people, normally peaceful and harmless, seems to baffle ordinary understanding. Nevertheless, the colonial administrator, who has for many years been in contact with the mystic spirit of the country and the race, and perceives a deep cause behind this temporary craze, explains 'Les esprits détestent les coupes de bois, les routes, les semailles tout ce qui amoindrit la vie magique.' [36]

The process of simplification and generalization used by Morand in *Magie Noire* to account for so many apparently heterogeneous and irreducible actions and impulses may seem at first somewhat arbitrary and superficial. Yet it has the merit of rendering intelligible facts which have a mysterious common root in the deep consciousness of the whole race, beyond the reach of the ordinary casual observer. The very speed with which Morand—as he proudly informs us [37]—visited '28 pays nègres,' covering '50,000 kilomètres,' enabled him to grasp, behind changing exteriors, some elements which are probably truly fundamental. Moreover, as he retained throughout this varying pageant all the vivid colours tingeing each particular scene, the book is on the whole one of unusual interest and no little fascination.

Champions du Monde is an attempt to characterize some features of American civilization. Morand follows the parallel lives of four young Americans, who have graduated from Columbia University a short time before the World

36. *Magie Noire*, III, Afrique, 2. Le Peuple des Etoiles Filantes, IV, p.276.
37. *Ibidem*, Avant-propos, p.9.

War. Jack Ram becomes a prize-fighter and has a meteoric
career, ending in catastrophe. Max Brodsky is a little
Bronx Jew—temperamental and idealistic—who gets involved in 'big business,' finds himself in jail, and finishes
up as an exile in Bolshevist Russia. Ogden Webb, a thin-
lipped and puritanical diplomat, efficient and dry, virtually kills himself with overwork and exaggerated nervous
strain. Clarence Van Norden, who is intelligent and—as
he showed during the war—is the stuff of which heroes are
made, fails to achieve anything, prematurely exhausted
by the wearing *tempo* of the civilization to which he belongs. Each of these four men is finally overshadowed—
either driven to ruin or carried through to the completion
of a grandiose task—by the intervention of a woman; the
book which had begun with the life story of four American
men significantly ends with the life story of four American
women. Though every one of these characters is supposed
to illustrate a typical aspect of modern America, Morand
had not the ambition to present in this book a complete
and detailed picture of life in the United States today. He
merely tried to throw some light on two specific points of
particular interest: the influence of American women on
the life of their husbands, and the reaction of average
American people to French civilization and culture. Even
within these natural and rational limits, however, the
book seems to be sketchy. The characters, it is true, appear
to be convincing enough and Morand himself said they
corresponded to actual persons he had known while a
student at the *Ecole des Sciences Politiques*. [38] But the
episodes in their lives often seem more fanciful than real
and above all the social background against which they
move is so inadequately evoked that the reader almost

38. *Les Nouvelles Littéraires*, Paris, 14 juin 1930, Pierre Descaves, 'Confidences
de M.Paul Morand.'

completely fails to perceive behind their actions the spirit
of America.

'Portraits de Villes' (*New-York*, *Londres*, *Bucarest*)
offers a most original combination of geography, historical survey, picturesque description—and psychology. The
blending of these various elements is so harmoniously
achieved that at the end of each book the 'personality' of
the city with which it deals stands revealed—as real,
intense, and complex as that of a living human being.
Though Morand does not rigidly follow the same method
in each case, he begins normally with a study of the primary physical conditions, the cradle of the infant city, as
it were; then he follows step by step the growth of the
developing organism, and finally presents in rich and
varied display its present, multiple aspects. At each stage
of the exposition, Morand is not content with merely
stating the facts—which he does with commendable precision; he is above all anxious to explain their meaning and
full significance. His penetrating and intelligent interpretation excels in establishing the constant, interlocking
relationship between the material elements and the human
factors, in emphasizing the spiritual value of each feature,
and also in indicating the relation of the urban development to its national and moral surroundings. New York is
shown as a representative and yet abnormal element of
American life, London as a faithful expression of English
ideals and culture, Bucharest as a mirror of Roumania's
unhappy history and everlasting charm. So the very spirit
of a city gradually emerges from a multitude of seemingly
insignificant details and is vigorously summed up at the
end in telling and pungent phrase.

There is nothing theoretical or abstract in these studies
of urban phenomena. On almost every page Morand sets
forth an original impression, strikes a personal note. Each

city is considered from a thoroughly individual angle. Of
New York Morand knew very little when he undertook to
write about it, and his sojourn there was much too short
to allow him to acquire more than a rather superficial
knowledge of that huge *ensemble*. Yet his picture of it, in
spite of a few unavoidable inaccuracies and omissions, is
remarkably clever and even brilliant. The great essential
features, which alone Morand could observe, seem to flash
out from his pages like a marvellous and dazzling display
of fireworks. 'Should our planet grow cold, this city will
have been, notwithstanding, the warmest moment in the
experience of man. Besides, its brightness is never extin-
guished. . . . Light, movement! No shadow anywhere, no
tree, no wasted space, nothing of what Nature put there
remains.' [39] New York, Morand likes 'because it is the
largest city on the globe and because it is peopled by the
strongest nation . . . the only nation that is not living on
the credit of its past; the only one . . . which does not
demolish but on the contrary has been able to construct.' [40]
Nevertheless, he cannot help experiencing a feeling of
mingled anxiety and awe in the contemplation of this overwhelming city. 'All is gay and yet terrible. The lights and
the fanfares of Broadway are not destined to make people
forget life but to intensify it for them tenfold. . . . It is a
terribly wearing life; people fall by the way and are removed, and the game goes on. . . .' [41] Finally he seems
concerned about the future of that splendid and gigantic
metropolis and even at times to doubt its actual reality.
'Will New York . . . one day crash to pieces? This ver-
tical city will perhaps collapse and we shall wake up. . . .
I do not always feel quite sure about that marvellous gift

39. P.Morand, *New-York*, Flammarion,Paris, 1929, IV, p.273.
40. *Ibidem*, IV, p.262.
41. *Ibidem*, IV, p.278.

that is New York. What if it were only a dream, an avatar, an ephemeral rebirth, a magnificent purgatory?' [42]

In London Morand lived for many years; he knows it intimately in all its details. His description is full of particulars—indeed there are almost too many of them sometimes—but they are all exact and significant, unobtrusively and yet powerfully re-creating the very atmosphere of the place. 'The beauty of London is its naturalness; there everything is simple, even that which is extraordinary; its orderliness is not administrative, it is moral. . . . Despite its indefinite profile and its irregular planning it is the most permanent of realities. But it is hard for a stranger to discover that reality among the fogs, in the course of a year made up of three months of winter and nine months of bad weather. To our fathers, London was a city . . . devoid of spirit; and indeed it weighs heavy on the ground; but it has a soul; its low-built houses do not conceal the sky. It gives forth a sound that is low but resounding; its colours are subdued yet delicately clear.' [43] While Morand's picture of London is less spectacular than his presentation of New York, one feels nevertheless that he has a most sincere appreciation, a deeper attachment, for the centuries-old capital of the British Empire than for the bustling metropolis of the New World. He glories in the tremendous epic of the seas associated with the great port of London embracing the story, throughout the world of 'six hundred years of blockades, embargoes, police, ransoms, searches, boardings and captures on all the seven seas; . . . six centuries of scurvy, fever, pressgangs, hangings, floggings, uncertain navigation in uncharted seas, of shipwrecks and nameless perils. . . .' [44] And he is

42. *New-York*, IV, p.281.
43. *Londres*, V, pp.327–328.
44. *Ibidem*, IV, p.324.

fully alive to the subtle charm of this city which lives
'according to the scarcely perceptible rhythm of a slow
and secret development. She does not throw her past over-
board—that past made up of a thousand memories which
seem ridiculous only to those who do not feel the poetry in
them. . . . London is full of commonplace objects, the
wonder of which is apparent only to the initiated.' [45]
Morand's book constitutes an initiation into the mysterious charm of these ordinary, every-day things. This is
achieved not by means of lyrical effusions but by the evocation of many well chosen, concrete examples—and in
this lies its essential merit.

Morand was well qualified to write of Bucharest. His
numerous journeyings to and fro had taken him frequently
to this Balkan capital where many roads meet, while his
marriage to a Roumanian had linked him more closely to
it. Yet, as he says, 'Les Roumains vous diront que Bucarest n'est pas la Roumanie, qu'il en est même souvent le
contraire.' [46] It behoved Morand to explain the paradox
wherein this comparatively small town, after centuries of
mediocrity in the midst of rich plains but perpetually
desolated by a chaotic oriental rule or even by down-
right plundering, suddenly blossomed into the voluptuous,
lively, and brilliant capital of a great modern nation.
In fact, 'Bucharest is a meeting place, rather than a
capital. It is like a public square where people come to
settle their business matters, to protest or to beg, to knock
at the door, yesterday of the Prince, today of the State.
There they empty their pockets and take their fill of
western ideas and manners. The most beautiful residences
were for a long time nothing but the *pied-à-terre* of rural
land-owners. . . . The agitation of the west, the tense

45. *Londres*, v, p.326.
46. P.Morand, *Bucarest*, Plon, Paris, 1935, Bucarest, Ville gaie, p.281.

faces of speculators are absent. . . . People do not live on their nerves here. . . .'[47] A cheerful, careless, and frivolous city, Bucharest displays the characteristic aspect of a people which, thanks to its adaptability and resilient optimism, has succeeded in outliving a tempestuous and tragic destiny. 'The lesson that Bucharest offers us is not a lesson in art but a lesson in living; it teaches one to adapt oneself to everything, even to the impossible. In this respect it well embodies the soul of a people whose patience is infinite, sublime like that of animals. . . . The capital of a tragic land where things are often reduced to a farce, Bucharest has allowed itself to be carried along by events without that stiffness—hence without that brittleness which comes from anger. That is why, throughout the ups and downs of a picaresque destiny, Bucharest has retained its gaiety.'[48]

All the way through Morand's description and interpretation of Bucharest, a sentimental attachment is faintly though definitely perceptible. This affection seems to be compounded of a number of ingredients—compassion for the past ordeals of the people, indulgence towards their present amiable failings, poetic appreciation of the subtle spiritual charm of the race—and perhaps also some more directly personal elements. Yet these individual sentiments of the author, far from impairing his faculty of vision, seem only to have increased his power of sympathetic understanding.

This is true, in different degrees, of all the 'Portraits de Villes.' The author's obvious sincerity helps the reader to make the acquaintance of each city presented, almost as he would that of an actual living person. Morand makes the necessary introduction; he summarizes the indispen-

47. *Bucarest*, Bucarest, Ville gaie, pp.289–290.
48. *Ibidem*, p.291.

sable biography and then places us in direct contact with
a magnificent and disturbing personality—that is New
York; with a reserved and trustworthy partner—that is
London; with a charming friend, who knows how to take
his bad luck nonchalantly and with a smile—that is
Bucharest. These impressions are Morand's own, of course;
but he seems to have grasped with striking accuracy what
are truly the fundamental characteristics of each of the
great cities he has studied—and as these great cities are
typical and essential features of the civilization of today,
Morand, in giving first hand testimony concerning each,
and a portrayal that is vivid and almost alive, has ful-
filled an important part of his programme, which was to
paint a true picture of the modern world.

What is the objective value of this portrayal of the
modern world, as represented in the evocation of the post-
war period, in the various accounts of travels up and down
the globe, in the specialized studies of Asia, Africa, and
America, and in the 'Portraits de Villes,' which constitute,
so far, the main divisions of Paul Morand's work?

Perhaps the most outstanding feature is the wealth of
documentation accumulated on all these subjects. Morand
is a keen observer, a man of broad and extensive views;
every possible aspect of reality appears to him to be of
interest and worthy of attention. Hence his présentation
of a mass of notes on every aspect of human life: on people,
their manners and ideas; on countries, their poetical charm
or their economic products; on national emotions and conflicts, be they mere vanity or deep racial antagonism; on
past events and traditions, either for the sake of telling an
entertaining anecdote or of getting at the very roots of
some contemporary problem.

When confronted with this medley of information, one
sometimes wonders if Morand has not been a victim of his

own universal curiosity or if he has not allowed himself to record certain facts not so much on account of their intrinsic worth as because he felt loath to leave them unused once he had discovered them. For instance, in *Rien que la Terre* there are long chapters on Siamese festivals, on the temples of Bangkok, and on white elephants, which have little more than a purely local interest. In his choice, Morand seems to be guided much more by a desire to paint striking and colourful pictures than by a care in presenting deeply significant points. Thus in *Bouddha Vivant* he writes that 'the bodyguards are tattooed all over, save on the palms of their hands and the soles of their feet.' [49] Again, describing Bangkok in *Rien que la Terre* he explains 'The sport of kite-flying takes place principally in March, on the lawn before the Palace. In order to get the better view people lie on their backs.' [50] Such information is obviously not intended to impart any definite knowledge concerning the mentality of the natives, but is given only for the sake of picturesqueness. His taste for the picturesque and the striking sometimes leads Morand to generalize an observation or to exaggerate it up to a point at which it becomes grossly inaccurate or at least highly improbable. For instance, he declares that 'Window-glass is unknown from Aden to Shanghai'; [51] in speaking of Vancouver he affirms, 'One sees houses being moved to the suburbs on passing trucks. In British Columbia people sometimes change their place of habitation, but never the habitation itself; each one carries his shell along with him.' [52] Further he declares that Siamese nurslings smoke cigars, and interrupt their smoking to take the breast of their mother; 'ils fument un cigarre et ne s'interrompent

49. P.Morand, *Bouddha Vivant*, Grasset, Paris, 1927, i, 2, p.53.
50. *Rien que la Terre*, Jeux, p.173.
51. *Ibidem*, Bangkok, p.129.
52. *Ibidem*, Adieux à l'Occident, p.22.

que pour téter.' [53] Apart from a few such exaggerated statements, which, it must be said, are by no means numerous in his books, Morand is as a rule reliable. Not only does he possess an exceptionally sharp and penetrating mind which enables him vigorously to attack all aspects of reality and to grasp and retain their most essential characteristics, but he spares no effort in verifying every piece of information that may come his way by all the means at his disposal.

He has a special predilection for old memoirs and rather musty archives, and he likes to compare his personal impressions with those of his predecessors. As a rule he does not display his erudition for its own sake but rather with the idea of illustrating a change, a transformation, in order to stress the modern aspect of what he describes. ' Niagara Falls: when our missionaries from Saint-Sulpice, led by Indian guides, beheld them, they fell on their knees and intoned the *Magnificat*. Today the coloured waiter in the dining-car just says: "Niagara Falls, boss!" ' [54] But it sometimes happens that Morand cannot refrain from unloading on his reader bookish knowledge of very indifferent interest. For example in *Rien que la Terre* he goes out of his way to give a detailed account of the audience once granted by the King of Siam to the ambassador of the French King Louis XIV.[55] Again in *Air Indien*, he enumerates the various laws relating to coca that were passed in Peru in the seventeenth and eighteenth centuries; [56] and he even inserts the names of the various explorers in the nineteenth century who went in search of the ruined city of Picchu-Macchu.[57]

53. *Rien que la Terre*, De quelques coutumes, p.181.
54. *Ibidem*, Atlantique-Pacifique, p.17.
55. *Ibidem*, Les Temples, pp.149–150.
56. P.Morand, *Air Indien*, Grasset, Paris, 1932, p.127.
57. *Ibidem*, p.173.

In spite of these little blemishes, the whole picture which Morand has given us of the modern world is remarkably clear and precise. The irregular and discursive pace of the presentation leaves the reader with an impression of the complexity and disjointedness of the universe; yet there is never any confusion or vagueness in Morand's descriptions. With cool and alert intelligence he arranges all his details, setting each in its proper place and in the light that will most vividly reveal its character. There is no sign of any artificial organization or distortion of facts for the sake of a thesis. Sometimes a warm flash of imagination illuminates one aspect or another of his subject; but more often the facts are left exposed under the cold hard glare of Morand's relentless scrutiny. Frequently the scrutiny does not penetrate much beneath the surface; indeed it would be difficult for anyone to cover as much ground as Paul Morand did and to penetrate far beneath the surface at the same time. True, in places, Morand has shown that he is capable of delving deeply, but such 'excavations' are not much to his taste. He prefers to travel fast, to take a general, broad, synthetical view of the most striking aspects of our contemporary world and to bring home to his readers the results of his life-long enquiry into the mentality of the various nations and races he has had the opportunity of observing;—and while exposing the hardness and ferocity of our modern civilization to display its often unsuspected, yet peculiar and compelling beauty.

Paul Morand's remarks on the psychology of different races and nations are among his most original contributions to contemporary literature. He knows of course that certain fundamental traits are common to practically all normal men in all parts of the world; but he is not greatly interested in the abstract types of universal humanity, which the French writers of the classical school have studied with so much predilection in past centuries. In point of fact, these universal elements of human psychology often lie so deeply buried in our consciousness that they are scarcely noticeable from the outside, and have little bearing on our outlook or our actual behaviour; if they were the dominant factor of our mental life, a general understanding between people would be fairly easy of attainment. But the essentials of a man's attitude towards his fellow men originate, according to Morand, in external, almost superficial characteristics—characteristics which are stamped on each individual by national and racial influences. Such characteristics are to a large extent inborn, though environment also plays an important part in their formation and in the determination of their various modalities. Yet whatever their origin, they undoubtedly represent the most active and sensitive part of the modern man's reaction to the universe; and to them Morand has devoted much care and attention, as being perhaps the outstanding typical features of our contemporary world.

In his studies of racial and national psychology, Morand's most original method is to take the case of a human being who has been uprooted and transplanted into foreign surroundings; the most typical traits of national or racial character become, for a while at least accentuated, almost exaggerated, in opposition to unfamiliar circumstances. So they are shown up more clearly to the observer against the contrasting background of different manners and alien mentalities. Sometimes also, Morand looks at people deliberately from the standpoint of a foreigner and thus easily perceives the most striking and individual points of their national character. These features are illustrated in Morand's tales and novels mainly by the action and speech of his individual characters themselves, but often he presents also in a few short, sharp statements a gem of keen and shrewd observation.

The Japanese are set down in a few telling words, as 'those Japanese . . . so perplexed at the greatness of Western inventions and the smallness of the inventors; proud and shy Japanese who are like animals at bay when I ask them what they are thinking of.' [58] The Germans are subjected to more careful and detailed analysis: 'This country [Germany] is full of amateurs, resolved to live their own life and yours as well. You have to resign yourself to this when living in Germany. People pin you immediately on a cork, turn you over and over, and take notes. The Germans are haunted by the desire for information and the craving for analysis. But their information is so warped by the excess of detail, their conclusions so disconcerting and their blindness so complete as they plunge towards the light that they are all out of condition when they reach the proximity of a fundamental truth.' [59] And again: 'The Germans have a taste for what is strange and ferocious, which is manifested in their literature, their manners and their religion. It must not be forgotten that we are pagans at bottom. Here it was necessary to massacre in order to convert people.' [60]

The English he treats more kindly: 'How is it possible,' says Morand, 'not to render thanks to Almighty God that England has never ceased to be an exclusive club; that there kindness prevails over equality; that the sneer of Voltaire has become the smile of Mr. Punch; that the solid and the simple have conquered rhetoric, pathos and affectation; . . . that hypocrisy is respected according to its merits. . . . ! How is it possible not to pray . . . that

58. *Rien que la Terre*, Nara, p.45.
59. *Fermé la Nuit*, La Nuit de Charlottenburg, p.89.
60. *Ibidem*, p.91.

the English may persist in their delicate habit—noted aforetime by Froissart—of enjoying themselves sadly; that they may go on refusing to explain everything, yet understanding all. . . . I would finally thank God that the English . . . do not go with their hand on their heart, but with their heart on their hand . . . that they are the oldest freemen in the world and yet know how to say "Thank you" . . . that with them it takes ten years to produce a technician but ten centuries to make a gentle man.' [61]

With regard to the United States he has some misgivings: 'An America, full of outward egotism and of generosity within, Puritan at heart, Slavic in its senses, Greek in its muscles—a country I admire for its ostrichlike stomach, which absorbs everything and returns nothing, —an America, creating nothing as yet, just manufacturing, but at any rate perfectly happy. For how long will it remain so?' [62] (Written in 1926.) Beneath the superficial happiness of prosperous times in America Morand perceived deep lying causes of disturbance. 'If a whole continent is the victim of speed, that is because it is running away from itself and seeking speed for its own sake rather than money, in order to keep from thinking and to avoid a number of painful subconscious problems and hidden complexes. . . . Often I have had the impression, over there, of a civilization not advancing towards progress but flying before ghosts.' [63] One of the probable causes of that profound lack of balance and of harmony, to quote the words of Brodsky in *Champions du Monde*, is that there are 'too many women; our political system has all the defects which are attributed in history to petticoat rule: capriciousness, outbursts of anger, sentimental thrills, extravagant spend-

61. *Londres*, v, pp.332–334.
62. *Rien que la Terre*, Adieux à l'Occident, pp.24–25.
63. *Papiers d'Identité*, De la vitesse, p.292.

ing—not to mention that marriage with materialism, which is industry; that prostitution, which is commerce; that excess of amorous ardour, which is overproduction. . . . America is a woman . . . a woman who loves soldiers, boxers, mascot bears, youth . . . tenors and gospel preachers, ecstasies, silk and kisses on the lips!' [64] Though this outburst is put in the mouth of a paradox-loving and, moreover, intoxicated Jew, one cannot help feeling that it does represent one side at least of Morand's opinion of modern America.

France has to take an even more severe judgment from him. Morand has been frequently denounced in France for drawing an unflattering picture of French life; some of his compatriots have even accused him of not being a good Frenchman. In actual fact, he is deeply attached to his country, but as he has lived abroad for a long time, he has had the opportunity of seeing France from the outside, as most of his fellow countrymen could not do. He must often have suffered inwardly from criticisms levelled at the French by foreigners, and being very clear sighted he must have recognized that many of these criticisms were not without foundation. Being fully aware of France's failings and defects as well as of her grandeur, he prefers, instead of advertising the well known charm of 'la belle France,' to rid the French of the illusion that they are universally beloved and admired; also to open their eyes to their own essential weaknesses. Some of the indictments of France contained in his books, which have aroused the ire of many Frenchmen must not be considered as the expression of Morand's personal opinion, for they are simply statements of what certain foreigners believe. 'Webb . . . had no sympathy for the French. He found them to be vague, great talkers and gesticulators, full of useless ideas, in-

64. P.Morand, *Champions du Monde*, Grasset, Paris, 1930, ii, pp.78–79.

clined to Bolshevism and yet backward, miserly and yet
spendthrift, scoffers, yet credulous.' [65] Further, 'French
culture seemed to her [Mrs. Webb] an ensemble of formal
rules, of old amatory stratagems and academic knick-
knacks for the exclusive use of the privileged classes, a
kind of code that was childish, immoral and out-of-date.' [66]
The French may challenge the accuracy of such unkind
and partial strictures. But one cannot fail to recognize the
stamp of truth and the accent of sincerity in the following
assertions: 'Paris is stifled by the spirit of criticism and
overcome by the fear of being silly.' [67] 'France is a country
that has always stinted herself so as to be able to afford
brilliant personalities and has sacrificed herself for them
for centuries.' [68] And again, '"So states may suffer from
disease," said the Prince.—"Yes, and from old age also;
constitutions grow old; administrations have hardening of
the arteries; there is no money for remedies and at the
same time a senile craving for thrift prevails; the open air
is held in horror and poisons are used to excess; alcohol is
on sale at every street corner but never any milk; soon the
reflexes become disordered, the healthy organs try to save
themselves at the expense of the others; then follow
prostration, persecution-mania, misery—I saw this happen a short time ago."—"Where was that?"—"In France,
Monseigneur. . . ."' [69] Then there is the advice heavy
with revelation: 'The French must be taught to accept
change joyfully; they always submit to it with ill-humour
and after much delay. Are they then so happy that they expect from commotion only the worst possible outcome?' [70]

65. *Champions du Monde*, iii, p.192.
66. *Ibidem*, iii, p.193.
67. *Bouddha Vivant*, iii, 2, p.191.
68. *Ibidem*, iii, 2, p.155.
69. *Ibidem*, i, 1, p.35.
70. *Rien que la Terre*, Yokohama, p.32.

Besides such serious and somewhat stern appraisals of the characteristics of leading modern nations, Morand at times strikes a more humourous but no less effective note, as when for instance he endeavours to show how the spirit of a country is exemplified in the atmosphere of its ocean liners. 'The American ship is powerful, gay, vulgar. The jazz band plays twenty hours out of the twenty-four. You enter and leave port, amidst a din of music. Within fifteen minutes after the boat docks you can phone from your cabin to the town. The English ship is well kept, elegant, the service excellent, the crew a model of its kind, the games varied, the food terrible; one has to dress for the evening; strictly correct behaviour seems, outwardly at least, to prevail, and on Sundays everyone attends divine service. The German and the Dutch ships are polished like fine furniture; the meals are too heavy and too numerous; the passengers deadly boring. The French ship is the image of our political paradise: a "southern" forgathering of pals which is disturbed by the presence of a number of "lousy" paying passengers. . . . Untidiness reigns. Everything one wants is, as a matter of principle, "forbidden" or "impossible." There is no going ashore at ports of call because it is expensive, no change of bed-linen, no cinema, no music, but the cellar is excellent and people have a good time at night in the cabins. . . .' [71]

However, Morand is not only a psychologist, he is also— and even essentially—an artist. Like his father, the painter, he knows how to appreciate and to enjoy the varied aspects and forms offered to our eyes by our own surroundings. In fact the contrasts in outlook and mentality found among the denizens of the modern world interest him, not so much on account of their bearing on social or political problems, as because they constitute in

71. *Rien que la Terre*, Malle des Indes, pp.237–238.

themselves the most colourful and striking element in the
rich and checkered pageant presented by our planet today.
And this pageant Morand, the artist, finds at every point
fascinating. The denunciation of the modern world as
harsh and unpoetical has become a commonplace in literature; in particular those aspects of contemporary civilization which are linked with labour and machinery are
usually accepted as unavoidable and perhaps even convenient, but they are not as a rule held to be beautiful.
Morand feels their beauty keenly and sincerely and one of
the great merits of his works is that he makes us aware of
the inherent poetry in the most decried spectacles—the
feverish atmosphere of a six-day bicycle race,[72] the garish
display of a bullfight,[73] the doubtful appeal of a night club.[74]

He has evoked too the strange charm and the true
romantic flavour of a grand hotel *de luxe* 'The great modern hotel . . . dates from the end of the nineteenth century. It is not the descendant of our old inns; it is, properly speaking, a caravanserai—that is to say, a place where
in the Orient caravans stop—with all its conveniences, its
merchants, its relays of donkeys, its money-changers, its
go-betweens—the annex of the bazaar, as one encounters
it . . . in the "Arabian Nights" or in the Indian story-
tellers.' [75] The spell of an air-port at night,[76] the gaudy and
stirring bustle of an international train, like the Orient
Express,[77] the swift and powerful lines of a modern ship,
have found in Morand not only a painter but almost a
lyric bard; 'To those who say that beauty is disappearing,
one can forthwith reply: What about the liners? The liner

72. *Ouvert la Nuit*, La Nuit des six Jours.
73. *Ibidem*, La Nuit Catalane.
74. *Ibidem*, La Nuit Hongroise.
75. *Rien que la Terre*, Hôtels d'Asie, p.240.
76. *Flèche d'Orient*, III, pp.31–38.
77. *Ouvert la Nuit*, La Nuit Turque, pp.75–77.

has not the romance of the sailing boat but it represents the great return to the classic line, that of the temples and of the most exacting architecture. . . . The vertiginous flight of the parallel lines of the promenade decks and of the rubber-covered passages, the single sweep of the ceiling, from side to side in the public lounges and dining saloons, unbroken by supporting columns, the depths of the swimming pools, the play of electric light, the reflectors, the searchlights which suddenly illumine the ship as for a *fête* when entering port, revealing in the darkness all its purest lines and causing astonishment on shore—these are so many pictures in our epoch.' [78]

Even the bleakest aspects of a huge modern city during a shower are transfigured by Morand's poetical vision. 'Paris was swamped by the rains of a muggy November, the houses being reflected to their very roofs on the wet asphalt. The foggy mist around the street lamps was turned into a rose-hued dust. Along the flooded side-walks battered trees were bending themselves in the wind.' [79] A fog at sea, and a ship sailing for Japan, acquire the symbolic value of magic: 'Twelve days of white fog, lilac-tinted towards evening, impenetrable, without a star to show the position, during this midsummer December. A few yards of sea at the sides of the ship and one horizontal abyss succeeding another. Never a ship met with. For six days the shrieking siren has drilled through these pale vapours that guard the approach to Asia and seem as if issuing from the mouths of dragons. . . . Evil omens: entrance to a forbidden world. . . . Our long ship makes its magical progress towards another planet like a sonorous flute pierced with its round holes.' [80] In this frame of mind

78. *Rien que la Terre*, Malle des Indes, pp.235–236.
79. *Ouvert la Nuit*, La Nuit Catalane, pp.48–49.
80. *Rien que la Terre*, Océan Pacifique, pp.27–28.

Morand appears not as the chronicler of a decaying universe but as the pure artist, the great poet of the modern
world he loves so well.

3. *A Philosophy of Modern Life*

IT is Morand's own conviction that he is primarily an
artist and that in his works ideas take a subordinate
place; they come after direct and honest observation of
reality and as the result of that observation. 'I rely on my
senses only. They have never betrayed me. After rapid
and copious observation, the ideas come.' [81] In fact, from
the picture of the modern world drawn by Morand, an
original conception of life, almost a philosophy, can easily
be deduced.

His attitude towards life is fundamentally pessimistic.
He may have been by nature inclined to sadness and
despondency. He says of himself: 'J'ai toujours eu un
goût profond pour le néant. Je suis une nature paresseuse,
pessimiste.' [82] But the circumstances of his life and especially the influence of the war and the post-war period on
his moral development are undoubtedly to a large extent
responsible for his deep-rooted conviction that life in our
days is a disastrous adventure and that every individual
tries to escape and to save himself if he can from the
universal shipwreck. ' "Pourquoi allons-nous si vite?" asks
Prince Jâli practically of his chauffeur and friend—"puis-
que nous ne nous rendons nulle part?"—"Pour avoir plus
frais," answers Renaud—and he adds symbolically: "et
aussi parce que notre époque est un sauve-qui-peut général,
Monseigneur, et que les plus mobiles d'entre nous seuls se

81. *Les Nouvelles Littéraires*, 14 juin 1930, Pierre Descaves, 'Confidences de
    M.Paul Morand.'
82. *Ibidem*, 8 fév. 1930, Nino Frank, 'Rien que la Terre', Reported statement
    of P.Morand.

tireront d'affaire." ' [83] And on his own account, Morand
repeats and subscribes to the cynical statement of Voltaire
as being perfectly true today: 'C'est le 20 septembre 1766,
c'est-à-dire aujourd'hui, que notre contemporain Voltaire
écrit, "Comptez que le monde est un grand naufrage et
que la devise des hommes est sauve-qui-peut."' [84]

Morand does not accept evil with resignation; yet there
is nothing in him of the reformer either. His reaction to
suffering is one of spontaneous individual defensiveness,
instinctive in origin, nevertheless perfectly conscious and
even rational in its manifestation. He believes that no
section of society is exempt from the universal strain and
unhappiness of these unsettled times. In every country and
in every station of life people are beset by the same feeling
of inward discontent and distress. According to his view
also, there is very little hope of improvement within the
life span of the present generation, since the most disturbing of our problems are related to the evolution and adaptation of the whole human race.

There is only one possible relief for worried humanity:
if a man passes from one uncomfortable or painful situation to another which is in itself no better, the pain or dis-
comfort subsides or even vanishes temporarily during the
actual time when the change takes place. In the same way,
a patient on his sick bed turns over in order to allay his
suffering; it does not improve his condition at all, but his
fretting makes him forget momentarily his ailment and so
renders it somewhat more bearable. This is the explanation
and the justification of modern restlessness, love of movement and craving for change. ' "You will change," says
the *Imitation of Christ*, "and you will be no better off."
This is obvious; it is as much as to say that one is equally

83. *Bouddha Vivant*, i, 1, p.31.
84. *Rien que la Terre*, p.16.

badly off anywhere. But what our age has discovered is that, during the moment of change, when man himself became movement, he was better off.'[85] The idea that change constitutes the only good thing in life, the only known remedy to the moral ills from which our age suffers —though the remedy be a very elusive one—is the general foundation of Morand's view of the world as well as of his personal conception of art: 'Un seul point fixe: l'idée de changement. Mon art imparfait n'est que la mesure prise entre deux points qui changent.'[86]

Extensive travelling is but a manifestation, perhaps the most striking manifestation, of this universal desire for change. Travel, in Morand's opinion, is one of the few privileges exclusive to our time. In our fathers' days, a trip abroad was a costly, difficult, and sometimes dangerous undertaking. For our children, travel will hold no attraction; it will be too easy and banal, and by that time also the whole planet will have been standardized and rendered uniform. 'Our fathers were sedentary. Our sons will be even more so, because they will have only the earth on which to move about. To take the measure of the globe is still interesting for us—but what after we have gone? . . . We are approaching the time when a trip round the world can be made for eighty francs. All that has been said of human misery will not be really true until this price is attained.'[87]

Meanwhile modern mankind is free to indulge in travel —that potent and intoxicating drug. The aspects of modern travel are manifold. In spite of what is often said about the 'educational value' of travelling, in spite of what many travellers may themselves sincerely believe, very few

85. *Rien que la Terre*, Yokohama, p.31.
86. *Ibidem*, p.32.
87. *Ibidem*, pp.11–12.

people travel for the sake of instruction. The desire for objective investigation and knowledge is exceptional and is becoming rarer every day. 'It is no longer a question of discovering something, but much more of losing oneself.' [88] A man will start on a journey so that he may leave his troubles behind and forget them for a time. 'The reason why people move about so much nowadays, is that they are unhappy; hence the pleasure trips. . . . The Cook's agencies are visited less by people who are happy, wealthy, in love, than by people who want to be helped to forget. . . .' [89]

How does the miracle work? To begin with, there is in distance, in remoteness, a magic—not unlike that of time —which transforms the most ordinary sights into something fascinating, ideal, and poetic. The origin of this lure of things far away has not yet been clearly analysed, though Morand mentions 'the strange optical illusion created by travel—a mirage of remoteness in space which, less fortunate than the mirage of time, still awaits its Proust.' [90] But the fact remains patent: when we are far from our customary surroundings for a while 'the external world will cease to be a greyish, dull and passive background.' [91]

Morand thinks that, when the universe is transfigured in this way in the eyes of the traveller, it is owing simply to excitement. 'The change acts on us like a mental counter-irritant; curiosity relieves the congestion of the sore place in our hearts or in our minds. A punched ticket is enough to break our habits, so that the lazy man gets up at dawn, the anæmic person feels hungry, the miser spends his money. What would one not give for these

88. P.Morand, *Le Voyage*, Hachette, Paris, 1927, I, p.16.
89. *Ibidem*, I, p.16.
90. *Rien que la Terre*, Malle des Indes, p.239.
91. *Le Voyage*, I, p.17.

few magic hours? Magical hours but with no morrow.' [92]
The tonic effect of change does not outlast the period
of change itself—sometimes it even becomes exhausted
sooner: 'To travel is to flee one's familiar spirit, to out-
distance one's shadow, to give one's double the slip. One
may succeed in getting ahead of it for a few hours or a
few days. Then troubles fall away, the chronic ills that all
nervous people drag along with them vanish. What joy!
But already the enemy is closing in on you again, he is on
you: it is all over.' [93] The only remedy seems to be: more
speed—and that is why life in this mad modern world of
ours has become such a frenzy of delirious haste.

Speed in itself possesses a strange and compelling fascination: 'There is in speed something irresistible and forbidden, a tragic beauty with incalculable consequences,
a necessity and a curse.' [94] Speed is the main characteristic, perhaps the chief grandeur of our age. 'The notion of
speed was born of the notion of progress' [95]—which ety-
mologically signifies a march forward. Speed and progress,
so closely linked together, constitute Western civilization's
gift to the world—the underlying strength of the Western
peoples—the dazzling beauty of the Western world. Thanks
to speed, parts of the earth naturally remote and different
from each other are easily brought together. Just as the
simultaneous perception and comprehension of apparently
distinct and unrelated features of reality are a fundamental aspect of intelligence, so the colourful meeting of
vividly contrasing elements is the foundation of all artistic
enjoyment and creation. Being both clever and artistic,
Morand loves speed, which breeds these intoxicating and
illuminating contrasts.

92. *Le Voyage*, I, p.17.
93. *Ibidem*, v, p.57.
94. *Bouddha Vivant*, I, 1, p.38.
95. *Papiers d'Identité*, De la Vitesse, p.272.

At least he loved speed at one time. 'It has often been said that I was a worshipper of speed. Indeed I did love it greatly once, but later on not so much. In trying to understand it better, I realized that it is far from acting always as a stimulant; it also has the effect of a depressant, a corrosive acid. . . .' [96] Speed is eating up our planet, and the earth actually seems to be becoming smaller every day— to mankind's irretrievable loss and distress. 'To so many reasons for considering life impossible will soon be added the torment of a cramped existence on a ball whose watery area . . . covers, alas, three quarters of its surface. Man will succumb to the finite, will perish in a locked compartment, sealed up in the one-class coach of this little sphere lost in space; for the earth is astonishingly small.' [97] Within its narrow limits man's hereditary demesne is growing more uniform and monotonous every day. International communications are so easy and so rapid that the innumerable differences of customs and manners which made one country contrast picturesquely with another are gradually disappearing and the prospect of a world completely standardized and dull is looming alarmingly near.

Speed, which creates contrasts, also destroys contrasts, when it is carried to extremes: 'Speed . . . kills colour; the gyroscope, when turning at full speed, shows up grey.' [98] And in that paradox lies the curse of modern existence: speed, which is the symbol of Western efficiency and power—speed, which seems at first to hold the promise of vivid, intense, and varied perception and enjoyment of the universe, finally disorganizes all personal autonomy, annihilates every individual shape, and dissolves every in-

96. *Papiers d'Identité*, De la Vitesse, p.271.
97. *Rien que la Terre*, p.11.
98. *Papiers d'Identité*, p.289.

dependent aspect of reality into a confused mass of swiftly
moving and soon indistinguishable elements. It is with a
strange and yet perfectly logical revulsion that Morand—
long an apostle of speed—concludes his essay 'De la
Vitesse' with the exhortation to put on the brakes.[99]

But is such a thing possible? Except this obvious general
advice Paul Morand offers no practical suggestions for
checking or slowing down the rush of modern life. It is
very probable that even in his own case, a change of
tempo was hardly conceivable since he approached all the
topical problems raised by the hegemony of speed with
the implicit assumption that the present trend will continue indefinitely.

Great contemporary problems are examined and discussed in Morand's books in the spirit of modern human
geography. History, the consciousness of the past, has
probably been the dominant factor in the formation of the
mentality of the different nations during the nineteenth
century. But today, in the twentieth century, the consciousness of the present, as conditioned to some extent
by the past, but also principally by topographical or
climatic features and likewise by the mutual economic
relationship between countries and between continents,
tends more and more to impose itself on the attention of
the world at large. This is a direct consequence of the ever-
increasing speed of communication which has compelled
peoples, hitherto more or less isolated, to become more
fully aware of the existence of other nationalities, to trade
with them, to fear their competition or oppression. All of
them, in the midst of the universal distrust and apprehension born of these new and unexpected circumstances, feel
more than ever dependent upon their own material possibilities and natural resources.

99. *Papiers d'Identité*, De la Vitesse, p.296.

Morand, in his literary presentation and artistic rendering of the present state of affairs in our modern world, has
employed very aptly the methods of geographical science,
the object of which is precisely the technical study of these
very same conditions. The 'Portraits de Villes' are the
most typical instances of his effort in this direction; but
throughout all his writings are to be found remarks or
descriptions showing that he possessed a very keen geographical sense. His talent for evoking the physical aspect
of a given region appears for example in this description
of the Danube valley above Budapest: ' . . . The Hun-
garian plain, with the dazzling reflection of its ripe wheat
fields,—broken by farms rimmed with acacias,—bearing
on their surface heavily laden corn-stacks, plastered over
with manure, gave place to the mountains. The river became narrower. Woods of fir unrolled themselves, keeping
to a straight line in spite of the slope of the ground, dark
from the very edge, like vast "cup-boards" in which were
set tidy little villages, each nestling round a bulbous
steeple.' [100] Morand's capacity for grasping the essential,
dominant features of a particular region is well illustrated
in this analysis of Siam: 'Rice and water: that is Siam.
Rice that is water grown—whose cultivation is more like
fishing—whose growth and harvesting determine the
rhythm of the whole country. Rice fields cracked in the
summer like pottery, flooded during the rainy season—
rice fields which, when seen on a horizontal plane are like
green lawns, and when seen vertically are lakes. Twenty
kinds of rice exist in Siam; all are sown and harvested as
they were two thousand years ago. . . . Finally water, the
second element of wealth, water which spreads in fertilizing floods, seeping into thousands of canals, soaking like
good soup into this immense triangular cloaca of Siam,

100. *Ouvert la Nuit*, La Nuit Hongroise, p.161.

closely shut in between the equatorial forests to the east and west and the mountains to the north.' [101]

Nevertheless Morand does not believe that simple geographical background offers an adequate explanation of all the complex difficulties of our modern world. Geography, especially economic geography, does account for certain fundamental elements, but besides there are moral forces which may transcend them so much as almost to nullify their influence. Morand possesses marvellous psychological intuition which enables him to catch the most elusive whiff of a moral atmosphere; and he knows how to make perceptible to his reader the subtle, powerful, yet imponderable influences which—more effectively and dangerously than any definite opposition in material interests —threaten almost every day to throw nation against nation, race against race. 'The mercantile explanation of the world which about 1900 made the task of our professors so easy is no longer accepted. Now the universe is led by spiritual forces, and it is a mystic struggle that is being waged.' [102] Morand duly acknowledges the importance of the economic and material causes of expansion or crisis; but he perceives also the tremendous power of public opinion, racial prejudices, religious aspirations, collective fear, class hatreds, national pride, petty jealousies, superstitions, beliefs, or devotion to an ideal, which variously sway human emotions and bring about stupendous achievements or equally great disasters.

One great new fact, in his opinion, dominates the whole evolutionary trend of contemporary mankind. Speed in travelling and, speaking more generally, the sudden startling development of international communications have multiplied and accelerated human contacts to a point

101. *Rien que la Terre*, Arrivée à Bangkok, pp.121–122.
102. *Ibidem*, Hong-Kong, p.81.

formerly undreamed of and heavy with consequences for the future. The application of scientific technique to transportation has completely revolutionized the relations between human beings. A complex situation where material features occupy a primary place but where moral elements tend to play an ever increasing part, has developed within the last few decades. The great tragedy of our age is that different peoples and races have been brought into close material contact before they have had time to learn to put up with each other. Centuries of constant mutual intercourse are necessary before two nations can understand one another; or at least accept in a more or less disgruntled manner the fact that they have mutual differences. But when groups of unrelated human beings are unexpectedly brought face to face, the obscure consciousness of their mutual irreducibility inclines them to fly at each other's throats. Hence the suspicion, contempt for foreigners, national irritability, which characterize our age of cosmopolitanism. 'La beauté affreuse de notre époque c'est que les races se sont mêlées sans se comprendre ni avoir eu le temps de se connaitre et d'apprendre à se supporter. On est arrivé à construire des locomotives qui vont plus vite que les idées.' [103]

The causes of the antagonism between different nationalities brought together suddenly and without any preparation are many and weighty. Among others, Morand mentions the thousand annoying regulations concerning passports, customs, police, which in every country embitter the relations with foreigners from start to finish. He also points out that the main agents in furthering mutual acquaintance between nations are tourists and politicians. Representatives of these two classes are not likely to convey a flattering idea of the nations they repre-

103. *Rien que la Terre*, p.13.

sent; nor are they capable, as a rule, of adequate and intelligent appreciation of any country they visit. More often
than not, when a foreign visitor is attracted to a city—such
as Paris—or to a people, it is not because of their best
features, but because of their very worst aspects. 'Every
virtue is an obstacle. As for the defects, the foreigner
easily accommodates himself to them; nations are loved
for their faults even more than are individuals. . . . The
France that is appreciated abroad is the France of Louis
XV or of the Second Empire; it is not the France of
Louis XIV or that of Verdun.' [104] Under such circumstances
mutual ignorance would undoubtedly be better, Morand
thinks, than that questionable familiarity—but there is
no turning back on the road of 'progress' and the inevitable results of the overthrow of the balance between
technical discoveries and moral adaptation have to be
faced calmly and clear-headedly.

The most important result of the rapidity and facility
attained in transportation is that mankind is heading
towards general confusion and intermingling of all races.
'It seems probable to me that the day will come when,
as a result of migrations, wars, under the pressure of in-
vasions, peaceful or otherwise, the various races of the
universe will melt into a single type, although a re-differ-
entiation may set in later on.' [105] Morand even insists, in
speaking of the 'Vaudou' doctrine, that 'the world will
eventually turn into a general fusion of races'—and he
adds—'my favourite theory.' [106]

Morand does not seem to think that this eventuality
would be an unmixed blessing. Of course, as an artist, he
cannot help rejoicing at the thought of the many curious

104. *Rien que la Terre*, pp.14–15.
105. P.Morand, *Hiver Caraïbe*, Flammarion, Paris, 1929, pp.52–53.
106. *Ibidem*, p.121.

combinations and the countless psychological possibilities to which this would give rise. But, as a moralist, he is obliged to admit that, 'If, as Emerson says, nature delights in mixtures, she does not delight in *all* mixtures.' [107] In most cases the soul of human mongrels is torn perpetually between antagonistic desires and contradictory aspirations. This may seem very interesting to an observer, but it is tormenting and even tragic for the subject himself. It will often happen, even as Morand has shown in *Magie Noire*, that the least trace of an almost obliterated cross-breeding will all of a sudden, imperiously assert itself and irresistibly draw the unwilling victim into a display of the most compromising behaviour. Such anomalies arouse in Morand a feeling of 'pitié angoissée mêlée de répulsion.' [108] One must face the prospect of the whole of humanity inwardly divided against itself and writhing under the torture of irreducible and conflicting hereditary tendencies.

This prospect, however, is remote and after all uncertain. Of much closer concern to ourselves are several specific problems which are among the main causes of modern restlessness. The problem of race has been approached repeatedly by Morand from different angles, but his chief conviction in regard to the subject seems to be that the different race mentalities are absolutely impenetrable one by another. Any attempt at a *rapprochement*, either moral, intellectual, or physical, ends inevitably in misunderstanding and finally in hostile separation of all the parties. Yet, even if a possible ultimate intermixture of races is left in the lap of the future, modern mankind must face the fact that, in spite of instinctive mutual revulsion, material progress in trans-

107. *Hiver Caraïbe*, p.51.
108. *Ibidem*, p.51.

portation irresistibly draws races more closely together
today—and will probably throw them against one another
tomorrow. Even should the final intermingling of humanity predicted by Morand become a fact, it will not be
realized without collisions and struggles. The present generation will probably bear the brunt of the first major on-
slaught. 'Les conflits de race seront les véritables crimes
passionnels du XXᵉ siècle.' [109]

The fate of Europe in the course of the probable coming
conflagration, has often been viewed with pessimism by
casual political prophets. The enormous mass of the
Asiatic and American continents seems to portend for
the small peninsula of Europe almost unavoidable de-
cline and overthrow. Yet, on this particular point, Morand
displays for him an unwonted optimism. In his opinion,
if—as it seems likely—speed and efficiency should one
day conquer the whole of this planet, which people would
be better able to control the development of these tremendous forces than the one that unleashed them upon
the world? There are in Europe reserves of energy, dormant and hidden most of the time, yet capable when necessary—precisely when things are at their worst—of
sudden and formidable awakening. 'These desperate attempts to right things, this frantic struggle against
chaos . . . this worship of heroic personalities—does
not all that spell Europe?' [110] Even the present unrest
and general anxiety, the ominous rumblings, which seem
to presage the coming of a great disaster, are they not
but the forerunners of a new period of creation and power?
'This taste for speed, these cravings for material things,
this over-production of commodities for which it [Europe]
is blamed, are perhaps nothing but evidences of growth.

109. *Bouddha Vivant*, IV, 1, p.229.
110. *Rien que la Terre*, Détroit de Messine, p.252.

Perhaps they should be considered not as toxins but as ferments.' [111]

One of the main causes of perturbation in regard to the fate of Europe and also of the rest of the world is that past and present are constantly encroaching on each other. Formerly the past used to be forgotten very quickly, annihilated as it were, and every day went forward untrammelled towards the future at a moderate and dignified pace. In our age the past is artificially kept alive by history and is even resurrected from its grave and forcibly injected into the present. The present, on the other hand, has nowadays a tendency to move forward far in advance of past conditions with breath-taking speed. So in our modern society are to be found side by side outmoded relics of a past which has not been eliminated and prefigurations of future forms of life still in the making. This dramatic conjunction of a stubborn, useless past and a hastily conceived future constitutes the spirit of our age. 'The contrast between yesterday and today is sharper than it has ever been at any time in history. On the one hand new facts are being accumulated and, on the other, old facts insistently refuse to disappear. Formerly what did any man, who was not a scholar, know about the past? A few oral tales, a few vulgarized versions of scientific or literary works. . . . In our epoch, on the contrary, if we but travel we live simultaneously the present, the past and the future.' [112]

Paul Morand adds soon afterwards, 'Le philosophe se désespère, mais l'artiste se réjouit.' [113]—which gives the key to his own attitude towards the modern world. As an artist, he loves the pageant of this age; no era has been richer in contrasts, in vibrant colours, in strange and

111. *Rien que la Terre*, p.252.
112. *Papiers d'Identité*, Mélodie du Monde, pp.258–259.
113. *Ibidem*, p.259.

striking spectacles, in ever renewed and gripping conflicts of interests. As a moralist, as an understanding
and sympathetic human being, he realizes that this brilliant display betokens unsettled conditions, perplexity, disorder, and suffering. He can see clearly the problems
which beset our world, but like the rest of us, he cannot
see the solution; hence his pessimism and his sadness. So
his writings as well as his personality present a seemingly
disconcerting complexity; he is aware of the beauty of
our modern world and also of its distressing moral squalor.
He describes both aspects with the passionate intensity
of a deeply sensitive man; but at the same time he protects his personality and he achieves a measure of artistic
unity in his work by systematically putting on the deceptive mask of a cynic.

4. *The Art of P.Morand*

'IL reste la littérature. Elle vit de contrastes.' [114] Contrasts are the very life of literature, so thinks Paul Morand. All his own literary achievements illustrate this
theory of his. The mere juxtaposition of elements which
are not usually found in association arouses his interest
and his artistic curiosity. He is prompt to discover beauty
in all the colourful and variegated aspects of modern
reality, as when nations and races mingle or clash violently together, or when past, present, and future come
into collision and overlap one another in picturesque confusion. The æsthetic value of these contrasts is brought
out and enhanced in Morand's works by the forceful presentation of the characters, the rich quality of the background against which they move, and the intensity and
vividness of his own literary expression and style.

114. *Papiers d'Identité*, Trois Préfaces: Sous pavillon noir, p.218.

The characters which he depicts are, in most cases, drawn from direct observation of life. But he never merely transfers bodily into his books the actual portrait or biography of any person he has known in his own experience. A measure of artistic and imaginative elaboration goes into the transposition, whereby the original data are combined and transformed into an entirely new character. Actual human beings have provided him with a mass of working material, but not with definite individual models. This material is, of course, entirely distinct from Morand's own personality and remains so even when the artistic creation is completed. It would be idle to attempt to find in Morand's characters any reflection of his own obsessions, aspirations, or desires. Those who have tried that experiment have only succeeded in fabricating a composite figure, either grotesque or odious, according to the aspect considered—but in no wise related to the man's own idiosyncrasies. The characters presented by Morand are objectively constructed; they stand each for some aspect of the modern world and not for the moods and opinions of their author. Yet the author does not disappear altogether behind the characters of his creation; rather he remains at their side, in the modest and subordinate capacity of a witness, pursuing them with his sharp irony, and his subdued emotion, in all their antics and adventures. We learn very little about the personality of this unassuming companion—in fact, we are not interested in him; the characters portrayed readily concentrate upon themselves all our direct curiosity.

As a rule, Morand's heroes are not too easily understood. He does not draw a full length, self-contained portrait of any of his characters after the manner of La Bruyère. Their personality is revealed to some extent by their behaviour; but their behaviour is often so strange

and disconcerting that it calls for an explanation instead
of providing the reader with one. Morand does not em-
ploy the hackneyed subterfuge of unveiling the innermost
thoughts and intentions of his characters, as if he had the
magic power of reading their minds and hearts. His
method is more natural and at the same time more complicated. Almost every character feels impelled to talk,
to explain his actions, to present himself as he sincerely
believes himself to be, or as he wants other people to
think he is—but not as he really is. Such information is
not always reliable, being generally but a network of misrepresentations and illusions; yet from their very nature,
these misrepresentations often reveal the most fundamental aspects of a personality. The remarks of the
witness who faithfully accompanies them, listens to their
confidences, and observes their deportment, serve as a
check and a control, revealing how they actually appear
to the people around them. This witness's judgment is
superficial and incomplete, as must inevitably be the
testimony of an outsider; yet it is objective and accurate.
The points of view of the witness concerning the characters
and that of the characters concerning themselves of course
do not coincide, but they correct and supplement one
another; and with these elements to go upon, the reader
is free to reconstruct for himself the actual personality
which is brought to his imagination. The very fact that
one has to take an active, creative part in the psychological evocation of fictitious individuals aids in imparting to them a life and a reality which a more finished and
definite picture would fail to convey.

The physical aspect of each of Morand's characters
often stands out almost with the expressiveness of a
caricature. For instance, young Isabelle in 'La Nuit
Romaine' is described thus: 'Immediately below her

shoulders she appeared divided into two thin, tapering
legs, like a pair of compasses, and she moved forward by
sticking the points into the pavement.' [115] The face of
the Levantine, Habib, in 'La Nuit de Putney' is depicted
in the following manner: 'From a point just below the
hair-line there appeared one single streak of eyebrow
and a hook-like nose, holding up thick lips resembling a
piece of red butcher-meat. Below this, was a full, heavy
chin, and bluish cheeks which, under their coating of
rachel face-powder, took on a shade of verdigris.' [116]
Prince Jâli in *Bouddha Vivant*, when he is first introduced
to the reader, appears in this guise: 'All that could be
seen of his face was an oval of burnished copper; a triangular nose, broad at the base; curling, violet lips; and
two flat eyelids, over which the head-dress fell so low
that they seemed stretched sideways and nearly closed,
save for two lines of enamel gleaming beneath.' [117]

Notwithstanding the diversity of their external appearances they possess a number of characteristics in common.
Most of them have been uprooted from their natural environment. As a rule they are sharp and clever, showing
more cunning and shrewdness perhaps than broad human
intelligence. Generally they display excessive sensuality,
but they lack the frank, natural—even if over-rich—vitality which is to be found for instance in the powerful
creations of a Rabelais. They seem to live in a perpetual
state of excitement, and they are inclined, all too often,
to follow devious and abnormal paths in seeking to satisfy
their cravings. Moral scruples do not stand in their way;
religions hardly seem to exist for them; superstitions
beset them on all hands. They are seldom moved by any

115. *Ouvert la Nuit*, La Nuit Romaine, p.111.
116. *Fermé la Nuit*, La Nuit de Putney, p.149.
117. *Bouddha Vivant*, I, 1, p.26.

deep sentiments; their affectation is to be rather 'matter
of fact,' though, being highly emotional and rather unbalanced, they often act on sudden and violent impulse.
They rarely indulge in analytical or contemplative moods;
they belong to an era in which action seems to have first
claim; and they throw themselves into activity, if not
with any definite and clear purpose, at least with all the
impetus of a dramatic destiny.

Upon this common background are superimposed in
each particular case the more specific traits which go to
complete the picture of the revolutionary agitator, the
political *émigré*, the professional sportsman, the beauty
specialist, the decayed aristocrat, the successful business
woman, and so on—all representative types of our age.
The writings of Paul Morand could furnish a gallery of the
most striking and typical characters of the modern world.

Yet these characters by no means represent average or
normal types of modern humanity. They are all exceptional, and in cases abnormal, specimens of their kind.
But precisely because they are exceptional, they perhaps
disclose more truly the most fundamental aspects of our
society, which cannot be readily detected in the 'average'
man. Modern psychologists have shown that our most
basic tendencies are normally concealed and only appear
in exceptional circumstances when some mistake, some
unforeseen slip unexpectedly betrays us, thereby revealing their existence; it is therefore necessary to concentrate
attention on these apparently insignificant symptoms of
an important hidden reality. Morand employed a very
similar method: the unusual people he has chosen to
depict are not presented as normal types; but through
them he is able to disclose the hidden substrata of modern
civilization. 'I am often accused of keeping to the exceptional and not seeking in my writings to establish the

human and permanent elements. . . . Is it possible to-day, when all the new psychology teaches us that the deepest abysses of our moral life are never revealed on the surface but are revealed by actions that have apparently miscarried—actions that are illogical, unexplainable—is it possible to take young writers to task for commencing on the same lines? For me the study of the exceptional is a way of reaching the permanent.' [118]

The artistic setting in which Morand places these exceptional yet typical human examples is no less exceptional and at the same time no less typical than they themselves are. He overlooks the familiar and common-place aspects of the surroundings he describes. He retains and evokes only those which are highly coloured, rich in contrasts—those which surprise the reader and strike the imagination because of their novelty or their strange-ness. The word 'exotic' has sometimes been employed by critics with reference to the literary effects achieved by Morand when describing the bizarre habits of some little known group of people, either near or remote—or when painting peculiar features of scenery in strange and dis-tant lands. He has vehemently protested against the use of such a term in criticism of this phase of his art. Indeed the term 'exotic' has become associated with the idea of a rather gaudy ornament, added more or less artificially to a description for the sake of picturesqueness, and having neither meaning nor value in itself. For that kind of local colour, plastered only too often on the surface of modern novels, Morand has nothing but contempt. He avers that in his own case every detail presented expresses a sig-nificant aspect of reality and helps us to grasp the funda-mental relationship between ourselves and the outside world. 'Pour ma part, je serais très heureux si j'avais pu

118. *Papiers d'Identité*, Interview, pp.26–27.

contribuer à démoder *l'exotisme*. . . . L'exotisme c'est l'utilisation littéraire de ce qui se trouve au loin, hors de nos frontières, par exclusion et *aux dépens* de ce qui est au dedans. Or, ce que nous voulons faire, c'est justement le contraire: établir pour nous-mêmes et pour autrui des rapports nouveaux, exacts et constants entre notre pays et le reste de l'univers.' [119] Thus his intentions are clear; yet one may wonder if the spontaneous love of colour which undoubtedly does exist in him has not induced him more than once to use his brush, not so much for the purpose of conveying an idea or an impression, as for the sheer artistic joy of spreading on his canvas the magnificence of a rich and entrancing hue.

In Morand's short stories and novels the action usually presents the same surprising singularity in characters and in environment. The progress of events is neither definite nor logical. Adventure, with its complex and alluring possibilities, seems to lead on at random the shiftless and ill-conditioned individuals. The plot in each case follows a sinuous course, sometimes turning aside abruptly, sometimes stopping for no obvious reason, sometimes branching off by way of a detour, as it were, and then picking up again the original direction. Important, dramatic sequences do occur; but in Morand's presentation of them, chance seems to be the only arbiter of their occurrence. Is this, we may ask, the fitting and adequate interpretation of an age in which facts tumble over one another, unforeseen, unconnected, and yet compelling? Or is it that Morand is displaying merely the modern gambler's love and expectation of sheer luck? 'I like to obey the dictates of chance,' he says, 'and I always have forty-eight hours to spare for that friend who is so dear to me.' [120] Or once

---

119. *Papiers d'Identité*, Interview, pp.19–20.
120. *Ibidem*, Le Rhône en hydroglisseur, p.300.

more, does it arise from an artistic predilection for the colourful web of events that only chance can produce? 'Events . . . when allowed to combine freely together create the most harmonious designs, the rarest iridescences, the most fanciful arabesques.' [121] Or again is not it rather that Morand's instinctive feelings coincide with the very spirit of our time, expressing both the fundamental impotence of man to control his own destiny and the fantastic beauty of the capricious patterns into which our life is woven by some mysterious, all-powerful influence?

Morand's style to a large extent reflects this conception of existence. His sentences are not at all regular, organized, or well composed. They sparkle with intelligence; but the grammatical construction is constantly dislocated for no obvious reason. He pays little attention to the rhythmic cadence of his phrases; he never cares to round off a nice period with well chosen and sonorous words. From time to time, however, there surges up unexpectedly some intense, rich, pungent expression in which all the evocative and suggestive power of the passage is concentrated, giving the reader the shock or the thrill of a direct and entirely unconventional vision of reality.

To achieve these effects, Morand uses the following method: he first writes in a connected manner a full and fluent account of what he has to relate. Then, in the very middle of his text, he deliberately cuts out all the transitions and connexions,—all the spontaneous but superfluous literary padding that has grown round his original, simple, clear thought. He goes even further and strikes out a number of those words that find their way into a clause in order to satisfy the exigencies of the syntax but which do not in themselves carry any particularly interesting signification. For instance, the verb *est* and the

121. *Flèche d'Orient*, IV, p.97.

expression *il y a* are very often omitted, and many a formal sentence is cut down to a noun followed by several grammatically unconnected attributes. Approximately one third of a first version is eliminated by this method; the rest is given to the public untouched and unpolished, in a sketchy but extremely arresting form.

This manner of composition conveys to the reader an impression of great rapidity. The mind has to leap quickly from one idea to another; all the intermediary stages of thinking have been suppressed; in many a clause only the indispensable element has been retained; throughout the whole the reader is rushed along at full speed as though by a telegraphic impulsion. Yet speed must not be taken here as a synonym for conciseness. Morand does not possess the art of expressing a great deal in a few well chosen and highly significant words. His technique is one of suppression rather than of compression—though the result for the casual reader amounts to practically the same thing.

The reader is not led step by step along an easy and well defined road. He receives naturally indications and hints, all perfectly clear and fairly numerous; but nevertheless his mind has to be constantly on the alert in order to keep on the right path, to supply the missing links in the development of the tale, or to turn sharply and without much warning, should Morand suddenly take a fancy to explore some secluded nook or corner by the wayside. So the reader is made to collaborate, as it were, with the author, and the mental activity required of him, which is tactfully measured to keep his mind nimble and yet is not so arduous as to make him feel unpleasantly taxed, goes far towards imparting to Morand's writings a remarkably stimulating, enlivening quality.

But the most striking feature of Morand's style is his

abundant, queer, and aggressive imagery. The most surprising, far-fetched yet often illuminating comparisons
give his prose an entirely personal accent. Many critics
have protested against his extraordinary metaphors—
among others Marcel Proust, who wrote: 'Le seul re-
proche que je serais tenté d'adresser à Morand, c'est qu'il a
quelquefois des images autres que des images inévita-
bles.' [122] The literary images presented by Morand are
certainly not inevitable ones; they cannot even be called
natural; they rest upon artificiality. For instance, he will
quite systematically assimilate some physical feature of a
human being, or some normal aspect of natural scenery,
to a manufactured object,—and invariably to one, not
only of the most trivial use, but also of the most emphatically modern application. Yet after the first shock of
surprise one is bound to recognize that these seemingly
irrelevant suggestions often indeed disclose subtle, realistic
affinities between persons and things apparently very far
remote from each other. Thus Morand compares the dis-
coloured eyelids of a *femme galante* to the yellowish-grey
French fifty-franc notes. 'J'aimais ses mains plébeien-
nes, ses paupières de la couleur des billets de cinquante
francs.' [123] A former Prime Minister, overthrown by
the Chamber of Deputies stays, discarded, in a corner
like a spittoon. '. . . Un ancien Président du Conseil . . .
qui se tenait modestement dans un coin comme un cra-
choir.' [124] Dense, white clouds look like great masses of
whipped cream: 'Nuages en crême fouettée.' [125] During a
storm the sky is split by a flash of lightning as if it were a
piece of silk suddenly rent in twain. 'Le ciel se fendit

122. P.Morand, *Tendres Stocks*, Nouvelle Revue Française, Paris, 1921, Préface
  de Marcel Proust, p.35.
123. *Ouvert la Nuit*, La Nuit des six Jours, p.138.
124. *Lewis et Irène*, IV, p.31.
125. *Hiver Caraïbe*, p.20.

comme une pièce de soie.' [126] The watery eyes of a bilious
and observant professor are likened to a photographic
plate in the yellow fluid of a developer. 'Il descendait le
boulevard Saint-Michel . . . posant sur le monde des
yeux gris et noirs pareils à une plaque de photographie et
qui baignaient dans l'eau jaune d'un révélateur.' [127] To
the same class of comparisons belong the frequent references to works of art, both ancient and modern. Speaking
of living snakes he has seen in Singapore, Morand writes:
'Ils sont peints en losanges verts sourds, ocres, bruns
arides, qui font penser aux compositions très modernes
d'un Braque ou d'un Juan Gris.' [128] Curling waves remind
him of some old Japanese print: 'De grosses vagues frisées
à la manière d'Hokusai. . . .' [129]

In his early books Morand used to indulge frequently
in such plays upon words as 'Evitez qu'on invite le
soleil,' [130] or 'Léa était toujours belle et rebelle.' [131] But in
his later productions this type of mediocre pun has practically vanished from his prose. On the other hand, the
tendency to make long, impressive enumerations seems to
have grown and developed increasingly. In *Rien que la
Terre* he attains a curious, provocative literary effect
simply by listing all the varieties of cocktails served in
Shanghai. 'Without mentioning all our ordinary cocktails, we have here the Bamboo cocktail of the Anglo-
Indians; the Blenton—the Royal Navy cocktail; the
Hula-Hula from Hawaii; the gin-fizz, brought in by the
towering P. and O. liners. Sometimes also sweet cocktails

126. *Ouvert la Nuit*, La Nuit Catalane, p.16.
127. *Ibidem*, p.23.
128. *Rien que la Terre*, Bestiaire de Singapore, p.109.
129. *Hiver Caraïbe*, p.18.
130. P.Morand, *Feuilles de Température*, Au Sans Pareil, Paris, 1920, Syncope,
    p.20.
131. *Ouvert la Nuit*, La Nuit des six Jours, p.139.

from the South: the Sol y Ombra from San Sebastian, the chocolate cocktail of the Brazilians,—chartreuse, port and powdered fresh chocolate shaken together; then the Gibson from Yokohama, so strange with its white onion; . . . the Matila cocktail, made with white rum; . . . the Handicap, the cocktail favoured by the Bubbling Well Road polo players of Shanghai; the Deep Sea, the drink of the Merchant Marine; the snobbish cocktails: the Mayfair and the Luigi . . . ; the naughty cocktail, Kiss-me-quick; the sentimental Love's Dream; the poetical September Morn. . . .' [132] But when in *Air Indien* he spins out over six solid pages [133] the nomenclature of all the birds, real or mythical, which have played a part in the history of America, a sense of fatigue irresistibly pervades the reader at this too obvious literary *procédé*.

Fatigue and strain too often result from prolonged contact with Paul Morand's works. A multiplicity of vivid splashes of colour, brilliant touches, and startling contrasts, more or less disconnected, without any toning down whatever of their lurid intensity, flash past our eyes at almost cinematographic speed. The spectacle is exciting, fascinating, intoxicating; but even if new aspects of beauty are revealed now and then, the hard, pitiless light falls more often than not on dismal and distressing objects. The quickness of the pace seems to multiply their occurrence. Contrasts are too sharp, clashes too frequent, changes too rapid—the procession dissolves itself into a dizzy, fluttering show. But who among us would not recognize in these features the very characteristics of our modern times? Morand offers a typical case of perfect adaptation of an author to his chosen topic. His defects and his merits, are they not the defects and merits of the

132. *Rien que la Terre*, Le plus grand bar du monde, pp.75–76.
133. *Air Indien*, l'Air, pp.12–17.

world today? That is why he has been able to express so well its anxieties and its forebodings. That is why his recording of our ordeals and woes will remain permanently one of the most invaluable and illuminating testimonies of the spirit of our age.

BIBLIOGRAPHY

I. Marcel Proust

1. WORKS BY MARCEL PROUST

Portraits de Peintres
Au Menestrel, Paris, 1896.

Les Plaisirs et les Jours
(Preface by Anatole France. Illustrations by Mme Madeleine Lemaire. Includes four pieces for piano by Reynaldo Hahn.)
Calmann-Lévy, Paris, 1896.

John Ruskin: *La Bible d'Amiens*
Translation, Notes, and Preface by Marcel Proust.
Mercure de France, Paris, 1904.

John Ruskin: *Sésame et les Lys*
Translation, Notes, and Preface by Marcel Proust.
Mercure de France, Paris, 1906.

Pastiches et Mélanges
Nouvelle Revue Française, Paris, 1919.

Jacques-Emile Blanche: *Propos de Peintres*
Preface by Marcel Proust.
Emile-Paul, Paris, 1919.

Paul Morand: *Tendres Stocks*
Preface by Marcel Proust.
Nouvelle Revue Française, Paris, 1921.

Chroniques
(A Collection of articles previously published in the *Figaro*.)
Nouvelle Revue Française, Paris, 1927.

A la Recherche du Temps Perdu:

    I. DU CÔTÉ DE CHEZ SWANN
        Bernard Grasset, Paris, 1913 (one vol.).

    I. DU CÔTÉ DE CHEZ SWANN
        Nouvelle Revue Française, Paris, 1919 (two vols.).

    II. A L'OMBRE DES JEUNES FILLES EN FLEURS
        Nouvelle Revue Française, Paris, 1918 (two vols.).
        (Not placed on the market until 1919.)

    III. LE CÔTÉ DE GUERMANTES, I.
        Nouvelle Revue Française, Paris, 1920 (one vol.).

    IV. LE CÔTÉ DE GUERMANTES, II; SODOME ET GOMORRHE, I.
        Nouvelle Revue Française, Paris, 1920 (one vol.).

    V. SODOME ET GOMORRHE, II.
        Nouvelle Revue Française, Paris, 1922 (three vols.).

    VI. LA PRISONNIÈRE
        Nouvelle Revue Française, Paris, 1923 (two vols.).

    VII. ALBERTINE DISPARUE
        Nouvelle Revue Française, Paris, 1925 (two vols.).

    VIII. LE TEMPS RETROUVÉ
        Nouvelle Revue Française, Paris, 1927 (two vols.).

II. CORRESPONDENCE OF MARCEL PROUST

The following books and articles contain a number of letters written by Proust to his friends and acquaintances.

'Hommage à Marcel Proust,' *La Nouvelle Revue Française*, Paris, January 1, 1923. (Reprinted in book form—N.R.F.; Paris, 1927.)

E.de Clermont-Tonnerre: *Robert de Montesquiou et Marcel Proust*, E.Flammarion, Paris, 1925.

L.Pierre-Quint: *Marcel Proust*, Kra, Paris, 1925.

L.de Robert: *Comment débuta Marcel Proust*, Nouvelle Revue Française, Paris, 1925.

'Lettres de Marcel Proust à Jacques Emile Blanche,' *La Revue Juive*, Paris, February 1, 1925.

C.Vettard: *Marcel Proust—Lettres Inédites*, Bagnères de Bigorre, 1926.

R.Dreyfus: *Souvenirs sur Marcel Proust*, B.Grasset, Paris, 1926.

J.M.Pouquet: *Le Salon de Mme de Caillavet*, Hachette, Paris, 1926.

Lettres à Mme Sheikévitch, Librairie des Champs-Elysées, Paris, 1928.

'Lettres de Marcel Proust,' *La Revue Universelle,* Paris, April 1, 1928.

Lettres et Vers à Mmes Laure Hayman et Louisa de Mornand, recueillis et annotés par Georges Andrieux, Paris et Valenciennes, 1928.

Quelques lettres de Proust, précédées de remarques . . . par L.Pierre-Quint, E.Flammarion, Paris, 1928.

Quelques Lettres de Marcel Proust à Jeanne, Simone, Gaston de Caillavet, Robert de Flers, Bertrand de Fénelon, Hachette, Paris, 1928.

Six Lettres de Marcel Proust, Les Amis du Dr. Lucien Graux, Paris, 1929.

L.Daudet: *Autour de soixante lettres de Marcel Proust,* Nouvelle Revue Française, Paris, 1929.

B.Crémieux: *Du Côté de Marcel Proust, suivi de lettres inédites de Marcel Proust à Benjamin Crémieux,* Lemarget, Paris, 1929.

47 lettres inédites de Marcel Proust à Walter Berry, (with English translation), The Blacksun Press, Paris, 1930.

Comment parut ' Du Côté de chez Swann.' Lettres de Marcel Proust, Kra, Paris, 1930.

R.de Billy—*Marcel Proust—Lettres et Conversations,* Editions des Portiques, Paris, 1930.

Lettres à la 'Nouvelle Revue Française,' Nouvelle Revue Française, Paris, 1932.

Correspondance générale de Marcel Proust (published by Robert Proust and Paul Brach until 1935, then by Suzy Proust-Mante and Paul Brach)—

I. Lettres à Robert de Montesquiou (1930).

II. Lettres à la Comtesse de Noailles (1931).

III. Lettres à M. et Mme Sydney Schiff, Paul Souday, J.E.Blanche, Camille Vettard, J.Boulenger, Louis Martin-Chauffier, E.R. Curtius, L.Gautier-Vignal (1932).

IV. Lettres à P.Lavallée, J.L.Vaudoyer, R.de Flers, la Marquise de Flers, G.de Caillavet, Mme G.de Caillavet, B.de Salignac-Fénelon, Mlle Simone de Caillavet, R.Boylesve, E.Bourges, Henri Duvernois, Mme T.J.Gueritte, Robert Dreyfus (1933).

V. Lettres à Walter Berry, Comte et Comtesse de Maugny, Comte V.d'Oncien de la Batie, Pierre de Chevilly, Sir Philip Sassoon, Princesse Bibesco, Mlle Louisa de Mornand, Mme Laure Hayman, Mme Sheikévitch (1935).

VI. Lettres à Mme et M. Emile Straus (1936), Plon, Paris.

III. ENGLISH TRANSLATIONS OF PROUST'S WORKS

A la Recherche du Temps Perdu—Translated as REMEMBRANCE OF THINGS PAST.

Du Côté de chez Swann—Translated by C.K.Scott Moncrieff as SWANN'S WAY, Chatto & Windus, London, 1922; Henry Holt & Co., New York, 1922.

A l'Ombre des Jeunes Filles en Fleurs—Translated by C.K.Scott Moncrieff as WITHIN A BUDDING GROVE, Chatto & Windus, London, 1924; Thomas Seltzer, New York, 1924.

Le Côté de Guermantes—Translated by C.K.Scott Moncrieff as THE GUERMANTES WAY, Chatto & Windus, London, 1924; Thomas Seltzer, New York, 1924.

Sodome et Gomorrhe—Translated by C.K.Scott Moncrieff as CITIES OF THE PLAIN, Chatto & Windus, London, 1927; A.&.C. Boni, New York, 1927.

La Prisonnière—Translated by C.K.Scott Moncrieff as THE CAPTIVE, Chatto & Windus, London, 1929; A.&C. Boni, New York, 1929.

Albertine disparue—Translated by C.K.Scott Moncrieff as THE SWEET CHEAT GONE, Chatto & Windus, London, 1930; A.&C. Boni, New York, 1930.

Le Temps retrouvé—Translated by Stephen Hudson as TIME REGAINED, Chatto & Windus, London, 1931; and by Frederick A. Blossom as THE PAST RECAPTURED, A.&C. Boni, New York, 1932.

IV. WORKS OF CRITICISM ON PROUST (selection)

Raitif de la Bretonne: 'Pall Mall Semaine,' *Le Journal*, Paris, February 3, 1897. (Raitif de la Bretonne was the pen-name of Jean Lorrain. This article was the cause of the duel between its author and M. Proust.)

P.Souday: *Les Livres du Temps*, Emile-Paul, Paris, 1913.

J.Boulanger: *Mais l'art est difficile . . . I.*, Plon, Paris, 1921.

Ch. du Bos: *Approximations*, Plon, Paris, 1922.

'Hommage à Marcel Proust,' *La Nouvelle Revue Française*, Paris, January 1, 1923. (Reprinted in book form—N.R.F., Paris, 1927.)

Marcel Proust. An English Tribute, Collected by C.K.Scott Moncrieff, Chatto & Windus, London, 1923.

B.Crémieux: *XXe Siècle*, Nouvelle Revue Française, Paris, 1924.

F. Lefèvre: *Une heure avec* . . . (SERIES I), Nouvelle Revue Française, Paris, 1924.

A. Gide: *Incidences*, Nouvelle Revue Française, Paris, 1924.

E. de Clermont—Tonnerre: *Robert de Montesquiou et Marcel Proust*, E. Flammarion, Paris, 1925.

L. Pierre-Quint: *Marcel Proust, sa vie, son œuvre*, Kra, Paris, 1925; enlarged ed. 1929. English translation: A. A. Knopf, New York, London, 1927.

P. Rosenfeld: *Men Seen*, L. MacVeagh: The Dial Press, New York, 1925.

A. Laget: *Le roman d'une vocation*, Les Cahiers du Sud, Marseille, 1925.

F. Lefèvre: *Une heure avec* . . . (SERIES II AND III), Nouvelle Revue Française, Paris, 1925.

L. de Robert: *Comment débuta Marcel Proust*, Nouvelle Revue Française, Paris, 1925.

J. Benoist-Méchin: *La musique et l'immortalité dans l'œuvre de Marcel Proust*, Kra, Paris, 1926.

G. Turquet-Milnes: *From Pascal to Proust*, Jonathan Cape, London, 1926.

R. Dreyfus: *Souvenirs sur Marcel Proust*, B. Grasset, Paris, 1926.

J. M. Pouquet: *Le Salon de Mme de Caillavet*, Hachette, Paris, 1926.

Ch. Daudet et R. Fernandez: *Répertoire des personnages de 'A la Recherche du Temps Perdu,'* Nouvelle Revue Française, Paris, 1927.

P. Souday: *Proust, Gide, Valéry*, Kra, Paris, 1927.

M. L. Bibesco: *Au bal avec Marcel Proust*, Nouvelle Revue Française, Paris, 1928.

E. R. Curtius: *Marcel Proust* (translated into French by A. Pierrhal), La Revue Nouvelle, Paris, 1928. (The German original was published in 1925.)

L. de Robert: *De Loti à Proust*, E. Flammarion, Paris, 1928.

L. Pierre-Quint: *Comment travaillait Proust*, Editions des Cahiers Libres, Paris, 1928.

C. Bell: *Proust*, Harcourt Brace & Co., New York, 1929.

L. Daudet: *Autour de soixante lettres de Marcel Proust*, Nouvelle Revue Française, Paris, 1929.

B. Crémieux: *Du Côté de Marcel Proust*, Lemarget, Paris, 1929.

A. Dandieu: *Marcel Proust—sa révélation psychologique*, F. Didot, Paris, 1930; H. Milford, London, 1930.

P. Abraham: *Proust, Recherches sur la création intellectuelle*, Rieder, Paris, 1930.

R. de Billy: *Marcel Proust. Lettres et Conversations*, Editions des Portiques, Paris, 1930.

J.W.Krutch: *Five Masters*, Jonathan Cape and Harrison Smith, 1930.

E.Seillière: *Marcel Proust*, Nouvelle Revue Critique, Paris, 1931.

L.Chaigne: *Vies et Œuvres d'ecrivains*, P.Bossuet, Paris, 1933.

F.Hier: *La Musique dans l'œuvre de Marcel Proust*, Publications of the Institute of French Studies, Columbia University, New York, 1933.

A.Feuillerat: *Comment Marcel Proust a composé son roman*, Yale University Press, New Haven, 1934.

Havelock Ellis: *From Rousseau to Proust*, Houghton Mifflin Co., New York, 1935; Constable, London, 1935.

R.Celly: *Répertoire des thèmes de Marcel Proust*, Nouvelle Revue Française, Paris, 1935.

D.Saurat: *Modernes*, Denoël et Steele, Paris, 1935.

G.Cattaui: *L'Amitié de Proust*, Nouvelle Revue Française, Paris, 1935.

R.Brasillach: *Portraits*, Plon, Paris, 1935.

R.Le Masle: *Le Professeur Adrien Proust*, Lipschutz, Paris, 1936.

II. André Gide

I. WORKS BY ANDRÉ GIDE

Les Cahiers d'André Walter (Anonymous)
Librairie Académique Didier-Perrin, Paris, 1891.

Les Poésies d'André Walter (Anonymous)
Librairie de l'Art Indépendant, Paris, 1892.

Le Traité du Narcisse. Théorie du Symbole
Librairie de l'Art Indépendant, Paris, 1892.

La Tentative Amoureuse
Librairie de l'Art Indépendant, Paris, 1893.

Le Voyage d'Urien
Librairie de l'Art Indépendant, Paris, 1893.

Paludes (Sotie)
Librairie de l'Art Indépendant, Paris, 1895.

Les Nourritures Terrestres
Mercure de France, Paris, 1897.

Réflexions sur Quelques Points de Littérature et de Morale (Anonymous)
Mercure de France, Paris, 1897.

Feuilles de Route (1895–1896)
Undated; place and publisher not given. [Vandersyper, Brussels, 1899.]

Philoctète ou le Traité des Trois Morales—El Hadj ou le Traité du Faux Prophète
(Published in One Volume, along with a reprint of 'Le Traité du Narcisse' and 'La Tentative Amoureuse')
Mercure de France, Paris, 1899.

Le Prométhée Mal Enchaîné (Sotie)
Mercure de France, Paris, 1899.

Lettres à Angèle
(First appeared separately in the review *L'Ermitage*, 1898, 1899, 1900.)
Mercure de France, Paris, 1900.

Le Roi Candaule
La Revue Blanche, Paris, 1901.

L'Immoraliste (Récit)
Mercure de France, Paris, 1902.

Prétextes
(A collection of essays including: 'Réflexions sur quelques points de littérature et de morale' (Mercure, 1897); 'Lettres à Angèle' (Mercure, 1900) and 'De l'Influence en Littérature,' 'Les Limites de l'Art,' 'Oscar Wilde,' the three latter having previously appeared in the review *L'Ermitage*, in 1900, 1901, and 1902 respectively.)
Mercure de France, Paris, 1903.

Amyntas—Mopsus—Le Renoncement au Voyage
(All three published in one volume, together with a reprint of 'De Biskra à Touggourt,' which had appeared previously in the review 'L'Ermitage' (1904), and of 'Feuilles de Route' [Brussels, Vandersyper, 1899].)
Mercure de France, Paris, 1906.

Le Retour de L'Enfant Prodigue
(Had appeared previously in the review *Vers et Prose*, 1907.)
Bibliothèque de l'Occident, Paris, 1909.

La Porte Étroite (Récit)
(Had appeared previously in the review *Nouvelle Revue Française*, 1909.)
Mercure de France, Paris, 1909.

Nouveaux Prétextes
Mercure de France, Paris, 1911.

Isabelle (Récit)
Nouvelle Revue Française, Paris, 1911.

Dostoïevsky, d'après sa Correspondance
Figuière, Paris, 1911.

Bethsabé
(Originally appeared in the review *L'Ermitage*, 1903, and again in the review *Vers et Prose*, 1908–1909.)
Bibliothèque de l'Occident, Paris, 1912.

Souvenirs de la Cour d'Assises
Nouvelle Revue Française, Paris, 1914.

Les Caves du Vatican (Sotie)
Nouvelle Revue Française, Paris, 1914.

La Symphonie Pastorale (Récit)
Nouvelle Revue Française, Paris, 1919.

Morceaux Choisis
(Including many hitherto unpublished fragments)
Nouvelle Revue Française, Paris, 1921.

Pages Choisies
(Including several hitherto unpublished fragments)
Crès, Paris, 1921.

Dostoïevsky. Articles et Causeries
Plon-Nourrit, Paris, 1923.

Incidences
Nouvelle Revue Française, Paris, 1924.

Corydon
(Privately and anonymously printed—12 copies—Imprimerie Sainte Catherine, Bruges, 1911. New, enlarged edition privately and anonymously printed—21 copies—Imprimerie Sainte Catherine, Bruges, 1920.)
Nouvelle Revue Française, Paris, 1924.

Les Faux-Monnayeurs (Roman)
Nouvelle Revue Française, Paris, 1925.

Si le Grain ne meurt
Part I privately printed—12 copies—Imprimerie Sainte Catherine, Bruges, 1920.
Part II privately printed—13 copies—Imprimerie Sainte Catherine, Bruges, 1921.
Partial reprint—Champion, Paris, 1924.
Partial reprint—Clarendon Press, Oxford, 1925.
First complete edition:
Nouvelle Revue Française, Paris, 1926 (bearing date 1924, but not placed on the market until October, 1926).

Journal des Faux-Monnayeurs
Editions Eos, Paris, 1926.

Numquid et Tu . . .?
Privately printed—Imprimerie Sainte Catherine, Bruges, 1922.
J.Schiffrin—Editions de la Pléiade, Paris, 1926.
Voyage au Congo
Nouvelle Revue Française, Paris, 1927.
Retour du Tchad, Suite du Voyage au Congo. Carnets de Route
Nouvelle Revue Française, Paris, 1928.
L'Ecole des Femmes
Nouvelle Revue Française, Paris, 1929.
Essai sur Montaigne
J.Schiffrin—Editions de la Pléiade, Paris, 1929.
Un Esprit Non Prévenu
Kra—Editions du Sagittaire, Paris, 1929.
Robert, Supplément à l'Ecole des Femmes
Nouvelle Revue Française, Paris, 1929.
L'Affaire Redureau, suivi de Faits Divers
Nouvelle Revue Française, Paris, 1930.
La Sequestrée de Poitiers
Nouvelle Revue Française, Paris, 1930.
Œdipe
J.Schiffrin—Editions de la Pléiade, Paris, 1931.
Pages de Journal
Nouvelle Revue Française, Paris, 1934.
Les Nouvelles Nourritures
Nouvelle Revue Française, Paris, 1935.
Retour de l'U.R.S.S.
Nouvelle Revue Française, Paris, 1936.
Nouvelles Pages de Journal
Nouvelle Revue Française, Paris, 1936.
Geneviève
Nouvelle Revue Française, Paris, 1936.
N.B. The 'Œuvres complètes' of A.Gide are in course of publication,
under the supervision of L.Martin-Chauffier, at the 'Nouvelle Re-
vue Française'; twelve volumes have appeared so far (1937).

II. TRANSLATIONS (FROM THE ENGLISH) BY A.GIDE

Rabindranath Tagore: L'OFFRANDE LYRIQUE
Nouvelle Revue Française, Paris.

Rabindranath Tagore: AMAL ET LA LETTRE DU ROI
Nouvelle Revue Française, Paris.

Joseph Conrad: TYPHON, Nouvelle Revue Française, Paris.

Shakespeare: ANTOINE ET CLÉOPÂTRE, Nouvelle Revue Française, Paris.

William Blake: LE MARIAGE DU CIEL ET DE L'ENFER, Aveline, Paris.

III. ENGLISH TRANSLATIONS OF GIDE'S WORKS

Oscar Wilde—Translated by Stuart Mason as OSCAR WILDE, Holywell Press, Oxford, 1905.

Le Prométhée mal enchaîné—Translated by Lilian Rothermere as PROMETHEUS ILLBOUND, Chatto & Windus, London, 1919.

La Porte Étroite—Translated by Dorothy Bussy as STRAIT IS THE GATE, Jarrolds, London, 1924; A.A.Knopf, New York, 1924.

Les Caves du Vatican—Translated by Dorothy Bussy as THE VATICAN SWINDLE; also as LAFCADIO'S ADVENTURES, A.A.Knopf, New York, 1925.

Dostoïevsky—Translated by Dorothy Bussy as DOSTOEVSKY, J.M.Dent & Sons, London, 1925; A.A.Knopf, New York, 1926.

Les Faux-Monnayeurs—Translated by Dorothy Bussy as THE COUNTERFEITERS, A.A.Knopf, London & New York, 1927.

Essai sur Montaigne—Translated by H.Guest and Trevor E.Blewitt as MONTAIGNE, The Blackamore Press, London, 1929; Horace Liveright, New York, 1929.

L'Ecole des Femmes—Translated by Dorothy Bussy as THE SCHOOL FOR WIVES, A.A.Knopf, London & New York, 1929.

Voyage au Congo

Le Retour du Tchad—Translated by Dorothy Bussy (and published together) as TRAVELS IN THE CONGO, A.A.Knopf, London & New York, 1929.

L'Immoraliste—Translated by Dorothy Bussy as THE IMMORALIST, A.A.Knopf, London & New York, 1930.

Isabelle—La Symphonie Pastorale—Translated by Dorothy Bussy (and published together) as TWO SYMPHONIES, Cassell, London, 1931; A.A. Knopf, New York, 1931.

Si le Grain ne meurt—Translated by Dorothy Bussy as IF IT DIE . . . AN AUTOBIOGRAPHY, Random House, New York, 1935.

iv. Works of Criticism on Gide (selection)

E.Gosse: *Portraits and Sketches*, Heinemann, London, 1912.

G.Gabory: *André Gide, son œuvre*, Nouvelle Revue Critique, Paris, 1924.

H.Massis: *Jugements*, Plon, Paris, 1924.

P.Souday: *Proust, Gide, Valéry*, Kra, Paris, 1927.

R.Lalou: *André Gide*, J.Heissler, Strasburg, 1928.

P.Lièvre: *Esquisses Critiques*, Le Divan, Paris, 1929.

Ch. du Bos: *Le Dialogue avec André Gide*, Au Sans Pareil, Paris, 1929.

R.Fernandez: *André Gide*, R.A.Corrêa, Paris, 1931.

E.Martinet: *A.Gide, l'amour et la divinité*, V.Attinger, Paris, 1931.

R.Schwob: *Le Vrai drame d'André Gide*, B.Grasset, Paris, 1932.

H.Drain: *Nietzsche et Gide*, Editions de la Madeleine, Paris, 1932.

L.Chaigne: *Vies et Œuvres d'ecrivains*, P.Bossuet, Paris, 1933.

L.Pierre-Quint: *André Gide, sa vie, son œuvre*, Delamain et Boutelleau (Stock), Paris, 1933. (English translation by D.M.Richardson—Jonathan Cape, London, 1934.)

E.Gouiran: *André Gide: Essai de psychologie littéraire*, J.Crés, Paris, 1934.

M.H.Stansbury: *French Novelists of Today*, University of Pennsylvania Press, Philadelphia, 1935; Oxford University Press, London, 1935.

M.Sachs: *André Gide*, Denoël et Steele, Paris, 1936.

A.Rousseaux: *Le Paradis Perdu*. B.Grasset, Paris, 1936.

III. Jean Giraudoux

i. Works by Jean Giraudoux

Le Dernier Rêve d'Edmond About
Marseille-Etudiant, Marseille, 1904.
(Reprinted as 'Premier Rêve Signé'—Emile-Paul, Paris, 1925. Also included in 'Provinciales.')

Provinciales
B.Grasset, Paris, 1909; enlarged edition, 1922.

L'Ecole des Indifférents
B.Grasset, Paris, 1911.

Retour d'Alsace
   (Reproduced later in 'Lectures pour une Ombre.')
   Emile-Paul, Paris, 1916.
Lectures pour une Ombre
   Emile-Paul, Paris, 1918.
Simon le Pathétique
   B.Grasset, Paris, 1918; enlarged edition, 1926.
Amica-America
   Emile-Paul, Paris, 1918.
Promenades avec Gabrielle
   Nouvelle Revue Française, Paris, 1919.
Adieu à la Guerre
   (Reproduced later in 'Adorable Clio.')
   B.Grasset, Paris, 1919.
Elpénor
   Emile-Paul, Paris, 1919.
Adorable Clio
   Emile-Paul, Paris, 1920.
Suzanne et le Pacifique
   Emile-Paul, Paris, 1921.
Siegfried et le Limousin
   B.Grasset, Paris, 1922.
La Prière sur la Tour Eiffel
   (Reproduced later in 'Juliette au Pays des Hommes.')
   Emile-Paul, Paris, 1923.
Visite chez le Prince
   (Reproduced later in 'La France Sentimentale.')
   Emile-Paul, Paris, 1924.
Juliette au Pays des Hommes
   Emile-Paul, Paris, 1924.
Hélène et Touglas, ou Les Joies de Paris
   (Reproduced later in 'La France Sentimentale.')
   Au Sans Pareil, Paris, 1925.
Le Couvent de Bella
   (Reproduced later in 'La France Sentimentale.')
   B.Grasset, Paris, 1925.
A la Recherche de Bella
   La Lampe d'Aladin, Liège, 1926.
Le Cerf
   Cité des Livres, Paris, 1926.

Les Hommes Tigres
  Emile-Paul, Paris, 1926.
Bella
  B.Grasset, Paris, 1926.
Première Disparition de Jérôme Bardini
  Kra, Paris, 1926.
Anne chez Simon
  Emile-Paul, Paris, 1926.
Eglantine
  B.Grasset, Paris, 1927.
Le Sport
  Hachette, Paris, 1928.
Le Signe
  (Reproduced later in 'La France Sentimentale.')
  Les Cahiers du Sud, Marseille, 1928.
La Grande Bourgeoise
  Kra, Paris, 1928.
Marche vers Clermont
  Les Cahiers Libres, Paris, 1928.
Siegfried
  B.Grasset, Paris, 1928.
Amphitryon 38
  B.Grasset, Paris, 1929.
Aventures de Jérôme Bardini
  Emile-Paul, Paris, 1930.
Mirage de Bessines
  (Reproduced later in 'La France Sentimentale.')
  Emile-Paul, Paris, 1931.
Bêtes
  Firmin Didot, Paris, 1931.
La France Sentimentale
  B.Grasset, Paris, 1932.
Berlin
  Emile-Paul, Paris, 1932.
Judith
  Emile-Paul, Paris, 1932.
Fugues sur Siegfried
  Lapina, Paris, 1933.
Intermezzo
  B.Grasset, Paris, 1933.

Combat avec l'Ange
  B.Grasset, Paris, 1934.
Fin de Siegfried
  B.Grasset, Paris, 1934.
Tessa, La Nymphe au Cœur Fidèle
  (Adaptation of 'The Constant Nymph,' by Margaret Kennedy and
  Basil Dean.)
  B.Grasset, Paris, 1934.
La Guerre de Troie n'aura pas Lieu
  B.Grasset, Paris, 1935.

II. English Translations of Giraudoux's Works

Lectures pour une Ombre—Translated by Elizabeth S.Sergeant as
  CAMPAIGNS AND INTERVALS, Houghton Mifflin Co., New York,
  1918.
Siegfried et le Limousin—Translated by Louis Collier Willcox as MY
  FRIEND FROM LIMOUSIN, Harper & Brothers, London & New York,
  1923.
Suzanne et le Pacifique—Translated by Ben Ray Redman as SUZANNE
  AND THE PACIFIC, G.P.Putnam's Sons, London & New York, 1923.
Bella—Translated by J.F.Scanlan as BELLA, A.A.Knopf, London &
  New York, 1927.
Siegfried—Translated by Philip Carr as SIEGFRIED, L.MacVeagh—
  The Dial Press, New York, 1930; Longmans Green & Co., London,
  1930.

III. Works of Criticism on Giraudoux (selection)

A.Gide: *Nouveaux Prétextes*, Mercure de France, Paris, 1911.
F.de Miomandre: *Le Pavillon du Mandarin*, Emile-Paul, Paris, 1921.
F.Lefèvre: *Une heure avec . . .* (SERIES I), Nouvelle Revue Française,
  Paris, 1924.
J.Boulanger: *Mais l'art est difficile* (SERIES III), Plon, Paris, 1924.
B.Cremieux: *XX⁰ Siècle*, Nouvelle Revue Française, Paris, 1924.
P.Lièvre: *Esquisses critiques* (SERIES III), Le Divan, Paris, 1924.
L.Dubech: *Les chefs de file de la jeune génération*, Plon, Paris, 1925.
P.Humbourg: *Jean Giraudoux*, Les Cahiers du Sud, Marseille, 1926.

G.Truc: *Quelques Peintres de l'homme contemporain*, Editions Spes, Paris, 1926.

F.Lefevre: *Une heure avec* . . . (SERIES IV), Nouvelle Revue Française, Paris, 1927.

M.Bourdet: *Jean Giraudoux*, Nouvelle Revue Critique, Paris, 1928.

M.H.Stansbury: *French Novelists of Today*, University of Pennsylvania Press, Philadelphia, 1935; Oxford University Press, London, 1935.

P.Brasillach: *Portraits*, Plon, Paris, 1935.

A.Rousseaux: *Le Paradis Perdu*, B.Grasset, Paris, 1935.

IV. Paul Morand

1. WORKS BY PAUL MORAND

Lampes à Arc, Poèmes
  Au Sans Pareil, Paris, 1919.
Feuilles de Température, Poèmes
  Au Sans Pareil, Paris, 1920.
Tendres Stocks (With Preface by Marcel Proust)
  Nouvelle Revue Française, Paris, 1921.
Ouvert la Nuit
  Nouvelle Revue Française, Paris, 1922.
Fermé la Nuit
  Nouvelle Revue Française, Paris, 1923.
Poèmes, 1914–1924
  (A reprint of 'Lampes à Arc' and of 'Feuilles de Température,' with the addition of 'Vingt-cinq Poèmes sans Oiseaux.')
  Au Sans Pareil, Paris, 1924.
Lewis et Irène
  B.Grasset, Paris, 1924.
La Fleur Double
  Emile-Paul, Paris, 1924.
L'Europe Galante (Chronique du XXᵉ Siècle—VOL. I)
  B.Grasset, Paris, 1925.
Rien que la Terre
  B.Grasset, Paris, 1926.
Siam
  Aux Aldes, Paris, 1926.
L'Avarice
  Kra, Paris, 1926. (Coll. Les Sept Péchés Capitaux.)

408 BIBLIOGRAPHY

La Mort de l'Amour
   Emile-Paul, Paris, 1926.
Bouddha Vivant (Chronique du XXe Siècle—VOL. II)
   B.Grasset, Paris, 1927.
Le Manuscrit Autographe
   J.Royère, Paris, 1927.
Mr. U.
   (Later reproduced in 'Rococo.')
   Les Cahiers Libres, Paris, 1927.
Tableaux de Paris (Containing contributions by several authors, in-
   cluding LA TOUR EIFFEL by P. Morand)
   Emile-Paul, Paris, 1927.
Le Voyage
   Hachette, Paris, 1927.
U.S.A., Poèmes. Album de Photographies Lyriques
   Au Sans Pareil, Paris, 1928.
Charleston
   (Short story—later reproduced in 'Magie Noire.')
   Liège, 1928.
Syracuse
   (Short story—later reproduced in 'Magie Noire.')
   B.Grasset, Paris, 1928.
Magie Noire (Chronique du XXe Siècle—VOL. III)
   B.Grasset, Paris, 1928.
Poesie Noire
   Les Nouvelles Littéraires, Paris, June 23, 1928.
Paris—Tombouctou, Documentaire
   E.Flammarion, Paris, 1928.
Foujita
   Chroniques du Jour, Paris, 1928.
Nœuds Coulants
   (Later reproduced in 'Rococo.')
   Lapina, Paris, 1928.
Rain, Steam and Speed
   Champion, Paris, 1928.
Hiver Caraïbe, Documentaire
   E.Flammarion, Paris, 1929.
Le Rhône en Hydroglisseur
   (Later reproduced in 'Papiers d'Identité.')
   Emile-Paul, Paris, 1929.

De la Vitesse
  (Later reproduced in 'Papiers d'Identité.')
  Kra, Paris, 1929.
Le Voyageur et l'Amour
  (Later reproduced in 'Papiers d'Identité.')
  Grande Maison de Blanc, Paris, 1929.
Ma Légende
  (Later reproduced in 'Papiers d'Identité.')
  Champion, Paris, 1929.
New-York
  E. Flammarion, Paris, 1929.
Comment Voyager sans Argent
  Hazan, Paris, 1930.
Champions du Monde (Chronique du XXe Siècle—VOL. IV)
  B. Grasset, Paris, 1930.
A la Frégate
  Ed. des Portiques, Paris, 1930.
Route de Paris à la Méditerranée
  Firmin-Didot, Paris, 1930.
Papiers d'Identité
  B. Grasset, Paris, 1931.
Flèche d'Orient
  Nouvelle Revue Française, Paris, 1931.
1900
  Editions de France, Paris, 1931.
Londres
  Plon, Paris, 1931.
L'Art de Mourir (Followed by 'Le Suicide en Littérature')
  Les Cahiers Libres, Paris, 1932.
Mes Débuts
  Denoël et Steele, Paris, 1933.
Air Indien
  B. Grasset, Paris, 1933.
Rococo
  B. Grasset, Paris, 1933.
France-la-Doulce, Satire
  Nouvelle Revue Française, Paris, 1934.
Bucharest
  Plon, Paris, 1935.

Rond-Point des Champs-Elysées
  B.Grasset, Paris, 1935.
La Route des Indes
  Plon, Paris, 1936.
Les Extravagants
  Nouvelle Revue Française, Paris, 1936.
Le Réveille-Matin
  B.Grasset, Paris, 1937.

II. ENGLISH TRANSLATIONS OF MORAND'S WORKS

Ouvert la Nuit—Translated by H.B.V. as OPEN ALL NIGHT, Chapman &
  Dodd, London, 1923; Thomas Seltzer, New York, 1923.
Tendres Stocks—Translated by H.I.Woolf as GREEN SHOOTS, Chapman
  & Dodd, London, 1923; Thomas Seltzer, New York, 1924.
Fermé la Nuit—Translated by G.P.G., C.B.P., and H.M. as CLOSED ALL
  NIGHT, G.Chapman, London, 1924; Thomas Seltzer, New York,
  1924.
Lewis et Irène—Translated by H.B.V. as LEWIS AND IRENE, Chatto &
  Windus, London, 1925; Boni & Liveright, New York, 1925.
L'Europe Galante—Translated by Guy Chapman as EUROPE AT
  LOVE, A.A.Knopf, London, 1926; Boni & Liveright, New York,
  1927.
East India and Company (Twelve short stories written in English),
  A.&C.Boni, New York, 1927.
Bouddha Vivant—Translated by Eric Sutton as THE LIVING BUDDHA,
  A.A.Knopf, London, 1927; and by Madeleine Boyd as THE LIVING
  BUDDHA, H.Holt & Co., New York, 1928.
Magie Noire—Translated by Hamish Miles as BLACK MAGIC, Heine-
  mann, London, 1929; The Viking Press, New York, 1929.
New-York—Translated by Hamish Miles as NEW YORK, Heinemann,
  London, 1931; H.Holt & Co., New York, 1930.
Champions du Monde—Translated by Hamish Miles as WORLD
  CHAMPIONS, Heinemann, London, 1931; Harcourt Brace & Co.,
  New York, 1931.
1900—Translated by Mrs. Romilly Fedden as 1900 A.D., W.F.Payson,
  New York, 1931.
Flèche d'Orient—Translated as ORIENT AIR EXPRESS, Cassell & Co.,
  London, 1932.

Paris to the Life, A Sketch-Book by P.Morand and Doris Spiegel—Translated by Gerard Hopkins, Oxford University Press, London & New York, 1933.

Air Indien—Translated by Desmond Flower as INDIAN AIR, Impressions of Travel in South America, Cassel, London, 1933; Houghton Mifflin Co., New York, 1933.

Londres—Translated by Desmond Flower as A FRENCHMAN'S LONDON, Cassell & Co., London, 1934.

Rien que la Terre—Translated by Lewis Galantière as NOTHING BUT THE EARTH, R.M.McBride, New York, 1927; and by E.E.Roche as EARTH GIRDLED, A.A.Knopf, London, 1928.

France-la-Doulce—Translated by Stuart Gilbert as THE EPIC-MAKERS, L.Dickson, London, 1935.

III. WORKS OF CRITICISM ON MORAND (selection)

F.Lefèvre: *Une heure avec* . . . (SERIES II), Nouvelle Revue Française, Paris, 1924.

P.Dominique: *Quatre hommes entre vingt*, Le Divan, Paris, 1924.

B.Crémieux: *XXe Siècle*, Nouvelle Revue Française, Paris, 1924.

L.Dubech: *Les chefs de file de la jeune génération*, Plon, Paris, 1925.

G.Truc: *Quelques peintres de l'homme contemporain*, Editions Spes, Paris, 1926.

P.Lièvre: *Esquisses critiques*, Le Divan, Paris, 1929.

Nino Frank: 'Rien que la Terre,' *Nouvelles Littéraires*, Paris, February 8, 1930.

P.Descaves 'Confidences de M. Paul Morand,' *Nouvelles Littéraires*, Paris, June 14, 1930.

A.Rousseaux; *Ames et Visages du XXe Siècle*, B.Grasset, Paris, 1932.

A.Maurois: 'Londres,' *Nouvelles Littéraires*, Paris, June 3, 1933.

M.H.Stansbury: *French Novelists of Today*, University of Pennsylvania Press, Philadelphia, 1935; Oxford University Press, London, 1933.

R.Brasillach: *Portraits*, Plon, Paris, 1935.

INDEX

The titles of books by Proust, Gide, Giraudoux, and Morand are printed in italics.

413